YUGOSLAVIA

PATTERNS OF ECONOMIC ACTIVITY

PRAEGER SURVEYS IN ECONOMIC GEOGRAPHY

General Editor

PROFESSOR R. O. BUCHANAN

GEOGRAPHY AND ECONOMICS

Michael Chisholm

PLANTATION AGRICULTURE

Philip Courtenay

NEW ENGLAND

A Study in Industrial Adjustment

R. C. Estall

YUGOSLAVIA

Patterns of Economic Activity

F. E. Ian Hamilton

AN ECONOMIC GEOGRAPHY OF EAST AFRICA

A. M. O'Connor

AN ECONOMIC GEOGRAPHY OF OIL

Peter R. Odell

AGRICULTURAL GEOGRAPHY

Leslie Symons

YUGOSLAVIA

PATTERNS OF ECONOMIC ACTIVITY

F. E. IAN HAMILTON

FREDERICK A. PRAEGER, *Publishers*
New York · Washington

BOOKS THAT MATTER

Published in the United States of America in 1968
by Frederick A. Praeger, Inc., Publishers
111 Fourth Avenue, New York, N.Y. 10003

Printed in Great Britain

TO
J.B.

Preface

The writing of this book has been encouraged by the scanty knowledge in the Western world of the processes, results—and factors influencing the results—of decision-taking relating to economic development strategy and to the location of economic activities in a socialist state. The initial seeds of the idea of studying Yugoslavia were sown in 1957 during a summer expedition, curiously enough, across the Norwegian mountains with Krsto Cvijić of Zagreb, then a fellow undergraduate at the London School of Economics. Practical realisation of the idea began one year later when, as a Gerstenberg postgraduate scholar at the School, I was encouraged by Professor M. J. Wise to pursue my interest in the area and to undertake research on the problems of industrial location in postwar Yugoslavia. Naturally this initial research inspired many of the themes that are set out here, but the scope of this book is much wider, being concerned with all the major economic activities and with economic development generally. Although work on the book began in 1963, it was interrupted by lengthy and extensive travels in the other countries of East-Central Europe. The passage of time, and the wider experience gained have, however, permitted the constant reappraisal of the original themes, especially in the light of more recent changes in Yugoslavia itself.

The research embodied in this book could not have been accomplished without adequate periods of residence in Yugoslavia, nor without assistance in many forms from many quarters. I acknowledge, with thanks, therefore, the assistance of first, the British Council, under whose auspices I was a Yugoslav government scholar during the academic year 1959–60, and second, the Yugoslav authorities who organised my sojourn in Zagreb then and who facilitated extensive travel throughout the federation on field research in the spring and summer of 1960. I gratefully acknowledge also the financial assistance granted by the University of London from its Central Research Fund to enable me to revisit the federal republic in 1962, as well as by the Joint School of Geography, King's College, London/London School of Economics for a return there in 1966 to supervise a student expedition on the island of Hvar.

I am indebted to very many Yugoslavs who have arranged access to source material, who have given their guidance and who have given me an insight into the Yugoslav system as well as the 'Slav soul': to Branko Horvat, Kosta Mihailović, Jakov Sirotković, Borisav Srebrić and many others in Belgrade; to Franjo Gašparović, Dragomir Gorupić, Branka Habek, Ivan Krešić, Branko Kubović, Josip Roglić, Nikola Sekulić, Dragomir Vojnić and Stanko Žuljić in Zagreb; to Svetozar Ilešić, Vladimir Klemenčić and Vladimir Kokole in Ljubliana; to Dušan Brkić and Divna Jagodić in Sarajevo; to Nikola Ključev in Skopje; and to city and commune officials, factory and farm managers, and simple working folk up and down the country. In particular I wish to remember the invaluable assistance and advice of Professor Rudolf Bićanić, University of Zagreb, as well as the fine teaching of Serbo-Croatian that I received from Slavko Stojčević, also in Zagreb.

Words cannot express adequately the debt that I owe, from my student days, to colleagues at the London School of Economics, and particularly to Professor R. O. Buchanan and Professor M. J. Wise, for their inspiring teaching of economic geography. To them, in addition, I wish to convey my deepest gratitude for their part in the preparation of this book, for their constant encouragement and for sacrificing their precious time to read and comment upon the manuscript. A very special word of thanks is due to Professor R. O. Buchanan for his masterly and painstaking editorship of the final draft. I wish to record my appreciation also of the advice that Professor Doreen Warriner gave to me during the earlier stages of preparation. Any shortcomings in the book, however, are entirely my own responsibility.

Credit is due to Miss Elizabeth Crux and Miss Stephanie Hall for drawing the maps and to Mrs. E. Wilson for her advice on cartographic presentation. Miss Judith Tagg, Miss Diane Dubury and Miss Angela McLennan skilfully typed the manuscript, despite the frequent occurrence of unfamiliar terms and place-names.

Finally, I express special gratitude to Justyna, my wife, who constantly spurred me on during the preparation for and the writing of this book, and to my parents for their help and encouragement in earlier years.

London, 1967   F. E. Ian Hamilton

Contents

Maps and Diagrams

Tables

PART I

THE BACKGROUND TO MODERN DEVELOPMENT

CHAPTER 1

Introduction

'*Most koji je prelaz od Zapada na Istok, i obrnuto . . . Ali tu . . . dozrevali su plodovi novih vremena.*'* These words, written by Ivo Andrić, sum up certain features relevant to the area that we call 'Yugoslavia' today. The bridge was built by the Turks in the sixteenth century over the swift and dangerous river Drina at Višegrad to replace the old ferry and to provide better transit facilities along the caravan route from Constantinople, Sofia, and Salonika, to Sarajevo and Travnik in Bosnia. Locally the bridge functioned as the meeting place for people from Višegrad and villages on both banks of the river. Yet this was no ordinary meeting place. Christians living on the west bank met Muslims from the other side, people different in clothing, in customs, even in mentality and the very words they spoke, although all were the same South Slavs. When Austrian armies advanced and annexed Bosnia in 1878, the bridge became a strategic gateway for Hapsburg power against the independent state of Serbia and the Ottoman outpost in the Sandjak of Novi Pazar.

The drama enacted on the bridge epitomises the history of the Yugoslav peoples. It expresses their geographical position in relation to the shifting influence of different alien cultures associated with areas in Central Europe to the west and north, and with Asia Minor to the east. This work begins with history, for while there is much geography behind that history, past events are imprinted boldly on the Yugoslav landscape and its peoples, and find expression in modern regional and national economic problems.

The prime object of this study is to present the aims and

---

* 'A bridge that is the crossing place from West to East, and vice-versa . . . Yet here . . . ripened the fruits of modern times.' Ivo Andrić, *Na Drini Ćuprija* (The Bridge on the Drina), Zagreb, 1962.

methods of planning in this socialist state, and to assess its achievements in the distribution and location of economic activity. The validity of these aims, and their success in practice, can be judged only against the patterns and problems that the present Yugoslav government inherited from the past. The comparison involves an assessment of the impact of the new socialist system, based on a formulated ideology, on a pattern of activities which had evolved within the framework of feudal and capitalist economies. One cannot start, therefore, with the economic geography of Yugoslavia in 1939 alone. The postwar government inherited not only economic, but also social and political problems and patterns which have their roots deep in a complex history and which in many ways made difficult the fulfilment of socialist aims.

Moreover, the pre-war economy of Yugoslavia cannot be understood in terms of theories of areal specialisation and comparative advantage. The pattern of exploitation of the country's resources bore little relation to local possibilities and needs, or to world markets. Economic factors are allowed reasonably full play only where political unity or stability and unhampered internal and external economic forces prevail. The Yugoslav peoples never enjoyed such stability or freedom, and were not even brought into one Kingdom until fifty years ago. Their history before 1919 was dynamic, full of conflict and power politics, so that political, rather than economic, factors have shaped their economy. The historical drama on the land bridge between west and east, played out over the last five centuries, goes a long way towards explaining three major problems with which postwar planning in Yugoslavia has had to contend.

First, Yugoslavia is an under-developed country which inherited an economy maladjusted to domestic resources and needs—a country where there exist reserves of energy, mineral and vegetable resources awaiting use in production, and which, when brought into use, will contribute towards absorbing the surplus of poverty-stricken peasant labour still living on the land.

Secondly, Yugoslavia is a land of cultural contrasts which are fossilised in the architecture of buildings, and in the ways of the people. There can indeed be few sharper differences

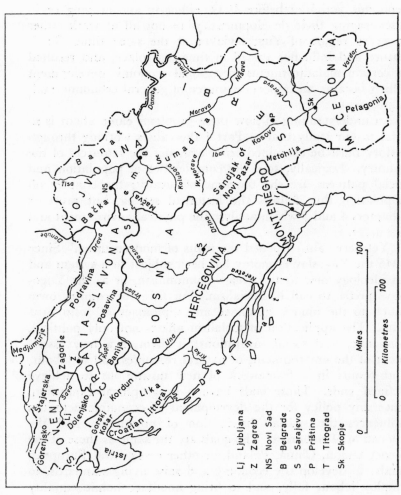

Figure 1. A Location Map of the Six Republics and Capitals, Major Provinces and Major Rivers

in any small country than that, for example, between the old towns of Ljubljana and Sarajevo, the former a miniature Salzburg, the latter more oriental than Istanbul.

Thirdly, the factors that had affected the character of economic activities before 1939, either in encouraging or in discouraging their development, were not all at work either in every region of Yugoslavia or at the same time. Their nature and influence varied in time and place, and resulted in certain maladjustments in regional economic development which became an important source of general economic maladjustment.

An understanding of how these problems came about is so vital to our study that in Part I the causes working through history must be examined *before* assessing the resources of the country. Logically, too, the complexities of population and social patterns are the outcome of history; the chapter on population thus follows the historical setting, but precedes Chapters 4 and 5 which analyse the physical environment and resources.

'Yet here (also) ripened the fruits of modern times.' Since 1945 the Yugoslav economy has been subject to a system and an ideology new to the area—Communism, or as the Yugoslavs prefer to call it, Socialism. For this, the country owes much to the unique guidance and diplomacy of Josip Broz Tito. The application of socialism affects not only political, economic, and social institutions; it involves a new assessment of the environment, of natural resources and of labour, and results in a framework of new institutions to achieve defined ends. Those ends have a geographical expression, since any policy for the development of economic activities influences the spatial distribution of production and the allocation of resources. The goals are the same as those of the Soviet Union, China, Poland, or other east-central European lands: to develop the economy and raise living standards, to employ labour fully, and to bring about economic equality within the country. Tito and his advisers, however, have evolved and applied a socialist system which is different in mechanism and is constantly changing, and they have earned Yugoslavia an international position which many envy.

It may be argued that the fruits of the new system have

not yet ripened, still less been harvested, but the crop has certainly made considerable growth. In internal policy the aim of the Yugoslavian government is to decentralise the power of decision-taking in economic and social fields to as many people as is feasible or desirable, and to operate the market mechanism of demand and supply within set limits. The resulting pattern of investment allocation plays an important part in the location of production and services. The foreign policies of Yugoslavia have placed her among the leaders of the 'uncommitted' nations, in large measure the 'Third World'. This has given the Yugoslavs important advantages as well as problems in economic development. In a sense, therefore, Yugoslavia lies politically between 'West' and 'East' in the popular meaning of those terms. Ideologically the country belongs to the communist world, but her government was the first to become fully independent of the Soviet Union and to open a new era of socialist thinking. The result has been the evolution of a system of economic planning which draws on the experience of both the Soviet Union and the capitalist world; but these borrowings are adapted to the specific cultural, historical, and political experience of the Yugoslavs themselves, and bear their own interpretation of Marxist-Leninist ideas. Part II (Chapters 6, 7 and 8) thus presents an analysis of the Yugoslav planning system, setting out its aims, methods, periodic modifications, and achievements in so far as these relate to the problems of the development and the location of production and services.

Part III is devoted to an examination of the patterns of growth, change and location of production in primary, secondary and tertiary activities, stressing the effects of government action in these sectors since the Second World War. Special attention is paid to the collectivisation of agriculture, to the factors that influence industrial location and to the rôle of transport in economic development in a socialist economy.

Part IV provides an introduction to the problems of economic regionalisation and regional planning in Yugoslavia, emphasising that the significance of economic regions for planning purposes has not always been realised by the government despite the fact that the trend from centralised towards decentralised planning has increased the need for a scientific approach to this problem.

This work, then, breaks new ground. Yet, while lessons may be drawn from Yugoslavia in respect of the geography of economic activities in other communist countries, it is essential to emphasise that differences in area, resource endowment, history, population density, and the stage of economic development, make generalisations about other countries dangerous. Yugoslavia is unique.

CHAPTER 2

The Historical Setting

Yugoslavia—'land of the South Slavs'—belongs to the Old World. Situated in southeastern Europe between the centres of Greek and Roman civilisation and settled by Slavs in the seventh century A.D., the region in medieval times was culturally more advanced than western Europe.[1] Nevertheless the Yugoslav state was not created until 1918–19, being then constituted as the 'Kingdom of Serbs, Croats, and Slovenes', and including areas which had been administered by non-Slav powers before the Great War. In 1929 it became the Kingdom of Yugoslavia[2] with an area of 95,571 square miles (247,542 sq. km.). In 1943, at Jajce, Marshal Tito proclaimed Yugoslavia a Federal People's Republic. This was formalised in the 1946 Constitution, as was also the division of the state into six federated republics.* The addition of territory from Italy in 1945 and of Zone B of Trieste in 1954[3] enlarged the republic to its present area of 99,000 square miles (255,804 sq. km.).[4] Yugoslavia became a Federal Socialist Republic in 1963.

The kingdom enjoyed only twenty three years' independence between the two World Wars. Those were years of economic stagnation. Agriculture was everywhere the principal source of livelihood, employing 6·2 million people or 81 per cent. of the working population in 1941, and the total number of people dependent on it increased substantially from 9 million in 1921 to 12·5 million in 1941.[5] This situation reflected neither good farming conditions, nor the attractiveness of a prosperous activity. Agriculture was bankrupt. Overpopulation was acute, resulting in extreme subdivision of holdings. About

---

* These are: Slovenia, Croatia, Bosnia-Herzegovina, Serbia, Montenegro and Macedonia. Serbia is subdivided into Serbia Proper and two autonomous areas, Vojvodina in the north, and Kosovo-Metohija in the south (Figure I).

9

6·5 millions persons,[6] or 61·5 per cent. of the rural population, were surplus to agricultural requirements in 1930. Conditions further deteriorated with the rapid growth of population and the economic crisis after 1931. The population increased by four million persons, or 34 per cent., in two decades, most of the increase occurring in the countryside. Emigration to the New World—the 'safety valve' before 1914—was no longer either possible, because of immigration restrictions, or attractive, because of depressed farming and export industries overseas. So, while the agricultural land area increased by 4 per cent. between 1931 and 1941, the total agricultural population increased by nearly 20 per cent. in that decade.

The increasing surplus had nowhere to go and nothing to do. Between 1921 and 1941, employment in handicrafts and industry expanded from 522,000 to 750,000 workers, mostly in tiny workshops, for employment in mining and manufacturing increased only from 200,000 to 240,000 persons in the same period.[7] About 29 per cent. of industrial capacity was idle in 1940 as a result of shrunken markets for materials abroad, and declining surpluses of food for processing at home. Urban unemployment increased also and in 1938, a year of economic expansion, the Labour Exchanges could find work for only three out of every 100 applicants for jobs;[8] the great majority of unemployed, however, did not register. The increase in non-agricultural employment barely kept pace with the growth of the working population. A persistently backward agriculture created a vicious circle which paralysed the whole economy, for an impoverished peasantry had nothing to invest and very little to spend. Restricting capital inputs and markets, this made any expansion of trade, industry, building and services impossible.

Just how backward Yugoslavia was economically may be judged from the following indices of national income per head of population for selected European countries in 1938:[9] France 100, Great Britain 98, Germany 96, Belgium and Netherlands 87, Norway and Sweden 83, Baltic Countries 60, Austria and Czechoslovakia 58, Italy 49, Hungary 45, U.S.S.R. 42, Spain 41, Poland 35, Rumania 33, Greece 29, Bulgaria 27, Portugal and Yugoslavia 25. Clearly Yugoslavia was among the poorest countries of Europe. The per capita value of crop and livestock

production—to which the majority of the population contributed—and of timber felling and processing, mining,
quarrying and manufacturing in Yugoslavia generated an
income equal to only one quarter of that of developed countries
in north-western and central Europe, and to only one half of
that in neighbouring Austria, Italy, and Hungary.

The government realised in the 1920s that in the absence of
private entrepreneurs the state had to take the initiative to
stimulate progress. Nationalisation of the railways, coal mines,
heavy industries and tobacco-processing, and government
investment in new steel, engineering and paper works brought
many non-agricultural activities under state control before
1939. High protective tariffs, introduced in 1925, encouraged
industrial development, but only three industries made much
headway: textiles, requiring little capital; shoes, mass-produced
by 'Bata'; and mining, financed from abroad to supply raw
materials to overseas markets. Government policy also
hindered progress as much as it encouraged it. High indirect
taxation fell heavily on the peasantry, increasing their poverty
and reducing their purchasing power so that they could
afford to buy only simple, cheap consumer goods. The
Agrarian Reform, although politically necessary, subdivided
commercial holdings in Vojvodina and Slavonia* into peasant
holdings and so diminished food surpluses and capital accumulation in the best agricultural areas. The state was obliged
to depend more on foreign capital, but as this involved either
repayment with interest or the exploitation of resources for
export it offered no long-term stimulant to Yugoslav economic
progress.

Enormous tasks had faced the government in 1919. The
Great War had caused tremendous damage and loss of life.
But national integration was a more intractable problem.
Yugoslavia was an entirely new amalgamation of areas with
peoples diverse in character, culture and language, who,
having lived variously in the control of Austria, Hungary or
Turkey, had come to know of each other rather than to know
each other. Satisfactory integration required enlightened

* Slavonia is the name applied to the area that lies between the Drava and Sava
rivers from east of the Ilova river (i.e. between Kutina and Virovitica) to the
Croatian Republic boundary with Serbia.

policies; above all, it required time. None of these requirements was met. A start was made in 1919 with the Agrarian
Reform, which did give a greater measure of social and
regional equality, at least in landownership. State investment
in railways contributed towards creating one economic area
out of a series of formerly disconnected areas by linking
western with central and eastern Yugoslavia, and the interior with the coast. Any success these measures might have
had, however, was compromised by domestic politics, in
which a clash between centralist and federalist movements
became identified with the leading national groups, respectively the Serbs and the Croats. To paper over the
cracks, King Alexander changed the state title from the
'Kingdom of the Serbs, Croats, and Slovenes'—emphasising
varied nationality—to the 'Kingdom of Yugoslavia', to stress
unity. Nevertheless, a Serbian dictatorship, characterising
the decade 1929–39, made efforts to Serbianise non-Serbs and
to channel investment into Serbia while neglecting Croatia,
Dalmatia and the poorest regions of central and south-eastern
Yugoslavia. Not surprisingly, increasing tension and instability at home weakened the ability of the state to control
domestic affairs and to attract foreign capital.

Internal social and economic distress resulting from the
economic crisis of 1931 further weakened Yugoslav bargaining
power internationally. Export markets for primary produce
shrank, impeding the importing of manufactures and the
borrowing of capital. After 1933 Nazi Germany began to gain
economic hegemony over Yugoslavia by buying food and
materials from her to accumulate credit balances in her
favour.[10] When Austria and Bohemia-Moravia were incor-
porated into the Reich in 1938 Germans gained control of
75 per cent. of Yugoslav trade and a large part of foreign-
owned industry in Yugoslavia. Thus, with subservience to
Germany and acute poverty everywhere, the economic situation
in 1941 was little different from what it had been before 1914.

THE ROOTS OF THE PROBLEM

Economic backwardness reflected underdevelopment of the
economy in relation to both the resources available and the
needs of the population. Structural maladjustment was clear

in several ways. Agriculture employed too many people. This manifested itself in overpopulation. Whereas 80 per cent. of the people depended upon agriculture only 60 per cent. of all land was used for agriculture. Conversely, industry was underdeveloped compared with available domestic resources. That existing industrial capacity was idle merely reflected the structural maladjustment of industry: the dominance of food-processing, which relied upon a declining food surplus, of consumer goods, for which the home market was shrinking, and of mining which served shrinking overseas markets. Yet whereas in 1941 Yugoslavia had the eighth largest population in Europe (excluding the U.S.S.R.), her reserves gave her a place between first and third in non-ferrous metals and hydro-electric power potentials, fifth place in iron-ore and timber and eleventh place in coal. Use of these resources would have provided employment in industry and supporting services for a substantial proportion of the six million 'surplus' people. The failure of the government to stimulate the growth of manu-facturing encouraged exploitation of resources for supply in raw or only semi-processed form to industry abroad.

Equally serious, however, was the government's failure to realise the regional problem underlying general maladjustment in the economy. Very sharp differences in levels of economic development and national income existed among regions. These were matched by local economic maladjustments which were consequent upon a discord between the distribution of population and the availability of resources. Three types of regional maladjustment were, and still are, distinguishable. First, central, eastern and south-eastern Yugoslavia commands most industrial resources, yet an overwhelming majority of people living there were engaged in a pitifully backward agriculture. Second, the karst regions lack most resources, yet overpopulation there, too, was serious. Third, in northern Yugoslavia fertile land was plentiful and overpopulation unimportant, yet agriculture was extensive, and industry was developed despite local scarcities of natural resources. The solution to the problem of underdevelopment, therefore, hinged not only on changes in economic structure but also on achieving better harmony between the character and location of production on the one hand, and the possibilities and economy of production on the other. Regional differences in economic development cannot be explained by reference only to resource endowments and comparative advantages. Account must also be taken of historical events, partly political, partly social and partly economic in character, which led, first, to a marked imbalance between the location, distribution and growth of population on the one hand, and the opportunities provided by nature and harnessed by man to gain a living on the other; and, secondly, to an irrational use of those resources which *were* exploited. These historical factors were war, political instability, strategy and foreign administrative control and investment—factors which were partly consequent upon the position and accessibility of the South Slav lands.

POSITION AND ACCESSIBILITY

Yugoslavia lacks the internal physical conditions that favour the development of strong unified states. Complex mountain-and-basin relief, with underground streams isolating basins in some areas, and irregular and anomalous river systems giving indeterminate watersheds and easy passages in others, encouraged and conditioned, but did not determine, the confused political and social geography of Yugoslavia.[11] Confusion has caused internal instability. By contrast, regions which were conducive to the growth of strong states surround the South Slavs: the Pannonian plain on the north, the Po basin and the Adriatic Sea on the west, and the Maritsa plain and the Sea of Marmara on the south-east. Three features of the Yugoslav lands, moreover, encouraged conquest by powers centred on these regions. Firstly, their location on that part of the strategic 'land-bridge' between central Europe and Asia Minor where the valleys of the Morava, Vardar and Nišava rivers provide the only easy routes through the mountainous Balkan Peninsula. Secondly, their separation of a more powerful and more advanced Austro-Hungary from its nearest and easily accessible Adriatic Sea outlets.[12] Thirdly, their openness to the north as the Hungarian plain grades gently into the hill country of the Dinaric and Rhodope systems, and to the south where the Vardar corridor provides easy entry from the Aegean, whereas high mountains make entry difficult from the Adriatic.

Modern Yugoslavia lies astride two major European divisions and comprises areas characteristic of each division: the northern areas belong to 'Central Europe'; the remainder is part of the Balkan Peninsula. The east-west dividing line is drawn from the Iron Gates along the Danube, Sava and Kupa rivers, and continues to the Adriatic coast near Rijeka.[13] Northern Yugoslavia comprises a western area of Alpine topography and German-inspired culture, and an eastern area of plains and mixed culture characteristic of the Danubian lands. The Balkan[14] part comprises two distinct areas: an interior of complex physique and social instability (associated with the penetration of influences from north, west and east) in the Dinaric and Rhodope regions, and the Mediterranean coastal belt. These geographical divisions correspond in large measure to the political divisions shown in Figure 2: the north-west dominated by Austria, the north and north-east by Hungary; the interior area under changing administration, and the coast under Italian influence.

THE IMPACT OF WAR, INSTABILITY AND STRATEGY

Internal physical disunity, a strategic situation and easy accessibility from external centres of power explain the frequent wars on, and subsequent foreign domination of, Yugoslav territory. Having crushed Serbia, the last South Slav medieval state, at Kosovo Polje in 1381, the Turks gained dominion over Macedonia and Serbia by 1485, Bosnia-Herzegovina by 1463, and Vojvodina and Slavonia by 1541. Only Slovenia and extreme western Croatia,[15] lying north-west of a line drawn from Senj via Sisak to Kotoriba, escaped Turkish control (Figure 2). The Hapsburg counter-attack recovered Croatia-Slavonia and Vojvodina by 1718, after which the Sava and the Danube rivers formed the boundary between the Hapsburg and the Ottoman Empires for 100–160 years.[16] Only the Serbs, however, gained any measure of independence from foreign rule before 1914.

Unrest and instability increased in the crucial period of modern economic development before the First World War. Increasingly onerous social and economic conditions accompanying the decline of the Turkish Empire caused frequent

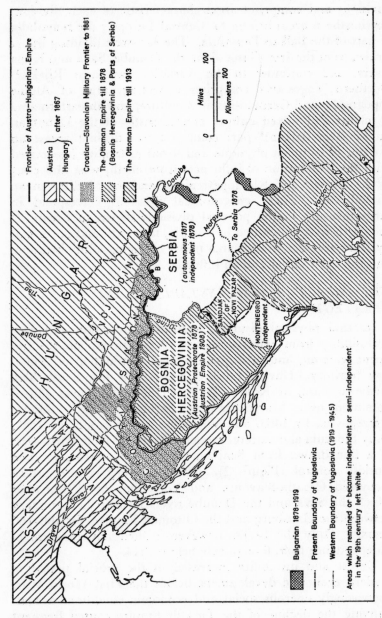

Figure 2. The Pattern of Foreign Domination before 1914

violence and counter-terror which destroyed livestock and settlements especially along the Military Frontier (Figure 2) and in Bosnia-Herzegovina, southern Serbia[17] and Macedonia. Feuds among Albanian clans in Kosovo-Metohija (henceforth referred to as 'Kosmet') channelled investment into the construction of fortified dwellings. War and terror contributed much to regional backwardness since on every occasion an alternation of construction, devastation and reconstruction incurred heavy costs in using and losing capital, materials and youthful manpower. The grant of independence by Turkey to diverse peoples inhabiting badly defined or disputed areas increased the likelihood of conflict after 1878. Within forty years the eastern and south-eastern regions were involved in six wars: the Serbo-Turk wars (1876, 1878), the Serbo-Bulgarian war (1885), the Balkan Wars (1912, 1913) and the Great War of 1914–18. Serbia suffered most since her resources were small and her independence was threatened. Indeed, she was spending 25–35 per cent. of her total annual budget between 1900 and 1912 simply on repaying foreign loans, borrowed chiefly from Russia for buying arms.[18] Money needed for economic development was being drained away for very costly defence. In contrast, Slovenia and west Croatia long enjoyed peaceful conditions which facilitated the operation of regular productive activities and the accumulation of capital for local reinvestment.

War and instability affected the distributions of population and land use. Northern and eastern plains and fertile valleys, most frequently the scene of battle, were left thinly populated. Livestock-rearing became dominant because low population density encouraged extensive grazing. Livestock mobility moreover, was an advantage while insecurity made uneconomic the investment of money, effort and materials in farm buildings or sown crops which might only benefit some foreign marauder. Insecurity discouraged anything but a minimum of subsistence activity and so prevented capital accumulation. Many fertile areas were left uncultivated, and even good pasture was rarely grazed, so that living standards remained extremely low. Improvements were discouraged by the depredation of bands of *hajduks*—Serbs and Montenegrins who had sought refuge from the Turks in isolated central and

C

southern mountain areas which were not worth foreign exploitation or close supervision. A proportionately greater concentration of population developed in these areas of poor soil, harsh climate and broken relief, where life was difficult and where the people were isolated from knowledge of the new techniques and industry developing elsewhere in Europe. The use of medieval methods persisted, while population increased, overpopulation emerged, inducing soil erosion in these areas; dire poverty resulted.

The Austrian Military Frontier along the Sava valley was created to contain Turkish incursions and to provide men for Imperial armies. Danger discouraged[19] settlement in this fertile belt even though the frontiersmen were free of the *corvée* which burdened their brethren elsewhere. The work of cultivation fell upon the womenfolk, which, with persistence of the three-field system, resulted in food shortages while land lay fallow. Neighbouring areas in Hrvatsko Zagorje, by contrast, became overpopulated just because they were peaceful. The presence of areas of instability alongside areas of relative security led to a distribution of population which was not adjusted to regional productiveness, thus giving irrational land-use patterns and preventing progress.

As wars were frequent, strategy often determined which activities were developed and where they were located. Slovenia and Istria, being Hapsburg areas which were safe from attack and yet lay in proximity to trouble spots in Italy and the Balkans, were favoured as areas where the long-term operation of trading establishments, industries and ports guaranteed a return on investment. Thus the fine natural harbour at Pula became the major Austro-Hungarian naval port. Industries producing steel, lead-shot, explosives and woollen clothing were located in alpine valleys in Slovenia to form vital links in supply between Vienna, the Slavonian frontier and the Trieste shipyards. Austria developed similar industries in Bosnia and Slavonia after 1878. Strategy was also important in Serbia, which, despite her small size, had four frontiers to defend. Between 1830 and 1878 armament, metal, shoe and coal industries were developed near Kragujevac, the geometrical centre of the Kingdom.

THE EFFECTS OF FOREIGN RULE

Yugoslav history has until very recently reflected one theme, foreign domination. Serbia was first to gain her independence after 360 years of Turkish rule, the former Belgrade Pashalik being freed between 1815 and 1830, followed by Niš Pashalik in 1878. Three foreign powers—Austria, Hungary, and Turkey—governed the remainder of Yugoslavia virtually until 1918. Slovenia having belonged to German princes since A.D. 700, was absorbed by Austria in the Middle Ages. Hungary extended her territory to include Vojvodina—the 'Duchy'—in A.D. 900 and Croatia-Slavonia in 1102. Apart from the Ottoman interlude (1530–1718) these areas remained part of Hungary until 1918. Venice ruled Istria and much of Dalmatia until 1797, when these, too, came under the Hapsburgs. Bosnia-Herzegovina, under Ottoman hegemony for 400 years, was occupied by Austria in 1878. Five hundred years of Turkish rule in south Serbia, the Sandjak of Novi Pazar, Kosmet and Macedonia ended only in 1912.

The Yugoslav lands were thus divided for a long period among several occupying powers whose diverse and concurrent administrations differed, not least in economic structure and orientation. Figure 2, showing nineteenth-century political boundaries is basic to understanding the present geography of economic activities, for 'the economic and social history of Yugoslavia is involved—in some regions completely identified—with that of the several states and provinces into which the country was formerly divided'.[20] That division operated in the century after 1815, when the rise of modern capitalism, industry and transport began to alter the nature, scale and pattern of economic activities and the assessment of the physical environment. The degree and the speed of adoption of these changes varied with the occupying power and with the nature and situation of its south Slav lands, giving differential regional progress, including complete stagnation. Economic and social differences, sharpened in the nineteenth century, however, had their origins in foreign colonisation, cultural influences, social systems and economic policies in earlier periods.

(1) Colonisation and Culture

The Danube and Sava rivers form a major cultural divide between the European and Turkish spheres of influence. Turks parcelled out the lands to the south as fiefs to the *spahis* —Islamised warriors—who with Turkish administrators, artisans, and traders established an oriental culture. Turkish colonisation was small, yet the impact was profound, for the culture was identified with a strict religion—Islam—which was a way and a philosophy of life given force by the rulers through sharp social and economic discrimination against those, the Christian Slavs, who did not adopt it. Many people living in central and south-eastern areas were converted to Islam, making them reactionary, distrustful of innovation and education. For them the Koran sufficed. This sowed in these areas the seeds of economic backwardness, of stagnation at levels of knowledge and technique common before the Turkish conquest, and later, with an increase of population, of economic degeneration.

Serbia, alone among lands long under Ottoman control, made some progress in the nineteenth century after her liberation. Serbs began resettling their *domovina* (homeland) after 1830, encouraged by virgin or depopulated land and by freedom from the feudal obligations that existed elsewhere. Some, returning from isolation in Montenegro, contributed little to progress for they still practised medieval methods. Others, whose ancestors had fled the Turks and crossed the Danube three centuries earlier to live in Austro-Hungary, brought skills, and established crafts new to Balkan towns (baking, tailoring, printing, and carpentry)[21] and improved farm techniques. These elevated Serbia above her neighbours while population remained small. Yet 360 years of Turkish domination had strengthened the Serb's devotion to the land he had lost, or had worked for someone else, for so long. This sentiment was supported by the Minimum Homestead Laws of 1836 and 1873-74.[22] Subsistence peasant farming persisted. When subject to rapidly increasing population after 1870, Serbia became overpopulated. A similar story emerges from the Pashalik of Niš after 1878, although severance of the area from main Turkish markets caused some depression in handicrafts in Niš and Pirot.

Despite changes in Serbian life, the Danube and Sava rivers continued to be a major cultural divide up to 1914 and indeed even to the present day. Having crossed the Sava from Slavonia to Bosnia in 1887, Émile de Laveleye wrote: 'I have never seen the contrast between the west and the orient so sharply. Two civilisations, two religions, two ways of life, and two completely different mentalities are separated only by a river. . . . For four centuries, this river, in reality, has divided Europe from Asia.'[23] Writing sixty years later Grdjić observes that 'it would be difficult to find in all Europe two neighbouring and ethnically kindred areas that developed to so great an extent under such different conditions as did Vojvodina and Serbia'.[24]

Germanic and Magyar cultures dominated the northern areas. Depopulation of Vojvodina and Slavonia before 1699 enabled the Hapsburgs to settle Germans and Hungarians on the empty plains later. A Viennese 'Colonial Commission', for example, settled 60,000 Germans from Cologne, Ulm, Schweinfurt and Regensburg in Vojvodina between 1768 and 1789, and provided them with the means for progress: large land areas, houses, implements, money, and equipment for draining land and building canals. Serbs, Slovaks, and Russians also settled and, with the Germans, they applied new methods, knowledge of which came from western Europe. Agriculture in Vojvodina thus reached an economic and technical level far above that of other Yugoslav areas. By contrast, Slavs in Croatia were divorced from change either in the Military Frontier or because Germans and Hungarians monopolised economic life. The Croat was a foreigner in his own capital, Zagreb, where, until 1880, he bought wares at 'Kindermann und Storf' and 'Dömöterffy', drank 'Zum Weissen Ochsen', and tried to read the local newspaper, the *Agramer Zeitung*! Teutonic influence was strongest in the north-west where one thousand years of contact were apparent in the education, skill, inventiveness, efficiency and thrift of the Slovenes which had enabled them to accumulate and invest capital in factories, water mills and furnaces.

The Hapsburg lands thus contained some seeds of progress; elsewhere Islam stifled all possibilities of it.

(2) Economic and Social Systems

Foreign powers succeeded in maintaining feudalism, the mechanism for the continuation of their power, until 1815 in Serbia, 1848 in Slovenia and Pannonia, 1878 in Dubrovnik and south Serbia, and almost until 1913 in central and southeastern Yugoslavia. The longer feudalism persisted, the later economic development was deferred. Virtually no progress took place in Balkan Yugoslavia until after 1919, and thereafter, for reasons already stated, until 1945.

German, Hungarian, and Muslim landlords had no incentive to improve production methods as they did no work, but by taking up to one half of the crop, they obtained a surplus of food to barter or sell. The serf Slavs had neither the knowledge nor the resources to make improvements; and their socially inferior position discouraged effort to produce bigger crops from which they derived little benefit. Feudalism preserved a subsistence economy and, thus, the inefficient use of land and resources. Nevertheless, outside Serbia where peasant proprietorship was dominant, feudal systems varied from large latifundia in Pannonia and central Dalmatia which lent themselves later to commercial production, to fragmented, share-cropped land around Dubrovnik which offered no basis for progress. The čiftlik system replaced the timar system in Macedonia,[26] intensifying agriculture through irrigation, but paradoxically the severity of the new corvée led, by 1900, to depopulation and abandonment of fertile areas. In Bosnia, the legacy of Turkish feudalism was shifting cultivation, with a long fallow on the larger vakf lands in central Bosnia.[27]

The growth of capitalism brought changes which affected Austria after 1800, Hungary after 1867 and Bosnia after 1878. The impact varied regionally. Latifundia in the north began producing, and later processing, food and timber for the market, a process greatly accelerated after 1870 by the railways.

Competition from the latifundia created a growing landless labour force among the peasantry, who as a source of cheap labour discouraged further investments in, and intensification of, agriculture. In Serbia, Croatia, and Dalmatia, most money became tied up in peasant debts to traders who lent money at high interest rates. Austrian occupation of Bosnia merely

introduced the use of money to the old order, causing bankruptcy as peasants had to borrow money from *begs* and *agas*
to pay new state taxes and then to pay more produce—up to
three quarters—to cover these commitments. However, the
abolition of feudalism and the spread of capitalism in Slovenia
never led to the farm fragmentation, consequent upon debt
and rising population, common elsewhere, because inheritance
was based on primogeniture.[28] People left the land for other
occupations, for Vienna or Trieste or abroad.

(3) *Economic Policy*

The Imperial governments treated their South Slav territories as colonial sources of food, materials and manpower.
But whereas the Sultan's economic policies were conspicuous
by their absence, those of governments in Vienna and Budapest
were complex, all pervasive, and required a sizeable bureaucracy. Ottoman policy rarely went beyond establishing and
maintaining feudal institutions. It did very little to improve
agriculture or transport and was apathetic to industrialisation. Certain trade and craft centres—Sarajevo, Vučitrn and
Pirot[29]—prospered under the Turks, and Dubrovnik undoubtedly benefitted from its commercial position between
land and sea, Turkey and Italy, Orient and Occident. By
1900, the roads that the Romans had built and that had
throbbed with trade until the seventeenth century, were over-
grown, disconnected, unsafe, and were not followed by any
railway.[30] Similarly the mining of ores, which had a long
tradition in the Balkans, had declined. Turkish neglect, however, preserved valuable resources of timber and minerals for
use in modern Yugoslavia.

Hapsburg economic policy was centralised, at first in
Vienna, and after 1867 also in Budapest. Absolute monarchy
in the eighteenth century was replaced in the nineteenth
by the bureaucratic state, which applied administrative and
fiscal instruments to regulate the development and distribution of economic activities within the Empire. This was
supported by central banks in Vienna and Budapest with
branches in the South Slav lands. Attempts were made
between 1740 and 1867 to weld the heterogeneous Empire
into an economic unit with specialisation in its constituent

areas which were decided according not to resource availability but to the needs of Austrian *Weltpolitik*. Rivalry between Austrians and Hungarians caused division of the Monarchy in 1867, but the same mercantilist doctrines were applied to discriminate against the South Slavs, a logical corollary of their political inequality in the Empire.

Although the grant of monopoly privileges for practising trade or industry in defined places followed no plan, Maria Theresa stipulated that none would be granted for production in Hungary (i.e. including Croatia-Slavonia and Vojvodina), which might compete with manufactures from her 'German lands', Austria, Bohemia-Moravia and Slovenia.[31] Tariffs on trade were introduced after 1754 to ensure the success of this policy. Joseph II in 1786, for example, protected Austro-Czech interests by prohibiting imports of 200 products and subjecting the rest to 60 per cent. duty; imports of Austro-Czech products into Hungary were kept duty free. These laws continued to operate until 1853, fostering the localisation of 60 per cent. of the metals and machinery, 75 per cent. of the textile, leather and paper, 95 per cent. of the ceramics and glass of the entire Empire[32] in Bohemia-Moravia and conversely discouraging investment in Hungary. Only silk, hemp, flax and cotton textile industries were permitted in Croatia, Slavonia and Vojvodina.[33] Slovenia was never as favoured as the Czech lands, although free of such control; industry developed there rather because of its position between Vienna, the capital, and Trieste, the main Imperial port.

After independence in 1867 the Hungarian government protected its own market from Austrian 'dumping'. Independence now permitted, and the market encouraged, the inflow of foreign capital for railway- and factory-building in Hungary, but not in 'inferior' Croatia-Slavonia. The exception in Croatia was Rijeka which, as an Adriatic port in proximity to Central Europe, could serve Hapsburg interests. Rijeka thus became the Austrians' free port in 1719, the Hungarians' only seaport in 1867 and, as the *separatum corpus* within the Empire, also the centre of foreign-owned sugar-refining, paper and vegetable-oil industries, which could serve the Imperial market duty free.

The Hapsburgs began to improve communications after

1785, making cheaper and faster bulk transport a powerful factor in regional economic development. The regulation of the Danube and Tisa rivers and the building of 123 miles of canals after 1793 gave Vojvodina distinct advantages for commercialising agriculture, expanding trade, accumulating capital and developing industry. Non-improvement of the Sava and Drava waterways left Croatia-Slavonia backward, without competitive ability. Such discrimination was explained by the greater convenience of the Danube for direct transport of foods and materials to Vienna and Budapest, by Austrian *Drang nach Osten* towards the Serbian 'corridor lands', and by the instability of the Military Frontier along the Sava. Similarly, an Austrian monopoly of Adriatic shipping after 1797 ensured an economic stranglehold of transit traffic by Trieste and Rijeka. When the monopoly was relaxed in the 1850s Dalmatian ports could compete neither for trade nor for market-oriented industries. Dalmatia, therefore, remained backward.

More marked differences followed the construction of the railways. Most lines were built by Austro-Hungary, and to the north of the Danube and Sava rivers. Their construction was used for Imperial ends, to link, first, markets and industries in Vienna and Budapest with Yugoslav sources of cheap food and materials; second, the capitals with the ports, Vienna with Trieste (1860), Budapest with Rijeka (1873), incidentally encouraging division of labour between the ports as markets and sources of imported materials and Slovenia-West Croatia as sources of labour, timber and minerals; third, occupied Bosnia and Serbia[34] with the imperial network to make the 'push to the east' easier; and finally, to preserve the isolation of the Yugoslav lands one from another for political reasons, and all from the Dalmatian ports for economic reasons. Only in the north-west was a true railway network developed—to serve the main ports. Numerous lines served Slavonia and Vojvodina, yet these were aligned south-north towards Budapest, so isolating Bačka from Banat, eastern from central Slavonia and, for long, Slavonia from Croatia. Bosnia was left isolated physically and commercially from Serbia, Dalmatia and Ottoman areas by a lack of railway links, and from Slavonia by a difference of gauges.

Even where railways did exist, differential tariffs were applied to give advantages to some areas and disadvantages to others. Hungarian tariff policy illustrated 'the misuse of railway tariffs to control both passenger and freight traffic, and to steer that traffic along defined lines without reference to distance, accessibility or location'.[35] Tariffs encouraged the movement of materials and semi-manufactureres from Hungarian-controlled mines, forests, and factories in Croatia-Slavonia, Vojvodina and Bosnia to Hungarian towns, especially Budapest, for processing. Rates between a Yugoslav town and Budapest were fixed at little more than the rate between two nearby Yugoslav towns, making manufacturing uneconomic locally, and stimulating industrial agglomeration in Budapest. 'Fixed' tariffs, subsidised rates to particular foreign firms, and other similar measures, made real transport costs an insignificant factor in the location of economic activities.

(4) Capital Investment

For centuries Dubrovnik was the chief source of capital in Yugoslavia, but Trieste and Rijeka began to replace her by 1800. Capital elsewhere was lacking. Money was used to repay heavy debts so that the peasant had nothing to save and nothing to invest. Most capital came from foreign sources.

The pattern of foreign rule was instrumental in channelling foreign capital into some areas rather than others (Figure 3). The decaying Ottoman Empire invested little in central and south-eastern regions; and no capital was forthcoming from overseas to prop up the 'sick man of Europe' on his death bed, least of all from the Hapsburgs, who were ready for the kill. Austria-Hungary, in contrast, invested in railways, land-drainage, agricultural improvement and industry in their respective administrative areas. Figure 3 shows how Austrian capital dominated industry in Slovenia, and Hungarian capital in Croatia-Slavonia. Only after 1878 did investment penetrate into Bosnia and Serbia. German and Italian capital, now in search of materials for industries serving enlarged and unified markets, joined much Austro-Hungarian state investment in Bosnia. Accessibility determined the location of these investments (Figure 3): Austro-Hungarian along

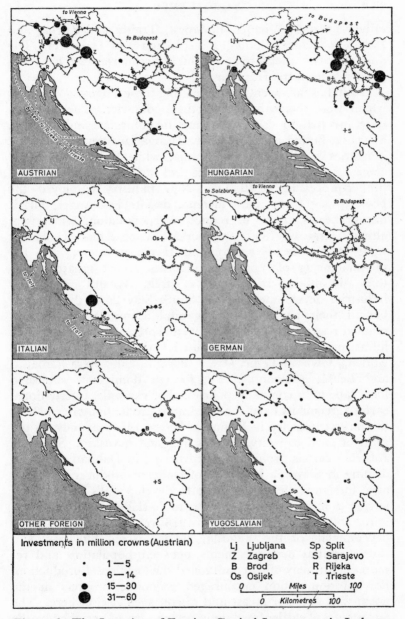

Figure 3. The Location of Foreign Capital Investment in Industry and Mining in Slovenia, Croatia-Slavonia, Dalmatia and Bosnia-Herzegovina in 1914

railways serving Vienna, Budapest, Trieste and Rijeka, and Italian in central Bosnia, Herzegovina and Dalmatia. The dominance of other foreign capital in Serbia reflected her independence from the Hapsburgs.

Capital usually went into exploiting those Yugoslav resources which were scarce in the 'mother' countries. The Austrian state invested in coal-mines and metallurgical industries in Slovenia, Bosnia and Dalmatia. Hungarians developed forest industries in Slavonia and Bosnia, while Italians developed cement, chemical and bauxite industries in Dalmatia and timber-processing in Bosnia. New industry employed the poor, giving them more income, despite low wages, but it hardly began either to reduce overpopulation, which was already large by 1890, or to create a local market. Profits went to Austria, Germany and Hungary where, also, the manufacturing of Yugoslav resources added greater value than did mining in Yugoslavia itself. Wealth created by industrial development in the South Slav lands did little to benefit their progress; local capital accumulation thus remained restricted. A few larger entrepreneurs did provide an infrastructure for future industrial development in small workers' towns at Teslić, Drvar (Bosnia), Duga Resa (Croatia) and Belišće (Slavonia). Yet foreign dominance subjected local labour to company policies. For example, international cartel agreements fixed the maximum production of cement— the largest industry in Dalmatia before 1914—at only 16 per cent. of local capacity, causing regional hardship. Similarly Austrian cartels prohibited salt-working in Dalmatia and oil-drilling in Slavonia in favour of Galician producers.[36] Often, also, foreign industry did little to develop skills locally, preferring to import trained workers to do skilled work.

Instability and war before 1918 retarded the economic development of the Yugoslav lands, except Slovenia, and caused spatial maladjustments between population and resources. Strategy often conditioned the location of production. Foreign domination encouraged economic progress in the north-west and north-east and discouraged it elsewhere. The advantages of earlier freedom in Serbia were outweighed by the military drain on her resources. The creation of Yugoslavia in 1918 raised problems of finding new markets and material suppliers, Slovenia being severed from Austria and Croatia-Slavonia and Vojvodina from Hungary, and of integrating these more advanced regions with the very backward southern regions.

REFERENCES

1   The richness of inscriptions and decorations in monasteries and other monuments of the 13th and 14th centuries confirms this.

2   Before 1950 this was often spelt 'Jugoslavia', from the Serbo-Croat 'Jugoslavija'.

3   Zone B of Trieste was administered by the Yugoslavs between 1945 and 1954 as part of the Free city of Trieste; Zone A was under British and American administration, but became linked to Italy in 1954.

4   Yugoslavia is thus somewhat larger than Great Britain with Northern Ireland (94,280 sq. m.), is a little larger than the Federal Republic of Germany (95,700 sq. m.), and is about the size of the states of Oregon or Wyoming in the U.S.A.

5   *Definitivni Rezultati Popis Stanovništva 1921, 1931; Jugoslavia, Vol. III, Economic Geography, Ports and Communications*, Geographical Handbooks Series, Naval Intelligence Division (U.K.), 1945, p. 73.

6   Based on W. E. Moore, *Economic Demography of Eastern and Southern Europe*, League of Nations, Geneva, 1945, p. 72.

7   Based on *Statistika Kraljevine Jugoslavije: Rudarstvo i Industrija 1938*, Belgrade, 1940.

8   *Jugoslavia, op. cit.*, p. 172.

9   Based on: Ludwik Landau, *Gospodarka Światowa*, Warsaw, 1939, pp. 126–32; League of Nations, *Statistics of National Income 1938*, Geneva 1940.
    Since these figures relate to per capita national income accruing from agriculture, forestry, mining and industry only, the assessment is most accurate for countries with low indices (except Greece where shipping was important); it underestimates real income in developed countries, where services add considerably to the national income. The Baltic Countries here include Denmark, Finland, Estonia, Latvia and Lithuania.

10 A. Basch, *The Danubian Basin and the German Economic Sphere*, London, 1944.

11 Marion I. Newbigin, *The Geographical Background to Balkan Problems*, London, 1916.

12 Harbours in the bays of Trieste and Kvarner were easily accessible from Austria via longitudinal and transverse valleys through the Slovene Alps and from Hungary across the narrow neck of Karst mountains separating Rijeka from the Pannonian Plain.

13 Four other variants of this line are recognised by geographers. They are drawn along the following lines: firstly, from the Sava at Brežice

(Slovenia) through Postojna to Trieste (after Filip Lukas); secondly, from the Sava at Ljubljana through Vipava to Trieste (J. Cvijić); thirdly, from Škofja Loka along the Sora valley to Trieste; and fourthly, from the source of the Sava along the Soča valley to Trieste. See Vladimir Blašković, *Ekonomska Geografija Jugoslavije*, Zagreb 1962, pp. 20–21.

14 The word 'Balkan' is Turkish for 'mountain'.

15 A tiny part of the principality of Montenegro was never actually conquered, while the Republic of Ragusa (Dubrovnik) paid dearly to Turkey, and later to Venice, to maintain her independence.

16 After 1815 the rivers formed the boundary between an independent Serbia and the Hungarian Empire in the east, but the middle Sava continued to be the boundary between the Turkish Bosnia and the Hapsburg lands until 1878.

17 'Southern Serbia' in this context refers to areas lying along the Upper Morava system to the south of Niš as far as the watershed with the Vardar river system, but lying to the east of Kosovo. It is not to be confused with the name 'Southern Serbia' applied to Macedonia during the period of the Serbian dictatorship between 1929 and 1941.

18 Mijo Mirković, *Ekonomska Historija Jugoslavije*, Zagreb 1954, p. 322.

19 It is estimated that in the revolutionary years 1848–49 alone, some 30,000 men from the Military Frontier zone died out of a total Imperial Army of 80,000 men.

20 E. D. Teppe, G. F. Cushing, V. de S. Pinto, and P. Auty, *Contrasts in Emerging Societies*, edited by D. Warriner, London, 1964, p. 283.

21 *Proizvodne Snage Srbije*, Ekonomski Institut, Belgrade, 1953, p. 6; Ljubija Protić, *Razvoj Industrije u Srbiji u Vremenu Kneza Miloša, 1815–1839*, Belgrade, 1948.

22 These laws were introduced to protect the peasant from indebtedness and to limit the subdivision of holdings and property. The law of 1836 prescribed that the peasant could not sell his house or garden, two oxen and two cows to obtain credit to pay off debts. A new 'minimum' was introduced in 1873–74 which stipulated that 'in a bankruptcy court one could not take from the peasant: one plough, one cart, two oxen or two buffalo and two horses, a mare with a foal up to one year old, a cow with a calf up to one year old, ten sheep, five pigs, five goats, . . . or as much food as is necessary for him, his family, and his livestock.' *Proizvodne Snage Srbije*, pp. 5, 9.

23 Baron Émile de Laveleye, *La Péninsule des Balkans*, Tome I, Paris, 1889, p. 143.

24 G. Grdjić in: *Proizvodne Snage Srbije*, p. 26.

25 Gjuro Szabo, *Stari Zagreb*, Zagreb, 1938, pp. 117–20.

26 T. Stoianovitch, 'Land Tenure and Related Sectors of the Balkan Economy', *Journal of Economic History*, 1953, pp. 398–411.

27 These lands belonged to mosques and were most common in Bosnia where population was less dense and where forests occupied a large percentage of the land. The distribution of these holdings can be traced in such present place names as *Donji Vakuf* (the lower *vakf*), *Gornji Vakuf* (the upper *vakf*), *Kulen Vakuf* (the castle *vakf*) and *Skender Vakuf*.

28 A. Melik, *Naše Selo*, Ljubljana, 1949.

29   Vučitrn was the 'half-way house' on the main caravan route through the central regions of Yugoslavia between Salonika and Sarajevo. Pirot became a famous centre of 'Turkish' carpets.

30   These routes were: firstly the *Via Ignatia* from Durres (now an Albanian port) via Struga, Bitola, and Ostrovo to Salonika, linking the Adriatic with the Aegean; secondly, from Alassio via the Drin valley through Prizren, Kosovo, Niš, the Timok valley, and so to Vidin, linking the Adriatic with the Danube; thirdly, from the mouth of the Neretva valley in Dalmatia through Sarajevo and Višegrad, with a northern branch to Belgrade, and a southern one to Skopje and Salonika. Political boundaries in the nineteenth century were partly responsible for the lack of continuous roads along these lines, notably after 1788, when Austria occupied Bosnia, leaving the vital link in the Sandjak of Novi Pazar to decay under Ottoman rule.

31   The 'German lands' were defined as those areas, firstly, where a large proportion of the population were German; secondly, where the people had been subject to a process of assimilation to German ways and language since the Middle Ages; and thirdly, which had become regarded as 'hereditary' to the Hapsburg Empire, following their inclusion in that Empire for more than 200 years.

32   A. Wrzosek, *Czechoslowacja*, P. W. N., Warsaw, 1960, p. 137.

33   R. Bićanić, *Doba Manufakture u Hrvatskoj 1760-1860*, Zagreb, 1950, pp. 189-96.

34   Austria had obliged Serbia, through the provisions of the Berlin Treaty of 1878 to construct, at her own expense, a railway between the Imperial network at Zemun in the north and her borders with Bulgaria and Turkey in the south east and south so that Austria had direct rail access to the Orient.

35   Mirković, *op cit.*, p. 267.

36   J. Lakatoš, *Industrija Dalmacije, i Bosne i Hercegovine*, Belgrade, 1926, p. 29.

CHAPTER 3

The Demographic Factor

Population size and distribution define the volume and location of market demand only broadly, purchasing power per head determining the volume, type and range of goods demanded. Yet purchasing power expresses productivity, the people's ability to produce or to exchange goods for what they need. The quality of labour, expressing a knowledge of environment and of techniques, conditions productivity through its use of resources and combination of production factors. Thus consumption and production by the community are closely linked, economically and spatially. J. S. Mill wrote, in answer to Thomas Malthus, 'with every mouth God sends a pair of hands', but the productivity of the hands determines the ability to consume. Historically, only the independent Serb farmer influenced consumption by his production. Elsewhere in Yugoslavia land and labour were used as vectors for production and consumption by foreign states or magnates, the Slav consuming the residue. Only when full Yugoslav independence was achieved under Tito after 1945 could population influence more fully the size and location of economic activities through its own ability to produce, exchange, earn money, and so consume in any place or region.

THE SIZE AND GROWTH OF POPULATION

At the 1961 census 18,549,291 people were living in Yugoslavia, placing her eighth in Europe by population size.[1] The first full census was made in 1921. Earlier returns exist only for Serbia and Austria-Hungary, but reliable estimates give the population in Yugoslavia[2] in 1880 as 8,851,000. Table 1 shows that population has more than doubled in 85 years, giving an average annual growth rate of 12 per thousand. Until 1948 growth, however, has been below the natural

32

TABLE 1

THE GROWTH OF POPULATION IN YUGOSLAVIA, 1880–1964

CENSUS YEAR	Total Population (000s)	VITAL STATISTICS (PER THOUSAND)			
		Birth Rate	Mortality Rate	Natural Increase	Actual Increase
1880	8,851 ⎱	39·0	24·0	15·0	10·5
1910	11,698 ⎰⎱	—	—	—	6·5
1921	12,529 ⎰⎱				
1931	14,517 ⎰⎱	34·5	18·5	16·0	15·1
1938ᵃ	15,630 ⎰⎱	29·0	17·0	12·0	11·9
		—	—	—	1·4
1948	15,842 ⎱	28·8	12·4	16·4	16·0
1953	16,937 ⎰⎱	24·0	9·7	14·3	14·2
1961	18,549 ⎰⎱	21·8	9·0	12·8	12·8
1964ᵃ	19,200 ⎰				

Sources: *Statistički Godišnjak S.F.R.J.*, 1964, pp. 82–83.
Die Ergebnisse der Volkszahlung von Austria, Wien, 1880, 1910.
Die Ergebnisse der Volkszahlung von Bosnien und Herzegovina, 1910, Sarajevo, 1912.
Miloš Macura, *Stanovništvo kao Činilac Privrednog Razvoja Jugoslavije*, Belgrade 1958, p. 7.
ᵃ The figures for 1938 and 1964 are official estimates.

increase. Emigration and war account for the slow growth during the periods 1880–1910, 1910–21, and 1938–48. Emigration to the New World was high until 1930, especially from poor, Karst areas accessible to the sea. Serbia and Montenegro[3] lost 800,000 people through war and reduced reproduction between 1914 and 1918, and about 1,706,000 Yugoslavs (12 per cent. of the population) were killed in the Second World War.[4]

In peacetime, 1919–40 and after 1945, a high birth rate, and a lower (but still high) mortality rate were characteristic, giving a high natural increase and rapid population growth. Birth and death rates have been falling, yet they remain among the highest in Europe.[5] Death rates have declined more rapidly since 1945 so that, with minimal emigration, population growth is faster now than it was before 1939. Every four or five years adds another million people to the country. To maintain existing living standards, therefore, supplies of food and consumption goods must expand by 2 per cent. annually. New employment must be found, chiefly outside agriculture, for 130,000 school-leavers each year. A high birth rate means that more people are dependent on a proportionately smaller working population. These problems are

D

TABLE 2

POPULATION GROWTH BY REPUBLICS, 1880–1961

	CENSUS 1800		CENSUS 1921		CENSUS 1961	
	Population (Thousands)	Per cent. of Yugoslav Population	Population (Thousands)	Per cent. of Yugoslav Population	Population (Thousands)	Per cent. of Yugoslav Population
Slovenia	1,085	12·9	1,288	10·3	1,592	8·7
Croatia	2,494	28·1	3,422	27·4	4,160	22·4
Serbia	3,324	37·4	4,830	38·6	7,642	41·2
Bosnia-Herzegovina	1,158	13·0	1,884	15·0	3,277	17·7
Macedonia	595	6·5	792	6·3	1,406	7·5
Montenegro	195	2·1	313	2·4	472	2·5
TOTAL	8,851	100·0	12,529	100·0	18,549	100·0

Sources: M. Macura, op. cit., p. 8.
Statistički Godišnjak S.F.R.J., 1964, p. 351.

serious where capital is lacking and productivity low, and hence where production is restricted and consumption per capita low.

Such problems do not impinge equally on all areas, for regional population growth is far from uniform (Table 2). War temporarily reduced population in Bosnia-Herzegovina, Macedonia[6] and Serbia (1914–18), and in Croatia, Slovenia and Montenegro (1941–45). More important, however, are two long-term trends: the slower growth and declining importance of the population of Slovenia and Croatia; and the more rapid growth and increasing importance of the population of Bosnia-Herzegovina, Macedonia and Serbia.[7] These diverging trends result from incredible interregional differences in natural population increase. Vital statistics given in Table 3 reveal two sharply contrasted demographic groups: first, the people of Slovenia, Croatia, Vojvodina and Serbia Proper, with natural increases averaging 9·9 per 1000 since 1950; and second, the people of central and south-eastern Yugoslavia with natural increases averaging 23·4 per 1000. These trends are divergent because in the first zone birth rates have declined more sharply than mortality rates, giving a rapidly declining rate of natural increase while mortality has declined as quickly as, if not more quickly than, the birth rate giving a slowly declining natural increase in Bosnia-Herzegovina, Macedonia, and Montenegro, and actually an increase in Kosmet.

Great as these differences are, there is also much diversity within republics. Natural increase is very high (20–32 per 1000) in a crescent from west Bosnia to western Macedonia, a distribution which, reflecting the distribution of muslim Slavs and Albanians, delineates, even today, the Turkish Empire of a century ago. A high natural increase (15–20) is characteristic in south-central Yugoslavia and parts of southern Serbia and northern Macedonia. Increases are moderate (10–15) in Croatia, western and south-eastern Serbia, Vojvodina, east Slavonia and southern Macedonia, and small (0–10) in Slovenia, western Slavonia, Vojvodina and central and eastern Serbia where western civilisation, Christianity and a tradition of smaller families to prevent excess farm subdivision has encouraged low birth rates. Deaths exceed births

D*

TABLE 3

VITAL STATISTICS OF THE POPULATION LIVING IN THE SIX REPUBLICS AND TWO AUTONOMOUS REGIONS OF YUGOSLAVIA, 1950–64

(Figures per 1000 population)

AVERAGES FOR 5-YEAR PERIODS	YUGOSLAVIA	Bosnia Herzegovina	Croatia	Macedonia	Montenegro	Slovenia	SERBIA Serbia Proper	SERBIA Vojvodina	SERBIA Kosovo-Metohija
1950–54:									
Birth Rate	28·8	38·2	23·2	38·4	32·1	22·8	26·1	23·3	43·5
Death Rate	12·4	13·9	11·7	14·5	10·0	10·9	11·3	12·4	18·0
Natural Increase	16·4	24·3	11·5	23·9	22·1	11·9	14·8	10·9	25·5
1955–59:									
Birth Rate	24·0	38·5	20·3	34·0	29·9	19·8	19·6	18·3	42·5
Death Rate	9·7	14·8	10·1	11·6	8·3	10·2	9·3	10·2	15·9
Natural Increase	14·3	23·7	10·2	22·4	21·6	9·6	10·3	8·1	26·6
1960–1964:									
Birth Rate	21·8	32·0	17·5	29·8	27·0	18·0	16·9	16·6	42·0
Death Rate	8·9	9·2	9·6	10·1	7·2	9·4	8·6	9·7	11·3
Natural Increase	12·9	22·8	7·9	19·7	19·8	8·6	8·3	6·9	30·7

Based on: *Statistički Godišnjak S.F.R.J.*, 1964, p. 359.

giving a natural decrease in the Timok valley (east Serbia). The economic significance of these differential growth rates is, thus, notable. The areas with population increases over 15 per 1000 containing 50 per cent. of the total population in 1953, but contributing 70 per cent. of the population growth after 1953 lie in central and southern Yugoslavia where physical, social and economic conditions are least able to support the increase. Conversely, the remaining areas, also with half the population, but giving only 30 per cent. of the increase, lie in the north and east where better environments can support greater growth. This is the continuing source of a problem which aggravates the inherited economic dichotomy between north and south.

POPULATION DISTRIBUTION & SETTLEMENT

The average density of population, 73 persons per sq. km. (189 sq. m.) in 1961, is low for Europe.[8] Figure 4 shows, however, that the distribution is very uneven. The densest populations are along a coastal strip varying in altitude from 10 to 100 m. in Central Dalmatia (300 per sq. km. or 750 per sq. m.) and in the Croatian Zagorje and Medjumurje areas (100–200 per sq. km., 250–500 per sq. m.).[9] High densities (100–175 persons per sq. km.) occur also in northern and central Bosnia, Šumadija and the Morava valleys, west-central and southern Vojvodina and in the Kosovo and Metohija basins. Densities are about average (60–100 per sq. km.) along the borderlands of Croatia and Slovenia, in the Danube-Tisa plains, in north-west Bosnia and in north-west and central Serbia. Over large areas of the Dinaric Karst, the coast and islands, Alpine Slovenia, central Slavonia, east Vojvodina and peripheral Serbia and Macedonia, densities are below 60 per sq. km. and may be as low as 10 per sq. km.

These distributions can be correlated only partially with natural environments. Higher population densities in Bačka, Šumadija, the Morava valley, central Slovenia, central Bosnia and around Belgrade and Zagreb coincide with good agricultural or industrial resources. Equally, low densities occur where relief, soils, and water supplies are unfavourable, as in the karst regions; here, however, the only meaningful measure of density is the area of agricultural land per head of

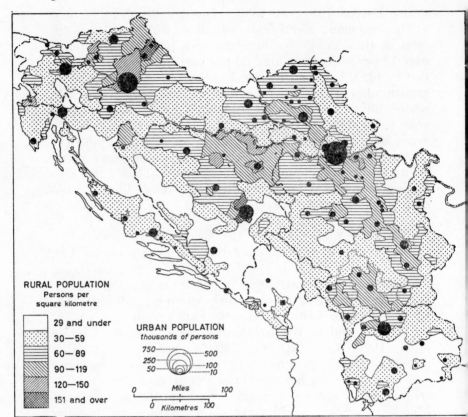

Figure 4. The Distribution of Urban and Rural Populations, 1961
Census

agricultural population. Elsewhere, high densities occur
where there are neither good soils nor industrial resources
but where living was relatively peaceful and reproduction
high: in Zagorje (outside the Military Frontier) and in northern
Bosnia (the less terrorised and attractive periphery of the
Ottoman Empire). The existence of the Military Frontier,
seasonally reinforced by floods, kept densities low along the
Slavonian bank of the Sava river, in Srem and southern Banat.
In addition to population density, the settlement pattern

conditions the character and location of labour and of consumer markets. Large labour supplies and concentrated markets occur where densities are high and large settlements are frequent; labour is scattered and markets diffused where densities are low. In 1961 there were nearly 27,900 settlements in Yugoslavia, 27,550 of them rural, housing 72 per cent. of the population. That 19,170 settlements averaged fewer than 500 inhabitants and another 7,700 averaged 500–2,000 inhabitants, underlines the dispersion of population. This has importance for the scale and location of developing secondary and tertiary activities in relation to labour supplies, demand, and the choice between the costs of commuting labour from widespread settlements and investment in housing in a central place.

Most scope for development is offered by the 350 'urban' settlements which housed 28 per cent. of the population in 1961, but only 58 towns had over 20,000 inhabitants.[10] History and man's use of environment account for regional differences in the broad distribution and scale of settlements: small and dispersed in Slovenia, Bosnia-Herzegovina, Montenegro and Karst areas, Croatia; small but closely packed in Zagorje; average in the plains of Slavonia, Kosovo and Macedonia; large and frequent in Serbia; and very large (over 3,000 inhabitants) in Vojvodina. Each region offers different opportunities in planning location in relation to labour supplies. Although rural population is scattered and the urban population and towns are relatively small, the distribution pattern reveals a surprising degree of concentration in larger towns. About 2,527,000 people (48·2 per cent. of all town-dwellers or 13·6 per cent. of the total population) were living in the 18 towns with near or over 50,000 inhabitants in 1961. By far the largest concentrations of population, and hence labour and markets, are Belgrade, the federal capital, (population in 1961, 600,000), and Zagreb (460,000). They are followed by other republic capitals, Sarajevo (200,000), Skopje (170,000), Ljubljana (160,000) and Novi Sad (111,000), by the chief ports, Rijeka (101,000) and Split (85,000) and by regional centres, Maribor (85,000), Niš (85,000), Subotica (75,000), Osijek (73,000), Zrenjanin (56,000), Tuzla (53,000), Kragujevac (53,000), Banja Luka (51,000), Bitola (50,000) and Mostar (49,000).

NATIONALITIES, LANGUAGES & MINORITIES

The South Slavs have a saying: 'Yugoslavia comprises *six* republics in which live *five* nationalities who speak *four* languages. They have *three* religions and write in *two* alphabets, but there is only *one* desire: independence.' Complex as this seems, and broadly accurate as it is, it leaves out of account several minorities which pose their special problems. The 'five nationalities' (the 'Yugoslavs'),[11] comprising 7,806,000 Serbs, 4,294,000 Croats, 1,589,000 Slovenes, 1,046,000 Macedonians and 514,000 Montenegrins, made up 82·2 per cent. of the population in 1961; the remainder included 1,290,000 muslims, and mainly non-Slav minorities, the most prominent being 915,000 Shiptars (Albanians), 504,000 Hungarians and 183,000 Turks. In no other continental European country do minorities account for such a large proportion of the population, nor is the ethnic variety of the population so great.

Serbs and Croats, the two main groups, form two-thirds of the population. They speak two very similar languages which, together as 'Serbo-Croatian', are compulsory in schools everywhere. Although Serbs readily understand Croats in speech, and vice versa,[12] they read and write totally different alphabets. Serbs use cyrillic (associated with the Orthodox church), Croats use latin (associated with the Catholic church). Communication in writing or print is often difficult, even among postwar university students. Montenegrins speak a language which is close to Serbo-Croatian, but they write with cyrillic characters. The Slovenes and Macedonians speak Slav languages which are not only different from each other, but are different also from Serbo-Croatian,[13] thus isolating them more from their Yugoslav brethren. Slovenes write in latin script, Macedonians in cyrillic. These two alphabets divide Yugoslavs between the Orthodox east and the Catholic west.[14] Islam, the relic of Ottoman days, blurs the division, however, since muslims live chiefly in Bosnia, and in Herzegovina, Sandjak, north-eastern Montenegro, Kosmet and north-western Macedonia. When these major divisions of religion and nationality are identified with conflicting politics, they are explosive elements in the national life. The social tragedy of two World Wars for the country was that Yugoslavs fought Germans *and* among themselves: Croats and Slovenes were conscripted by Austria to fight Serbs and Montenegrins in 1914; Croats fought Serbs in the Nazi-inspired religious-civil war of 1942–44. In peacetime social differences permeate economic matters.

Federalism has attempted to resolve these differences. The six republics, and the tripartite division of the Republic of Serbia (into Serbia Proper, Autonomous Province Vojvodina and Autonomous Kosovo-Metohija District), are delineated ethnically. The republics are truly 'national'[15]: Slovenes comprise 95 per cent. of the population in Slovenia; Serbs 92 per cent. in Serbia Proper; Croats 80 per cent. in Croatia, and Macedonians 70 per cent. in Macedonia. Sixty-five per cent. of the people in Bosnia-Herzegovina are Serbs and Croats; the remainder are muslims. Many Serbs, however, live in Lika (Croatia) and Slavonia, having fled the Turks after 1400. Vojvodina and Kosmet are defined as autonomous regions of Serbia partly because non-Slav peoples are very important in those areas. Albanians (Shiptars) account for two-thirds of the population of Kosovo-Metohija, and Hungarians for one-quarter of the people living in Vojvodina.[16]

Complex as the ethnic structure is now, it is less complex than it was thirty years ago when, in addition, Germans (510,000), Rumanians (250,000), Ruthenians (26,000), Russians (21,000), and Poles (15,000) lived in Yugoslavia, chiefly in the Pannonian plain and its borderlands. Most were repatriated to their homelands in 1945.

THE IMPACT OF MIGRATION

Statistics of migration have become available only since 1948. Before then, some 400,000 peasants from Montenegro, Sandjak, Herzegovina, and Croatia (Lika, Banija, and Kordun) were resettled in Vojvodina[17] under the agrarian reforms 1945–47. Postwar census figures permit accurate assessment of migration movements at the following levels: local (intra-district or intra-commune), inter-district (but intra-republic), and inter-republic. The autochthonous population has increased but slowly, rising by 608,000 (from 10·9 million to 11·58 million) since 1948. This compares with a total population increase of 2,708,000 in the same period. Yugoslavs are becoming more mobile. Local migration is difficult to

measure because of the reorganisation of small local government (i.e. statistical) units—the communes—between 1953
and 1961. Between 1948 and 1961, however, about 1·4
million people moved from one district to another within
the same republic, while 500,000 moved to another republic.
Migration, then, involved about 1 person in 10 in this period.
The volume of intra- and inter-republic movement given in
Table 4 throws light on the geography of economic and social
conditions. Clearly, relatively more people (65·7 to 72·4 per
cent.) living in central and south-eastern Yugoslavia still live
where they were born. People in these regions are poorer,
less adaptable, less affected by change elsewhere, and fewer
have the choice of moving as regional employment opportunities are restricted. More people are also too young to
participate in migration processes. While average conditions
obtain in Serbia, the low percentages of autochthonous population in northern and north-western areas indicate a greater
mobility which is clearly facilitated by greater knowledge,
higher standards, and better communications, and encouraged
by widespread secondary and tertiary activities.

Migration within communes and districts, and between
districts, traditionally consists of 'marriage migration' by a
newly-wed from one village to that of the partner. In recent
years, however, migration by unskilled workers to the mine,
railway, or forestry centre, or migration into towns, has become more common. Intra-commune migration is important
in Slovenia and Montenegro, where settlements are small and
dispersed, but it is low in Vojvodina and Croatia where
settlements are larger. Inter-district migration is greater than
local movement in Croatia, Slovenia, Macedonia, Serbia and
Vojvodina, where varied activities—more localised in capital
cities, regional centres, or ports—attract large numbers of
migrants. Table 4 indicates that Vojvodina has attracted
proportionally most migrants from other republics. Bosnia-
Herzegovina, Montenegro, Slovenia and Kosmet, have been
least attractive.[18] The table also gives the proportion of people
migrating away from the commune where they were born,
who moved to another republic, thus indicating the attraction
of other republics for employment relative to other districts
in the republic concerned. High percentages for Montenegro

TABLE 4

PERCENTAGE AUTOCHTHONOUS AND MIGRANT POPULATION (1961 CENSUS) AND INTER-REPUBLIC MIGRATION 1921–61 (THOUSANDS)

1961	YUGOSLAVIA	Bosnia Herzegovina	Croatia	Macedonia	Montenegro	Slovenia	SERBIA Serbia Proper	Vojvodina	Kosovo-Metohija
% Autochonous Population 1961	62·5	72·4	60·0	65·9	65·7	46·9	62·8	54·9	70·6
Local Migrants (i.e. Intra-commune)	11·1	10·9	9·6	9·1	17·4	18·9	11·6	5·5	12·4
Intra-District Migrants	18·7	13·1	23·3	17·9	11·2	27·8	17·4	15·7	10·8
People from another Republic	7·7	3·6	7·1	7·1	5·7	6·4	8·2	23·9	6·2
Total Migrants (%)	37·5	27·6	40·0	34·1	34·3	53·1	37·2	45·1	29·4
	100	100	100	100	100	100	100	100	100
Proportion of migrants who moved to another republic	—	46·3	23·6	22·1	65·2	13·2	22·3	31·7	41·9
Volume of Inter-Republic Migration 1921–61 (000's) Emigrants from: Immigrants to:	1,359 1,359	370 109	301 257	71 65	99 24	67 66	240 372	137 410	74 56
Balance of Migration	—	−261	−44	−6	−75	−1	+132	+273	−18

Based on: *Statistički Godišnjak SFRJ*, 1964, p. 352.

(65·2), Bosnia-Herzegovina (46·3) and Kosovo-Metohija (41·9) clearly show that many migrants in these areas had to seek employment in other republics.

The low percentage for Slovenia reflects sufficient local employment opportunities. The relatively high figure for Vojvodina expresses the attraction of nearby Belgrade. Some 1,359,000 people migrated to another republic between 1921 and 1961 (Table 4). Broadly, migration is from the south to the north and north-east. Bosnia-Herzegovina and Montenegro lost heavily in net emigration. Croatia also lost population, chiefly from its poor Karst areas to Vojvodina, despite heavy immigration into Zagreb and Slavonia from Bosnia. Only two regions gained by immigration: Vojvodina and Serbia Proper (chiefly Belgrade). These movements are a response to regional economic conditions and contribute towards equalising regional population characteristics. Young immigrants swell the population in Vojvodina and Serbia where small natural increases occur; emigrant youth partly relieves the pressure of population growth in backward areas where natural increase is high (Bosnia-Herzegovina and Montenegro).

Otherwise, however, inter-republic migration is not a good barometer of economic conditions. Migration to Slovenia, the most developed region, is small, and that on balance from Macedonia and Kosmet, the most backward areas, is also surprisingly low. The reasons are these. First, Slovenia has been the main source of skilled labour which has migrated to assist development elsewhere, especially in new towns in Bosnia. Second, Kosmet and Macedonia lie adjacent to each other, and are separated from more developed or developing areas by another discouraging zone of underdeveloped country in Serbia Proper. Third, differences in language and customs make Slovenes, but especially the Macedonians and Albanians, less ready to move to areas inhabited by Serbo-Croatian speaking people. For Slovenes, migration can only take them to poorer areas. Serbs, Croats and Montenegrins move readily in central, eastern and northern Yugoslavia, but rarely to Slovenia or the south-east. Thus, social factors partly modify the effects of varying economic conditions upon migration patterns.

A more detailed study of migration is essential for planning the acceleration or deceleration of movements between particular areas. For want of statistics one must approach this problem indirectly by comparing actual population changes with natural increases. This has been done, with great labour, for the communes of Yugoslavia for the period 1953 to 1961, a period when the number of communes declined from 1479 to 759. The pattern of, and reasons for, change are shown in Figure 5. Six groups of areas are defined. Three groups comprise areas which are sources of net emigration: areas of depopulation resulting from natural decrease and emigration; areas of depopulation where emigration offsets natural increase; and areas of population increase, but where emigration slows growth. The fourth group comprises those areas in which population increase approximately equals natural increase, i.e. where migration has a minimal effect. The last two groups include regions where immigration has contributed to population growth to a greater or lesser degree than the natural increase.

Depopulation is widespread (Figure 5) from the Karst areas stretching from western Slovenia south-eastwards to the Albanian frontier, from west-central, eastern and south-eastern Serbia and from Macedonia. These are problem areas, for although depopulation expresses backwardness or unfavourable environment, it erodes away the younger generation, leaving the older people who are less capable of making changes and improvements. Emigration is also serious from some areas of high population increase (group 3), especially from parts of Bosnia-Herzegovina, Kosmet and Sandjak. So long as large-scale emigration does not completely offset the high natural increase, this may not be critical for the propensity of the population to produce, adapt and consume. Stable population conditions occur chiefly where economic opportunities expand in step with the local labour market, as in Vojvodina, parts of Slovenia and around developing centres in Bosnia-Herzegovina, Kosovo and Macedonia. Immigration plays an important role in population increase where there are medium or large urban centres, good agricultural land, or expanding secondary and tertiary sectors: the Adriatic port areas, the Sava valley, central Vojvodina,

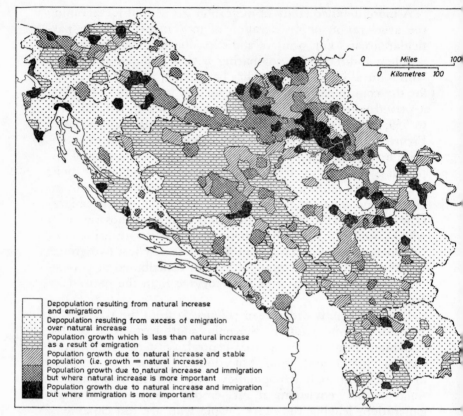

Figure 5. Emigration, Immigration, Natural Increase and Spatial
Population Change, 1953–61

the Morava valley, the Sarajevo area, and scattered centres in
the south-east. These areas gain more than just numbers of
people. They gain the youth who are more productive, and
who are (or can be) educated and can apply change and
quicken economic growth. Migration is thus contributing to
changes in the propensity of the populations of particular areas
to produce, trade and consume: they reduce it in areas of
depopulation or high emigration (where it is low anyway
because of over-population, the predominance of agriculture,
and a high proportion of dependents), and they increase it
sharply in the smaller areas of Yugoslavia (where it may be

high or low but where it has the greatest possibility of being high as a result of the predominance of secondary and tertiary activities).

Urbanisation has been an important feature in areas in groups 5 and 6. In 1961, some 5,242,000 people lived in towns in Yugoslavia, compared with 3,117,000 in 1948, an increase of 2·1 million. Since the total population increased by 2·7 million in the same period, the population living in rural areas and settlements has continued to increase, though slowly. The more developed areas, with a higher proportion of town-dwellers in 1948 and with a lower natural increase of population, show the greatest increase in urbanisation. In Croatia, Slovenia, Vojvodina and Serbia, the rural population is actually declining. Migration into towns is most important in these republics. It is estimated that 1·3 million people migrated to towns between 1948 and 1961, about half of the total number of migrants. There is still much migration between non-urban settlements, therefore, a fact which underlines the slow growth of urban population (from 21 to 28 per cent. 1948–61). Since employment in towns has often expanded more rapidly than housing, Yugoslavia has a serious problem of commuting labour.

THE POPULATION AS CONSUMER & PRODUCER

All census returns since 1921 show the effects of war in an abnormally low proportion of people in the 20–41 age groups and in a high ratio of females to males (1081:1000 in 1948 and even 1136:1000 in Croatia). The heavy burden of reconstruction and expanded production has fallen on a smaller population of working age which must also support a high proportion of young dependents. The burden falls unevenly as Table 5 shows. Striking regional contrasts in the proportion of people engaging in production are closely related to differences in age composition and the employment of women. Although too much should not be read into the relative size of the working population (because employment in an underdeveloped country often grades into under-employment and concealed unemployment), nevertheless, high birth rates in central and south-eastern Yugoslavia mean that the proportion of people of working age is low, and that frequent pregnancy

TABLE 5

SALIENT FEATURES OF THE POPULATION OF WORKING AGE BY REPUBLICS, 1961

	Population of Working Age (15–64 years) (Percentage of Total Population)	Working Population (Percentage of Total Population)	Female Working Population (Percentage of Working Population)	Proportion of Females of Working Age who work
YUGOSLAVIA	62·6	44·9	37·6	31·7
Slovenia	64·9	48·3	40·9	38·6
Croatia	65·4	46·9	37·5	35·3
Vojvodina	65·8	44·0	29·9	25·8
Serbia Proper	65·7	51·1	38·6	39·1
Kosovo-Metohija	53·2	34·7	24·7	17·1
Bosnia-Herzegovina	57·9	39·2	31·9	24·4
Macedonia	57·5	39·4	29·7	23·2
Montenegro	56·5	34·2	25·4	19·1

Source: Statistički Godišnjak S.F.R.J., 1964, pp. 82, 84, 351–2.

reduces the female working population to a minimum.[19] As capital scarcities are greatest in the same areas, the unusually small labour force must substitute for capital and yet be used efficiently enough to raise per capita production and consumption despite the rapid increase in numbers of young dependents.

(1) Unemployment & Agricultural Overpopulation

Wholly or partially unemployed labour is a major productive resource in Yugoslavia, even though it implies a restricted market for production. Statistics of unemployment are neither comprehensive nor continuous, and they give no indication of the concealed unemployment inherent in agricultural overpopulation. This was the central economic problem of pre-war Yugoslavia. To a large degree it still is. Agriculture is virtually the only large source of labour for employment in secondary and tertiary activities; and labour is the only abundant factor of production. The existence and volume of overpopulation or 'surplus' agricultural population is thus important, yet it can be established only indirectly and imperfectly. Calculations made for the 1930s estimate the 'surplus' in Yugoslavia by comparing the actual agricultural population (and their production) with that which could be expected to depend on agriculture assuming European or French standards of productivity per hectare of arable equivalent[22] and per capita production levels. These estimates are set out in Table 6. The figures are hypothetical, yet those given in column 2 appear to be a reasonable guide. It is generally accepted that, where peasant subsistence agriculture prevails, considerable overpopulation exists wherever there is less than one hectare of arable land (or arable equivalent) per head of agricultural population; only areas with over 1·5 ha. arable equivalent per capita do not suffer overpopulation.[24] By any standard, Yugoslavia before 1940, ranked as one of the most overpopulated countries in Europe, disposing of only 0·5 ha. arable land per head of agrarian population.[25] According to Moore, between 4·0 and 6·5 million people were 'surplus'. This included 1–2 million *active* people. War-time losses and postwar economic progress in branches outside agriculture have contributed to a reduction of the 'surplus', but

Table 6

AGRICULTURAL OVERPOPULATION IN YUGOSLAVIA ABOUT 1930
(thousands and per cent. of agricultural population)

Area[23]	Method of Calculation: 1		2		3		4	
	Surplus (000s)	%	Surplus (000s)	%	Surplus (000s)	%	Surplus (000s)	%
YUGOSLAVIA	6,532	61·5	4,122	38·8	8,301	78·1	6,932	65·2
Slovenia	452	65·9	307	44·8	553	80·6	470	68·5
East Bosnia and West Serbia	817	64·9	518	41·2	1,007	80·0	838	66·6
Vojvodina and Sumadija	543	30·5	180	10·1	1,077	60·5	870	48·9
Central and East Serbia	822	66·8	566	46·0	998	81·1	853	69·3
Dalmatia and W. Herzegovina	585	78·4	361	48·3	655	87·7	528	70·7
Croatia-Slavonia	1,237	61·1	1,303	64·3	1,578	77·9	1,615	79·7
Macedonia, S.E. Serbia, Southern Kosovo-Metohija	879	71·9	511	41·7	1,029	83·9	820	66·9
N. and W. Bosnia, East Herzegovina, Montenegro	625	68·6	360	39·6	748	82·2	598	65·7
Sandjak and Metohija	572	75·7	386	51·1	652	86·2	546	72·2

Source: W. E. Moore, *Economic Demography of Eastern and South-Eastern Europe*, League of Nations, Geneva, 1954, pp. 64, 72, 206, 208.

METHODS: (1) 'Surplus' assuming existing Yugoslav production and European average output per capita.
(2) 'Surplus' assuming French productivity per hectare arable equivalent and European per capita output.
(3) 'Surplus' assuming existing production and French per capita level.
(4) 'Surplus' assuming French production, French productivity per ha. arable equivalent and French output per capita.

it remains high because natural increase in rural areas is high. Postwar estimates give the 'surplus' for Yugoslavia as around 3·2 to 3·3 million persons (1953) or 31 per cent. of the farm population, and for Serbia Proper and Kosmet 765,000 or 36 per cent. in 1948 and 642,000 or 33 per cent. in 1961.[26] A survey of agriculture in 1960 gives 1,069,000 private peasant holdings 'with an excess labour force'[27] unemployed for much of the year.

Whatever the estimates are, the geographical pattern of overpopulation before and after 1939 remains virtually the same. Moore's estimates showed that overpopulation was least in north-eastern Yugoslavia and greatest in Dalmatia, Herzegovina, Montenegro, and Croatia. Figure 6 shows the pattern for districts in 1957, giving the density of agricultural population per 100 ha. (1 sq. km.) of agricultural land expressed in arable equivalents. The minimum for reasonable subsistence

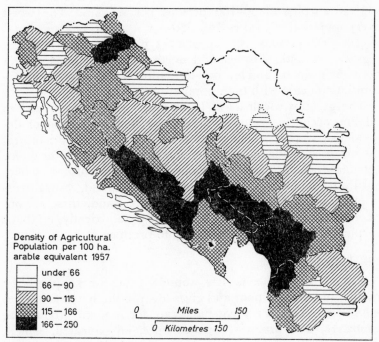

Density of Agricultural
Population per 100 ha.
arable equivalent 1957

under 66
66 — 90
90 — 115
115 — 166
166 — 250

0   Miles   150
0   Kilometres   150

Figure 6. Regional Patterns of Population Pressure on Agricultural Land

assumed is 1·5 ha. arable equivalent per capita (66 farm population per sq. km.). Clearly, only Vojvodina and eastern Slavonia, with densities ranging between 50–60 per sq. km., do not suffer overpopulation. A labour 'surplus', however, exists in all other regions of Yugoslavia. Figure 6 indicates the areal incidence of the 'surplus' by showing four types of overpopulated area. First, the more fertile lowlands of northern Serbia, central Slavonia and horticultural areas in Istria and Dalmatia where densities of 66–90 per sq. km. give a small surplus up to 25 persons per sq. km. Second, the hilly areas in north-west and central Serbia, west Slavonia, the Adriatic littoral, central Slovenia, northern and central Bosnia and Macedonia with densities of 90–115 per hectare, have a moderate 'surplus' (25–50 persons per sq. km.). Third, the broken uplands in central and southern Serbia, Croatia, eastern Bosnia-Herzegovina, Montenegro and Prekomurje (Slovenia) with 115–66 farm people per sq. km. arable equivalent suffer a large surplus of 50–100 persons per sq. km. The worst overpopulation (densities 166–250 per sq. km., i.e. 'surpluses' of 100–200 persons per sq. km.) typify the Dinaric Karst regions, Sandjak, Kosmet and north-west Macedonia, where poor environment and few non-agricultural employment opportunities coincide with high population growth.

The greatest surpluses of labour, i.e. least efficient uses of labour, occur in regions where there is a high ratio of dependents: workers. The greatest concentration of agricultural labour in Yugoslavia is in areas where neither physical nor economic conditions are favourable to agriculture, where agrarian labour supply does not reflect demand. Since overpopulation and malnutrition go hand in hand, these regions have least propensity to consume, but paradoxically, a labour surplus which has little propensity to produce.

(2) Illiteracy

Although Yugoslavia has abundant labour supplies, the quality of labour is poor and gives low productivity even when employed. This is a great handicap, for modern production, exchange, and progress depends upon an educated, skilled, and productive labour force with the ability to appreciate environment to apply new techniques designed to raise productivity and consumption per capita, and to pass on its knowledge to the younger generation who are the consumers of today and the producers of tomorrow.

Despite pre-war government school building programmes, only 56 per cent. of the children of school age were then receiving elementary education; nearly half the population of school age between 1919 and 1939 had no education. Illiteracy has been reduced by postwar compulsory education, but is still high, especially among the peasant labour force (10 per cent.), people of middle and older age (35 per cent.), and among women (39 per cent.). The weight of learning, applying and innovating thus falls heavily on the young; yet here the youthfulness of the population is an advantage. Illiteracy is a special problem in the agricultural population and in certain regions. The agricultural population is the largest single working and managing force in the economy, and the main force of labour for other activities; yet in 1953 some 2·4 million peasants, agricultural workers and proprietors (out of 5·2 million) could neither read nor write. Sharp contrasts exist, even today, in the levels of literacy of the people living in different regions. Illiteracy is virtually non-existent among the Slovenes (only 1·5 per cent.), is low among the people of Croatia and Vojvodina (10–15 per cent.), is higher in Montenegro, Herzegovina and Serbia Proper (15–25 per cent.) and very high in central and south-eastern regions (25–57 per cent.). These variations, closely related to historico-cultural and national characteristics are partly an effect of economic conditions. This is most apparent along a line from Črnomelj (Slovenia) to Cazin (Bosnia) only 40 miles apart. Illiteracy increases from 3 per cent. in Slovenia to 14 per cent. around Duga Resa (Karlovac, Croatia), to 32 per cent. around Slunj (in Croatia but bordering Bosnia), to 44 per cent. at Velika Kladuša (Bosnia) and 51 per cent. in Cazin.

Many skilled and educated workers were killed in the second World War. A major postwar problem has been the training of youth especially in economics, technology and natural sciences. As recently as 1961, 57 per cent. of Yugoslav's labour force had no more than elementary education, but at present 41 per cent. of all workers attend training courses. Ten years ago over one quarter of the labour force

E

had never been to school, half had had elementary education, and only 12 per cent. had received secondary education. Agriculture fared worse with one third, one half, and 1·5 per cent. respectively. Naturally the geographical pattern of unqualified and unskilled labour largely repeats the pattern of illiteracy: the proportion of unskilled workers is higher in central and south-eastern Yugoslavia (but also in Vojvodina) where it ranges between 31 and 38 per cent., than in the north and north-west (25–30 per cent.). Postwar efforts to develop southern Yugoslavia have demanded the provision of modern housing in new or expanded towns as a means of inducing skilled labour to move from the north to the skill-deficient areas.

'SELJACI-INDUSTRISKI RADNICI'—Peasant-Industrial Workers

Not all people who are employed full time (or part time in overpopulated areas) do only one job. The term 'peasant-industrial worker' denotes the peasant who works permanently outside agriculture, but who lives, and works in his spare time, on his land in the countryside. Usually these people commute to and from work daily over distances of two to twenty-five miles in one direction. Their exact numbers are unknown, but may be 900,000.[28] 'Peasant-industrial workers' have become important for a number of reasons: the growth of new urban employment, for which the countryside is the main source of labour; the attachment of peasants to their land, which discourages permanent migration;[29] and finally, the lag in urban housing facilities, which strengthens that discouragement and necessitates a large number of commuters. Travelling time reduces the time available for working their land (often throwing a heavier burden on the womenfolk) or for learning their new trade. This is not serious for agricultural production where there is overpopulation, but it means lower productivity in the factory or shop through fatigue and malnutrition. Travel is less onerous where communications are good, as in Slovenia; but where they are poor, as in central, eastern, and south-eastern regions, workers' fatigue after walking miles and travelling in overcrowded trains or buses becomes a serious matter. Where overpopulation is minimal, however, development of non-agricultural activities may adversely affect agricultural land use and production through the maladjustment between place of work and place of residence of the peasant-industrial workers.

Population is thus a complex factor, yet a clear distinction emerges in the greater ability of the population to produce, trade and consume in the northern, western, and eastern regions, and its restricted ability elsewhere, particularly in the regions most recently freed from Ottoman rule.

REFERENCES

1 Europe does not include the U.S.S.R. in this context. The seven states with larger populations in 1961 were: German Federal Republic (54 million); United Kingdom (52 million); Italy (50); France (47); Spain (31); Poland (30); and Rumania (18·7 millions).

2 The area referred to throughout is that of Yugoslavia since 1954.

3 These two areas shared the tragic distinction of the heaviest losses per 1000 population of all participants in the war, *Popis Stanovništva Kraljevine Srba, Hrvata, i Slovenaca 1921, Prethodni Rezultati*, Sarajevo, 1924, p. XIV.

4 M. Macura, *Stanovništvo kao Činilac Privrednog Razvoja Jugoslavije*, Belgrade, 1958, p. 10.

5 The birth rate among Yugoslavs between 1948 and 1962 was, on average, second in Europe only to that of the Poles. See *Statistički Godnišnjak S.F.R.J.*, 1964, p. 83 and *Rocznik Statystyczny P.R.L.*, 1963, p. 38. Mortality rates have been higher in Yugoslavia than in other European countries except Bulgaria.

6 The decline of population in Macedonia was partly a result of Turkish emigration.

7 Montenegro has shown a stable population as a result of high rates of emigration which reduce the effects of a high natural increase within the republic.

8 Only eight countries (Albania, Bulgaria, Finland, Greece, Iceland, Norway, Spain, and Sweden), out of a total of 26, have lower population densities.

9 I. Rubić, 'Planimetrijska i Altimetrijska Razdioba Naselja i Stanovništva Dalmacije', *Krš Jugoslavije*, Zagreb, 1957, pp. 63–108.

10 *Jugoslovenski Pregled*, 5, 1964, pp. 191–4. The precise definition of 'urban' settlements in Yugoslavia is difficult because of the continued importance of agriculture; settlements are thus designated 'mixed' if agriculture employs under 30 per cent. of the people in settlements with 500–2000 inhabitants, rising progressively to 60–70 per cent. of the population of settlements with 10–15,000 inhabitants. Macura, *op. cit.*, p. 90.

11   Few people call themselves Yugoslavs. Tradition, language, and dialect strongly identify people with a region, so that regional consciousness is well developed. People identify themselves as Serbs, Croats, Dalmatians, Herzegovinans, Bosnians or Slavonians etc.

12   Yugoslavs often stress that the differences between Serbian and Croatian are limited to dialects and pronunciation; for example, the 'e' sound in Serbian as in 'belo' (white) becomes 'ije' or 'je' in Croatia as in 'bijelo'. Many words in use every day, however, are quite different, especially the names of months, the words for time, place, items of food, furniture, and clothing. Apart from original Croatian or Serbian words, Croatian shows links with Slovak and the influence of German and some Italian, while the Serbian language contains words bearing the stamp of Turkish and French.

13   The Slovene language is closer to the western Slav group of languages (especially Slovak), but many words testify to centuries of German and Italian influence. Macedonian is related to Bulgarian and includes many words of Turkish origin.

14   The Orthodox religion is supreme in Serbia Proper, Montenegro, and much of Macedonia; Catholicism dominates Slovenia, the coastlands, Croatia and Slavonia. Where Serbs and Croats mingle, as in Bosnia, Vojvodina, and Lika, so do religions, alphabets, and customs. The dualism of the alphabets is emphasised by the fact that throughout the Serbo-Croatian areas, the names on railway stations are duplicated in cyrillic and latin.

15   The six republics were known as 'national' or 'people's' republics until 1963; since then they have been called officially socialist republics.

16   Albanians also live in western Macedonia and Hungarians along the Drava valley. Several lesser minorities are distributed as follows: Italians live mainly in Istrian and Dalmatian towns, the Rumanians in Banat (Vojvodina) and the Timok valley (E. Serbia), the Czechs in Slavonia and Bosnia, Slovaks in Vojvodina, and Bulgarians in eastern Serbia and Macedonia.

17   R. Petrović, *Ekonomska Geografija Jugoslavije*, Zagreb, 1958, p. 120.

18   If, as seems likely, most immigrants into Bosnia-Herzegovina, Montenegro, and Kosovo-Metohija have average Yugoslav natural growth rates, their relative importance is reduced by high local birth rates. The exception is Slovenia.

19   The fact that overpopulation is greater where the percentage of working population is lower places these regions in a worse position so that production, and hence consumption, per head is minimal.

20   This is a fair percentage because only insured persons could register, and only those who worked outside agriculture were usually insured. These figures, therefore, do not include 'surplus' agricultural workers; but they also give no record of uninsured workers who were unemployed.

21   *Statistički Godišnjak S.F.R.J.*, 1964, p. 380–1.

22   The 'arable equivalent' of land is an attempt to interpret different qualities of land in different uses by a comparable measure. The equivalents of 1 ha. arable land are: 0·33 ha. of orchard, garden, or vineyard; 2·5 ha. of meadow; and 5·0 ha. of pasture. For a recent

discussion, see: R. Bićanić, 'Three Concepts of Agricultural Over-population'; in: Roger N. Dixey (ed.) *International Explorations in Agricultural Economics*, Ames, Iowa, 1966, p. 9–22.

23 These areas are described here for the sake of clarity; the actual areas quoted by W. E. Moore were the official administrative areas for the period 1930–41 which were called 'banovina'.

24 This average is realistic because Yugoslavia is a land of small peasant proprietors; there are few medium or large farms.

25 This compares with 1·2 ha. in Hungary, 1·1 ha. in Czechoslovakia, 1·0 ha. in Rumania, and 0·9 ha. in Bulgaria.

26 N. Čobeljić and K. Mihailović, 'Agrarna Prenaseljenost', *Ekonomist*, Belgrade, 1, 1953, pp. 16–17, and D. Stanković and M. Popović, *Rezerve Radne Snage u Poljoprivredi S.R. Srbije*, Institut za Ekonomiku Poljoprivrede, Belgrade, 1965.

27 *Statistički Godišnjak S.F.R.J.*, 1964, p. 415.

28 *Ibid*, p. 415.

29 The phenomenon arises only where private peasant proprietorship exists; state agricultural enterprises employ workers who do not own land.

CHAPTER 4

The Physical Environment

Spatial variety in historical experience, in social environment and in social change is matched by no less vivid areal contrasts in physical environment. Broadly, a position in south-eastern Europe, in the same latitudes as Catalonia, Languedoc and Italy, and bordering the Adriatic Sea for 400 miles, should provide Yugoslavia with a distinctly Mediterranean environment. In fact, mountains which rise abruptly in an almost unbroken 'wall' to 6,000' from the coast and the Greek Macedonian plain restrict such an environment to the narrow western and south-western littoral, the Adriatic islands, and the lower Vardar valley. This 'wall' is not itself an important watershed, yet the major divide between Mediterranean and Danubian drainage is sufficiently far to the west, south-west and south for 70 per cent. of Yugoslavia to be drained by the Danube and its tributaries. Since the tributary valleys broaden and descend generally northwards and eastwards to the Pannonian plain, which itself is open to the north and north-east, continental influences pentrate into most regions. Within these broad physical divisions locally varied geological conditions, relief, climatic influences and aspect give marked regional differentiation of environment. Overall, however, the opportunities that nature offers to the South Slavs are moderately favourable for long-term economic progress in all branches of the economy.

GEOLOGY & STRUCTURE

Three main structural units dominate the physique of Yugoslavia: the Rhodope massif, the fold mountains and the Pannonian basin. Crystalline and metamorphic rocks (gabbros, gneisses, granites, schists and slates) characterise the ancient structural nucleus of the Balkans, the Rhodope massif.

These outcrop widely in the east and south-east, within a broadly triangular area lying between Kragujevac in the north, Bitola in the south and Trn (on the Bulgarian-Yugoslav frontier) in the south-east. During the Tertiary orogeny the massif was arched and fractured, giving complex faulting and much volcanic activity. To the north-west, towards the ancient Alpine cores, crystalline and volcanic 'islands' occur along a N.W.–S.E. axis as outliers of the Rhodope, forming isolated massifs that rise from the Pannonian plain between Medvednica (Zagreb) and Fruška Gora parallel to ridges through central Bosnia to Slovenia.

In Mezozoic times, in seas which surrounded these massifs, were accumulated the great thicknesses of Triassic, Jurassic and Cretaceous sediments which cover much of Yugoslavia today. Tertiary earth movements raised, intensely folded and crushed these sediments as fold mountains against both sides of the Rhodope block. Simultaneously, the Pannonian basin sank within the Carpathian arc. Fold mountains dominate the area to the west and south of a line drawn Maribor-Karlovac-Kragujevac-Bitola, but comprise four distinct structural units. First, the Alps extend along a west-east axis into Slovenia, the Julian Alps continuing the southern limestone Alps, the Pohorje continuing the central crystalline Alps and the Karavanke forming the division between them. Secondly, the Dinaric mountains commence southward of the Tolmin (Soča valley)—Ljubljana tectonic line and follow the N.W.–S.E. trend that characterises the entire region between the Adriatic coast and the rivers Soča, Sava, Ibar and Drin. The western and south-western zone, however, consists of limestones of great purity and thickness which give rise to the renowned Karst (*Krš* or *Kras*); except for flysch and marl in synclines, this zone lacks impervious outcrops. In contrast the eastern Dinaric fold region comprises a variety of rocks besides limestones: volcanics, schists and serpentines, and shales and sandstones, with Palaeozoic rocks exposed by erosion in the east. Thirdly, the Pindus (western Macedonian) mountains and Šar Planina are geologically akin to the eastern Dinarics, but they are separated from them by the river Drin and trend N–S. Fourthly, eastward of the Rhodope massif lie the East Serbian ('Balkan') mountains, the Yugoslav portion of the

Carpathian arc comprising limestones, sandstones and volcanics. All the mountain regions have been fractured since
Tertiary times to produce fault basins and *polja* along tectonic
lines.

During the Eocene period the sea overflowed the Pannonian
basin and peripheral Mediterranean areas, penetrated the
mountain valleys and submerged interior synclines and lower
tectonic basins. Marine and lacustrine sediments accumulated
to give fertile land (marls, flysch) in the heart of limestone
mountain country and to form Tertiary areas adjoining the
Dinaric and Rhodope systems along the margins of the Pannonian basin. This basin, the third major structural unit,
continues to subside. Its surface today comprises Quaternary
loess blown off central European ice-sheets in the Pleistocene
period and river alluvium, except where isolated crystalline
massifs break the surface.

STRUCTURAL INSTABILITY

Regional and local tectonic lines are widespread southward
of the Sava and Danube rivers and have a dual importance.
Often they have become mineralised zones during periods of
igneous activity. Yet they indicate structural weakness and,
as a result of proximity to the active zone of Mediterranean
earth movement, potential and actual instability over large
areas. Tremors are frequent. Fewer than 50 tremors may be
recorded annually in 'quiet' periods (1941–48 and 1956–60),
but in the 'active' periods, 1938–40, 1949–55 and 1962–63
some 820, 585 and 885 tremors respectively were recorded!
Earthquakes of force V and over occur every year and may
strike virtually anywhere. Especially vulnerable regions are
Macedonia and southern Serbia, centring on Skopje, 'whence
there is a fan-like divergence of the main tectonic lines in the
Balkans, coupled with transverse faulting',[1] and the western
Dinaric zone, where eleven tremors of force VI–IX in 25
years emphasise the dangers to hydro-electricity barrages.
Earthquakes may have short-term effects where they strike
but their persistent occurrence represents both an investment
and a maintenance cost risk to the state. The 1963 Skopje
earthquake, causing damage equivalent to ten per cent. of the
Yugoslavian annual national income, is still fresh in the minds

of many; and other large towns also lie within the zone of frequent earthquakes.[2]

RELIEF

Uplands and mountains dominate the Yugoslav scene. Less than one third of the land is lowland (below 650′, 200 m.), while over one half lies above 1,000′ (305 m.) and one fifth above 3,000′ (915 m.). Although the lowlands are most favourable for agriculture, cultivation, in existing climatic conditions, is possible up to 3,000′, depending upon aspect, slope and soils. Forest and pasture dominate above that level. Extremes of relief and altitude is a recurrent theme. Broadly, a highland zone contrasts with a lowland zone. Neither, however, is uniform. From the extensive Pannonian plain rise bluffs and terraces eastward, and also imposing uplands westwards, of the Danube. True Alps alternate with deep glaciated valleys and tectonic basins in Slovenia. The Dinarics comprise alternating *planina* ridges and synclinal depressions, the former dissected by river gorges, the latter broken irregularly by tectonic basins and marked by complex drainage. Karst plateaux, pitted, broken and dissected by *polja, doline, uvale, ponore*[3] and dry valleys, add variety in the western Dinaric zone and partially also in the Carpathians. Much of the east, however, comprises broad valleys, interlinking fault basins and contrasting with multi-directional uplands in the Rhodope massif and broad valleys, platforms and rolling hills in the Tertiary country of Šumadija.

Past uplift of peneplained surfaces and of folded mountains above deep valleys and down-faulted polja 'accounts for the youthfulness of relief. Relatively steeply sloping land is common everywhere, making much land below 3,000′ unsuitable for cultivation, unless the risk of soil erosion is countered by terracing or by planting trees. Slopes at lower levels often remain forested. In the Alps and Dinarics, however, more slopes have a north aspect and are forested than in the Rhodope and Pindus systems, where more slopes face east or west and are cultivated or under pasture. Steep slopes subject large areas in Yugoslavia to soil creep, gullying and rapid erosion with large-scale flooding and deposition beyond the break of slope on the plains, valley floors or polja.

The dominance of youthful relief enhances the value of flat or gently sloping land and lowland for agriculture and for siting modern industries, transport facilities and urban building. The most extensive lowland is the Pannonian plain, which covers one quarter of Yugoslavia. Three level surfaces are important for human activity here: the flood plains of the major rivers, the higher and drier alluvial terraces, and the extensive loess terrace. These offer the best areas for large-scale mechanised farming in Yugoslavia; the plain is also a natural focus for valley routes from most regions and permits easy intercommunication over a wide area. Elsewhere only the valleys of the lower Neretva (Herzegovina), Morača (Montenegro) and Vardar (Macedonia) are important. Flat land is very scarce along the coast. Within the fold mountains and Rhodope systems level surfaces, *polja*, various terraces and uplifted peneplains, are at a premium. Tectonic movements from Tertiary times, followed by erosion, produced the *polja*, a feature that is typical of Balkan relief. *Polja* are sunk within synclines or broader plateaux and clearly demonstrate local structure lines; hence the *polja* of Lika, Livno and Popovo have a Dinaric trend and Polog or Pelagonia a Pindaric trend. Filled with lacustrine and fluvial deposits and situated at altitudes up to 3,000', *polja* form the most important—in the Karst the only—areas of fertile land amid the mountains. Terraces, developed by lacustrine abrasion and river erosion during intervals of stillstand in the recession of the Tertiary seas, break the mountain slopes and provide fertile areas for agriculture (if aspect is favourable) above the *polja* which may be liable to seasonal flooding. Seven to fifteen terraces[4] are recognisable between 300' and 3,000'; in the Tertiary hill country of Šumadija and north Bosnia they remain as dissected, yet extensive platforms. At higher altitudes, up to eleven peneplain levels are discernible as accordant *planina* summits or as extensive plateaux of *humina*[5] which are well preserved in the Karst; these surfaces provide useful upland pastures.

Relief is an important obstale to interregional and local communications. The Dinaric Alps can be crossed only with great difficulty since they lie transverse to Pannonian-Adriatic routes, they range in breadth from 25 miles (near Rijeka) to 175 miles eastwards, they comprise up to eleven parallel planina ridges which rise to between 3,000' and 8,000' over much of their length, and generally they end in very abrupt slopes to the sea. They present three further obstacles. First, the Una, Sana, Vrbas and Drina rivers, draining northward, cut transversely through the planina in narrow gorges, permitting only tenuous, or totally preventing, contact between lower and upper valley sections and *polja*. Second, no passes cross the Danubian-Adriatic watershed below 2,000'; most lie between 2,500' and 3,500' and are exposed to severe climatic conditions in winter. Third, karst country makes transport extraordinarily difficult between this watershed and the sea, leaving many areas isolated locally because surface drainage is lacking or discontinuous and tectonic and karstic processes have produced very irregular and abrupt dissection and perforation of rocky surfaces. Only the Neretva provides a moderately easy route across the Karst to the Ivan Saddle and the Bosna valley. Except here, and where the Karst narrows between Pannonia (in the upper Kupa valley) and Rijeka, interior Yugoslavia is effectively isolated from its coast. In contrast, communications from the northern plains easily penetrate the longitudinal and transverse alpine valleys of Slovenia, the broad and inter-linked basins of the Morava system in Serbia and cross the low, indistinct watershed to the Vardar valley.[6] Such, then, is the Dinaric barrier that the best routes are peripheral, lie near the northern and eastern frontiers and terminate in foreign ports (Trieste, Salonika and, till 1945, Rijeka). Certain other important valley routeways are both vulnerably near frontiers and are relatively isolated in Yugoslavia by rugged relief: the Soča, the Timok, the Radika-Drin (west Macedonia). The Bistrica-Lim-Morača route around northern Albania, providing the shortest link between Kosmet and coastal Montenegro, crosses four passes between 2,500' (760 m.) and 5,800' (1,770 m.) above sea level!

CLIMATE

The location of relief forms in relation to the Mediterranean Sea and major air streams explains the broad patterns of climate: a Mediterranean type along the littoral, a cool wet transitional type in the western and southern mountains and a drier continental type in the north and east.

The area from Sardinia to the Kvarner Bay (Rijeka) is a major centre of cyclogenesis between September and May as cold dry air from the Russian anticyclone is drawn into contact with warm moist air in the Mediterranean low and meets the southern branch of the European jet stream moving eastward from the Atlantic. Very frequent depressions diverge from Kvarner across lower Slovenia north-eastwards, along the Sava valley eastwards or along the Adriatic to the Aegean.[7] Pressure and temperature gradients between the adjacent cold lands and the passing 'warm' depression induce strong local winds. Most important are the north-easterly *Košava* ('mower') of eastern Vojvodina, the *Vardarac* and the *Bora*. Blowing with terrific velocity down precipitous coastal slopes, the 'bora' brings all land, sea and air communications to, from and along the Adriatic coast and islands to a standstill, isolating local communities for days. In summer winds are light, as the Azores anticyclone extends across the region, giving high temperatures and reducing land-sea differences.

Temperatures amply demonstrate the prevalence of continental conditions. Annual *ranges* of temperature, moderate (ranges of 14–16°C, 25–29°F) along the Adriatic, become continental (ranges of 20–21°C, 36–38°F) already along a line Tolmin-Delnice-Gospić-Mostar-Titograd, 15–30 miles inland, as relief shuts out maritime influences and induces winter temperature inversions of up to 18°C (equal to 32°F) in basins.[8] Extremes are greatest in Vojvodina (23–24°C, 41–43°F). Everywhere north-east of this line *absolute* winter temperatures are below 0°C (32°F), while the coast enjoys temperatures of 5–9°C (41–48°F). Temperatures rise rapidly through the spring to July maxima, averaging 24–26°C (75–79°F) in Dalmatia, 20–24°C (68–75°F) in Pannonia and 18–20°C (64–68°F) in interior *polja*. High 'anomaly' coastal temperatures in summer result from the high insolation and lack of cloud, the heat of the barren Karst and isolation from Atlantic influences. Inversions, frequent and severe in depressions and valleys throughout highland Yugoslavia, encourage settlement and cultivation on valleysides and terraces where snow melts earlier, frost-free periods are longer and fogs are fewer.

Frost-free periods with 'growing' temperatures of 6°C

(43°F) permit cultivation below 3,000' in all regions, but their length, combined with insolation and cloudiness, conditions regional crop potentials. Outstanding are the coastal lowlands south of the Velebit and south-eastern Macedonia, where 275–315 consecutive frost-free days, 2,300–2,750 hours of sunshine per annum and high spring and summer temperatures permit the cultivation of sub-tropical fruits, rice, cotton and tobacco. Elsewhere the frost-free period is shorter, averaging 180–220 days, cloudiness is greater and temperatures lower as summer rain becomes prevalent and insolation provides only 1,500–1,800 hours of sunshine throughout the highland zone and 1,900–2,200 in Pannonia; temperate crops predominate, therefore. Late spring frosts at or near ground level, however, often damage cereals, vegetables and vines in northern and eastern lowlands.[9]

Annual and seasonal precipitation varies regionally, too (Figure 7). Abundant precipitation falls in the western and southern fold regions, the coastal lowlands receiving annually 700–1,400 mm. (28–56") and the high mountains averaging 2,000–3,000 mm. (80–120") rising to 5,300 mm. (210") above Kotor. The remainder of Yugoslavia lies in a marked rain shadow, annual precipitation declining sharply north-eastwards to 600 mm. (24") in Vojvodina and eastwards to only 400–500 mm. (16–20") in central Macedonia. The most even seasonal distribution, with equal maximum precipitation in early summer and late autumn, occurs along a line Varaždin-Banja Luka-Foča-Uroševac-Vranje shown in Figure 7. Seasonal amplitudes increase with distance from this line, with more marked autumn maxima to the south-west (including the 'Mediterranean' area) and summer maxima to the north-east. Average precipitation everywhere between April and June is usually adequate for crops. A disturbing feature, however, is the increasing uncertainty of late spring and summer rainfall towards the east and south-east. This becomes critical precisely in the best agricultural regions from Vojvodina to Macedonia and in the coastal lowlands on account of the very much lower rainfall (summer drought along the coast), higher evaporation and fewer rainy days than farther west. Droughts are frequent, sometimes of long duration (up to 55 days)[10] and cause catastrophes for agriculture in Vojvodina one year in

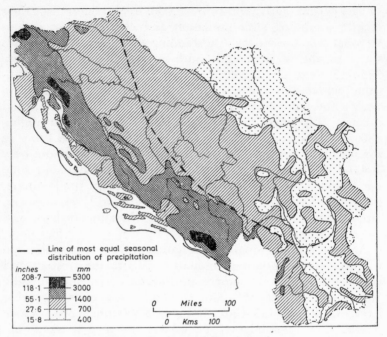

Figure 7. Annual Precipitation

every four. By contrast, these same parched lowlands are partly flooded in autumn and spring.

HYDROLOGY

'Yugoslavia occupied a high place among European states regarding the natural abundance and economic importance of her water resources.'[11] Those resources, however, are distributed evenly neither in space nor in time; indeed, marked regional and seasonal surfeit and deficit are characteristic. Bedrock conditions ensure a dense network of surface drainage, except in the loess of Vojvodina in the Karst, where underground supplies attain prominence. Indeed the porosity of limestone is such that the region of highest precipitation, the Adriatic drainage basin, has a remarkable dearth of surface drainage. Rivers flowing away from the Dinaric watershed, the Sava tributaries and the Adriatic rivers, are well supplied by high runoff (60–90 per cent.) from high precipitation even, in the Karst where drainage underground minimises evaporation to 20–55 per cent. (i.e. 45–80 per cent. runoff).[12] These rivers have steep profiles in the fold regions and flow swiftly, offering widespread opportunities for power generation. Those that enter the northern plains suddenly become gently graded, the larger rivers Danube, Sava and Tisa being navigable. Runoff in eastern Yugoslavia does not exceed 30 per cent., a serious matter in view of the low rainfall and the critical agricultural importance of these regions; indeed potential evapotranspiration often exceeds precipitation. Vojvodina must rely on water brought from the mountain rim around the Hungarian basin by the Danube and its tributaries; the Morava and Vardar offer valuable, though less reliable and more meagre water supplies for the east and south-east.

River régimes show marked seasonal fluctuations, reflecting the rhythms of freeze, thaw, drought and maximum rainfall. Ratios of high:low water rise from an average of 2:1 in the Danube with its composite régime through 6:1 in the Sava to 18:1 in the Vardar. Such fluctuations cause problems for agriculture, navigation and power production, not to speak of ordinary water supply. The utility of the Pannonian rivers for navigation is considerably reduced by winter freezing (which averages 30–45 days on the Danube), by high water and shifting channels during the autumn rains and spring thaw and by shoals during the summer low water. The mountain sections of Pannonian rivers do not freeze in winter and power can be generated, but the water is dammed back by the ice downstream, causing extensive flooding in agricultural lowlands. This may be continued or repeated when, first, a heavy load, transported after heavy rain or the snow melt, is deposited as the river slackens upon entering the plain, or second, when all the water pouring into the Danube cannot get away through the Iron Gates.

Floods annually threaten 3·5 million ha. or 20 per cent. of all farmland. In 1964–65, for example, re-cropping was necessary on 500,000 ha. in the best agricultural areas of the Danube and Morava basins. Heavy rains convert tiny streams in the Adriatic and Aegean basins into raging, eroding torrents in winter. In late spring or summer rivers reach low levels everywhere just when agriculture and livestock need water most. The construction of artificial reservoirs and canals is often necessary to even out water supplies, even, for example, in the eastern Dinaric regions if industrial demands are large, as in the Spreča valley[13] supplying water to the Tuzla-Lukavac industrial basins.

Seasonal fluctuations do not encourage efficient power generation, although the summer minimum occurs when demand is low. Artificial barrages are often necessary to even out the flow, but climatic variety makes river regimes complementary regionally. Maximum flows progress chronologically from autumn and winter in the southern and south-eastern rivers to spring and early summer in the east, centre and north-west. Minima in the north-western rivers in winter are thus counterbalanced by maxima in the southern Dinaric zone, permitting exchanges of hydro-electricity to balance interregional demand and supply.

Yugoslavia abounds in lakes, though few are large by European standards; the glacial lakes Bled and Bohinj, tectonic lakes of Ohrid and Prespa, and the chain of Plitvice Lakes (dammed by calcareous material and of rare beauty amid the wooded Karst) have touristic and fishing importance. Heavy autumn rains, however, create temporary lakes in forty of the 220 karst *polja* (including 13 of the 28 that are over 15 miles square in area). Flooding may last up to six months and often reduce the growing season in these, the best agricultural areas of the Karst, so that crops may fail (as in Popovo *polje*) in up to seven consecutive years. The general problem of too much or too little water is amply shown in many *polja* both within and outside the Karst by the proximity of ill-drained areas and land needing irrigation. Skopje *polje* is an example.[14]

The Adriatic Sea is of immense importance for the economy of communities lying westward of the Dinaric 'wall', for transport, fishing and salt production; the water has a high salt content (38 per cent.) but the level areas required for salt extraction are limited to Istria, Pag and Ulcinj. Fishing is partly restricted by the limited development of plankton.

SOILS

Variety in geology, relief and climate make Yugoslavia 'truly the pedological museum of Europe'.[15] Three types of soil dominate, however: podsols, chernozems and terra rossa (Fig. 8). Less widespread, but of great local importance, are *gajnjaća* (brown forest soils), *crnice* (flood-plain or peaty black-earths) and *smonice* (valleyland forest soil).

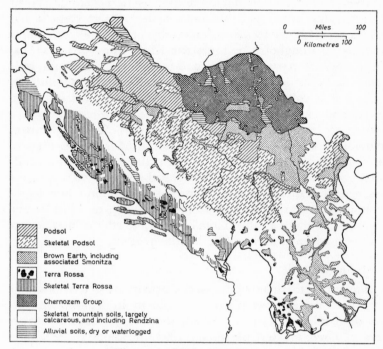

Figure 8. Major Soil Types

Podsols are by far the most extensive soils, dominating the uplands from the Alps to the Iron Gates and southern Macedonia, including the Croatia-Slavonian hills but excluding the Mediterranean region. Their quality varies from moderate fertility in Pannonia, to skeletal in the Dinaric and Alpine zone where rainfall is high, agriculture impeding over much of the state; only pine forests thrive on such soils above the valley lowlands. Locally, however, soils from alluvium, scree, serpentine or volcanic rocks offer more attractive conditions for arable farming; so do brown forest soils. Chernozems are localised in the dry steppe of Vojvodina and eastern Slavonia. West of the Danube these soils, which provide the richest agricultural

F

land in the state, become degraded as rainfall increases towards the Slavonian hills. Related fertile blackearths occur in the wetter flood plains of the great Pannonian rivers and in many *polja*. Their agricultural value in several *polja*, however, is severely reduced by high salinity, as in Pelagonia, or by waterlogging as in the Ljubljana marsh.[16] Terra rossa is, like chernozem, highly localised, especially in the hollows, valleys and *polja* throughout the limestone Karst from Istria to Prokletije and in parts of western Macedonia. Although only moderately fertile, terra rossa is so valuable that in the interior karst soil is collected from minute hollows, loaded into panniers, and carried by donkey to tiny fields where the soil is protected by stone walls. Yet karst soils are very varied, ranging from black humus-rich soils in dolinas to grey or brown soils on *polja* floors. *Gajnjača* and *smonice* are usually found together, the former higher up the valley side and more leached than the latter. These forest soils contain a fair degree of humus and are especially fertile in valleys, on hillsides and levels in Šumadija, the Timok valley, northern Bosnia, the southern Morava and middle Vardar regions.

SOIL EROSION

Several factors contribute to the gravity of soil erosion as a major economic and planning problem in Yugoslavia: the youthful relief and river profiles, the softer nature of terrace material over much of the upland zone, the abundant precipitation of the western regions or the high intensity of less reliable precipitation in drier regions, the marked seasonal changes in run-off causing rapid swelling in rivers, and the action of violent winds. The full erosive effect of these elements was unleashed in many areas as man exposed soil by felling or burning the forest, cutting out humus-bearing turf in limestone areas to improve the fertility of his arable, setting his goats to graze so destroying the ability of vegetation to regenerate, and by ploughing up and down slopes. The extensive, barren Karst, covering 10 per cent. of the state area, stands testimony to man's destruction of woodland to practise pastoralism and farming, to build ships and, during the Turkish occupation, to obtain clear views along the strategic south-western frontier ridges overlooking the Adriatic.

The result today is that 8 million hectares of agricultural and forest land, or one-third of the productive area of Yugoslavia, is subject to soil erosion. Much of this vulnerable area lies outside the fertile plains, except along the edge of the loess terraces of Vojvodina, in the upland regions. While much erosion is slow, soil creep or sheet erosion, more damaging are gully erosion, river abrasion causing caving-in and landslides. Soil erosion destroys or reduces the fertility of 100,000 ha. of productive land annually. Equal to only 0·4 per cent. of the total productive area this nevertheless adds up to a very serious cumulative loss ever since 1945. Soil erosion is less serious in the well-forested central and western regions. It is very serious, however, in eastern, south-eastern and south-western Yugoslavia, where forest cover is limited, rainfall and rivers more torrential, soils more fertile and less podsolic and softer Tertiary sediments more widespread. This is borne out by the fact that the Morava river carries more material in suspension (c. 13 million m.³)[17] into the Danube than do the Sava, Drava and Tisa together so that 'the need is urgent to regulate the Morava and its tributaries to protect land along its valley from erosion'.[18] Indeed, 10,000 ha. fertile land in Serbia Proper (0·2 per cent.) is totally lost every year. Conditions in Macedonia are worse still, for there some 32,000 hectares (2 per cent.) are endangered by erosion annually. Elsewhere soil erosion is most serious in the Karst and the Croatian hill country.

Gullying and changing river courses also make rational patterns of land use difficult. Soil erosion endangers upland communications, especially in gorges and deep valleys, incurring high maintenance costs; some 450 torrents for example, are potentially destructive to railway lines. The problem throws into sharp focus the need for greater regulation of rivers and for speedier reclamation of ill-drained *polje* land to offset losses.[19]

VEGETATION

The interaction of climatic and pedological conditions give certain well-marked vegetation zones in Yugoslavia which remain identifiable despite age-long human interference. The Vojvodina, characterised by chernozems and a dry continental climate, was covered before 1700 by natural steppe grasses. Very little woodland existed, except for willows, poplars and alders which still today form narrow borders along rivers, canals and ditches or shelter belts around fields and farms. Only 5 per cent. of Vojvodina is wooded. The steppe has been replaced by the seasonal cover of crops, chiefly cereals, lucerne, sugar beets, oil seeds and, locally, tobacco, vines, cotton and rice. The latter two here approach their northern limits of cultivation, i.e. 200–210 frost-free days for cotton and at least three summer months with average temperatures above 68°F (20°C) for rice. To the south lies the hilly Morava region where the natural vegetation comprised deciduous forests, especially oaks, at lower levels and conifers at higher altitudes, with pastures above. Forests have been cleared for agriculture and less than 20 per cent. of the region remains forested, chiefly in areas of poor soils or accessibility. Evidence of former extensive woodland must be sought in historical documents and in regional or local place names such as Šumadija (the 'forested land'), Topola (poplar), Brestovik or Brestovac (elm woods) and Bukovik (beech wood). The crops that have taken their place resemble those of Vojvodina, except that more moisture and hilly terrain have encouraged more maize and fruit cultivation here. The Morava region produces temperate fruits, plums, apples and pears. Further south lies the Vardar region where Mediterranean influences penetrate, providing, in southern Macedonia, a drier environment suitable for the cultivation of sub-tropical fruits, tobacco, cotton and rice as well as wheat. About 30 per cent. of Macedonia remains forested, despite large-scale clearance.

By far the most extensive forest region in Yugoslavia is the Alpine-Dinaric fold region with its broken relief, wet climate and predominantly podsolic soils. Forests remain throughout this region, especially on the higher, steeper and less sunny slopes, covering up to 45 or 50 per cent. of the land area. The forest region extends as far east as a north-south line drawn Novi Sad-Ohrid. Deciduous woods dominate up to 3,600' in Slovenia and 4,300' in the Šar Planina, conifers above these levels to between 5,700' in the north-west and 6,600' in the south-east. Pastures are found at higher altitudes. To the north of the fold region lies the Tertiary hill country. Partly covered with deciduous woods, this region is transitional to the Slavonian plains where higher rainfall and more podsolic or marshy soils than in Vojvodina allow forest to prevail. Slavonia was once renowned for its great oak forests; today these are restricted to marshier, low-lying regions along the Drava and Sava, having given way to agricultural land in drier areas. To the south-west of the upland forest is the Karst. Here evergreen aleppo and black pine form the taller forest stands at lower altitudes, above which the maquis and brushwood zone occurs, rising to 600′ along the northern Adriatic and to 1,150′ along the southern Adriatic coasts. Rock and drought resistant plants characterise the Karst, although the cooler, wetter, north-western Karst is heavily wooded. Palms and cypress have been introduced to give added distinctiveness to the coastal settlements. Because of drought conditions and steep rocky slopes the artificial cover planted by man is limited to well-watered areas of good soil and comprises chiefly tree crops, figs, olives, lemons, oranges and vines.

The physical environment thus offers man a variety of opportunities for the cultivation of agricultural crops.

REFERENCES

1 I. Kostov, 'Zoning in the Mineralisations of the Balkans', *Trudove V'rhu Geologiata na B'lgaria—Serie Geochimia, Mineralogia i Petrografia*, V, 1965, B'lgarska Akademia na Naukite, p. 21.

2 F. E. I. Hamilton, 'The Skopje Disaster', *Tijschrift voor Economische en Sociale Geografie*, 55 (3), 1964, pp. 78–80. A map of earthquake epicentres in Yugoslavia for the years 1945–64 may be found in: *Statistički Pregled: Jugoslavija 1945–64*, p. 20.

3 These four South Slav words have become part of the accepted international language concerning the Karst. A *polje* (plural *polja*) is a basin, large or small in size and often of tectonic origin; the alternative Serbo-Croat meaning of 'polje' is 'cultivated field', an indication of the individuality and importance of such depressions or basins amid mountain country. A *dolina* (plural *doline*) is a hollow; an *uvala* is a steep sided and deep hollow, while a *ponora* is a gigantic shaft-like aperture. *Planina* are long flattened ridges characteristic of the Dinaric regions.

4 A. Melik, *Jugoslavija: Zemljepisni Pregled*, Ljubljana, 1958, pp. 34–35. A very detailed account is given in B. Z. Milojević, *Les Vallées Principales de la Yougoslavie*, Belgrade, 1958, pp. 3–27.

5   The name *Humina* is applied to the area of coastal plateaux between the river Neretva and the Bay of Kotor; the word itself describes a plateau surface that is broken by abrupt isolated limestone hills called *hume*.

6   Chaotic relief, however, tends to isolate many parts of Macedonia in a manner similar to that of the Dinaric region.

7   P. Vujević, *Podneblje F.N.R. Jugoslavije*, Arhiva za Poljoprivredne Nauke, VI (12) 1953, pp. 7–8.

8   *Ibid.*, p. 19.

9   M. Milosavljević, 'Anomali Prolećnih Mrazova u Srbiji', *Zbornik Prirodne Nauke*, Novi Sad, 25, 1963, pp. 5–14.

10 N. Dundjerov and P. Katić, 'Periodi bez Kiše u Vojvodini', *Zbornik Prirodne Nauke*, Novi Sad, 24, 1963, pp. 153–62.

11 R. Petrović, *Ekonomska Geografija Jugoslavije*, Zagreb, 1958, p. 38.

12 D. Dukić, 'Vodni Bilans F. N. R. Jugoslavije', *Glasnik Srpskog Geografskog Društva*, 1, 1959, pp. 15–36.

13 *Yugoslav Life*, 4, 1965, p. 7.

14 T. L. Rakićević, 'Melioracije Skopskog Polja', *Glasnik Srpskog Geografskog Društva*, 1958, 2, pp. 81–96.

15 A. I. Stebut, *Nasi Glavni Poljoprivredni Reoni*, Beograd, 1926, p. 3.

16 D. Rodić, 'Pelagonia. Geografske Promene posle Drugog Svetskog Rata', *Glasnik Srpskog Geografskog Društva*, 2, 1964, pp. 119–140. Augustin Lah, *Ljubljansko Barje*, Slovenska Akademija Znanoste in Umetnosti, Institut za Geografijo, 9, 1964.

17 T. Koneski, 'Kompleksno Vodoprivredno Rešenje Slive Morave', *Ekonomika Poljoprivrede*, 11(11), 1964, pp. 3–18.

18 D. Dukić, 'Djerdapska Hidroelektrana', *Glasnik Srpskog Geografiskog Društva*, 44(2), 1964, pp. 97–117.

19 Ž. Jovičić, 'Potreba Organizovanog Proučavanja Erozije Tla u Jugoslaviji', *Glasnik Srpskog Geografskog Društva*, 40 (1), 1960, pp. 57–61.

CHAPTER 5

Energy and Minerals

In addition to water power and forest resources, to which some reference has already been made, Yugoslavia possesses many minerals and mineral deposits. These are the legacy of a diversified geological history embracing varied exogenic conditions and punctuated by periods of intense tectonic and igneous activity. Coal deposits developed throughout the Mezozoic and Tertiary periods from luxuriant vegetation growing in shallow waters along the margins of the Pannonian and Adriatic seas and in lakes in tributary valleys. Oil- and gas-bearing sediments were deposited, and rock salt formed, in these seas in late Tertiary times. Bauxite developed in limestones in the tropical conditions of the Trias, Cretaceous and Tertiary. Magmatic intrusions along tectonic lines in or near the contact zone between the Rhodope system, its outliers and the fold mountain systems, produced several mineralised belts during the Mezozoic and Tertiary eras: mercury, iron ore and manganese in the west and centre; chrome, asbestos, magnesite, iron ore, lead and zinc in the east centre; and copper and pyrites in the east.

The extent and value of these mineral resources were not appreciated before 1945. Intensive geological and hydrolological research has been carried out since then to establish their precise size, location and range. The result has been a very substantial increase in the extent of known, probable and economic reserves. As prospecting continues in this insufficiently documented land there is every chance of further upward assessments of the size, if not the quality, of nature's resource endowment.

ENERGY RESOURCES

The availability of sufficient domestic sources of good quality fuel and power is one important pre-requisite for the

75

development of industry and other activities. Known and probable energy reserves amount to 17,000 million tons coal equivalent, placing Yugoslavia among the first ten European states with 850 tons energy resources per capita. Water power and coal are of almost equal importance, accounting for 48 and 43 per cent. of the total reserves respectively. This seemingly favourable balance is more apparent than real, however, for the coals are generally more suitable for power generation than for industrial use. Oil and natural gas contribute modest reserves (2 per cent.) although new discoveries are being made continually. The remaining energy reserves (7 per cent.) comprise wood and small reserves of oil shale and nuclear fuels.

(1) Coal

Intensive geological prospecting during the 1950s raised official estimates of known and probable coal reserves from 12,800 million tons to 21,300 million tons.[1] Two-thirds can be mined economically using present-day techniques, so that at present extraction rates reserves are sufficient for 300 years. Ninety-nine per cent. comprises coals of low calorific value— Pliocene lignites (90 per cent.) and Oligocene brown coals (9 per cent.). Only one per cent. is relatively good bituminous coal, mainly of Eocene age.[2] The total heating value of coal is, therefore, low, amounting to only 7,300 million tons bituminous coal equivalent. Yet this is more than the combined coal resources of Yugoslavia's seven neighbouring states. On the other hand, the bituminous coal shortage is acute. High sulphur and ash content make domestic coals unsuitable for coke and gas manufacture, bituminous and brown coals being useful for steam-raising and burning, lignite for electricity generation. As Yugoslavia depends for fuel upon low quality, poorly transportable domestic sources or upon imports of high quality (especially coking) coal, efforts are being made to substitute domestic coals for bituminous coal in industrial processes and to improve their transport and storage properties by briquetting brown coal, by drying lignite, or by mixing domestic and imported coals.[3]

The problems of transport and storage are offset only partially by the widespread dispersal of coal basins, of which there are 130, throughout highland, and along the margins of lowland, Yugoslavia. Few areas lie more than 25 miles from a coalfield. However, most (117) are small irrespective of coal quality. Some of these (13) are virtually exhausted; 73 are unexploited because of isolation or of the high costs of investing in and working short-life mines. Only 32 small brown coal and lignite basins are productive, each giving 50–150,000 tons coal per annum; these are shown in Figure 9. Seventeen supply local markets only; the remainder serve larger areas with relatively good coal from thick seams.

In contrast, thirteen basins possess four-fifths of total coal reserves; these are numbered in Figure 9. Bituminous coals

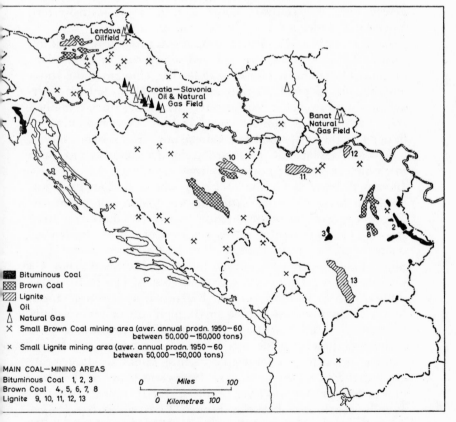

Figure 9. Major Producing Areas of Coal, Oil and Natural Gas

occur chiefly in the west at Raša (1) with one-third of the reserves (80 million tons) and in the east at Rtanj-Timok (2) and Ibar (3). Seventy per cent. of the brown coal (1,400 million tons) is localised in east-central Bosnia in the Zenica-Sarajevo (5) and Banovići (6) basins, 15 per cent. in east-central Serbia around Despotovac-Senjski Rudnik (7) and Aleksinac (8) and 8 per cent. at Zagorje (4) in central Slovenia. The greatest resources, however, are concentrated in five large lignite basins: Velenje (9) the smallest, with 1,200 million tons, Kreka (10) the second largest, Kolubara (11), Kostolac (12) and Kosovo (13). With 5,550 million tons reserves (1,900 million tons coal equivalent), Kosovo boasts the largest lignite basin in Europe. In sum, Serbia possesses nearly half, east-central Bosnia a third and north-western Yugoslavia under a tenth of total coal resources.[4]

Between 1939 and 1965 coal output was raised from 6 million tons to 30 million tons and played a key rôle in industrialisation. The acquisition of Raša, following changes in the Italo-Yugoslav frontier in 1945, only temporarily alleviated the shortage of bituminous coal, the output of which has since remained stable around 1·3 million tons. Indeed, the predominance of deep, highly disturbed and thin seams and problems of gas, water and collapsible overburden in the main basins limit maximum annual bituminous output to only 1·8 million tons. Increased demand for the best coal had to be met from imports, so tying industrialisation to the balance of payments. The entire growth of production has come, therefore, from brown coal and lignite mines which work more horizontal seams of up to 115 ft. thick and at depths of less than 500 ft. Since 1946 brown coal output has been increased from 4·3 million tons to 11 million tons and that of lignite from 1·3 million tons to 18 million tons. Expansion has been achieved by rationalisation—by closing small, high cost mines especially in Slovenia and Croatia, by channelling investment into existing or new long-life pits in the major basins and by replacing primitive underground lignite mines by large-scale mechanised opencast workings. Important shifts in the location of coal production have resulted. Production in 1946 was equally distributed between Bosnia, Croatia, Serbia Proper and Slovenia with 1·5 million tons (25 per cent.) each. By

1965 Bosnia was producing 11·5 million tons (38 per cent.), Serbia Proper 8 million tons (27 per cent.) and Slovenia 6 million tons (20 per cent.). Difficult mining conditions in small basins prevented much expansion in Croatia[5] where, since 1960, near exhaustion of brown coal and lignite deposits in Zagorje and Dalmatia has caused a decline from 2·5 to 2·0 million tons (6 per cent.). Kosovo and Montenegro, however, have emerged as significant new producers.

(2) Oil and Natural Gas

A decade ago the 550 million tons of oil shales of Zletovo (north-east Macedonia) and Aleksinac were the largest known sources of hydrocarbon fuels in Yugoslavia, containing some 42 million tons of oil;[6] combined reserves of crude oil and natural gas were estimated at less than 10 million tons oil. Subsequent drillings revealed much larger resources in the Miocene and Pliocene sediments underlying the Pannonian plain at depths of 1,000–4,500 feet; these contain 50 million tons crude, mostly light, oil and 150,000 million cubic metres of natural gas (equal to 150 million tons oil).[7] Stimulated also by expanding domestic fuel and raw material markets, production has risen from 20,000 tons oil and 2·5 million m.[3] gas in 1939 to 2·2 million tons oil and 320 million m.[3] in 1965. The centre of production has shifted eastwards with the discovery of new fields. Until 1950 output was localised at Lendava (Figure 9), but most oil and gas since 1950 have come from the Croatia-Slavonia fields which, opened in 1945, now produce three-quarters of the oil and half the gas output. A third field, in Banat, came into production in 1956; recently it became 'prolific', producing 500,000 tons oil and 130 million m.[3] gas in 1965. Good prospects of finding oil and gas reserves exist elsewhere in Pannonia and along the Adriatic coast.

(3) Hydro-electric Power

Water, for generating electricity, is the greatest single energy source in Yugoslavia. Indeed, it has assumed international importance since the United Nations Economic Commission for Europe began exploring the possibilities for exporting Yugoslav hydro-electricity to neighbouring countries.

Surveys of Slovenian and Dalmatian rivers, made in about 1900 by the Austrian Ministry of Agriculture and Water Management, were used to estimate countrywide resources after 1918; the dearth of detailed hydrological data, however, made accurate assessment impossible. After 1945 the Yugoslav Ministry of Public Works began and the Federal Institute for Electric Power Development completed (1954) exhaustive surveys of all rivers.[8] These put the technico-economic production potential at 66,000 million KWh per annum (8,250 million tons coal equivalent). In all Europe only Norway has a greater absolute potential and only Norway, Switzerland, Sweden and Finland have greater per capita potentials.

Over 70 per cent. of the potential is localised in the Alpine and Dinaric regions (Figure 10), where abundant precipitation and run-off and youthful river profiles provide a high potential power output per unit catchment area. This reaches a maximum in the Karst, where water is channelled from very extensive underground drainage networks and lakes into the surface and sub-surface canyons of a few large rivers (Cetina, Neretva, Trebišnjica and Morača). Potentials in Pannonia, Serbia and Macedonia are limited by small precipitation, little run-off and gentler river profiles, except at the Iron Gates where 10 per cent. of total Yugoslav water-power resources are localised. Nevertheless it is the Drina basin that boasts the greatest resources (17·5 per cent.), followed by the Neretva, Danube, upper Drava and Sava, Cetina, Morava, Vardar and Bosna (Figure 10).[9] Together, these rivers contain 80 per cent. of total resources.

The harnessing of this large potential has been a major planning priority which, since 1945, has consumed 16 per cent. of industrial and 6 per cent. of total federal investment. The results are spectacular. From 1946 to 1965 hydro-electricity output increased from 478 million KWh to 12,000 million KWh or from 30 KWh to 600 KWh per capita. Water power has replaced coal first, as the main source of electricity, coal generating 800 million KWh electricity in 1965, and second, wherever electrolytic or electric-arc processes can replace scarce bituminous coal in the metallurgical industries.[10] The increase has been achieved by constructing 60 new hydro-electric power stations of progressively larger size: whereas

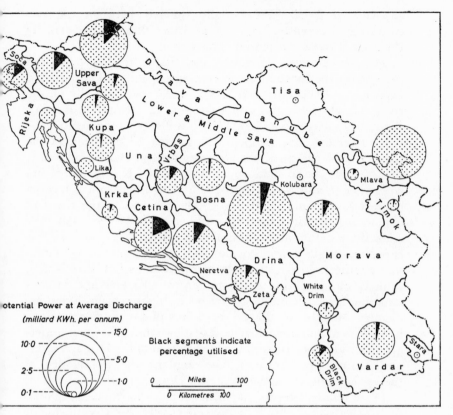

Figure 10. Water Power Potentials of the main River Basins

pre-war stations averaged 1 MW capacity postwar plants
average 65 MW capacity. Plants activated before 1953 were
generally small (up to 12 MW capacity) and used high heads
of water on small rivers. Between 1953 and 1961 sixteen
stations, involving the construction of dams, tunnels and
storage reservoirs on larger rivers or in the Karst, were completed with installed capacities ranging from 30 MW to
180 MW. More recently, four with 110–180 MW and six
with 210–460 MW capacity each began operating.[11] Meanwhile construction has begun on the joint Romano-Yugoslav
Iron Gates project which, when complete in 1971, will have a

capacity of 2,050 MW equally divided between the two countries. Currently, however, no more than 17 per cent. of the total Yugoslav potential is harnessed.

The development of many new plants readily permitted changes in the location of generating capacity. The installed capacity in 1939 (only 116 MW) was localised equally on the rivers Drava (Slovenia) and Cetina-Krka (central Dalmatia). Present capacity (about 3,600 MW) is dispersed throughout the upland regions, five regions each having 14 per cent. of the total: Alpine Slovenia, the Croatian-central Dalmatian Karst, the Neretva basin and south Dalmatian Karst, the Drina river system, and Montenegro; another 10 per cent. is located in west Macedonia (Mavrovo). The location in the Karst of ten hydro-electric power stations of 40 MW to 460 MW capacity, together accounting for 46 per cent. of total installed capacity, stands testimony not only to the success of Yugoslav engineers in constructing complex networks of channels, tunnels and pipelines to tap underground water and in constructing large accumulation basins in highly porous limestone country but also to the thoroughness of previous geological, hydrological and speleological investigations of the karst underground. This localisation, along with that of the Drina, Vardar and Drim power stations, also exploits the abundance of the water resources along the main Dinaric-Pindus watershed.

These changes represent an attempt to harmonise regional hydro-electricity output more effectively both with major consumption centres in Slovenia, Croatia, Dalmatia, central Bosnia and central Serbia and with regional water-power potentials. The new location pattern has also been encouraged by the opportunities that varied physical environments offer for inter-regional exchanges of hydro-electricity. During the rainy Mediterranean winter the karst stations supply maximum power to northern and central Yugoslavia where the load is at a peak and rivers in the Alps and Pannonia are frozen. Conversely, in summer, the snowmelt in the High Tauern maintains a high water level in the Drava from which power is transmitted to the drought-ridden karst regions.[12] Such exchanges have been effective only since 1955 when the coastal and northern regions were interlinked by high-tension grids.

(4) *Other Energy Sources*

Timber still contributes 10 per cent. of all the energy consumed in Yugoslavia, although its importance is far less now
than twenty years ago and its uses more limited to domestic
heating. Like the many tiny mechanical water mills that still
grind corn using the flow of Pannonian and Bosnian rivers, this
reminds us that the modern is only just replacing the ancient.
And just as the declining use of timber and mechanical water
power mark the passing of an era, so the recent discovery of
nuclear fuels heralds the coming of another. Uranium ores are
being mined and concentrated at Kalna (east Serbia) with a
view to 'including nuclear power plants in the power generating
system after 1970'.[13]

METAL RESOURCES

Yugoslavia possesses a wide range of commercially workable
ore deposits, including both ferrous and non-ferrous ores.

Postwar prospecting for minerals has increased the size of
known iron-ore reserves, and discovered new deposits. In
1966, reserves amounted to 464 million tons[14] or 167 million
tons iron. At present extraction rates (2·3 million tons ore
annually) this is sufficient for 200 years, but planned increases
in output to 9 million tons ore will shorten this period unless
new deposits are discovered. Seventy per cent. of the reserves
are located in Bosnia, at Vareš and Ljubija (Figure 11). The
Vareš deposit, reckoned at 200 million tons, comprises side-
rites and haematites with 33 and 37 per cent. iron content
respectively. Horizontal beds are worked by opencast mining
methods which have permitted an increase of production from
200,000 tons (1939) to 1,750,000 tons (1965). The Sanski
basin (Ljubija-Topusko) reserves, amounting to 140 million
tons ore, offer substantial scope for large-scale extraction since
their Fe content is relatively high (38–47 per cent.). However, production has increased only by a third since 1945
(450,000 to 600,000 tons per annum) because of wartime
damage and difficult underground mining conditions. Elsewhere, iron-ore deposits are virtually unworked, but include
low grade ores mainly in west-central Macedonia (Tajmište
and Demir Hisar), containing 130 million tons ore. Exploitation is hindered at present by their isolation, low quality

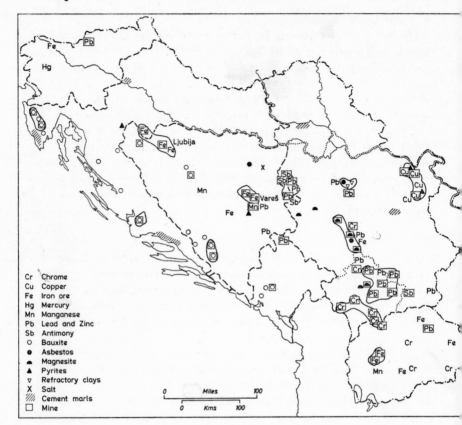

Figure 11. The Distribution of Metallic and Non-Metallic Mineral
Resources

(30–37 per cent. Fe) and high phosphorous content; ore-
preparation plants are planned to increase their utility.

Yugoslavia can also boast of self-sufficiency in a wide range
of alloying and non-ferrous metals.[15] Indeed, the republic
is the leading European producer of antimony, chrome, copper,
lead and molybdenum and a major producer of mercury,
bauxite and zinc. Her contribution to world production varies
from 1 to 3 per cent. copper, chrome and zinc to over 10 per
cent. antimony and mercury. The chief deposits occur along
tectonic lines in contact zones between major structural units,
chiefly in eastern Yugoslavia. Copper, commercially the most

important resource, is localised in north-east Serbia and mined at Bor and Majdanpek (Figure 11); undocumented deposits occur also in western Serbia and Macedonia. In contrast, lead-zinc ores are mined at many places (Figure 11), most production coming, however, from the Kopaonik region—the great Trepča mine. Other sources of lead and zinc are Mežica (Slovenia), Zletovo (Macedonia), Rudnik (north-central Serbia), Srebrenica-Veliki Majdan (Drina bend area) and Pljevlja-Mojkovac (Montenegro). Deposits of chrome are worked in the Šar Planina near Skopje, antimony at Zajača-Krupanj (Drina bend), mercury at Idrija (Slovenia), manganese at Čevljanovići (Bosnia) while pyrites, once mined only at Majdanpek, is now obtained as a by-product of lead-zinc flotation plants.

Since 1939–47 the output of all ores and metals, except latterly chrome and manganese, has increased. Unlike increases in energy and iron-ore production (which were intended for the expanding home market), the growth of non-ferrous and alloy metal output is a response to expanding markets abroad where supplies are scarce and prices remain high.

Increases in metal output, however, have been slow (Table 7). At current extraction rates, known reserves of all ores are sufficient for only a few years. Decades of mining have depleted the higher grade ores, leaving progressively lower metal:ore ratios in remaining deposits. The doubling of ore production has often been necessary (Table 7) simply to maintain metal output. Indeed, the production of one ton blister copper required 105 tons ore in 1965 as compared with only 25 tons ore in 1939 and 1947. Diminishing reserves and high investment costs per mine have led to the contraction of chrome and manganese output. Increases in production generally have been achieved only as a result of the opening of new mines and flotation plants to work and process newly-discovered reserves, the modernisation of existing mines and the improvement of refinery techniques. This has cost Yugoslavia 10 per cent. of her postwar industrial budget, money which, in view of the international importance of the metals concerned, has been obtained chiefly in loans from the United States' Import-Export Bank.

G

TABLE 7

PRODUCTION OF NON-FERROUS METALS AND ALLOYS, 1939–65

(Thousand Tons)

		1939	1947	1957	1965
Copper:	Ore	984	812	1,953	5,950
	Blister	41	32	33	51
	Electrolytic	13	14	30	49
Lead-Zinc:	Ore	775	739	1,764	2,375
Metal:	Lead	11	40	79	105
	Zinc	5	7	29	42
Antimony:	Ore	19	36	86	123
	Metal	1·5	1·4	1·8	2·7
Chrome Ore		45	76	120	94
Bauxite		791	88	888	1,250
Manganese Ore		6	13	10	8
Pyrites Concentrate		78	176	313	356

Source: *Statistički Bilten*, 357, 1965, pp. 20–22.
Statistički Godnišnjak S.F.R.J., 1966, p. 179.

The large increase in copper ore output and steady expansion of blister copper production since 1957 has been achieved by opening a new mine and flotation plant at Majdanpek to work a deposit of 130 million tons copper ore (1·2 million tons copper) which was discovered in 1949, raising total reserves to 200 million tons ore (2·2 million tons copper). Similarly, the discovery of lead-zinc deposits in Kosmet, central Serbia, the Drina bend and Montenegro, raising known reserves to 50 million tons (5 per cent. lead and 4 per cent. zinc metal), has facilitated a great increase in ore and metal output from new mines and flotation plants. Hence, also, the increased production of pyrites as a by-product.[16] Even so, at present extraction rates, all copper, lead and zinc resources will be exhausted within 25 years.

The reserves of one non-ferrous metal raw material, however, are outstandingly large: bauxite. This occurs in association with dolomite in karst hollows throughout the western Dinaric zone from Istria to the Albanian frontier and as far inland as central Bosnia. Reserves exceed 150 million tons with an average aluminium content of 55 per cent. Production has increased substantially since 1947, although pre-war output, for the Italo-German war effort, was quite large (Table 7). Until 1950 the major bauxite mines were at Drniš (Dalmatia) and Rovinj (Istria); since 1950 new mines near Mostar (Herzegovina) and Nikšić (Montenegro), the latter deposits discovered only in 1949, have become more important.

NON-METALLIC MINERALS

The rapid expansion of mining and energy has increased the demand for building, refractory and insulating materials. Rising living standards, increasing urbanisation and developing manufacturing industries have expanded the markets also for ceramics, salt and limestone. Domestic resources are generally large and varied enough to make self-sufficiency possible. Production since 1947 has increased ten-fold.

Marls for cement manufacture are available in abundance in all regions: in the Soča valley, in Istria and central Dalmatia, in the Medvednica and Fruška Gora hills in Pannonia, and in eastern Šumadija (Figure 11). Brickmaking materials occur everywhere, while natural asphalt is worked in central Dalmatia. The Istrian quartzite-sands, the centuries-old source of raw materials for the Venetian glass industry, were augmented in 1964 by 53 million tons of new reserves; other sands are worked in Zagorje, eastern Šumadija and the Timok valley. Kaolin reserves, in contrast, are insufficient for needs and scattered production must be supplemented by imports. Four areas, producing various refractory materials, have increased output sufficiently to make imports of these materials unnecessary: the Arandjelovac basin in Šumadija (clays), west-central Serbia (magnesite), Polog polje (silica) and Prilep polje (diatomaceous earth). Post-war surveys discovered small deposits of asbestos in the serpentine massifs of central and eastern Yugoslavia; mining began in 1947. Finally, two very large resources exist primarily for chemical processing: salt and limestone. Salt is obtained by evaporating sea water at Piran, Pag, Ston and Ulcinj and by mining rock salt at Tuzla, where reserves are assessed at 360 million tons.[17] Limestone is widespread south of the Sava-Danube line.

Broadly, then, a great variety of natural resources is available and favours many-sided industrial development. Reserves, however, vary in size and quality. Low calorie coals, bauxite, salt and water-power resources are relatively large. Present known reserves of iron ore are adequate for over a century but are of low grade. Most non-ferrous ores, which are of only average or low grade, will be exhausted within three decades. Resources are dispersed, generally in small reserves, so that few regions lack local sources of energy or minerals. This permits the dispersion of economic develop ment, so avoiding the costs of agglomeration. Yet investment and production costs in mining, and sometimes in processing, tend to be high as a result of duplicated infrastructure facilities, shorter depreciation periods, fewer economies of scale and lower-grade resources.

REFERENCES

1 Savezna Narodna Skupština, *Industriski Razvitak Jugoslavije*, Belgrade, 1957, p. 15, and M. Hubeny, *Ekonomska Geografija Jugoslavije*, Odbor Udruženja Studenata Ekonomskog Fakulteta, Belgrade, 1958, p. 92. Coal equivalents of other energy sources in this chapter are based on the conversion figures contained in United Nations, *World Energy Supplies*, 1961–64, New York 1966.

2 A detailed analysis of the age, composition, quality and distribution of coal resources, as well as an inventory of coal mines for the early 1950's, may be found in: M. Mellen and V. A. Winston, *The Coal Resources of Yugoslavia*, New York, 1956.

3 Aleksander Blažek, 'Ugalj', *Tehnika*, 15(3), 1960, pp. 502–4.

4 *Industrije Uglja u F.N.R. Jugoslavije*, Monograph II, Ekonomski Ekonomski Fakultet, Belgrade, 1955, and *Razvoj Privrede F.N.R. Jugoslavije*, Belgrade, 1956, pp. 139–44.

5 *Materijal o Privrednim Razvitku Hrvatske: II-Industrija, Rudarstvo, Gradjavinarstvo i Zanatstvo*, Ekonomski Institut Hrvatske, Zagreb, 1959, pp. 76–78.

6 'Nalazište Uljnih Škriljavaca Kod Aleksinca', *Tehnika*, 10(9), 1955, pp. 513–15.

7 Sources of information on oil and natural gas are: *Industrija Nafta u F.N.R. Jugoslavije*, Monograph I, Ekonomski Fakultet, Belgrade, 1954; M. M. Radovanović, 'Geografiski Razmeštaj i Reonizacija Naftonosnih Polja u Jugoslaviji', *Glasnik Srpskog Geografskog Društva*, 1, 1958, pp. 29–50; *Yugoslav Life*, 2, 1966, p. 6; and *Politika*, 29 June 1960, p. 8.

8 Jugoslovenski Nacionalni Komitet Svetske Konferencije za Energiju, *Energetski Izvori Jugoslavije, I: Vodne Snage Jugoslavije*, Belgrade, 1956, 456 pp.

9 *Ibid.*, p. 226.

10 F. E. I. Hamilton, 'Yugoslavia's Hydro-Electric Power Industry', *Geography*, 48 (1), 1963, pp. 70–73 and 'Location Factors in the Yugoslav Iron and Steel Industry', *Economic Geography*, 40 (1), 1964, pp. 46–64.

11 *Yugoslav Life*, 12, 1963, p. 5 and 3, 1965, p. 5; 'Razvoj Elektroenergije', *Jugoslovenski Pregled*, 10, 1964, pp. 365–70.

12 J. Jerić, *Prilog o Izučavanju Elektroenergetskih Problema u Dalmaciji*, Ekonomski Institut Hrvatske, Zagreb, 1956.

13 *Yugoslav Life*, 12, 1963, p. 4.

14 United Nations, Secretariat of the Economic Commission for Europe, *Economic Aspects of Iron-Ore Preparation*, Geneva, 1966, pp. 279–80.

15 Bogdan Djaković, *Yugoslavia's Non-Ferrous Metals*, Belgrade, 1958, 24 pp.

16 Very small quantities of gold and silver are obtained as by-products of copper, lead and zinc.

17 *Yugoslav Life*, 7, 1965, p. 3.

18 *Politika*, 14 March 1960, p. 4.

PART II

POLICY AND POSTWAR
ECONOMIC CHANGE

CHAPTER 6

Economic Policy and the Evolution
of the Planning System

Yugoslavia suffered more material damage during the Second World War than any other nation in Europe except Poland and the U.S.S.R. Besides the loss of one person in every twelve the Allied Reparations Commission in Paris established that direct war damage to buildings and functional installations amounted to $9,000 million, or nine times the total estimated Yugoslav national income for 1937. Agriculture was deprived of two-thirds of what little machinery and implements had existed on farms before 1941 and over half the livestock. Two factories in every five had been destroyed, over half the land and sea transport vehicles were lost and there were few continuous miles of either undamaged railway track or road anywhere. In 1945, then, economic base level, particularly in the most devastated areas (Croatia and Bosnia-Herzegovina) was far below what it had been in 1939 and a frighteningly difficult reconstruction period lay ahead. Yet there was the challenge to begin afresh, the possibility of developing along new lines. And there had emerged a remarkable group of leaders with new ideals, fresh ideas and a strong will. Under Josip Broz Tito they were to rise to the occasion, to accept the challenge and to organise the means to meet it.

THE FRAMEWORK FOR CHANGE

Those means consisted in the confiscation of certain property, nationalisation and the reorganisation of the economic system. Confiscation in 1944–45 gave the new federal state control over land and property, including industry, owned by citizens of the Third Reich, by the former *Volksdeutsche* living

93

in Yugoslavia and by other people who had co-operated with the Nazis. All remaining foreign-owned properties and investments were sequestered by the state, thus eliminating dominant foreign control of Yugoslav mining, manufacturing, banking and finance. This measure prevented the further use of the natural resources and labour of the country 'for the benefit of overseas companies, the steady outflow of dividends, the long-term drain on reserves and the direction of basic company policy as a constant threat to the ability of government to control events.'[1] That in 1939 foreign capital had controlled no less than 75–90 per cent. of all mining, metallurgy and chemicals, 50–75 per cent. of all metal-working, timber and textile industries and 25–50 per cent. of all ceramics, glass, food, leather and electrical production in Yugoslavia,[2] and no doubt would have re-established those percentages in 1945–46, emphasised the necessity for nationalisation simply to enable the Yugoslavs to manage their own economy in their own interest.

Full state control of the economy became a *fait accompli* in 1947 when nationalisation extended state management to more than 90 per cent. of all industry, internal and external trade, finance and transport. In 1948 small private workshop industries, hotels, catering establishments and social services were also nationalised. By then, with only a negligible proportion of total money flows outside the control of the state budget, the Yugoslav government was in a position to formulate its policy for the future and to put that policy into effect by strict and comprehensive controls over the allocation of investment. Nationalisation, therefore, was the logical prelude to the emergence of a competent state in a war-devastated and backward country as the only entrepreneur that could succeed in initiating development without invoking dependence upon foreign management. It also provided the framework for planned economic development and the practical possibility of minimising the discrepancy between the rate of change and growth planned and those achieved. Nationalisation *per se*, however, guaranteed neither rational economic development nor rational spatial planning; that depended upon the ability and knowledge of the planners and upon the order of their priorities.

One important economic sector remained outside direct

state control: agriculture. Agrarian reform in 1945 had transferred only 6 per cent. of all agricultural land from large landowners to state farms. The planning of change in agriculture,
with its highly dominant private sector and several million
illiterate and conservative peasants, seemed likely to prove
difficult. It was certain to make land-use planning of any
scale a very long-term process. The only consolation was that
two-thirds of the forest land (one quarter of the state area)
were already in state management. How successful agricultural
changes would be depended upon the aims of policy and the
economic measures adopted to realise them.

AIMS OF POLICY: A CONCEPTUAL APPRAISAL

This section examines neither development plans nor real
achievements; these are analysed in Chapters 7 and 8. Nor
does it attempt to analyse exhaustively the problems of developing an underdeveloped country, since these are covered
by an abundant literature.[3] Rather it attempts to underline
the Yugoslav approach to a practical solution of underdevelopment and to analyse briefly its conceptual rationality in
the socio-economic conditions of the immediate post-war years.

In formulating their policy the Yugoslav leaders derived
their inspiration from the writings of Marx and Lenin and
from the practice of the only socialist state then in existence—
the Soviet Union. The threads of a new policy became evident
during the post-war reconstruction in 1945–46. Systematic
codification, however, came only after the consolidation of
socialist power with the introduction of the first Five-Year
Plan in 1947. Extensive changes after 1949 both in the plan
and in the economic system did not lead to any modification
of the basic aims of policy, although some changes in interpretation have since been made. Broadly, that policy has
had three interrelated aims: the rapid economic development of
the country to achieve sustained growth, the maximum use
of domestic resources and the achievement of equality for all
people in all regions of the country.

(1) Rapid Economic Development

The most pressing problem was the need to break the
economy out of the vicious downward circle of poverty. In

the government's view any solution of this problem required radical changes which could be achieved only by rapid economic developments. Far-reaching structural changes were necessary to shift large, idle factors of production from agriculture into more productive and higher income-yielding non-agricultural activities. The government chose industrialisation as the vector of change, implying priority for investment in the construction of manufacturing plants over investment in other economic sectors. Such a policy implied also some geographical shift at least of the place of work, if not also of residence, from several thousand scattered villages and hamlets to the few hundred larger settlements localising more intensive secondary and tertiary industries.

There were good reasons for choosing such an economic strategy in 1946. Agriculture itself could contribute little to short-term economic progress either in increased production or in increased productivity because of limitations imposed by partially unfavourable and largely untamed physical environments, pitiful backwardness in techniques and management, the prevalence of illiteracy and poverty among the peasantry and a lack of even medium-sized farms. Indeed, except by using surplus rural labour in extending the cultivated area to expand production, agriculture could contribute nothing to progress without the provision of large quantities of fertiliser, equipment and improved seed and livestock. Supplies of these could be obtained only at high cost, if at all, because of underdeveloped industry at home and war devastation generally in Europe. Moreover, agricultural progress was impossible without consolidating thousands of tiny, parcellated holdings into larger farms. Such a policy was inopportune politically in 1946 and in any case it had to be preceded by the growth of attractive employment opportunities outside agriculture.

The key to economic progress thus lay with rapid industrialisation to provide employment quickly for part of the large and growing surplus of agricultural labour, the removal of which was the prerequisite of progress in agricultural organisation, techniques, land use and production. Equally, increased industrial demand for energy, materials and equipment and increased industrial supply of semi-finished and finished manufactures in a growing number of areas provided the sole large-scale means of multiplying secondary and tertiary employment opportunities to absorb progressively the remaining rural labour surplus by stimulating an expansion of productive trade and transport in goods and of building activity. Such employment guaranteed higher productivity, higher capital accumulation and higher purchasing power. In time mechanisation in agriculture could accelerate the transfer of labour from the countryside and would begin to substitute for labour when the rural labour surplus began to disappear. Industrialisation was also a means of achieving full economic independence from foreign aid and management and of backing political independence by defence.

Industrialisation as the vector of economic development was not only necessary, it was also possible. Supplies from existing mines and quarries of varied minerals which had been exported in raw form before the war could be diverted for processing in new manufacturing capacities at home. The extent to which this stimulated Yugoslav industrialisation—and at no extra capital cost in sinking new mines—can be grasped from the fact that inherited mine capacity was geared to sending more than 75 per cent. of the production of copper, antimony, pyrites, lead, magnesite, zinc, bauxite and chrome in raw or concentrated form to foreign markets. Such practical possibilities emphasise why economic theory has tended recently to attach greater importance than formerly to natural resources as a factor in economic development, a trend which conceptually supports Yugoslav policy.[4] And there were greater natural resources to be tapped. The aim then was to industrialise sufficiently rapidly to expand production and non-agricultural employment at rates above those of the growth of population and labour supply and hence of latent unemployment.

Limited supplies of capital, poor quality of labour and small markets restricted the rate of industrial and general economic development. Conceptually, however, the limits that these factors set on growth in post-war Yugoslavia are often over-rated. Capital supplies for investment within the country and increasingly within the control of the state budget, for example, were substantially higher than they had been in 1939. Large profits which were formerly channelled abroad by the foreign firms and investors that controlled much of the economy in 1939 were now available for domestic reinvestment. Costly repayments on foreign loans (even for Serbia's part in the First World War!), which channelled 10–12 per cent. of the Yugoslav state budget abroad in 1939,[5] were stopped, releasing more finance for domestic investment. The huge debt of the peasantry was cancelled, freeing money for productive use from their otherwise unproductive destiny— the pockets of usurers whose propensity to consume was low. By levelling incomes and by enforcing a high rate of saving from expanding and more productive activities outside agriculture, a further substantial increase in capital supplies could be achieved. This is not to say, however, that enough finance *would be* forthcoming.

The restriction of consumption, moreover, permitted a high rate of investment. Directed primarily to industry, such investment was the main factor in expanding existing and in creating new markets. Directly it stimulated the demand for capital goods; indirectly it created higher purchasing power for personal consumption, often much higher purchasing power since the wage of every newly-employed worker outside agriculture was equivalent in effect to the 'wage' shared by two or more surplus workers in agriculture. The production of capital goods could influence most the growth of markets immediately after the war, thus providing the logic of a policy which stressed investment in heavy industry while permitting the continued expansion of consumer markets despite restrictions. Thus the rates of regional industrial growth and market expansion depended upon the spatial allocation of investment. The critical pivot of policy here was that the regions with the greatest propensity to consume capital for economic development (the areas to the south of the Danube-Sava line with the largest natural resources and labour supplies) were those with the least propensity to accumulate it. Successful economic development seemed to demand, therefore, carefully planned capital mobility.

The importance of labour is often too unfavourably assessed, with insufficient emphasis upon the partial substitutability of the large labour surplus in growth (though not in the same occupations) for the lack of skilled personnel. Although,

strictly, industrial skills were rare in 1945, Yugoslav handicrafts provided a useful source of additional semi-skilled labour
which required relatively little re-training for factory employment. Yet overall expansion in the non-agricultural sector
certainly depended upon the employment of barely literate
peasant labour. This set important limits, but those limits
were capable of progressive removal through a massive effort
at rapid elementary training in existing schools, institutes and
'on the job'. Indeed, the mass harnessing of youth into the
education system and their awakening to the individual and
communal benefits that education is likely to bring with rapid
economic development, are themselves important growth
factors. The social environment in the most backward
regions, however, was least favourable to such enthu-
siasm; this further underlined the interregional problems
involved in attempting, let alone achieving, rapid economic
development.

If industrialisation placed investment priority on industrial
projects, then obviously surplus labour and other factors would
have to substitute for capital in the growth of other economic
sectors. The capacity of agriculture to expand output was
limited but its contribution to balanced growth could be
achieved in two ways: first, by diverting former export food
surpluses to home markets to feed the growing non-agricultural
labour force and the existing food-processing industries, and,
second, by employing surplus rural labour on land reclamation
and improvement schemes to increase the cultivable area.
Whatever capital was available for agriculture should go into
intensifying production. Transport, too, needed capital, but
UNRRA contributions of railway rolling stock virtually
provided for the re-activation of the entire railway system,
while new road and railway construction projects could be
completed by using surplus rural labour. This applied also to
building, trade and administration. In this way a substantial
expansion of tertiary activities could be achieved to support
early industrialisation without unduly restricting capital investment in industry.

Government policy stressed a further priority within industry for heavy industries. Conceptually, the choice of
'heavy' rather than 'light' industry is a matter of degree.

Strong emphasis on the former means a higher capital: production and employment ratio and a slower rate of growth as a result of longer periods of gestation given the same low level of development of both 'heavy' and 'light' industry. In fact much criticism of the government's 'ideological' emphasis on heavy industrialisation is groundless. The definition of 'heavy industry' adopted in Yugoslavia, following communist practice generally, is rather broad and includes mineral extraction, energy, metallurgy, chemicals, building materials, non-metallic mineral industries, metalworking as well as mechanical and electrical engineering. Only food-processing, textiles, leather, paper, timber and printing are considered to be 'light industries'. It is only natural that the heavy sector, capital-intensive as it is, should be allocated a large share of investment, even to achieve balanced industrial growth.

But in post-war Yugoslavia that growth did not begin on the same level for heavy and light industries. Following reconstruction the three leading industries in 1946 were consumer-goods industries: food-processing, textiles and timber. These far outstripped in importance any other industry, except engineering, which also catered largely for consumer markets. In the conditions of 1930–39 and 1945–46 these four industries were overdeveloped, up to half their capacity being idle because a poverty-stricken population provided an insufficient market. Food industries were idle also because agriculture supplied an insufficient commercial food surplus although surplus labour remained on the land. Industries were needed to produce the fertilisers which the intensification of agriculture and the raising of peasant incomes demanded. The engineering industry suffered a shortage of metal because of the large-scale exports of concentrates or raw materials, i.e. metallurgy was underdeveloped even in relation to the modest needs of the total domestic engineering industry. Initially, then, concentration of investment in heavy industries, where the highest labour productivity generated the highest incomes and propensity to consume, was the most logical way of achieving rapid economic growth, since the expansion of light industry depended upon eliminating bottlenecks in raw material, semi-finished material and machinery supplies as well as in consumer markets.

A substantial margin of economic development and growth, therefore, was *possible* simply by diverting formerly exported materials from export to home markets for domestic manufacture—primarily the metal and non-metallic mineral inputs of heavy industry—or, as with cement, for direct domestic marketing. To assist the growth of light industries at home only timber exports could be so diverted. The development of heavy manufacturing plants, however, required equipment which would have to be imported and paid for by exports of raw materials (especially timber) and surplus light industrial products. Nevertheless, domestic engineering plants, reorganised and reconstructed with war reparations and UNRRA equipment in 1945–46, could provide a significant proportion of the capital equipment required by Yugoslavia—hence the government's treatment of *engineering as the key heavy industry* to supply equipment and machinery for new manufacturing plants and other sectors of the economy. Capital-goods industries thus gained priority in order to remove imbalances within the industrial sector and to achieve most rapidly import-substitution and independence of costly foreign manufactures. The adoption of any other policy would have meant the continuance of the pre-war situation in which the ratio of the value of 1 ton of imported goods to 1 ton of exported goods[6] was almost 3:1.

(2) *The Utilisation of Resources*

Economic progress follows from three parallel improvements in the use of land, labour and natural resources: from an increase in the absolute amount of resources used, from an improvement in the quality of resources used and from a transfer of resources from less productive to more productive uses. In essence, 'the *maximum* use of resources', the aim of Yugoslav planning policy, implies the fullest application of resources in the most productive processes that available capital and existing markets will allow. Plans thus sought to reclaim land for cultivation, to fertilise and irrigate land to improve its quality and to increase productivity through changes in farm organisation and land use. Labour made its greatest contributions through improved skill and the large-scale transfer from agriculture to more productive secondary and tertiary activities. Industrial

H

employment, production, capital accumulation and income-generation, for example, could be rapidly increased over the 1939 level simply by taking up the 35 per cent. of idle capacity that had existed in industry as a whole in 1939 and by introducing two- and three-shift systems.[7] In this way about 400,000 workers could have been employed, as compared with only 197,000 in 1938, at no extra capital cost. Moreover, savings in capital in not having to build up extractive industries (except coal and water power) favoured the growth of heavy industries to process Yugoslav metal ore and non-metallic mineral output. Capital could be saved also by encouraging development as much where there was under-utilised social capital—transport, water supplies, power and housing—as where production was economic.

As industry was so underdeveloped, attention centred primarily on the more intensive use of the wide range of natural resources that was available within the state. Supplies of all known resources were to be increased to facilitate continued industrial expansion, while geological and hydrological surveying was intensified to discover and to assess accurately new resources. The 'maximum use of natural resources', however, requires that all resources which are exploited in the country should also be processed to the highest possible degree within the country. The concept of value added in manufacture is important here. Traditionally, Marxist economics stresses the significance of the value of production rather than the cost of production, price or profit, but it underlines the fact that in any economic system the rule is 'the higher the stage of manufacture the greater the value added and the higher the price of the product'. For an underdeveloped country like Yugoslavia, as we have seen above from pre-war trade relationships, the exporting of raw materials and semi-manufactures of low value in order to import finished manufacture from these same materials at far higher prices is an extremely expensive way of managing the economy. It was precisely this imbalance in Yugoslav industry which indicated underdevelopment before 1946 and which offered the greatest potential for development after 1947. As Kaldor stresses,[8] 'it is evidently in the interest of underdeveloped countries that the production of minerals be developed, and that this should be followed up by the development of processing facilities which give rise to industrial development; it is better to export aluminium than crude bauxite or refined copper than copper ore.' Until recently Yugoslav economists would have gone further to stress that exporting aluminium tubes, electrical components and copper cables is preferable to exports of aluminium or refined copper. This fact alone would stimulate the growth of metallurgical, engineering, chemical, timber-manufacturing and finished leather goods industries in Yugoslavia to eliminate exports of crude metals or ores, sawn timber, hides and livestock.

Such policies toward greater self-sufficiency conflict with the doctrine of comparative advantage, which implies that domestic resources may not be exploited or that domestic manufacturing may not be developed if semi-manufactured or finished products can be imported at lower prices. The answer seems to lie in allowing comparative advantage to operate in so far as the country must depend upon certain export markets for finished or semi-finished products or upon certain overseas suppliers of materials, while deriving simultaneously the greatest benefit (under protective tariffs, import quotas or bilateral trade agreements) from the opportunities for increased employment, capital accumulation and purchasing power that the exploitation of all domestic resources offers. In the last analysis, large home markets and capital supplies depend upon the creation, at lowest cost, of high added value at home; this is the crux of the problem of achieving self-perpetuating economic growth.

(3) The Quest for Equality

The best known aim of socialism is the achievement of equality among people, at least in opportunities if not in real income. Expressed geographically, this requires the exploitation of markedly unequal regional potentials to achieve a high degree of inter-regional and intra-regional equality of opportunity and income. Careful spatial planning is essential to allocate sector and branch growth, which is aimed at attaining rapid economic development by the more intensive use of resources, to reduce the spatial economic disparities that

simple

arise from the physical and human contrasts among the different regions of the state.

Meaningful regional divisions are required as a framework for spatial planning decisions. The 1946 constitution established six people's republics and two autonomous areas as administrative planning regions. These were delineated according to the national composition of regional populations and the accompanying contrasts in cultural and economic development arising from varied regional historical experience. The constitution conferred equal social and political rights upon all people living within Yugoslavia, i.e. upon the republics and their different national populations. This policy succeeded in achieving the political stability, the tolerance and the unity that pre-war Yugoslavia sadly lacked. Nevertheless, the government has consistently stressed that such social equality means little unless it is supported by substantial economic equality. This has gained force in the last decade with the devolution of more autonomy to the communes in which the provision of social and some tertiary services has depended increasingly upon the budgetary income that the commune derives from economic activities within its boundaries. The conscious aim was to reduce as far and as fast as possible the regional and the national economic inequalities that in the specific social and historical environment of Yugoslavia would stimulate nationalist tendencies and weaken the unity of the federation.

No-one can overestimate the critial importance that this assumes, for the economic disparities between the republics and autonomous areas expressed in indices of per capita national income are probably sharper than anywhere else in Europe. Estimates give the federal per capita income for the whole state in 1947 as $173. The corresponding values for the constituent areas were as follows:[9] Slovenia $272, Vojvodina $216 and Croatia $182 were above the average; Serbia Proper $171, Bosnia-Herzegovina $125, Macedonia $122, Kosmet $100 and Montenegro $74, were below average. Slovenia is sharply delineated as the most advanced republic with per capita income 50 per cent. above that in Croatia and Vojvodina, nearly twice the Yugoslav average and up to four times that of the most backward regions of the south-east.

Croatia and Vojvodina were far less developed than Slovenia, yet they were markedly better off than immediately adjacent areas in Bosnia and Serbia across the Sava and Danube rivers, and three times as advanced as Kosmet. Economic development in Bosnia-Herzegovina, Serbia and Macedonia was on a par around three-quarters of the federal average, but clearly Montenegro and Kosovo were *very* backward.

The magnitude of the difficulties of achieving inter-regional economic equality, even in the long term, is abundantly evident. Indeed, it was all the greater because the least favourable socio-economic environments, the greatest population growth and poverty, were precisely in those regions which were economically the most backward. Since 1947, therefore, the government has attempted 'to ensure the more rapid economic development of the backward areas'[10]—defined as areas where per capita national income is substantially below the federal or regional average—as compared with the advanced. Difficult as it would seem to attain inter-regional equality over many decades, the general *quest* for equality was in no way a dogmatic political concept. It was essential. It underlined the need for a purposive regional economic policy within the framework of general development and industrialisation policies to make certain that the most vicious circles of poverty in Bosnia, Serbia, Montenegro, Macedonia and Kosovo, which contributed most to Yugoslav poverty, were most effectively broken. These backward areas not only had the greatest need for rapid economic development; they also offered the greatest opportunities for such development through the employment of un- or under-utilised labour, fuel and water power, ferrous and non-ferrous metals, non-metallic minerals and timber. The provision of manufacturing plant in these areas would ensure local processing of 'export surplus' materials. At the same time it would increase substantially, first, the added value within the backward areas themselves, and second, the local industrial and tertiary employment, markets, average incomes and capital supplies. This argument was further strengthened by the fact that so long as the outflow of raw materials from the backward areas was continued with concomitant importing of finished goods any consequential stimulus to greater economic progress would be felt in the more

developed areas of the state, so that the regional economic disparities it was desired to get rid of would be actually accentuated.

This is not to say that economic development was not also
necessary in northern and western Yugoslavia. General development required the supply of materials from backward to
advanced regions in exchange for supplies of equipment for
new plant and infrastructure. An all-round development policy
was required, specifying differential regional growth rates.
Any policy which favoured growth in advanced areas on the
grounds of lower investment or production costs ran the risk
of slowing rates of progress as over-concentration there caused
costly shortages in labour supply, transport, power, water
supplies and 'unproductive' housing and communal facilities
for immigrants from backward areas while resources and reserves remained untapped in the backward areas. Herein lies
the logic of relatively dispersed economic development in an
underdeveloped, overpopulated country in which marked
economic differentials exist and may become more marked
through cumulative processes in contradiction to regional
economic potentials. Dispersion, in turn, is the logic of any
equalisation policy. Such a policy in Yugoslavia aimed at
avoiding the costs of unbalanced regional development and
taking advantage of the relative dispersal of resources. The
rapid development of backward areas, in the context of scarce
capital supplies, also seemed to demand, at least initially,
some concentration of investment upon those specialised
projects for which each backward area had the greatest comparative advantage and from which both the whole state and
the backward area concerned could derive greatest benefit.
Development policy thus required a careful analysis of the
inter-regional allocation of new projects. Such specialisation
again emphasised the critical importance of improving interregional transport services and of creating, through efficient
transport, an integrated federal market out of many scattered
and separated regional markets.

FROM MONOCENTRIC TO POLYCENTRIC PLANNING AND MANAGEMENT OF THE ECONOMY

Various mechanisms have been used to regulate the application of these concepts. The post-war period may be treated in

two distinct periods, 1947–51 and 1952 to the present, in which sharply contrasting economic mechanisms, based upon different concepts of the role of the state in socio-economic life, were operating. Details are readily available in a number of works;[11] attention here is focussed upon those aspects which are relevant to the location of activities.

Rigid centralised or 'monocentric' planning of economic development and day-to-day direction on the Soviet model, made feasible by nationalisation, became fact with the introduction of the first Five-Year Plan in 1947. The plan defined in detail the federal and the regional (i.e. republic) levels of production, turnover and employment in each economic activity for the plan period. The Federal Planning Commission (*Savezni Zavod za Planovanje*) in Belgrade decided the development and location of land use schemes, industrial plants and transport projects of federal importance in consultation with the Federal Executive Council (*Savezno Izvršeno Veče*). Republic Planning Commissions chose the locations of smaller-scale projects allocated to their particular republic by the central plan. Only then could the Republic Town and Country Planning Institutes (*Urbanistički Instituti*) advise on siting. As all accumulated capital was channelled into the federal budget, the allocation of investment from that budget guaranteed execution of the plan in so far as inter-republic rivalry encouraged each republic to use investment in the ways prescribed (otherwise scarce capital might be allocated elsewhere). It ensured the spatial mobility of capital from more advanced Slovenia and Croatia to finance projects in poverty-stricken Bosnia, Montenegro and Macedonia.

The Federal Planning Commission also determined the volume of production and trade of each state enterprise and specified the places from which it must obtain its raw materials and to which it must send its products. Directives replaced income and market demand as the link between production and consumption. There was no guarantee, therefore, that economic criteria would operate to bring about the close correlation of supply areas and market areas. Indeed, the physical planning of flows was more likely to be arbitrary, with uneconomic anomalies, for the price of most materials and products was fixed equally for the whole state area irrespective of production costs at different places and irrespective of distance between the places of consumption and of production. As prices, wages and transport tariffs were fixed arbitrarily or subsidised through the budget, it was impossible to compare the efficiencies of either planned or alternative investment allocations by branches and by locations. Since the operation of each enterprise was determined centrally in advance, the financial effects of that operation in profit or loss could not stimulate management to increase production efficiency, to improve the quality and range of products or to rationalise the space relationships of the enterprises with sources of materials, energy and labour and with markets. These disadvantages were magnified by an elaborate bureaucratic hierarchy which comprised no fewer than 217 federal or republic ministries for giving orders to enterprise directors and which were staffed largely by amateurs. In the conditions of a notably backward state, sapped of its energy by a terrible war, it was, however, probably the only system that could have succeeded in achieving rapid economic improvement by mobilising all resources.

Monocentric planning was short-lived. By 1951 its operation began to hinder, rather than to help, further development, which now seemed to require more incentives for and initiative by the people throughout the economic hierarchy. Realisation of this came when the Cominform resolution of June 1948, expelling Yugoslavia from the Soviet Socialist camp, gave the Yugoslav leaders an ideological shock amid increasing external political pressures and internal economic difficulties. Under Tito's shrewd guidance they began to re-evaluate and to re-think Marxism[13] to find 'a new road' for socialism to suit their own people and country. A unique system has been evolved which, incorporating fundamental theoretical and practical changes in management, in planning and in economic mechanisms for implementing plans is the most radical attempt ever made in a socialist country at decentralising social and economic decision-taking. Indeed, it is the only attempt to make management of the economy by ordinary people a vehicle of democracy to give greater meaning to social and political equality—to achieve really effective socialism.

Changes began in 1950 when laws replaced monocentric

'state capitalist' by polycentric 'social' ownership and administration which 'in the social interest' vested economic management or 'self-management' (*samoupravljanje*) in the workers
council (*Radnički Savet*) of every farm, factory, shop and service
enterprise in the socialised sector. In 1952 the 'new economic
system', based upon the 'market principle', was introduced to
apply economic criteria for achieving greater efficiency in investment allocation and to provide incentives to engage the
personal interest of the workers, the enterprise and the communes in increasing production efficiency. Fixed prices, production quotas and the physical direction of material and
product flows were gradually abolished. Within the limits of
certain 'ceilings' prices varied according to production costs
and wages according to productivity between enterprises and
locations. Increasing competition between enterprises on the
market encouraged rationalisation of space relationships, of
development and production policies. Workers' management
stimulated this process as each enterprise had a budget
which depended upon its profits; since wages in part also
depended upon profits, workers became interested in
minimising production costs and in achieving higher
productivity.

Acts passed in 1952 and the new constitution of 1953 established People's Committees (*Narodni Odbori*), or local councils,
in districts, communes and towns throughout the country.
Comprising elected politicians as well as separate Councils of
Producers—bodies of representatives of local economic activities by local employees—these councils were charged with
powers to initiate and to co-ordinate plans for economic development in their areas, to supervise the operation of local
enterprises, to maintain and improve local health, education,
roads, water supply and housing and to initiate economic
projects. Such decentralisation of planning and management
to many centres and enterprises was supported by a gradual
decentralisation of finance to give some effect to local planning and management. Each enterprise retains money from
its profits in a budget which the workers' council decides to re-
invest to improve competitiveness and to re-distribute to
workers as higher incomes. Each commune, which since 1955
has become the most important local government unit, raises

finance from taxes on the local population and enterprises; the council decides how to use that finance. Naturally the volume of taxation in part depends upon the volume of economic activity; this is stimulus enough for communes to be keen to initiate new economic projects to raise revenue. Communal banks set up since 1962, administer the local funds.

Decentralisation has reduced the proportion of funds at the disposal of the central government and national bank. For this reason considerable conflict developed after 1960-62 between those favouring greater centralisation and those favouring greater decentralisation. The latter won the day, but until 1965 the central government still maintained dominant control over the allocation of funds for developing heavy industries, large-scale transport and agricultural schemes and the electricity system.

With the official termination of the first Five-Year Plan in 1951, annual plans only were introduced between 1952 and 1957 to adapt planning to the new economic system and to solve the economic difficulties that arose from the Cominform blockade. By 1957, when the Second Five-Year Plan was introduced, the new planning system had crystallised as a two-way polycentric process. Plans, initiated simultaneously by enterprises, communes, districts, republics and the federation according to needs and possibilities, were, until 1964, co-ordinated at all levels until the Federal Planning Institute, in consultation with six republic planning institutes, drew up the final Five-Year Plan. When approved by Parliament, the plan was communicated down through the hierarchy as a framework within which communes and enterprises could revise or carry out their original plans, but neither the federal nor the republic planning authorities could impose plans on them. Federal plans did not specify details of production or location; they simply stated the aims of the plan, the expected trends in demography and productivity, the volume and allocation of investment, the increase expected from the different branches of production, the changes in national income anticipated, kind and amount of regional development through a given regional allocation of investment and of funds for developing backward areas, and trends in social services and foreign trade, and methods for implementing the plans. Further decentralisation in 1964 gave most planning power to the republic authorities.

The 'new economic system', regulating plan implementation, aims at achieving an optimum efficient balance of demand and supply through competition between producers (for supplying the market with goods and services) *and* between interested investors (for obtaining credit). Given the inter-branch alloca-tion of investment specified by the Federal Plan, spatial alloca-tion for purposes of economic expansion or new projects was decided, until 1964, by competition. The system was briefly this. Credit loans were (and remain) the chief means of financing investment, not the budget. The General (or Re-public) Investment Fund, from which credits might be allo-cated, was administered by Federal (or Republic) Investment Banks. These banks published competitions containing the conditions under which investment credit would be allocated for the several ends, i.e., given projects or expansions of capa-city, foreseen by the Federal and Republic plans. Parties interested in developing such projects—factory councils or commune or district councils—submitted to the banks their demands for credit. These had to be accompanied by detailed technical and economic documents giving production and in-vestment costs and the location of the project they wished to construct with the credit. A team of technical and economic experts analysed these demands for the Bank and then made a choice of project (and therefore location) according to the conditions of the competition. Usually demands for credit for a given purpose exceeded the supply, so that the Bank could effect a choice among competing alternatives. This system came into practice in 1954–55 and reached its prime during the Second and Third Five-Year Plans (1957–64); it was abandoned in 1964.

The new economic system operated through the criteria for selecting between projects. The most important criterion for investment allocation was the *rentabilitet* or *rentabilnost*, or what we may call the 'rentability', of the project.[14] 'Rentability' can be summarised as 'the relation of total income of a project (after the deduction of total costs) to the fixed and variable assets of the project'.[15] Accordingly, an analysis of investment programmes competing for a loan and the choice of the

location with the greatest 'rentability' required an assessment of
first, the comparative costs of production including the costs of
materials, fuel and power, transport and labour or other
input per unit output; and second, the comparative investment
costs of the project itself per unit capacity, including the cost
of erecting sufficient workers' housing and amenities. Where
differences in combined least costs between locations were
marginal, the effect of the project on employment and income
locally or its allocation to a backward region became decisive
in the choice of projects.

However, the system, left to work freely, would act against
the backward areas for the conditions of competition nearly
always stressed that credits would be allocated to those investors in those locations who could pay the highest rate of
interest on the loan as an expression of the 'rentability' of the
project, who could offer the largest contribution to the project
out of their own funds to reduce the drain on the General
Investment Fund, or who could repay the loan in the shortest
period. The location of projects (industries especially) in
backward areas generally incurred higher investment costs in
infrastructure while those areas had little capital to contribute
towards financing new projects. Development in backward
regions tended, therefore, to tie up a greater proportion of the
General Investment Fund in fewer projects in a given period
than if development had occurred elsewhere. A system of
guaranteed investments—tax-free and interest-free loans—
was introduced, therefore, in 1954 and continued until 1964 to
ensure that backward areas obtained a certain minimum of
investment capital.

In principle the system of polycentric planning, competition
and selection on the basis of 'rentability' provided an admirable
and original method for comparative sector and locational
allocation of investment according to the desirability, practi-
cability and effectiveness of particular projects. In practice
its ability to operate successfully was severely compromised by
the existence of fixed prices on some basic commodities including foods and electricity, price ceilings for many industrial
raw materials and semi-manufactures and special transport
tariffs on the railways. This is not to detract from the considerable flexibility in prices achieved through the operation of

market forces; yet it often made realistic comparative calculations of investment or production costs for different
projects and locations rather arbitrary. Human nature and
planning immaturity caused additional inefficiences. Often
the multiplier effects of projects were ignored. Often local
ambition rather than genuine economy stimulated applicants
to propose projects for their territories.[16] Often, through
pressure of work in analysing many projects for many competitions, the banks took decisions hastily without making
thorough comparisons. Many decisions were up to two or
three years overdue, thus slowing progress. Central control
remained most effective in industry where the competitive
system was applied most widely, causing conflicts between
decentralisation and centralisation and generating important
tensions which were not least regional tensions between those
republics that paid most to the General Investment Fund and
got least out of it (Croatia and Slovenia) and the remainder
who got most out of it. Often, therefore, banks adopted the
'diplomatic' line of sharing out projects between the republics
to offer the greatest good to the greatest number, without regard to the optimum socio-economic solution.

The latest reforms in the economic system, made in 1964,
have gone a long way to solve these problems. Prices have been
re-adjusted, none are now fixed and there is a good chance
that, with market forces in fuller operation than ever before,
they will facilitate complete comparability. The reforms,
however, have swept away the General Investment Fund and
the system of competitions. Decentralisation is almost complete. Very little money goes now to the central government
for redistribution, the largest funds being managed by the
enterprises and communes. Although it is too early to judge
the full effects of the reforms, certainly the principle of the
'rentability' of the direction and location of growth now
dominates the more vague but once important criteria of
'social interest' or of 'satisfying defined social needs'. The
reforms may thus accelerate overall growth. However, they
also jeopardise the policy of developing the backward areas and
encourage greater regional imbalances, for the greater the
dependence for economic growth upon autonomous funds, the
greater is the advantage to the developed areas.

REFERENCES

1 W. Davis, 'Should we sell more bits of Britain?', *The Guardian*, 16 June, 1966, p. 13.

2 S. Dimitrijević, *Strani Kapital u Privredi Bivše Jugoslavije*, Biblioteka Društva Ekonomista Srbije, Belgrade, 1952, p. 10.

3 For example: United Nations, *Processes and Problems of Industrialisation in Under-developed Countries*, Geneva, 1955. J. Bhagwati, *The Economics of Under-developed Countries*, World University Library, 1966. B. Datta, *The Economics of Industrialisation, Calcutta*, 1952. A. Mountjoy, *Industrialisation and Under-developed Countries*, Hutchinson 1963 (revised 1966). G. Myrdal, *Economic Theory and Under-developed Regions*, 1961. E. A. G. Robinson, ed., *Problems in Economic Development*, London, 1965.

4 E. A. G. Robinson, *op. cit.*, pp. 16–22, 35–37, 60–66 and 92–111.

5 Stjepan Lovrenović, *Ekonomiska Politika Jugoslavje*, Sarajevo, 1963, p. 82.

6 In 1938 Yugoslavia exported 3·7 million tons of produce to import 1·27 million tons of higher value products; one ton of exports then earned only 1393 dinars while one ton of imports cost 3917 dinars.

7 D. Krndija, *Industrializacija Jugoslavije*, Sarajevo, 1961, p. 19.

8 E. A. G. Robinson, *op. cit.*, p. 184.

9 I. Vinski, *Procjena Nacionalnog Bogatstva po Područjima Jugoslavije*, Zagreb, 1959, p. 40; B. Čolonović, 'Methods of Industrialising Underdeveloped Regions in Yugoslavia' in A. Winsemius and J. A. Pincus, *Methods of Industrial Development*, O.E.C. D., Paris, p. 155.

10 Introduction to the Five-Year Plan, 1947–51, Belgrade, p. 25.

11 A selection of works includes: C. Bobrowski, *La Yougoslavie Socialiste*, Paris, 1956. *L'economie Collective en Yougoslavie*, C.I.R.I.E.C., Geneva, 1959. G. W. Hoffman and F. W. Neal, *Yugoslavia and the New Communism*, 1962. E. E. Hagen, ed., *Planning Economic Development*, 1963, pp. 183–218.

12 E. E. Hagen, *op. cit.*, p. 189.

13 Leninism, upon which the Soviet system was based, went out of favour. Henceforth the Yugoslavs interpreted chiefly the concepts of Marx and Engels.

14 The origin of this word is the French *rentabilité* which, loosely translated, means 'profitability'. However it is felt that the literal translation 'rentability' is a more satisfactory interpretation since it avoids the pitfall of equating 'profitability' in the capitalist sense (economic profit of a project in isolation) with 'rentability' which devotes a balancing of the least investment and production costs of the project itself with the least costs of the macro-economic and macro-geographic situation of the project within the total system of the social and economic structure of the state. 'Rentability', therefore, is a broader concept than 'profitability'.

15 Momčilo Pejović and Radoslav Niketić, *Priručnik za Investitore*, Belgrade, 1958, p. 205.

16   Several basic textbooks on how to calculate 'rentability' for various
     types of social and economic activity were published to enable would-
     be investors, the majority of whom lacked anything but elementary
     education, to draw up better documented and more accurately assessed
     projects. Examples of these books are: Momčilo Pejović, *op. cit.*, 443 pp.
     which concerns primarily industrial and housing investment projects
     and Miloš Bogdanović, *Rentabilnost Investiranja u Poljoprivredi: Elementi
     za Izradu Računa Rentabilnosti, Praktični Primeri i Uputstva*, Zagreb, 1960,
     156 pp. for agriculture.

CHAPTER 7

Economic Development since 1945

The foregoing analysis establishes the conceptual and the practical rationale of the principles of the Yugoslav government's postwar economic policy. Yet implicit, too, are certain qualifications to the rationale of that policy as translated into actual development plans and to the success of the changing economic system in ensuring the implementation of those plans. The task, therefore, is to examine how far the government has achieved the economic development of the federation and an increase in the use of domestic resources. Chapter 8 investigates how far a greater measure of interregional equality has been achieved through a new geographical distribution of economic activities. Broad trends are indicated by changes since 1938, the year of greatest prosperity immediately before the war, in the occupational structure of the population, in production and in per capita national income. The speed and character of change, however, have varied through time, largely because the content and the balance of development plans made the Yugoslav economy unduly vulnerable to adverse external economic and political relationships and to internal environmental catastrophes.

THE COURSE OF ECONOMIC DEVELOPMENT

The government's postwar strategy has undoubtedly achieved outstanding economic progress. Real national income per capita in 1965 averaged some $480, which is four times as much as the estimated figure of $115 for 1938.[1] That such an increase has resulted from high and sustained rates of economic growth may be readily appreciated when it is considered that present national income is shared among 4 million or 25 per cent. more people than in 1947. Indeed, except for the years 1950–52, when the full impact of the Cominform blockade on the Yugoslavian economy abroad coincided with severe droughts which had disastrous effects on agriculture at home, the economy has been expanding at an average rate of 7 per cent. per annum while a rate of growth of 13 per cent. per annum, one of the highest in the world, was commonplace between 1957 and 1960. How sharply this focusses the vigour of postwar economic development against the depressing stagnation of the period 1919–39, when per capita income grew by 1·5 per cent. per annum!

Such rapid postwar economic expansion is attributable largely to a very much greater growth of output in the more productive branches of the economy, notably in modern industry, than in the more primitive agriculture and handicrafts.) This is clear from indices of the output of goods and services by different activities for 1965 as compared with 1939 (=100)[2]: agriculture 155, forestry 132, handicrafts 227, industry and mining 699, building 282, transport 366 and trade 392. Industry has more than doubled its contribution to national income (from 18 per cent. in 1938 to 42 per cent. in 1965), replacing agriculture as the major source of income; agriculture contributes now only 27 per cent. as compared with over 52 per cent. in 1938. Similarly, trade, transport, and building are now more important than formerly, while forestry and handicrafts are less important.)

These changes follow directly from the concentration of planned investment in non-agricultural activities and the accomplishment of considerable redeployment of the growing Yugoslav labour force (Table 8). Quite different trends in employment structure characterise the periods 1921–41 and 1945–65. During the former period the agricultural labour force not only continued to increase in absolute size, but between 1931 and 1941 it actually gained in relative importance as shrinking markets caused a contraction of employment opportunities in most non-agricultural activities. Only the expansion of a burdensome civil service maintained non-agricultural to agricultural employment in the ratio of 24:76. In contrast, the number of workers on the land has declined by well over a million since 1945, so that at present agriculture employs fewer people than it did in 1921. The reason lies in the spectacular growth of employment opportunities in non-agricultural

I

TABLE 8

THE OCCUPATIONAL STRUCTURE OF THE EMPLOYED LABOUR FORCE, 1931–61

	1931		1938		1953		1961	
	Thousands	%	*Thousands*	%	*Thousands*	%	*Thousands*	%
Agriculture & Forestry	5,163	76·3	5,900	77·8	5,361	66·9	4,748	56·8
Mining & Manufacturing	308	4·3	257	3·8	625	7·9	1,138	13·7
Handicrafts	445	6·5	365	4·9	366	4·7	379	4·6
Construction	—*		—*		206	2·6	318	3·8
Transport	99	1·3	81	1·2	168	2·1	250	3·0
Commerce & Tourism	198	2·8	165	2·4	241	3·1	351	4·3
Administration, Social Services & Other	551	8·8	750	9·9	1,004	12·7	1158	13·8
TOTAL	6,765	100	7,518	100	7,971	100	8,342	100

Sources: Defmitivni Rezultati Popisa Stanovištva od 31 Marta 1931 godine, Knjiga IV, Belgrade, 1934, pp. 4–17, 30.
S. Kukoleča, *Analiza Privrede Jugoslavije pred Drugog Svetskog Rata*, Belgrade, 1956, pp. 17–19.
Statistički Pregled: Jugoslavija 1945–1964, Belgrade, 1966, pp. 46, 58–59.

* Figures of the number of workers employed in Construction before the Second World War are included in 'Handicrafts' (private small businesses) and 'Other' (larger firms).

activities\from 1·7 million in 1938 to 4 million[3] in 1964. Over
half this increase occurred in mining, manufacturing and
building, one quarter in transport, trade and tourism and
one-fifth in the social service, administration and professions.
With ratios of agricultural : non-agricultural employment about
50:50, the Yugoslav economy today is a far better balanced
and a far more developed, more 'mixed', economy than it was
twenty years ago. Agricultural overpopulation has been
reduced by the outflow of labour into other occupations. Employment in administration has been stabilised. Yet industry,
crafts, building, transport, trade and tourism together still
employ under one-third of the working population; these
activities can clearly make greater contributions to further development of the country.

The main vector of postwar change has been the amount
and allocation of investment. A high rate of saving enabled
the government in every year after 1946 to sustain phenomenal
rates of investment in the Yugoslav economy equivalent to
27–33·3 per cent. of national income.[4] Reckoned at 1956
prices (300 dinars = U.S. $1), total postwar investment has
exceeded $35,500 million, the annual capital inputs rising, as
the national income and the availability of capital increased,
from around $940 million in 1947 to $3,125 million in 1965.
Over two-thirds has been invested in new projects, whence the
speed of structural change and economic growth and, potentially at least, of changes in the geographical distribution of
production. Mining and manufacturing have received the
largest single allocation of capital, amounting between 1946
and 1965 to 38 per cent. of all investment. This demonstrates
the determination with which the government has put its
economic policy into effect. It explains why industrial employment, output and social product have expanded so quickly
and have contributed most to general economic progress.
Another 15 per cent. has financed the new transport lines and
services required to cope with a growing volume and changing
pattern of trade both at home and abroad. That agriculture
has received barely 12 per cent. of postwar investment suggests
a lack of priority coupled with a need for gradual improvement
in the face of strong and unenlightened peasant resistance.
However, more money might have gone into this backward

sector. Trade and tourism received 3 per cent. of total investment, building 2 per cent., forestry 1·3 per cent. and handicrafts 1 per cent.; nearly 27 per cent. went into social infrastructure and housing.

Success has not been achieved without substantial setbacks.
The tempo of growth has deviated widely from the average
of 7 per cent. per annum. The lack of realism in certain
plans, the radical changes in the Yugoslav government's
international relations, the vulnerability of agriculture to
extreme climatic conditions, the varying emphasis on particular activities in successive development plans and the
frequent alterations in the economic system as the Yugoslavs
evolved their own 'road to socialism'—these factors explain
why the course of economic development, for all its achievements, has not been a smooth one. A brief survey must be
made, therefore, of the different stages of postwar change and
their salient features; a more detailed analysis unfortunately
lies outside the scope of this book.[5]

Five stages may be distinguished. The first, the reconstruction of war damage, embracing the years 1945–46, aimed
at re-establishing economic activities to their 1938 levels.
This was realised through the massive dual employment of
able-bodied people in normal and voluntary work, assisted by
reparations equipment, especially for factories, and by substantial supplies of transport vehicles, agricultural equipment,
food, seed and livestock, values at over $480 million, from
UNRRA. The transport system, however, was not completely renovated until 1950. Reconstruction reaffirmed the
status quo both in the structure and in the location of production,
the only important changes being the resettlement of peasants
from poorer to richer agricultural areas and Yugoslavia's acquisition from Italy of Fiume (Rijeka), Istria and the Soča valley.

The introduction of the first Five Year Plan, based on
assistance from the Cominform bloc, and of a centralised planning system in 1947 ushered in the second stage. This lasted
until 1952. The plan aimed at doubling per capita output
and income and at attaining sustained growth by 1951,
chiefly by implementing a very ambitious industrialisation
programme. A promising start was made. High rates of investment (3 to 9 times the 1939 levels) in all economic sectors,

extensions and modernisations of existing industrial plant and a rapidly increasing non-agricultural labour force achieved a growth rate of 14 per cent. per annum between 1947 and 1949. Growth was far more balanced than subsequently as investment in industry was less than planned (35 as against 42 per cent.) and in agriculture was more than planned (11 as against 7 per cent.). Yet there were serious weaknesses. Too many new industrial projects had been started (220 in 1947 alone) and depended upon imported capital equipment paid for by Yugoslavia in primary produce. Agriculture still produced less than it had in the 1930s because war destruction of cultivable land and livestock had not yet been made good. Compulsory food deliveries to the state at low prices and collectivisation discouraged peasant productivity. Exportable surpluses were inadequate, a trade deficit of $9 million emerged in 1948 and capital goods' supplies slackened, slowing industrial progress. Fulfilment of two-thirds of the plan depended upon capital and material supplies from Cominform countries,[6] especially Czechoslovakia and the Soviet Union. In 1948 the Cominform expelled Yugoslavia, instituted an economic blockade and all supplies from member countries ceased.

Like the bridge on the Drina at Višegrad after the coming of the railway, Yugoslavia 'was cut off from both East and West and left to its own resources like a wrecked ship. . . .'[7] Many projects were abandoned. The utmost resources were shifted into constructing defence industries in the face of Soviet threats. By 1952 industry was absorbing 61 per cent. of total investment (Table 9). And, as Yugoslavia sought new markets for two-thirds of her exports, her trade deficit rose in 1949 to $88 million. Catastrophic droughts in 1950 and 1952 severely reduced farm output and restricted incomes, productivity and home markets. Despite British, French and American supplies, the economy stagnated, thus reducing the overall growth rate for the period 1947–52 to 1·9 per cent. per annum. Clearly the planners had overestimated what Yugoslavia could achieve with her own resources in five years; and even with foreign help they had seriously underestimated the minimum requirements of agriculture. The Plan, officially extended until 1952, in practice embodied many changes which became the concern of stage three.

TABLE 9

THE ALLOCATION OF POSTWAR INVESTMENT BY ECONOMIC SECTORS, 1947–64

PERCENTAGE OF TOTAL INVESTMENT

YEAR	Total Investment at 1956 prices (million dinars)	Agriculture	Forestry	Mining and Manufacturing	Construction	Transport	Trade and Tourism	Handicrafts	Social Investment
1947	302	9	2	34	1	21	6	1	26
1948	413	12	3	32	2	22	2	0	27
1949	460	11	2	38	3	13	2	1	30
1950	413	9	1	42	3	13	2	1	29
1951	422	8	1	46	3	17	2	1	22
1952	357	10	0	61	2	9	1	1	16
1953	400	10	0	52	3	10	3	1	21
1954	452	11	0	44	2	13	3	1	26
1955	454	9	2	45	2	13	4	1	22
1956	462	12	2	37	2	15	4	1	25
1957	539	14	1	31	2	17	4	1	30
1958	604	16	1	27	2	17	4	1	32
1959	690	18	1	28	2	16	4	1	30
1960	818	14	1	32	2	15	4	1	31
1961	873	12	1	37	2	13	4	1	35
1962*	1,230	9	2	38	3	15	4	1	28
1963*	1,464	10	1	38	2	13	6	1	30
1964*	1,883	9	1	36	2	13	6	1	31

Sources: 'Investicije u Posleratnom Periodu', *Jugoslovenski Pregled*, 7–8, 1963, p. 299.
Statistički Pregled: Jugoslavija 1945–64, Belgrade, 1966, p. 282.

* Figures of total investment for 1962, 1963 and 1964 are given at current prices.

Although the Plan was hastily prepared, was based on insufficient experience and information, and was never fulfilled in many activities, it was of crucial importance for Yugoslav progress. Industrial output and employment were doubled and non-agricultural activities increased their share from 23·4 per cent. of the working population in 1938 to 35 per cent., so decreasing for the first time since the 1921 census both the employed and the dependent agricultural population (from 5·9 million workers and 6·3 million dependents in 1938 to 5·3 million workers and 5 million dependents in 1953). Moreover, the plan broke the circle of poverty and increased per capita income to $200 by 1954, so raising the economy above the level of economic backwardness as defined by the United Nations.

The third stage, 1953–56, saw the beginnings of substantial sustained expansion, which, averaging 8·4 per cent. per annum and consolidating the modified 1947–51 Plan, replaced central direction by workers' management and a new economic system involving greater efficiency incentives. Annual plans insisted upon fuller utilisation of existing capacities. They concentrated 45 per cent. of investment upon completing the 100 key industrial and defence projects that had been commenced between 1949 and 1952. As these were activated, industrial output rose by 62 per cent. between 1953 and 1956, employment and per capita consumption increased and more capital was released for opening bottlenecks notably in agriculture, forestry, transport and trade (Table 9). Liberalised agricultural policies and increasing fertiliser supplies stimulated some progress in agriculture, but droughts in 1954 and 1956 again necessitated food imports, causing trade deficits. Export promotion and limits on home demand for goods with a high import content (e.g. cotton textiles) received priority but now Yugoslavia's political position encouraged, and her shrewd leaders ensured, sufficient supplies of credit and foodstuffs from the West (amounting to $350 million) to eliminate deficits in these years. By 1956 a relatively broad industrial basis had been achieved, basic construction had been completed and many personnel had been trained; the way was prepared for a new medium-term plan.

That plan, the Second Five Year Plan (1957–61), marking

the fourth stage, was completed in four years (in 1960) and achieved the high average annual growth rate of 13 per cent. Many factors accounted for such success. Planners were more skilled in their art, were better informed in growth potentials and were more realistic in setting development goals. The plan itself was flexible, establishing only broad sector proportions and production targets which reflected the comparisons of costs and effects that were now possible within a partial market economy. Individual projects were judged by their 'rentability', but with an eye to reducing imports and increasing exports. A larger volume of investment was deployed more evenly (Table 9), priorities being shifted somewhat from industry towards agriculture, transport and social facilities to improve consumption and productivity, while within industry priorities went to food-processing and fertiliser industries. This policy paid off in faster and more balanced growth than ever before. Agricultural production expanded by 10·5 per cent. per annum (despite droughts in 1958 and 1960), permitting food export again. Industrial output rose by 14·2 per cent. per annum, building by 16·2 per cent. and transport by 13·3 per cent. Industry continued its rapid expansion as existing plant was modernised, as specialisation was increased, as agriculture demanded more reproductive goods, as expanding per capita income stimulated greater consumer demand, and as new industries, equipped with the most modern machinery to produce manufactures under licence from Western European and American firms, diffused technical knowhow. In addition, Tito's foreign policy of non-alignment began to pay economic dividends as the Third World (except China) sought Yugoslav industrial manufactures, capital goods and expertise.[8] Despite these improvements the balance of payments gap widened to $150 million annually, partly because some markets in Western Europe were lost with the creation of the E.E.C.

The last stage dates from 1961. Originally to be the period for fulfilling the Third Five Year Plan (1961–65), it proved to be one of instability. The plan aimed at continuing high rates of balanced growth, but with proportionally more investment in energy, metallurgy and transport, which had become serious bottlenecks and with less in agriculture. In practice, late frosts, floods, or droughts caused four bad harvests in six years (1960–65), causing greater trade deficits and slowing growth to less than 4 per cent. per annum, while acute inflation called forth deflationary action. The dinar was devalued and in 1965 radical economic reforms brought prices into line with world market prices, initiating a new phase in the pattern of economic development. Hitherto the economy had developed under a highly protective canopy of tariffs and quotas which permitted the maintenance of artificially low prices at home, encouraged autarky and facilitated arbitrary decisions concerning growth and location. By removing the protection the reform aims at increasing the efficiency of domestic actitivies and at encouraging competitiveness on the world market by modernising existing rather by developing new capacities, and by greater specialisation according to comparative advantage. The implications for the future economic geography of Yugoslavia are many but judgment of the outcome must wait until the new Five-Year Plan (1966–70) is completed.

THE USE OF RESOURCES

A brief examination must now be made of the results of planning in improving the use of land, labour and minerals. Further details are given in Part III.

In Yugoslavia, where agriculture remains the dominant occupation and where agricultural overpopulation has for long been a major problem, the use of as much land as possible, as intensively as possible, should be of primary concern. This assumed even greater importance after 1945 as a rapid population increase maintained overpopulation while economic development substantially increased the non-agricultural population living and working in towns. Yet by 1945 war operations had reduced the total area of the present state fit for agricultural use from 14·9 million to 13·4 million ha., and the same population had to be fed from an area that was smaller by one-tenth in 1946–48. The first Five Year Plan thus prescribed measures for regaining the pre-war agricultural area and for draining an additional 400,000 ha. of marshland to increase that area to over 15 million ha. Although surplus rural labour was available for such a task, sufficient money, materials and machinery were not. By 1951 no more than 14 million ha. were available for agriculture—small wonder, then, that production lagged. Greater investment after 1951, however, succeeded in raising the area to 15 million ha. in 1956, chiefly by draining half a million ha. Since then a further 500,000 ha. have been drained, but much has simply counterbalanced the loss of agricultural land to erosion, re-afforestation and building. As such land transfers will go on, and although there is scope for reclaiming 2·5 million ha., progress in agriculture will clearly depend upon the more intensive use of existing land.

It is in this direction that least has been achieved and that most remains to be accomplished. That widespread irrigation is essential in Yugoslavia needs no labouring: the high frequency and disastrous consequences of summer drought have been repeated often enough. Planners recognised this in 1947 and sought to increase the irrigated area from 32,000 ha. (1939) to 475,000 ha., with the possibility of extending it to 550,000 ha. later. Yet by 1965 barely 150,000 ha. were being irrigated. Such neglect is all the more surprising because large areas over much of the east and the south that are subject to extremes of seasonal precipitation lend themselves to dual purpose (water control/flood prevention or drainage and irrigation) schemes; and since also many adjacent areas require *either* drainage *or* irrigation, such schemes would seem to be inexpensive. At least 400,000 ha. remain to be irrigated according to original plans, yet those plans largely ignored the poor agricultural areas of the Karst that could derive most benefit from irrigation and where much *polje* land could be irrigated cheaply. Irrigation ought to receive top priority in the next few years.

Far more impressive is the utilisation of resources that is both a cause and an effect of a remarkable expansion of manufacturing. The proportion of the hydro-electric power potential utilised, for example, has been raised since 1945 from 0·72 per cent. to 17 per cent., making industrial progress possible and regulating river flow to increase the opportunities of using water also for irrigation in agriculture. Mining production has expanded markedly, too (Chapter 5). Present output is in few cases less than double the prewar level, while the production of key minerals (coal, oil, iron ore, copper, lead, zinc and refractory materials) has more than trebled. Clearly resources are being exploited more effectively. Yet the output of coal, oil, natural gas, iron ore, bauxite and several non-metallic minerals can be readily doubled or trebled again, without endangering known reserves within the next half century—a factor of crucial importance for future industrial development.

Nevertheless, increased domestic *exploitation* does not necessarily imply greater domestic *use* of these resources. Up to 1941 most materials were exported in raw form for use abroad. Postwar manufacturing capacities have made their greatest contribution to the use of domestic resources (including agricultural produce) by processing an increasing proportion and range of mineral and vegetable products into semi-finished goods at home, thus creating greater employment opportunities, adding greater value to industrial production, generating greater income and substituting exports of manufactures for exports of raw produce. The development and growth of ferrous and non-ferrous metallurgy, metal-working and engineering, timber manufacturing and tobacco processing has proportionally reduced exports of ores, timber and raw tobacco and has increased exports of refined metal, metal products, machinery, furniture and tobacco manufactures. Dramatic changes in the composition of Yugoslav exports have resulted. Thus in 1939, raw materials (minerals, logs and foodstuffs) comprised 55·4 per cent. of all exports, semi-processed goods (refined metal, sawn timber and processed foods) 39·2 per cent. and manufactures only 5·4 per cent. By 1965 raw materials accounted for only 17 per cent., semi-processed goods 38 per cent. and manufactures 45 per cent. of total exports. Thus the more intensive use of resources has reduced the ratio of the value of imports to exports, weight for weight, since 1946 from 3:1 to 1:1. One notable exception is bauxite, exports of which continue to absorb five-sixths of production. Limited progress in developing the aluminium industry has resulted from the lack of capital and the failure of the semi-controlled new economic system, prior to 1965, to stress the benefits of exploiting comparative advantage.

Limited investment has restricted the creation of jobs for

the large existing surplus agricultural population and for the rapid annual increase of the active population. Full employment has had to take its place among other priorities, including increased productivity. The stress laid upon the developing of the more capital-intensive energy and capital-goods' industries with a lower employment:capital ratio has also limited employment. Nevertheless, substantial substitution of labour for capital even in these activities, especially in the early years when capital was terribly short and when labour was trained during the plant construction period, greatly increased the numbers of jobs. So, too, did small investments in labour-intensive lighter industries and electrical engineering. The result has been a very balanced increase in employment, in basic industries from 96,500 in 1946 to 610,000 in 1965 and in light industries from 128,500 to 602,750. Total employment between 1946 and 1961 increased by a modest 1·3 million jobs, from 7·1 million to 8·4 million. This conceals the fact that the active agricultural population declined from 5·9 million to 4·7 million while the active non-agricultural population more than doubled, rising from 1·31 million to 3·7 million, an increase of 2·4 million in fifteen years. This rate of growth, 160,000 new jobs per annum, permitted the absorption of the entire growth of the active population *and* 30,000 of the agricultural surplus annually. An absolute reduction in agricultural overpopulation has therefore been achieved. This trend will continue as the active population grows more and more outside agricultural families and in the towns—and as the agricultural population gradually ceases to replace itself. Nevertheless, a 'real surplus' of 1·4 million workers still exists in Yugoslav agriculture.[9] At present economic growth rates, then, the rural labour surplus will remain until well after 1971. Indeed, in the next decade 150,000 new jobs must be found annually, otherwise a labour surplus will appear in the towns also. This explains why unemployment is serious.

In 1938, on average, 69,150 persons registered as unemployed were unable to find work—10 per cent. of the insured working population.[20] Unemployment was unknown before 1950 because feverish economic growth between 1946 and 1948 was accomplished chiefly by the phenomenal increase in non-agricultural employment of 500,000 in two years. Since 1950 unemployment has risen steadily as poor harvests (1950, 1952–53, 1956, 1962, and 1964) encouraged surplus farm workers to seek work in the towns, where (as a result of poor harvests) activities slacken and as average employment growth rates since 1950 have been 5,000 less below those of the active population. Labour exchanges were re-opened in 1952; their records indicate how many people sought and obtained employment in state enterprises.[21] Unemployment has increased from an average of 67,000 persons, or 0·8 per cent. of total employment in 1952, to 450,000 persons (7·1 per cent.) in 1966; over three-quarters of the unemployed are unskilled workers, few of them (6,000 in 1965) are school-leavers. The highest unemployment rates occur in Kosmet (20 per cent.), Macedonia (14 per cent.), Serbia Proper and Montenegro (12 per cent.); rates recorded in Croatia, Bosnia and Vojvodina are average (6–7 per cent.), but are very low in Slovenia (2 per cent.). Unemployment is thus widespread outside Slovenia. Some 360,000 Yugoslavs have emigrated to work in Western Europe since 1960.

Since 1958, however, the government has undertaken measures which profoundly affect the use of labour resources. Remuneration has been tied to productivity to raise low labour efficiency, to encourage full-time employment at one job and to eliminate practices of employing surplus labour in industry simply to provide jobs (especially for peasant-industrial workers). Higher prices have been introduced for marketable farm produce to raise farm incomes in order to reduce the rate of migration from the countryside and so reduce potential urban unemployment as well as numbers of peasant-industrial workers whose labour is least productive both in agriculture and in industry. Policy now aims at progress through higher productivity both in and outside agriculture, not simply through more non-agricultural employment.[10] Leading Yugoslav economists, however, continue to express dissatisfaction at the lack of a clear employment policy, particularly as population continues to grow rapidly in areas where employment opportunities are often lacking.

.

130   YUGOSLAVIA

REFERENCES

1 Figures for national income have been calculated from information
   contained in the following sources: *U.N. Statistical Yearbook 1966*,
   Geneva, 1967, pp. 550–4. *U.N. Planning for Economic Development*, Vol. II,
   Part 2, 'Centrally Planned Economies', New York, 1965, p. 236.
   Društveni Plan Privrednog Razvoja Jugoslavije od 1961 do 1965 godine,
   Belgrade, 1961, p. 16. Branko Horvat, 'Pitanja Razvoja Jugoslovenske
   Privrede', *Ekonomist*, 1963, 3–4, p. 597. *Jugoslovenski Pregled, op. cit.*
   pp. 299–300, 7–8, 1963, p. 295.

2 Indices of the growth of production were calculated from various
   statistics given in the Statistical Yearbooks for 1960, 1962, 1964 and
   1965.

3 Generally employment statistics for non-census years are not comparable with those of census years since in the former figures of peasant
   farm employment, private employment and state administrative
   employment are omitted from statistical tables in the various statistical
   publications; these are available only in census tables.

4 *Jugoslovenski Pregled, op. cit.*, pp. 299–300.

5 Readers who wish to gain a deeper knowledge of the process of change
   and the problems involved are referred to the following: U.N. Department of Economic Affairs, *Economic Development in Selected Countries*,
   1947, pp. 209–36. *U.N. Economic Survey for Europe*; notes on Yugoslavia have appeared in this survey during most years since 1952.
   Yugoslav Survey, a monthly journal of information, has been available in
   English since 1960 as a translation of *Jugoslovenski Pregled* (first published 1957). Translations of the Five Year Plans 1947–51, 1957–61,
   and 1961–65. A.A.L. Caesar, 'Yugoslavia: Geography and Postwar
   Planning', *Transactions Institute of British Geographers*, 30, 1962, pp. 33–45.
   P. Auty, *Yugoslavia*, 1964.

6 The members of the Cominform were then the U.S.S.R., Poland,
   Czechoslovakia, Hungary, Rumania, Bulgaria and Albania.

7 '... otsečen i od Istoka i od Zapada i prepušten sebi kao nasukarni
   brodovi...' Ivo Andrić, *Na Drini Ćuprija*, p. 257.

8 F.E.I. Hamilton, 'Yugoslavia's Hydro-Electric Power Industry',
   Geography, 48 (1), 1963, p. 73.

9 I. Klauzer, 'Viškovi Radne Snage u Poljoprivredi Jugoslavije',
   Sociologija Sela, 3 (718), 1965, pp. 101–13.

10 Miloš Macura, 'Politika Zaposlenosti i Proporcije Radne Snage',
   Ekonomist, 3–4, 1963, pp. 611–21 and Ivan Klauzer, 'Stanovništva,
   Regionalni Aspekt Plana', *Ekonomist*, 3–4, 1963, pp. 709–14.

CHAPTER 8

Changes in the Spatial Distribution of Economic Activities

Attention was drawn in Chapter 7 to the emphasis that the postwar government has placed consistently on the principle (but for practical reasons) of a rational spatial distribution of new productive and service activities as a means of achieving greater regional economic equality. Because of the inter-regional differences inherited from the past, the core of this policy has been the development of backward areas at rates above the Yugoslav average. Fashioning the general trends and areal details of the geographical pattern of economic development is thus an integral part of development planning, though it is by no means limited to the central planning authority. The very essence of the Yugoslav system is the de-centralisation of much locational decision-taking in line with the scale of activities. Assessments must now be made, there-fore, of the extent to which a new geography of economic activities is emerging and of the degree to which the govern-ment is succeeding in developing the backward regions and lessening—in twenty years it could be no more—regional economic disparities. Only broad changes are discussed here; detailed analyses of locational changes in various economic activities are to be found in Part III.

The comparison of occupational structures of the regional populations for 1965 with those for 1939, given in Table 10, provides the best introductory guide to broader economic changes. The simple classification of occupations adopted—distinguishing agriculture (with forestry and fishing), industry (mining, manufacturing and handicrafts) and services (trans-port, trade, professions and administration)—is intended to indicate trends in regional economic development. Clearly in

TABLE 10

CHANGES IN THE OCCUPATIONAL STRUCTURE OF THE POPULATION
by Republic and Autonomous Areas, 1939 and 1965 (percentages)

AREA	1939				1965			
	Agriculture	Industry	Services	Non-agricultural total	Agriculture	Industry	Services	Non-agricultural total
Slovenia[a]	65	18	17	35	37	34	29	63
Croatia[a]	76	10	13	23	52	24	24	48
Vojvodina	76	13	11	24	51	22	27	49
Serbia Proper (without Belgrade)	87	7	6	16	75	16	9	25
Serbia Proper (with Belgrade)	69	18	13	31	64	20	16	36
Kosovo-Metohija	90	6	4	10	70	16	14	30
Bosnia-Herzegovina	86	6	8	14	63	20	17	37
Macedonia	85	6	9	15	58	19	23	42
Montenegro	83	6	11	17	56	20	24	44

Sources: Calculated from figures in S. Kukoleća, op. cit. and Statistički Godišnjak Kraljevine Jugoslavije, 1940. Statistički Godišnjak S.F.R.J., 1966, pp. 295–304.

[a] The pre-war figures for Slovenia and Croatia relate to their contemporary areas, i.e. excluding the Julian March, Istria, Zadar and certain islands which were then under Italian control.

1939, Slovenia, with over one-third of the active population in non-agricultural activities, was the most advanced area, followed by Serbia Proper (including Belgrade), Vojvodina and Croatia. No area lying south of the Danube-Sava line (excluding Belgrade) had as much as one-fifth of the population employed in industry and services. Four conclusions about postwar trends emerge from Table 10. First, planning has succeeded in spreading the great expansion of industries and services widely throughout the federation, so reducing the relative importance of agriculture in all regions. Second, the very sharp structural differences in the regional economies of 1939 are now less pronounced as the proportion of the population dependent for a livelihood upon non-agricultural activities has less than doubled in Slovenia and in Serbia Proper (including Belgrade), while it has doubled in Croatia and Vojvodina and it has nearly trebled in Bosnia-Herzegovina, Kosmet, Macedonia and Montenegro. Nevertheless, since these rates of change start from different initial proportions it is clear, thirdly, that the same broad regional disparities remain as in 1939. The proportions of non-agricultural employment continue around the Yugoslav average (24 per cent. in 1939 and 49 per cent. in 1965) in Croatia and Vojvodina and well above it in Slovenia (35 per cent. and 63 per cent. respectively). Industries and services remain far less important sources of livelihood in central and eastern Yugoslavia, despite marked progress. Structural changes, however, have varied widely even within these areas. Economic development in Macedonia and Montenegro has raised the local balance of agricultural and non-agricultural activities much nearer to the federal average than formerly. Postwar changes in Serbia Proper have been apparently small (see Table 10) because of the localisation of prewar industries and services in the Belgrade urban area and the comparatively limited 'decentralisation' of new economic growth in Serbia outside Belgrade since 1945. Fourth, the postwar spatial development of industries and services has altered the balance of non-agricultural activities within each area. Industries have contributed much more than services to the growth of employment in Slovenia, Croatia, Serbia Proper (without Belgrade), Bosnia-Herzegovina and Montenegro while the opposite is true in Belgrade, Vojvodina and Macedonia.

K

A more detailed examination of the distribution of postwar economic development suggests that two conflicting locational trends, one towards greater dispersion and the other towards greater concentration, have been at work on both the inter-regional and the regional scales. Figure 12 attempts to synthesise such trends. Proportional pillars indicate how employment in secondary and tertiary activities increased in all districts between 1948 aud 1965, again underlining a certain dispersal of new activities. More evident, however, are the great spatial differences in the absolute increases of employ-employment and in the intensity of new job opportunities as

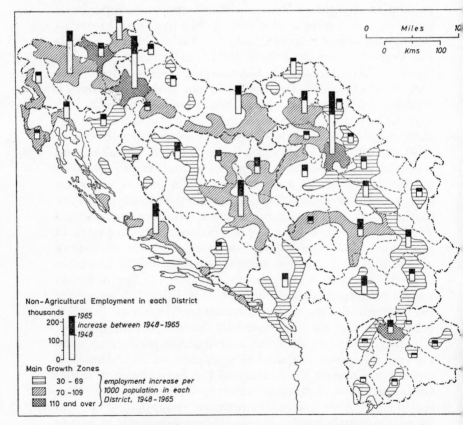

Figure 12. The Spatial Distribution of Growth in Employment in Industries and Services 1948–65

expressed by the number of new jobs created per 1,000 population. The use of this second, relative, measure obviates the difficulties of comparing simply the absolute employment increases for districts which are unlike in size and area and population. Although the index relates to each *whole* district, for simplicity it is shown in Figure 12 only in the main growth zones of each district where, in effect, secondary and tertiary activities have been localised.

Two broad regional types may be distinguished: first, regions where the intensity of new employment in non-agricultural activities since 1948 has exceeded, often substantially, the Yugoslav average of seventy new jobs per 1,000 population and where industries and services are becoming increasingly localised; and, second, regions where new employment per 1,000 population has been below that average and where, therefore, relatively less of federal non-agricultural activity is located. Five major growth zones localise 65 per cent. of all new employment in Yugoslavia since 1948, although only 47 per cent. of the total population lives there: (1) Belgrade with south-west Vojvodina and eastern Slavonia; (2) west Croatia and Slovenia; (3) east-central Bosnia linking with west-central Serbia; (4) Dalmatia; and (5) the Skopje region of Macedonia. More specifically, as Figure 12 shows, secondary and tertiary activities have been concentrated in and around the administrative capitals and larger towns. For instance, between 30 and 45 per cent. of all new jobs outside agriculture in Serbia (with Kosmet), Croatia, Macedonia, Bosnia-Herzegovina and Vojvodina have been located in or around Belgrade, Zagreb, Skopje, Sarajevo-Zenica and Novi Sad respectively. Indeed, since 1953 industries and services in these cities and in Rijeka and Celje have been providing new jobs at twice the Yugoslav average (95–139 compared with 50 per 1,000), so gaining most population from immigration.

The conflict between concentration and dispersion has taken different courses in different regions. Between 1948 and 1965 the shares of the Belgrade, Zagreb and Novi Sad areas in the non-agricultural employment respectively of Serbia and Kosmet, Croatia and Vojvodina increased from 36 to 51, 27 to 30 and 28 to 33 per cent. The shares of Sarajevo and Skopje in total non-agricultural employment in Bosnia-Herzegovina and Macedonia have declined from 44 to 33 and 35 to 31 per cent. respectively following proportionately greater growth elsewhere in those republics.

Clearly the most important growth areas lie northward of the Danube-Sava line in north-west and north-east Yugoslavia. As many jobs have been provided in these two areas (with only 25 per cent. of the total population) as in those extensive regions (containing 53 per cent. of the population) where, in contrast, the number of new jobs created has been below 64 per 1,000 (cf. the federal average of 70). Except for much of Slavonia, northern Bačka and Banat—the northern peripheral areas of the state—the regions of slower economic development, and hence declining relative importance, lie exclusively to the south of the Danube-Sava line. They include Herzegovina, Kosmet and most of Macedonia, where least expansion of employment has occurred (only 30–49 jobs per 1,000 population) and also west Bosnia, Montenegro and most of Serbia Proper (50–64 per 1,000). Since population growth and existing overpopulation are greatest here such slow growth accounts for the higher rates of unemployment in and emigration from these regions.

Similar trends occur on the local scale. Planning authorities from the federation downwards have taken the opportunity to develop new industries and services where formerly only agriculture provided employment. Such dispersal on any significant scale, however, has usually been restricted to towns and their tributary areas served by, and to zones along, transport lines which offer better accessibility to and from other districts and regions. This is because the shift of productive resources from the land into industries and services has involved, first, a shift from more extensive and highly dispersed forms of activity to more intensive and concentrated forms, and second, a shift from largely subsistence to largely commercial activities. The shaded areas in Figure 12 indicate clearly the basins and belts along the more important river valleys in which most development has occurred. These are not simply the areas of greatest employment; they are also the major zones of commuting labour. In northern and western Yugoslavia such growth zones are more extensive, since greater economic advancement means more growth points and also better communications and larger commuter zones. Elsewhere fewer growth points and poorer transport facilities restrict the size of growth areas. Beyond the growth and commuter zones are areas of greater inaccessibility where the provision of new employment in industries and services has been minimal. These are the white areas in Figure 12. Broadly speaking, their economies have stagnated, with the result that agriculture still dominates an occupational structure of the population which has changed little since 1948. Indeed statistical evidence shows that the rapid growth of agricultural population has combined with the emigration of youth (that formerly commuted to factories or to service establishments elsewhere) to give an *increase* in the proportion of population dependent on agriculture in many of these areas.

Hitherto, frequent references have been made to 'backward regions' without explaining, except broadly, what they are and where they are. Since 1947 'backward regions' have been defined as those areas in which the dominance of subsistence agriculture, the underutilisation of natural resources and labour and their corollary, the underdevelopment of industries and services, result in per capita income levels which are substantially below the federal average. Inspired by the federalism formalised in the 1946 constitution, the planners adopted a broad regional approach in the First Five Year Plan (1947–52) by delineating the three republics of Bosnia-Herzegovina, Macedonia and Montenegro as backward areas which would receive special financial aid to speed development. General federal backwardness at this stage precluded a more precise statement. After 1952 Bosnia-Herzegovina was omitted, as high rates of investment during the Plan had achieved notable progress there. Temporary aid was given to Slovenia and Croatia to develop northern Istria where unemployment became serious in 1954 following the separation of the area from the main sources of employment in Trieste, but this stopped in 1956. Macedonia and Montenegro continued to receive aid as backward regions and in 1957 they were joined, under the second Five Year Plan, by the formerly neglected area of Kosmet. These three regions remain the most important backward areas, receiving special federal investment grants.

Since 1961 the planners have become aware, through the

availability of better statistics, of the marked intra-republic differences in growth rates described earlier. Additional areas in southern Yugoslavia with lagging growth rates have thus been scheduled as backward regions, including: the Banija, Kordun, Lika and southern Dalmatian areas of Croatia; west Bosnia and Herzegovina; and the Sandjak, Leskovac, Pirot and Vranje areas of southern Serbia. These areas obtain capital from the republic government or from wealthier districts and enterprises within the republic to which they belong. Today, then, officially-designated backward areas comprise, as between 1947 and 1952, 40 per cent. of the area and 33 per cent. of the population of the federation; such proportions necessitate purposive regional economic planning.

In 1946 Boris Kidrič, then head of the Federal Planning Commission, formulated an ideal model of dynamic regional economic development according to socialist principles (Table 11). This has been the basis for all subsequent Yugoslav planning. The model established the need for rapid development of all regions but for faster growth in the backward areas and slower growth in the advanced areas in order to achieve an equal level of prosperity per capita everywhere by the nth year. Table 11 shows that the practical outcome of the government's development policy so far has been totally different. Only the changes in Vojvodina and in Montenegro fit into Kidrič's concepts. Elsewhere, rates of progress have been highest in Slovenia and Croatia and lowest in Serbia and Bosnia-Herzegovina, Macedonia and Kosmet, although in Bosnia growth was sufficiently near the Yugoslav average for this republic to maintain its relative position. Between 1947 and 1962, as a result, gross social product per capita increased by 109,000 dinars on average in the areas lying northward of the Danube-Sava line (including Belgrade), while it increased by only 49,000 dinars on average in areas lying southward of that line.[1] These broad findings are supported by Vinski's exhaustive analyses of regional changes in fixed assets since 1947. Contrary, then, to the aims of policy the economic difference between Slovenia, the most advanced region, and Kosmet, the most backward region, is now twice as great as it was twenty years ago. Interregional disparities have been increased, not decreased. Similar trends are evident

TABLE 11

A COMPARISON OF ACTUAL CHANGES IN PER CAPITA NATIONAL INCOME

in Republics and Autonomous Areas 1947–62 with the Ideal Model of Boris Kidrič

AREA	THE KIDRIČ MODEL					ACTUAL CHANGES				
	1947		Nth Year*		1947-Nth Index of Change	1947		1962		1947–62 Index of Change
	'000 Dinars	Index	'000 Dinars	Index		'000 Dinars	Index	'000 Dinars	Index	
Slovenia	82	157	530	100	675	82	157	265	197	336
Croatia	55.5	105	530	100	950	55.5	105	164	122	298
Vojvodina	68	127	530	100	775	68	127	140	104	206
Average Yugoslavia	53	100	530	100	1,000	53	100	135	100	255
Serbia Proper	51	97	530	100	1,050	51	97	124	92	243
Bosnia-Herzegovina	40	75	530	100	1,325	40	75	100	74	250
Macedonia	39	73	530	100	1,390	39	73	83	61	215
Montenegro	31	59	530	100	1,700	31	59	82	61	261
Kosovo-Metohija	38	71	530	100	1,875	38	71	42	31	150

Source: Ekonomist 1963, 3–4, pp. 608–9.

* Theoretical Figures.

from comparing smaller areal units. In 1965, for example, per capita national income in the most developed district of Ljubljana (Slovenia) was ten times greater than in the least developed district of Ohrid (Macedonia), giving conceptually a perfect economic gradient from extreme north-western to extreme south-western Yugoslavia.

The emergence of sharp differences within republics and districts can be attributed to a tendency towards greater localisation of activities, especially in underdeveloped regions where, by definition, economic growth occurs in fewer locations and contrasts more sharply with primitive subsistence agriculture. In 1965, for instance, in Serbia Proper per capita income was five times as large in Belgrade as in Valjevo, a neighbouring district, in Macedonia it was four times as large in Skopje as in Ohrid and in Bosnia-Herzegovina nearly three times as large in Sarajevo as in Bihać. Where economic development is greater and a wider range of industries and services, as well as commercial agriculture, is more dispersed, intra-regional economic differences are less—a fact which substantiates the rationale of the government's long-term development aims. In Vojvodina, for example, average per capita income in Novi Sad district was only 60 per cent. greater than in Pančevo district, while in Slovenia it was almost equal in the districts of Celje, Koper and Maribor and only 30 per cent. below that in Ljubljana district. Economic disparities may be extremely sharp between the communes of a given district, but since the general process of development involves inevitably a regrouping of both economic activities and population these microgeographical differences are less relevant to the problem of developing the backward regions successfully than are the broader, interregional disparities.

In view of the continual stress laid since 1947 upon the quest for greater interregional equality through the more rapid development of the backward regions, it may be asked why in practice rates of economic growth in all the backward areas (except Montenegro) were below average with, therefore, an increase and not a decrease in spatial economic disparities. The answers lie in the operation of a complex set of diverse, yet interacting factors.

The most fundamental and direct factor has been the

allocation of insufficient investment to the backward regions. The following indices[2] (Yugoslavia = 100) show that between 1947 and 1965 *per capita* investment in those regions (except Montenegro) fell substantially short of that in the advanced areas: Slovenia 157, Croatia 110, Montenegro 131, Bosnia-Herzegovina 83, Macedonia 81 and Kosmet 54. Although capital effectiveness varied with inter-branch allocation of investment from area to area, the range of levels of per capita investment nevertheless accounts basically for the range in rate of growth in per capita national income from high and above average in Slovenia, Croatia and only one backward area, Montenegro, to below average and very low in Serbia Proper, Bosnia-Herzegovina, Macedonia and Kosmet, and in only one advanced area, Vojvodina. 'To aim', as one economist observes, 'at achieving faster sustained development of the underdeveloped areas and to invest per capita continually less than average in these areas is to expect the impossible.'[3]

How is it possible for such a situation to arise in a planned economy? The order of planning priorities—the opportunity costs of various permutations of limited capital allocation—provides a partial answer. Throughout the postwar period top priority has been accorded to the economic development of the whole federation. Sector planning of growth has taken precedence over spatial planning. Indeed, regional growth rates have been largely by-products of growth rates in the various economic sectors. Above average investment per capita in Bosnia-Herzegovina (index 120) during the first Five Year Plan owed more to efforts to develop heavy and strategic industries in Yugoslavia, and the infrastructure to support them, than to efforts to develop this area more rapidly than others. Once, after 1953, federal economic progress demanded greater growth of manufacturing and consumer industries, investment in Bosnia began to lag while it increased in northern Yugoslavia where existing facilities could be expanded. This combined with the neglect of agriculture to cause low investment and slower growth in the more backward, agricultural areas of Serbia, Macedonia, Kosmet and also Vojvodina, while strategic consideration combined with the need to shorten land transport links between the southern Adriatic coast and Belgrade to ensure high rates of investment in Montenegro. In contrast, above average investment in Slovenia and Croatia resulted from the ease and lower costs of expanding a wider range of existing activities including heavy and manufacturing industries in Slovenia and manufacturing and port facilities in Croatia. Before 1960, therefore, when relatively more and new development occurred, the *spatial elasticity*[4] of that development was greater, but finance was scarcer so that sector planning, applied to branches or projects in isolation, tended to stress the cost savings of, and greater growth resulting from, the expansion of existing facilities in the more advanced areas. At times, however, it missed the greater benefits which could be derived from greater infrastructural investment in backward areas by integrated sector and spatial planning. Since 1960 growth in Slovenia and Croatia has gained ground as the third and fourth Five Year Plans stressed growth through the modernisation of the now greater number of existing plants rather than through new development.

The preponderance of the sector-planning approach induced (or misled) federal planners in formulating their plans to use, at least superficially, intra-regional and not inter-regional comparisons of the rates and sizes of growth. Thus the original 1961–65 Plan simply proposed average annual growth rates of 11 per cent. for the whole federation and 14 per cent. for the backward areas. Since the rate of 14 per cent. relates to a far smaller volume of income per capita in the backward areas than does the rate of 11 per cent. (or lower) in the federation and the advanced areas, this practice, begun in 1947, has been a direct cause of greater absolute and relative economic growth in the advanced regions.

A simple example will illustrate the point. Suppose that Five Year Plan X proposes a 5 per cent. growth rate per annum in developed area A (with a per capita income of $200) and a 10 per cent. rate in underdeveloped area B (with a per capita income of $60). Superficially, the latter appears to be the favoured region. If the plan is fulfilled, however, income in region A would rise in five years to $255 per capita, and in region B to $96·5. Although income increases by 60 per cent. in B and only 27 per cent. in A, the absolute growth in income is 50 per cent. more in A than in B, so widening the gap between A and B from $140 to about $160 per head.

Yugoslav economic planners have failed to realise that, *ceteris paribus*, an increase in per capita income by the same quantity in both developed and backward regions demands a far greater rate of growth in the latter than in the former. In 1963, it was calculated,[5] for example, that an increase in national income of 10,600 dinars (then about $15) per head per annum would require an annual growth rate of 19 per cent. in Kosmet and only 3 per cent. in Slovenia. To achieve this, however, the difference in per capita investment would have to be still larger since infrastructure absorbs a larger proportion of investment in backward areas (21–25 per cent. since 1947) than elsewhere (under 16 per cent.).

Neither plans nor planners have ever stated the obviously very different rates of growth that *would even begin to eliminate* interregional economic disparities. Kidrič as early as 1948 stressed that long-term regional 'phasing' of development was necessary because Slovenia and Croatia would have to continue to provide some capital goods for new development in the backward regions. Yet no geographical plan[6] for guiding such phasing existed in 1947; nor has one been drawn up since to establish *when* sufficient per capita investment would be allocated to the backward areas to enable them to begin to catch up the advanced areas. Purposive long-term regional development plans are lacking, reflecting a neglect of the regional approach to planning economic development, and resulting as much from the passing of centralised planning as from the preoccupation with the methodology of decentralised general and sector planning. No attempt has been made to devise a system of economic regions as a framework for assessing spatial development potentials and for formulating spatial development policies to exploit those potentials and to solve specific regional problems. Neither have the republics and autonomous areas been used for this purpose, although they are sufficiently large, their resources are sufficiently diversified and their economic development levels sufficiently different to provide a regional basis for development. Per capita investment in backward areas has lagged because no positive policies exist for deciding either the character or the speed of progress, whether these areas are treated individually or collectively. Indeed, 'Yugoslavia really has no long-term, logical and systematic development policy, not even at the Federal level.'⁷

The absence of a stated full employment policy has contributed to the absence of a regional development policy, for very marked areal differences in population growth cause great contrasts in supply in labour markets from area to area. This was not serious before 1952 while labour surpluses were widespread outside Vojvodina. It became serious after 1953, however, as collectivisation was abandoned, as development removed the surplus in the north and as the labour surplus became more and more an acute problem only of the backward regions from Banija (Croatia) south-eastwards to the Pirot (eastern Serbia) and Strumica (south-east Macedonia) basins. Subordination of regional employment problems to the needs of general economic growth has had a number of consequences. Investment has not been channelled specifically into labour-intensive activities in areas of large labour surplus—at least not until the 1960s. Indeed, an emphasis upon heavy industries to exploit resources in backward areas and on manufacturing in the advanced areas and neglect or urgent infrastructural projects (especially land transport) to employ labour in the backward areas has had broadly the opposite effect. Employment opportunities have increased more quickly in the advanced than in the backward areas. Now there are more vacancies than applicants to fill them in northern Yugoslavia, whereas the number of people without jobs is constantly increasing in southern Yugoslavia. In Macedonia, for example, where population growth is slow, unemployment averages 18 per cent. of the non-agricultural working population and 13 per cent. of the unemployed are skilled workers. This is evidence enough that insufficient investment in the backward areas has resulted in inefficiencies in the use of resources, not simply labour, but also educational resources. Had the provision of employment been given higher priority, per capita investment in the backward regions would have been undoubtedly higher and would have ensured the development in those regions of some of those manufacturing and tertiary activities that now lie partly idle because they were located in the advanced areas where there are labour shortages.

Efficient resource utilisation, however, does not necessarily involve the full employment of surplus labour only within the backward areas themselves. Unpublished analyses by the Federal Planning Institute show that, even with increasing capital availability, the highest per capita investment in industry and services in underdeveloped regions would still be insufficient to absorb entirely the surplus labour of Kosmet, Bosnia-Herzegovina, Sandjak and Macedonia.[8] It would be unfair to conclude, however, that the continued economic lag of investment and growth in the backward areas represents the government's unofficial conviction that the gap in interregional per capita standards may be reduced only through large-scale population migration from the backward to the advanced areas. Certainly thinking concerning the progress of the underdeveloped areas has been modified. Policies current until 1960 for dispersing activities to employ labour *in situ* as a means of economising on housing investment in areas of dense resident population surplus are being abandoned. The 1961–65 Plan for the Republic of Serbia, for example, states that people living in underdeveloped communes cannot necessarily expect the right to work where they are born;[9] they must be prepared to migrate to work in 'growth' or 'regroupment' centres where the existence of infrastructural facilities, the proximity of resources and markets and good communications provide a better basis for economic development.[10]

The solution lies in achieving faster economic growth in the backward areas by combining above average investment and employment in selected growth zones there with controlled migration to the more developed regions where slow progress would nevertheless provide more employment opportunities than local labour supplies would be able to meet. Despite large-scale migration from the underdeveloped areas since 1945, the labour mobility between regions is still insufficient but much wisdom is required in speeding it up, for: first, potential migration from Bosnia-Herzegovina and Serbia Proper is unhampered by language barriers and is traditional, yet these regions possess most of the country's resources for future manufacturing development; second, migration from Montenegro is likely to be substantial because few resources and opportunities exist there for creating growth zones to retain the population; and third, migration from Kosmet and Macedonia is most necessary since the resources and opportunities for growth are limited, but out-migration is least likely on account of powerful language barriers. Labour movement requires some broad guiding plan for the geographical employment of labour. None has been put forward so far, so the dichotomy between north and south will persist and deepen. The long-run solution, however, lies in substantially reducing the birth rate in most backward areas; and that depends upon sufficient education.

One temporarily operative factor was the Cominform Blockade during the years 1949–54. This has had long-term and complex consequences. While it discouraged industrialisation in the north, its stimulus to industrialisation in the backward centre and south was a mixed blessing. These areas received primarily strategic and heavy industries; their dispersal, their location sometimes in isolated areas to which people had to be brought and housed, and their slow growth rates have reduced the effectiveness of capital investment. Although certain key light industries were also located in Bosnia-Herzegovina, Kosovo-Metohija, Macedonia, Montenegro and southern Serbia, this gain was more than offset by the abandonment of a large number of manufacturing projects in these areas for lack of capital and equipment. The reorientation of trade from the Soviet bloc to the rest of the world following the Cominform Blockade also had multiple consequences. It reduced commercial activity in the north-eastern quadrant centring on the Danube artery and the Belgrade-Budapest/Bucharest/Sofia railways, but it strengthened tertiary activities in the north-western quadrant where railways provide the best links with West-Central Europe and with the best ports, Rijeka and Split. Of the backward areas only the Dinaric region has benefitted in employment in industry and services in forming the tributary area (in terms of trade and migrant labour) to the ports and to centres along the improved transport lines across the mountain barrier.

Since 1952, decentralisation and the new economic system have generally operated to the disadvantage of the backward areas. Whatever its faults, the centralised system of planning and finance did facilitate a high degree of interregional capital mobility by transferring a substantial part of the profits or 'accumulation' from activities in Slovenia and

Croatia to assist development in Bosnia-Herzegovina, Macedonia and Montenegro, and within Serbia from Vojvodina to Serbia Proper and Kosmet. Bosnia-Herzegovina then received above average per capita investment and, although other backward regions were less privileged, the system may be credited with achieving, between the two censuses of 1948 and 1953, many more new jobs (320,000) in industries and services in central and southern Yugoslavia (with 60 per cent. of the total population) than in the north (120,000) despite centralisation of the bureaucracy in Belgrade. Decentralisation has dissipated part of that bureaucracy, providing a marked increase in employment in administration, planning and banking throughout the hierarchy of administrative centres, from the republic capital to the commune centre, and so increasing the burden of 'non-productives' precisely in the backward areas where there are fewer 'productive' activities to support them.

This became serious with the evolution of the new economic system which has progressively increased the proportion of finance created locally which remains for re-investment locally with the enterprise, the commune, the district and the republic. Decentralisation has favoured the advanced areas directly, therefore, since the greater the amount of money and accumulation that is generated locally, the greater is the amount that remains for re-investment locally, and hence the greater can be the per capita investment and growth in those areas. The converse is true for the backward areas. This explains why, since 1953, in contrast to the period before 1953, the growth in non-agricultural employment has been greater in the areas lying northward of the Danube-Sava-Kupa line (500,000) than in the areas lying southward of that line (400,000). In the circumstances, the government achieved substantial progress in absolute, though not relative, terms in developing industries and services in the backward areas only by making additional finance from federal funds—'guaranteed investments', interest-free loans, cheap credit and subsidies—available in those areas. The complexity of financial arrangements evolved between 1952 and 1960, however, suggest a preoccupation of the planners with devising unique planning and management methodologies rather than with analysing the main problem and devising methods of fulfilling the aims of policy, especially the spatial aims, in order to solve the problem.

The greater growth of services in the more advanced north resulted directly from the full operation of decentralised decision-taking by republics, districts and communes in allocating their own budgetary funds, for the federal government interfered little except in allocating major projects. The greater growth of industry in the north, however, occurred while the federal government still maintained (until 1965) through the Investment Bank, much direct and indirect control over the use of finance for industry from any source. Three factors account for this paradoxical situation. First, rapid economic growth under the decentralised system was accompanied by marked inflation. This encouraged the channelling of more federal funds into, and the granting of permission for more investment from communes and enterprise, in manufacturing and consumer goods industries (located chiefly in the developed areas), in which high profits accruing from unpegged prices made investment more attractive. These activities, with high rates of accumulation, also generated a greater increase in the supply of funds locally. Second, in contrast, fixed prices (until 1964) and low profit margins in the heavy industries,[11] mining and power, made investment in the underdeveloped regions (where these industries are dominant) less attractive. Since these regions lacked funds and their industries provided only gradual increases in capital availability locally, growth generally was slower. This threw the central and southern regions into greater dependence upon scarce federal grants. Kardelj observes, moreover, that the process was often a circular one for such grants were allotted to the backward areas mainly for slow growth, heavy industries, which tended 'to contribute indirectly more to the rise in national income in other regions with developed manufacturing by supplying them with raw materials from less developed areas'.[12] Third, insistence upon the criterion of 'rentability' often put communes in the backward areas at some disadvantage in competing for federal investment loans, particularly since, unlike advanced communes, they could not offer to cover much of the costs of a project from their own funds. Backed by the continual liberalisation of prices and expansion of the market economy this criterion has put an end to the development of impressive 'political' or 'socio-economic' industrial projects like the metallurgical plants allocated to Montenegro and Macedonia in the 1950s.

This seems to indicate that backward areas have lagged also on account of unfavourable comparative advantage. Such a concept was applied little until the mid-1950s as economic policies demanded autarky while the administrative system made arbitrary decisions possible and realistic comparisons impossible. The Cominform Blockade substantially altered the order of priorities and led to the abandonment of projects, particularly the aluminium industry, which has obvious natural and economic advantages in Yugoslavia. The new economic system has made realistic assessments of comparative advantage feasible, especially since the reforms of 1965. Although the advantages of developing the backward areas—their substantial and varied natural resources, their large labour reserves and the savings they offer on housing investment—may now be given full commercial weight, the danger is that they will be over-shadowed by the disadvantages of underdeveloped infrastructure, poor transport facilities, less developed training facilities and insufficient skilled labour.

In this respect the division of Yugoslavia broadly along the Danube-Sava line (but omitting the Morava-Vardar corridor and the coastal ports from the south) is the division into two unequally competing worlds. Given that labour can be trained and illiteracy can be eliminated from the backward areas, the major handicap of these areas is the virtual lack of any real transport network to provide good accessibility to the main transport arteries along the Sava-Danube-Morava-Vardar axis and along the Adriatic coast, to the main urban-industrial centres, to sources of materials and to other underdeveloped areas. Even today, then, Yugoslavia cannot be viewed as one economic unit with a unified market. For this reason, and until such time as the backward areas are provided with satisfactory communications, comparative advantages for services and manufacturing lie decisively with the north-west, north-centre, north-east and east. Location here provides accessibility to a larger market at cheaper cost, permitting *ceteris paribus* larger scales of activity and lower production costs. Developments in the backward areas face the

L

serious disadvantages of poor transport and market accessibility, and hence higher transport costs, restricted market areas,
lower sales, smaller scale and higher production costs. In
these conditions certain regional monopoly elements exist and
in such a developing country as Yugoslavia make new entry in
production especially in the backward areas risky. Under the
old system of fixed prices operating up to 1957–64 locations in
backward regions were not placed in such a disadvantageous
position; now, with flexible prices, they are. Experience in
Yugoslavia amply bears out Myrdal's critique of the consequences that follow the operation of uncontrolled 'market
forces'.

Underlying, and sometimes stimulating, the development,
persistence and interplay of the factors that have contributed
to the lag in the development of the backward areas have been
'nationalism' and 'localism'. Tito's greatest achievement in
the political and social field was the generation of the 'Yugoslav idea' which was above nationality and which sought to
create coherence and unity among heterogeneous peoples who
were thrown together by the artifact of the Versailles Treaty.
The idea was strong enough to muffle localist tendencies until
the early 1960s when it was swept aside on a tide of decentralisation which has fanned the old nationalist embers to kindle
economic rivalry. Nationalism, however, has been powerfully
active in planning ever since 1945, in the form of pressure upon
actual planning decisions from republic interests in Parliament.[13] Local 'patriotism' and national—as opposed to federal
—interest have had a number of consequences for the course
and pattern of economic development. The Slovenes and
Croats, with most to lose from centralised administration of
the economy, have formed the vanguard of decentralisation,
while the representatives of the backward republics and the
Serbs have favoured the retention of a certain amount of
central economic power. Intense competition among the
republics for investment for given projects has dissipated limited
capital in the duplication of projects, giving lower intra-
regional effectiveness and losing economies of scale. Political
and social equality has made the levelling up of the backward
areas more difficult since the unity of the federation has been
maintained only by giving apparently *equal treatment* to the

republics, advanced and backward alike. While, however, the Montenegrins are well represented by strong interests in Belgrade, which may have served them in attaining high per capita investment, the Bosnians are not well served by the fact that they are either Serbs or Croats. Moreover, the dominance of planning by more educated Slovenes and Croats may also have operated, on balance, to the disadvantage of the central and eastern areas.

National pride in the republic capital has stimulated inter-city rivalry, encouraging greater localisation of industries and services in those capitals than in the smaller towns and the backward areas within republics. The counter-point has been provided at times by the communes which, in competing for loans, have exaggerated their comparative advantages in order to obtain projects to satisfy local pride and budgetary needs. In the last analysis, nationalism and localism have reduced the mobility of capital across administrative frontiers— to the disadvantage of the poorer areas—and have made impossible inter-republic co-operation in developing unified inter-republic growth zones which could be of mutual benefit. Administrative boundaries, therefore, have remained sharp economic frontiers between more advanced and rather backward republics. The Croatian-Bosnian frontiers provide a good example. Balkan politics, therefore, still provide a powerful, pervasive, if at present peaceful, under-current to economic planning.

The government, therefore, has been only partially successful in achieving the aims of spatial development. Absolute progress in increasing employment, production and income in the backward areas, with the sole exception of the Kosmet area has been very substantial—indeed, monumental when compared with the total neglect of these areas before 1945. Nevertheless, that progress has been insufficient, and with the rapid growth of population especially in central Yugoslavia vestiges of the poverty circle still remain. Two economic zones, more distinct than ever before, have been created. The first zone— lying northward of the Danube-Sava-Kupa line is developed, its economy is expanding faster, its income growing faster, and, despite immigration of labour and supplies of raw materials from backward areas, it is short of both labour and materials.

The second zone, lying southward of the line, is still under-developed, its economy and income are growing more slowly and despite the emigration of labour and outflow of materials it still possesses large reserves of labour requiring employment and reserves of materials which could be processes locally. The way ahead is still long.

REFERENCES

1 B. Čolanović, 'Organizacija Industrializacije Nerazvijenih Područja' in Radivoj Uvalić, ed., *Problemi Regionalnog Privrednog Razvoja*, Ekonomska Biblioteka 18, Belgrade, 1962, p. 155. I. Vinski, 'Regionalna Procjena Rasta Fiksnih Fondova Jugoslavije od 1946 do 1960', *Ekonomiski Pregled*, 1964, 7, pp. 417–49.

2 Calculated from all postwar sources giving figures of investment and population by Republics and autonomous areas, particularly from *Statistički Godišnjak*, years 1954–66 and *Vestnik Investicione Banke*, 1958–64.

3 Kiril Miljovski, 'Nedovoljno Razvijena Područja i Sedmogodišnji Plan', *Ekonomist*, 3–4, 1963, p. 671.

4 The concept of 'spatial elasticity' expresses the degree of locational choice that planned industrial investment programmes offer to regional planners. Plans are *spatially more elastic*, i.e. allowing a larger number of locational choices, the greater is the number of plants to be developed and the more 'footloose' they are in aggregate. Programmes are *spatially more inelastic* the smaller is the number of plants to be developed and the more 'localised' their location must be in aggregate. See: F. E. Ian Hamilton, 'Models of Industrial Location' in R. J. Chorley and P. Haggett, eds, *Models in Geography*, London, 1967, p 382; and A. Kuklinski, 'Glówne Problemy Przestrzennego Zagospodarowania Kraju', *Problemy Ekonomiczne*, 4, 1965; United Nations, Economic Commission for Europe, *Criteria for Location of Industrial Plants: Changes and Problems*, New York, 1967, pp. 66–68.

5 Kosta Mihailović, 'Varijante Plana i Regionalni Razvoj', *Ekonomist*, 3–4,, 1963, p. 610.

6 Boris Kidrič, *Odnosi Izmedju Narodne i Privredne Politike*, Belgrade, 1948, pp. 31–34.

7 D. Gorupić, *Problemi Sistema Investiranja u Industriji*, Ekonomski Institut N. R. Hrvatske, 1962, p. 90.

8 *Ekonomist, op. cit.*, p. 609, 709–13.

9 *Društveni Plan Privrednog Razvoja Narodne Republike Srbije 1961–65*, Belgrade, 1961, p. 69.

10 *Ibid.*, p. 24.

11 Vladimir Bakarić, *Aktuelni Problemi Izgradnje Naše Privrednog Sistema*, Zagreb, 1963, pp. 19–20, 42.

12 E. Kardelj, *Speech at the Plenary Session, Fifth Congress of the Socialist Alliance of Working People*, Belgrade, 1960, p. 162.

13 'In current practice . . . the elements of state-ownership monopoly . . .
    kept engendering aspirations towards nationalistic egoism, hegemony,
    towards the use of political pressure in dividing the "common pie".'
    Edward Kardelj, 'The Principal Dilemma: Self-Management or
    Statism', *Socialist Thought and Practice: A Yugoslav Quarterly*, 24, 1966,
    p. 20.

PART III

THE ECONOMIC SECTORS

CHAPTER 9

Agricultural Change

The importance of this primary activity in the Yugoslav economy and in government decision-making should not be underestimated. Fifty-eight per cent. of all land is used for agriculture, 35 per cent. is covered by forest and 7 per cent. is unproductive. Agriculture still employs half the working population, about 4·5 million,[1] and produces 27 per cent. of Gross National Product, although these proportions have declined since 1941 from four-fifths and one-half respectively.

Problems of land use and misuse have lain at the roots of Yugoslav economic difficulties for decades.[2] Insecurity induced uneven man/land ratios and irrational land-use patterns. Rising overpopulation decreased farm size, increased fragmentation and poverty, and entrenched extensive subsistence farming. Consequently, the overgrazing of pastures and the destruction of forests rendered both increasing marginal hill areas and fertile lowlands liable to soil erosion. Food exports continued until 1941, however, because the north-east produced a surplus which could not be purchased by the undernourished people of the overpopulated west, centre and south for lack of money and of interregional transport facilities. The need to solve the agrarian problem became ever more acute after 1945 as the population increased rapidly and the transfer of people from the land into urban occupations increased per capita demand for food in areas of food surplus and deficit alike. To solve the problem, the government has used direct legal, technical and economic measures related specifically to agriculture, and indirect measures, mainly industrialisation to reduce agricultural overpopulation and afforestation to reduce soil erosion. At every step, however, it has had to contend with the most numerous social force in the federation, the peasantry.

AGRICULTURAL PRODUCTION

In 1966 agricultural output was the highest on record, being almost double the average for the present state territory during the decade 1930–39. Progress, nevertheless, has been unsatisfactory by comparison with that in secondary and tertiary activities and particularly against growth in home markets. Demand for food has been expanding faster (6·4 per cent. per annum) than agricultural supply (5 per cent. per annum) throughout the postwar period as a result of rising per capita purchasing power,[3] causing rising food prices and food imports. Improved yields account for nearly four-fifths of the total increase in farm output, far outstripping the contribution of an expanded crop area (15 per cent.).[4] Indeed, yields per hectare are now generally 70 per cent. higher than in the decade 1930–39. Increased maize production accounts for one-third of the expanded total crop output, followed by wheat (one-quarter), vegetables (one-fifth), potatoes (one-eighth) and industrial crops (one-tenth). Improvements in livestock production and yields have been far more modest, largely because of frequent scarcities of fodder.

Trends in output, however, differ significantly before and after 1956.[5] As Table 12 shows, yields stagnated or declined between 1945 and 1956. Average farm production, 5 per cent. less than it had been between 1930 and 1939, had to feed 14 per cent. more people. By contrast, output has almost doubled since 1956. Marked increases in major crop yields (Table 12) are chiefly responsible: maize, wheat, sugar beet and potatoes directly, and silage maize, lucerne and clover indirectly (through higher livestock productivity). Although agricultural progress has not been uniform in time, it shows remarkable geographical uniformity. Production in the years 1962–66 was everywhere between 72 and 85 per cent. above the prewar average, except in Bosnia, where improvement (44 per cent.) was sluggish. Nevertheless, the broad pattern is one of greater expansion (80 per cent.) north of than (66 per cent.) south of the Sava-Danube.

Many factors have influenced the patterns of agricultural progress and change both in time and in place: land use, agrarian reform, economic policy and improved techniques; these must now be examined.

TABLE 12

INCREASES IN THE OUTPUT AND YIELD OF SELECTED CROPS 1930–39, 1947–56 AND 1957–66
(production in thousand tons and yields in quintals per hectare)

	Wheat		Maize		Barley		Oats		Sugar Beet	
	Production	Yield	Production	Yield	Production	Yield	Production	Yield	Production	Yield
1930–39 1939	2,430 2,910	11·4 13·1	4,300 4,070	16·4 15·1	410 424	9·7 10·2	310 348	8·5 9·3	616 922	176 200
1947–56 1956	2,040 1,600	11·3 9·9	3,370 3,370	14·2 13·1	332 344	10·1 9·7	285 324	8·3 8·7	1,240 1,130	151 163
1957–66 1966	3,800 4,450	17·1 20·0	5,750 8,000	22·4 26·3	540 620	14·6 16·3	309 400	11·0 14·0	2,210 3,240	256 316

	Potato		Tomato		Lucerne		Clover		Sunflower	
	Production	Yield	Production	Yield	Production	Yield	Production	Yield	Production	Yield
1930–39 1939	1,658 1,540	60 54	44 50	66 68	372 464	39 39	396 400	35 33	9 27	15·2 14·3
1947–56 1956	1,690 2,160	72 81	140 203	102 110	696 734	39 44	376 562	33 36	102 59	9·4 8·1
1957–66 1966	2,760 2,820	98 93	250 302	125 125	1,370 1,860	52 54	960 999	40 42	140 240	13·3 17·2

Sources: Statistički Bilten, 95, 'Ratarstvo, Voćarstvo i Vinogradarstvo, 1930–39, 1947–56', pp. 10–25.
Statistički Godišnjak, 1966, pp. 136–8.
Yugoslav Life, 11(10), 1966, pp. 1–4.

AGRICULTURAL LAND USE

Figure 13 summarises the distributions of arable land and gardens, orchard and vineyard, meadow and pasture in 1965. Arable farming dominates northern and eastern Yugoslavia, particularly the fertile lowlands of Vojvodina, the valleys of the rivers Sava, Drava, Morava, Timok and their tributaries, the depressions of Kosmet and adjacent hill country where annual rainfall is below 40″ (1,000 mm.). Field crops here occupy between 70 and 95 per cent. of all farmland, falling to 50–70 per cent., with pasture and meadow making up much of the rest, where lowlands are ill-drained (western Posavina, Baranija, Skopje Polje and Pelagonia), rainfall exceeds 40″ (Banija), and hill country is dry, dissected or gullied (the Carpathians, southern Serbia and Macedonia). Orchards and vineyards are extensive along the southern margins of this arable area from central Slovenia to east-central Serbia; they even penetrate the upland zone along the more sheltered Bosna, Upper Morava and Moravica valleys.

South-west of a line drawn through Maribor-Karlovac-Višegrad-Titov Veles arable land is restricted to flat *polje* floors, valleys or river terraces. It amounts generally to less than 30 per cent. of the agricultural area and in the Karst, with mountainous relief, harsher and wetter climate and poorer soils, falls below 10 per cent. Pastoral farming dominates here, chiefly on rough pasture, although meadowland is not unimportant, especially in Slovenia. Tree crops are also largely absent, but they become very prominent along the Adriatic coast (except for the inhospitable Velebit coast between Novi and Novigrad), where they are clearly associated with a Mediterranean-type climate. Generally, then, land use is closely adapted to physical conditions.

Superimposed upon the land-use distributions shown in Figure 13 is a scheme of five agricultural planning regions. Proposed in 1952 as a framework to guide the long-term development of agricultural specialisation, they were based upon the agricultural potentialities of regional physical environments although their boundaries followed those of contemporary administrative districts. Yet the correlations between planning regions and dominant, yet broad, agricultural

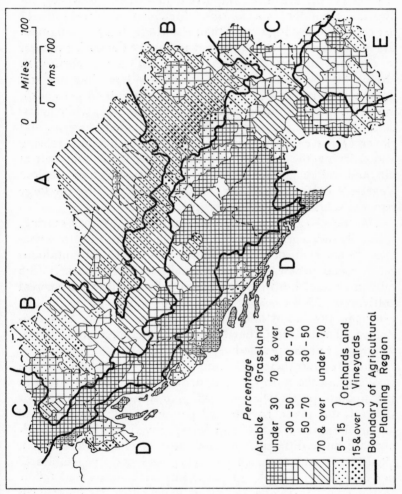

Figure 13. Agricultural Land Use Patterns and Agricultural Planning Regions

land uses, especially *arable* uses, are remarkably close. In region A, designated the *žitorodni* (cereal-growing) region, grains occupy 62 per cent. of all agricultural land. Industrial crops and vegetables (6 per cent. each) and sown fodder crops (10 per cent.), are more important here than elsewhere, indicating secondary specialisms. Meadows and pasture (12 per cent.) are less important than elsewhere, but they augment the mixed farming base required to supply livestock products to the four million consumers living within the north-east. Grains (45 per cent.) occupy much less land but are still dominant in region B. Orchards and vineyards (9 per cent.), in contrast, are the most extensive in Yugoslavia, while grassland (33 per cent.), arable fodder crops, chiefly lucerne and clover (7 per cent.), and grain-fodder make livestock-rearing and dairying the leading agricultural activities. This belt of hill and valley land is thus the 'fruit-vine-livestock' region. Vegetable cultivation (5 per cent.) is encouraged by the large regional market of 7 million people.

The most extensive form of land-use—livestock-rearing, primarily sheep-grazing, based on rough pasture—characterises over 70 per cent. of the farmland of region C. Mountainous relief, social backwardness and small, scattered markets (3·5 million people) limit cropland essentially to subsistence cereal cultivation (23 per cent.). Areas in other crops are negligible, except in the basins and valleys of Gospić, Livno, Sarajevo-Zenica, Drina-Lim, Ibar-Moravica, Metohija and Polog, where most of the people live.

The Mediterranean (D) and Vardar (E) regions are the smallest and the most specialised. Land use resembles that in the upland pastoral region, as poor grassland, mainly for sheep, is dominant, covering 63 per cent. and 50 per cent. of all farmland in regions D and E respectively. Otherwise land-uses are quite different. A dominance of vines (6 per cent.), citrus fruits and olives (4 per cent.) and early vegetables (7 per cent.) over grains (13 per cent.) with substantial fallow (6 per cent.) in region D reflects karst relief, Mediterranean climate, population pressure *and* rural depopulation. In region E, cereals occupy 30 per cent. of farmland but include substantial rice acreages, while of specialised importance are industrial crops (6 per cent.), such as tobacco, cotton, and oilseeds, vegetables, including paprika (3 per cent.) and vines and sub-tropical fruits (4 per cent.).

The structure of regional marketable surpluses,[6] indicates regional agricultural specialisms despite the continued importance of subsistence agriculture. In the north-east, grains provide directly 40 per cent. of all marketable surpluses by value; their full importance can be assessed only by adding the contribution of silage maize to the major commercial agricultural produce of this region, pork, beef and dairy produce (47 per cent.). Two thirds of marketable surpluses in region B comprise livestock produce (from cattle and pigs) with fruit, especially plums, and grapes in second place (18 per cent.). Sheep provide 60 per cent. of the produce sold off farms in region C, followed by arable, mainly industrial, crops. Fruits and grapes account for nearly half of the commercial agricultural produce of the Mediterranean region, industrial crops and cereals for two-thirds in the Vardar region. Wool and mutton are of secondary importance in both regions, providing respectively 35 and 28 per cent. of marketed farm produce.

Significant, though hardly far-reaching, changes have been made in land use since the war (Table 13). Reclamation of 1·6 million ha. of land, which had been devastated or abandoned between 1941 and 1945, restored the agricultural area by 1956 to its pre-war maximum of 15 million ha. This expansion in area contributed virtually the entire increase in agricultural output between 1946 and 1956 through increased arable and livestock-carrying areas (Table 13).

The major expansion, then, occurred in extensive farming: 895,000 ha. of reclaimed hill pasture and rough grazing and 245,000 ha. of new fallow arable. The striking increase in fallow land was an unpredicted side-effect of government policies, the peasant's response to the absence of fertilisers for maintaining soil fertility and to declining manpower availability on farms in areas of industrial development. Such extension of farming largely outweighed any increased agricultural production resulting from the substantially expanded fruit and vine area (Table 13) and the substitution of industrial crops, vegetables and fodder for grains on arable land (Table 14):

TABLE 13

TRENDS IN AGRICULTURAL LAND USE, 1939–65
(area in thousand hectares)

LAND USE	1939 Area	1939 %	1948 Area	1948 %	1956 Area	1956 %	1965 Area	1965 %
Sown arable	7,570	50·5	6,620	49·3	6,810	45·4	7,190	49·0
Orchards & Vineyards	560	3·7	565	4·2	665	4·4	710	4·7
Meadow	1,990	13·3	1,750	13·0	1,940	13·0	1,950	13·2
Pasture	4,500	30·0	3,865	29·2	4,760	31·7	4,480	30·3
Fallow	380	2·5	580	4·3	825	5·5	420	2·8
TOTAL FARMLAND	15,000	100	13,400	100	15,000	100	14,750	100

Source: Statistički Godišnjak, 1966, p. 144.
Statistički Bilten, op. cit.

TABLE 14

CHANGES IN ARABLE LAND USE 1930–39, 1947–56 AND 1957–65
(area in thousand hectares)

	1930–39		1947–56		1957–1965	
	Area	%	Area	%	Area	%
Grains	6,120	80·9	5,300	72·6	5,400	70·0
Industrial crops	152	2·4	374	5·1	375	4·9
Vegetables	435	6·1	446	6·1	540	7·3
Fodder Crops	333	4·8	523	7·1	825	11·4
Fallow	413	5·8	660	9·1	475	6·4

Source: Statistički Bilten 95, op. cit., p. 7.
Statistički Godišnjak S.F.R.J. 1966, p. 144.

The agricultural area remained stable at 15 million ha.
until 1961. Since then losses from erosion, abandonment of
upland pasture (Table 13), afforestation, building, and flooding
for hydro-electric power schemes, have offset gains of newly-
reclaimed land, reducing farmland to 14,750,000 ha. by 1966.
This confirms that higher yields have provided the dramatic
increase in agricultural output since 1956. Improved land
uses, nevertheless, have continued to play their part: an increase in arable, perennial tree crop and meadow areas at the
expense of marginal rough pasture and fallow (Table 13) and
a rising proportion of arable under vegetables and fodder
(Table 14).

Regional changes are more diversified and underline the
dualism of the Yugoslav economic and social environment. In
the north the agricultural area contracted by 350,000 ha.
between the averages in 1930–39 and 1957–65, involving decreases of 10 per cent., 5 per cent. and 4 per cent. in Slovenia,
Vojvodina and Croatia respectively. This reflects continued
economic development which stimulates greater demand for
building-land, more rapid rural depopulation, or more rapid
transfer of rural populations into non-agricultural occupations if not into towns, leading to farm labour shortages. Such
shortages induce net abandonment especially of upland pasture,
marginal land, labour-intensive vineyards and land which is
more distant from the farmhouse.[7] In contrast, in central,
eastern and south-eastern regions 600,000 ha. more land are
now farmed than were in the 1930s. Increases per cent amount

M

to 20 in Kosmet, 16 in Montenegro, 14 in Macedonia, 6 in Serbia Proper, but only 2 in Bosnia-Herzegovina. They reflect persistant, sometimes increasing, overpopulation which has caused an extension of rough pasture and marginal land, as well as the reclamation of much potential lowland arable and meadow. These changes now require further examination.

Alarmed by the rapid extension of fallow while food prices and imports rose steadily, the Yugoslav government in 1957 introduced a Law on the Cultivation of Fallow Land. This required private and co-operative landowners to sow crops on uncultivated land where this did not impair soil fertility. Additional control followed in 1959 with an Agricultural Land Use Law which gave commune councils power 'to acquire land compulsorily from private owners who do not use modern agro-technical methods to ensure the full and rational use of their land'.[8] In consequence, the fallow area has been halved since 1957 (Table 13). Cultivation, primarily for pulse-legumes as green fodder, has virtually eliminated fallow from northern Yugoslavia and Šumadija. Yet fallow is still very extensive in Macedonia, southern Serbia and Dalmatia, where its function of retaining moisture in the soils of drought-ridden areas is essential, and in Bosnia, where it forms part of a backward rotation system.

The contraction of fallow since 1957 has assisted the continuation of changes in arable land use (Table 14). The sown grain area has decreased from 6·1 million ha. (1930–39) to 5·4 million (1957–65), chiefly through contraction in rye (area decrease of 40 per cent.), barley (20 per cent.) and oats (15 per cent.). Much of the land so released and of newly cultivated fallow is sown with vegetables, industrial and fodder crops which now occupy 1,740,000 ha. (cf. 920,000 ha. before 1939). The greatest shift has been towards fodder crops—lucerne, clover, silage maize—indicating some increase in commercial mixed farming and permitting greater supplies of meat and dairy produce to growing urban markets. Areas sown with sugar beet, oilseeds and tobacco have also doubled to provide more domestic industrial raw materials. Similarly, 150,000 ha. of arable and former hill pasture have been planted with fruit trees. Vineyard areas have expanded more slowly: it is difficult to increase exports of wine.

Substitution of other crops for cereals has been most marked in Slovenia (Table 15) where cultivated fodder for mixed farming is the main substitute. Large decreases in grain areas occurred in Vojvodina, Macedonia and Kosmet in favour of industrial and fodder crops and in Montenegro in favour of early vegetables and fodder. In Serbia Proper, Croatia and Bosnia-Herzegovina, changes have been small, most increases in fodder being made at the expense of fallow.

For once patterns of change do not clearly differentiate north from south; greatest change has occurred in the north-west, north-east, south and south-east, least change in the north and centre. Levels of economic development, progress and education, though important, are not the only determinants. Very significant, too, are the degree of state influence on land use through local state and co-operative farms in bringing about more regional specialisation, of overpopulation and of opportunities offered by regional land reclamation for changing land use patterns.

Nevertheless, in comparison with needs and potentialities, improvements in land use in postwar Yugoslavia have been modest. Not until recently has land-use mapping been undertaken because of inconsistent base maps and the difficulties of representing diverse, fragmented land use patterns.[9] Land use often remains irrational. In overpopulated areas serious soil erosion and exhaustion result from continued degradation of woodland for pasture, extension of marginal cultivation, overgrazing of pasture and up-slope cultivation often on quite steep slopes. Such deterioration jeopardises increasing fertility and productivity in the plains by decreasing the stability of runoff and river régime and thereby increasing lowland flooding. Historically, strategic considerations combined with the forces of nature to encourage grazing of the valleys and cultivation of the hill slopes. In a broad belt of hilly country from Croatian Zagorje through northern Bosnia to the Morava-Vardar corridor, pasture dominates flat lowland while hill slopes are a chequerboard of tiny cultivated strips. Soil conservation requires integrated land-use planning to afforest much upland rough pastures, to drain and protect the bottom lands and 'to re-orient land uses by transferring arable crops from hill areas into the river plains and grass from lowlands

TABLE 15

CHANGES IN ARABLE LAND USE
by Republics and Autonomous Areas, 1930–39 and 1957–65
(in percentages of the total)

		Grains	Industrial Crops	Vegetables	Fodder Crops	Fallow
Slovenia:	1930–39	66·2	1·0	21·6	11·0	0·2
	1959–65	49·4	1·3	22·6	26·0	0·7
Croatia:	1930–39	72·8	1·8	8·0	10·2	7·2
	1957–65	68·5	3·8	9·7	12·8	5·2
Vojvodina:	1930–39	87·0	3·0	2·7	4·8	2·5
	1957–65	74·5	11·0	4·0	10·0	0·5
Serbia Proper:	1930–39	80·6	1·0	3·7	3·8	10·9
	1957–65	78·4	2·7	6·5	9·8	2·5
Kosmet:	1930–39	94·2	0·3	2·1	0·6	2·8
	1957–65	83·2	5·7	4·4	5·4	1·3
Bosnia-Herzegovina:	1930–39	72·3	1·3	5·3	2·3	28·8
	1957–65	69·1	2·1	7·8	6·5	14·5
Macedonia:	1930–39	70·4	3·2	3·6	1·4	21·4
	1957–65	53·4	10·1	6·7	6·2	23·6
Montenegro:	1930–39	79·7	1·0	8·5	3·0	7·8
	1957–65	67·5	1·4	13·8	9·7	7·6

Sources: Statistički Bilten 95, op. cit.
Statistički Godišnjak, op. cit.

into the hills . . . as well as by planting tree crops in terraces on hill slopes.'[10] Higher productivity would result, quite apart from any improvement in farm techniques, for 'yields of arable crops, especially of maize, are 30–50 per cent. lower on hill slopes than on level ground as a result of the constant loss of moisture from the cultivated soil horizon'.[11]

Planning of this kind is lacking in few areas; the reaching of such objectives, however, faces enormous long-term obstacles. The abandonment of marginal upland pastures for afforestation, chiefly in regions C, D and E (Figure 13), depends upon substantial industrialisation in or adjacent to upland pastoral areas to reduce rural population and numbers of livestock. Since 1945 this has been achieved only in Slovenia and Croatia where general economic development has advanced most. Over much of the centre, east and south-east marginal pasture areas are still increasing as insufficient urban employment has been provided to absorb surplus agricultural labour. Although the state has acquired large areas in the Karst where grazing by destructive goats has been banned in order to prepare land for afforestation, the most serious obstacle to the achievement of rational land use is farm fragmentation.

A large-scale reduction in natural pasture, however, would bring few benefits unless there were a complementary expansion of mixed farming in lowland arable areas. The major problem of the peasant sector continues to be 'the division of land use into two almost distinct patterns of exploitation of firstly crop production and secondly livestock-raising'.[12] Most peasant farms outside Slovenia grow mainly subsistence food crops and little sown grass or fodder. Cultivation of arable land exists almost independently of livestock, providing food for human consumption and receiving little manure while livestock graze on natural pasture or are fed in winter on hay from the meadows. This results in partial dependence upon fallow pasture, especially in central and south-eastern regions, to supplement feed in winter and spring, while shortages of both grass and fodder become acute during the summer and early autumn drought. In karst areas livestock in winter receive only leaves and young branches from oak trees or vines. Mixed farming, including arable fodder cultivation, offers an efficient solution of the problem and, moreover, is feasible in much of Yugoslavia without irrigation. Yet the turnover of arable land to fodder has been slow, except in Slovenia (Table 15). Peasants resist innovation because they know that cereals are commercially secure and can be subsistence crops; it is hard to convince them of the wisdom of producing feed for animals directly rather than for themselves. Moreover, tiny fragmented farms make impossible a system of farming which requires substantial capitalisation, frequent movement of fodder and livestock, controlled grazing, high livestock productivity and hence consolidated holdings. Fragmentation, therefore, adversely affects both crop and livestock farming. Combined with primitive techniques and persistent over-grazing of pasture it explains food shortages in urban markets. Improved land use, therefore, requires the integration of rural depopulation and afforestation in highlands with more mixed farming incorporating arable fodder in lowlands. Agrarian reform has been invoked as a method of establishing a social environment more favourable to such changes.

PEASANT FARMING

Yugoslavia is still predominantly a land of peasant farmers. At present, over 2·6 million private landowners own 10·5 million ha. (71 per cent.) of all farmland, 8·84 million ha. (85·8 per cent.) of all cultivated land, and 91 per cent. of all livestock in the federation. They produce 70–75 per cent. of total farm output, but they market only 55–60 per cent. of the net surplus, a fact which indicates the prevalence of subsistence farming. The reasons are simple. Farms are very small, averaging only 4·6 ha., of which 3·4 ha. are cultivated; indeed 72 per cent. of all farms possess under 5 ha. (Table 16). Farms are highly fragmented, and are worked primitively by draft animals and few tools. Yields and incomes, therefore, are low.

(1) Agrarian Reform

Agrarian reform has contributed to, but not caused, farm fragmentation, despite a long history dating back to Prince Miloš of Serbia in 1817. Surveys conducted between 1895 and 1902 indicate that 51–87 per cent. of all farms in Slovenia, Croatia-Slavonia, Dalmatia, Vojvodina and Serbia already

TABLE 16

PRIVATE FARMS AND AGRICULTURAL LAND BY SIZE OF HOLDING
1931, 1941, 1949, and 1963
(in percentages of the total)

YEAR	No. of Holdings	0–2 ha. a	0–2 ha. b	2–5 ha. a	2–5 ha. b	5–10 ha. a	5–10 ha. b	> 10 ha. a	> 10 ha. b
1931	2067000	34·3	6·5	33·6	21·5	20·4	26·6	11·7	45·4
1941	2636000	47·0	—*	24·0	—*	19·0	—*	10·0	—*
1949	2605000	37·2	10·4	34·7	26·2	19·6	27·5	8·5	37·5
1963	2618000	35·0	8·0	36·2	28·7	21·7	35·5	7·1	27·0

* = no data
a = the percentage of the total number of farms
b = the percentage of the total peasant farm area

Sources: P. Marković, 'Posedovna Struktura Jugoslovenske Poljoprivrede', Ekonomist, Belgrade, 1, 1960, pp. 108–27. Statistički Godišnjak 1964, p. 164.

comprised less than 5 ha. The first major reforms, initiated between 1919 and 1933, sought to remove the historical legacies of varied and inequitable land tenure systems. Serfdom was abolished in former Turkish regions and larger forests were nationalised. Land from large estates was expropriated above minima which varied from 90 ha. in the Karst to a generous 470 ha. in Vojvodina and Slavonia, where most large estates were located. Expropriated land, in all 2·5 million ha., was redistributed among 640,000 peasant families: in former Turkish areas, families received 6–12 ha. holdings, in Pannonia families received 2 ha. holdings, barely enough for subsistence. Vested interests in the north, however, succeeded in retaining 57 per cent. of estate land for their former landlords as late as 1936. Heavy taxation, inheritance laws and uncontrolled money-lending combined to increase farm numbers between 1931 and 1941 (Table 16) through subdivision into smaller units, and a general polarisation in land ownership towards dwarf farms (less than 2 ha.) and large farms (more than 10 ha.).

The postwar agrarian reforms affected directly a much smaller area, yet in many ways they were more radical. The 1945 Law on Agrarian Reform and Colonisation eliminated hired labour from private farms by expropriating all land above the low maxima of: 25–35 ha. of cultivated or 45 ha. of total peasant farmland, depending upon soil fertility and the ratio of arable/pasture; 10 ha. of land on estates belonging to banks, industries and churches; and 3–5 ha., enough only for subsistence, on the farms of absentee landlords (merchants, craftsmen and officials). The law also confiscated the entire property of Germans, Hungarians and Italians who had been expelled in 1945.

Some 1·57 million ha. were expropriated. Over 770,000 ha. became state property, to lay the foundations for large-scale socialised agriculture. Nearly 800,000 ha. were sold 'to those who till the land': to 316,435 families of landless labourers and smallholders. The land in dwarf and small farm management (less than 5 ha.) thus increased substantially by 1949, as Table 16 shows. Families generally obtained land in their own locality or republic, to reduce problems of social adjustment. Nevertheless, the location of most expropriated land in

Pannonia necessitated resettlement of 60,000 families from the overpopulated mountain core. Some 41,300 families (with 250,000 members) were resettled in Vojvodina, for example, mainly from Bosnia-Herzegovina (33 per cent.), south Serbia and Macedonia (25 per cent.), the Croatian Karst (20 per cent.) and Montenegro (15 per cent.).[13] Such subdivision of large commercial units and their resettlement by more backward people certainly held back food output in the late 'forties. In Vojvodina the number of holdings under 5 ha. increased by 84,000. Shepherds and hill farmers who could neither read nor write, impaired for years productivity in resettled areas in Banat and Bačka by continuing their customary extensive stockrearing, by their lack of plough-teams and farm implements and by their poor health and nutrition in the new environment.[14] Settlers refrained from growing the cereals, vegetables and industrial crops to which the Vojvodina is well suited because of the harder dirtier work involved; Montenegrins complained, for example, that 'sweet is the sugar, but slimey is the beet!'[15]

The reform limited maximum farm size and made illegal the sale or lease of land to prevent capitalist concentration of land and wealth. Numbers of farms were stabilised and the rapid subdivision of holdings, characteristic before 1941 (Table 16), was halted. Indeed, with time the pre-war trends were reversed. More land and holdings are being concentrated in 'medium' farms of 2–8 ha.; these now account for 64·2 per cent. of all land and 58 per cent. of all farms as compared with 53·7 and 54·3 per cent. respectively in 1949. Another reform in 1953 further restricted maximum private farm size to 10 ha. of cultivated land (15 ha. of karst land), decreasing the area farmed by larger units and again acting negatively upon those farmers generally most able to produce surpluses. The land thus acquired, 275,900 ha., became state property.

(2) The Changing Peasant Farm Economy

The 1953 reform also freed land sales and leasing, which, stimulated by industrialisation (which had induced movement into towns by nearly 4 million people causing labour shortages on peasant farms), have resulted in a steady transfer of land from dwarf and large farms (less than 2 ha. and more than 8 ha.

respectively) to 4–8 ha. farms.[16] This process, selective in time and place, has sharply focussed the contrasts within the peasant economy. Increasing opportunities for non-agricultural employment are drawing labour away from work, if not necessarily from residence, on farms of all sizes. The drain is greatest from farms with less than 4 ha. of cultivated land (up to 10 ha. in the Karst),[17] which cannot provide family subsistence. One half of all Yugoslav private farms are of this nature, and, working 36 per cent. of total farmland, yield *no* net marketable food surplus; indeed, their owners must buy 25 per cent. more food than they sell.[18] Needing money to subsist, the youth on such farms increasingly undertake off-farm work, leaving the same farmwork burden on progressively fewer older relatives. Such farms are called *mešovita domaćinstva* ('mixed households').

Since these farms yield no surplus income and are generally small, they usually lack draft power and agricultural implements (as did 50 per cent. of all farms under 3 ha. in 1957), in contrast to bigger farms (only 10 per cent. of all farms of more than 8 ha.).[19] Labour therefore becomes *the* critical factor as more family members engage in off-farm work, leaving progressively larger land areas uncultivated. Eventually farms become 'non-agricultural holdings', on which families ('peasant-industrial workers') live but work only part-time, or 'holdings without labour', on which the inheritors neither live nor work. The number of such farms grew rapidly[20] to reach 211,000 with an area of 354,000 ha. in 1960. It is their owners who are the most ready to sell or lease part, if not all, of their land, draft animals and tools. In 1960 over 400,000 ha. were leased and 100,000 ha. were sold in this way. Some land is bought or leased by socialist farms. Much, however, passes into the hands of peasants already owning 4–8 ha., who, except in mountain areas, both subsist from their farms and provide the total net peasant food surplus, or nearly 60 per cent. of all food marketed in Yugoslavia. Their farm incomes, often supplemented by some off-farm income, enables them to purchase additional land and the equipment to work it. A survey made of land leases in 1958 in 28 districts in Serbia Proper, Vojvodina, Croatia and Bosnia showed[21] that peasants leased out land because of insufficient manpower (34 per cent.), draft animals (19 per cent.) or implements (14 per cent.), because of sufficient supplementary income (21 per cent.) and because of old age (6 per cent.). Peasants leased in land because of insufficient land for subsistence (38 per cent.) and because of surplus labour (32 per cent.), draft animals (12 per cent.) or tools (9 per cent.).

In consequence, between 1949 and 1960 the number of dwarf farms (less than 2 ha.) decreased by 6 per cent. roughly in proportion to the net decrease of rural population, while numbers of draft animals and farm implements on those farms decreased by 50 per cent. Farms of over 4 ha. became more numerous, except farms larger than 10 ha., which, being chiefly marginal hill farms at greater distances from growth centres, tend not to become 'mixed households', but simply to lose labour to the towns. This process was accelerated in the Karst by state acquisition of extensive pastures for conservation and afforestation and by state prevention of goat-grazing, which greatly reduced the opportunities for subsistence.

This whole process is far more advanced in northern Yugoslavia and around larger urban-industrial centres where more farm inhabitants engage in non-farm employment. In Croatia and Vojvodina owners of even 5 ha. are selling or leasing out more land than they buy. Farms without active agricultural occupants account for up to one third of all farms around larger cities in Croatia-Slavonia, Vojvodina, north Serbia and central Bosnia. This feature is uncommon in Slovenia where good communications permit commuting from farms to dispersed non-agricultural employment on a much larger scale, so minimising farm labour shortages and land abandonment. By contrast the shortage and continued subdivision of land in overpopulated central, eastern and southern Yugoslavia is so acute that farmers with little over 2 ha. seek to lease or buy land from dwarf holdings. Since 1949, therefore, farm numbers have declined in northern areas from 1·19 million to 1·15 million, in Macedonia and in Montenegro from 238,000 to 220,000 where the socialist sector owns and can buy more land, and where rural depopulation and emigration are rapid. Numbers have continued to increase from 1·16 million to 1·25 million in Bosnia-Herzegovina, Serbia Proper and Kosmet.

These trends indicate progress within the peasant sector. More land and equipment is being transferred from a bare subsistence function to larger holdings which are better able to sell produce to, and are more influenced by, the market. Farms of more than 8 ha., for example, sell a food surplus, which by value is 6–10 times greater per worker and 4 times greater per hectare than that from farms of less than 2 ha. Thus the *volume* of marketed surpluses by *value* from the peasant sector has increased, while farms of more than 5 ha. have increased their surplus nearly twice as quickly as farms of less than 3 ha. Similarly, on average, larger commercial farming households (more than 4 ha.) reinvest 3–4 times as much money per hectare in their farms (in leasing land, buying fertiliser or equipment) as to dwarf or 'mixed households'. Larger farms can also be organised with longer crop rotations to benefit soil fertility, from two-field systems of wheat or maize and potatoes in the Karst to 6 year rotations on larger Slovenian farms. Nevertheless, 10–25 per cent. of farms with over 5 ha. lack draft animals and ploughs and, except for pastoral holdings, must depend upon assistance from other peasants or from the socialist sector.

The major obstacle to improvement, however, is farm fragmentation. In 1960, 2·6 million peasants worked a chequerboard of 20·8 million scattered parcels of farmland, or on average 8–9 per farm. Fragmentation results from over-population and the division of inheritance equally among all sons. The smaller is the farm the smaller are the plots into which it is fragmented: dwarf holdings comprise 4 plots of 0·22 ha. each on average, farms 2–5 ha. work 8 plots of 0·39 ha., farms 5–8 ha. 10 plots of 0·6 ha. and farms of more than 8 ha. 12 plots of 1 ha. each. Arable land is most fragmented in Macedonia, Montenegro, Dalmatia, parts of Slovenia, Croatian Zagorje, Central Serbia, north Bosnia and Herzegovina, where plots average only 0·32 ha. In overpopulated Medjumurje, farms average no fewer than 21 plots, 6 arable, the rest forest and pasture; in the Karst farms of 3–10 ha. may be divided into 35–65 plots (15–25 arable),[22] walled fields in *uvale* or on terraced slopes often being only a few yards square. Over much of Yugoslavia, then, conditions such as these make mechanisation, specialisation and mixed farming impossible.

Only in Vojvodina, where plots average 1·2 ha., are peasant farms better equipped to apply modern techniques. What is worse, 'fragmentation is greater on the more fertile soils of the plains, the hillsides and the terraces just where mechanisation is both essential and feasible . . . while more consolidated blocks of land are generally sited in less favourable upland areas fit only for pastoral farming.'[23]

Fragmentation reduces farm efficiency and influences patterns of land use on each holding and around each village. More distant strips are generally used for producing crops (hay) or for pasture which require least frequent attention or fewer man-days per ha. Nearer the farm, physique permitting, cereals, vines, fodder, vegetables and orchards which require more man-days per ha. progressively dominate. This pattern, which supports the concentric land-use concept of von Thünen, is more apparent on larger farms, producing more for the market, than on smaller, subsistence farms, whose owners, because of necessity, cultivate more land at greater distances from the homestead.[24] Broadly speaking, this reflects the tendency for the proportion of cultivated land to decrease from 95 to 48 per cent. and of pasture to increase from 5 to 52 per cent. as holdings increase in size from less than 2 ha. to more than 8 ha.

Industrialisation since 1950, however, has induced the abandonment of more distant strips belonging to 'mixed' and 'non-agricultural households', and important changes in land use. Increased selling and leasing of land, even distant strips, however, may increase the opportunities for consolidation. As long as agricultural population continued to increase, particularly before 1950, peasants devoted more land to bread cereals and less to meadow and pasture for livestock. This explains why productive livestock (cows and oxen), and not horses, are the main draft animals in overpopulated areas.[25] Since 1950, 'households which have become dependent on non-agricultural work engage less in farm activity, diminishing the area and the output of produce which demands more inputs of labour and more draft power, such as maize, wheat and other arable crops. They engage increasingly in livestock-rearing, which can be concentrated around the house and which can be supervised by children and by other people who are unfit for heavy farm work. . . . The farm is often trans-formed, therefore into an *okućnica* (garden plot) not only in a productive, but also in a spatial sense.'[26] Within city commut-ing zones, this type of farm (35 per cent. of all Yugoslav farms) has less land in cereals and industrial crops and more in fodder, vegetables and fallow, than any other type. Livestock products make up three-quarters of small gross agricultural surpluses, especially milk and meat for urban markets. Under 45 per cent. of total income is derived from selling farm produce. Although owners of these farms sell land most readily and work in towns, they live in the farmhouse and retain the *okućnica* for four reasons: low pay from unskilled work in factories or services; postwar inflationary food prices, necessitating some subsistence production; scarcity of urban housing; reluctance of peasants to leave their proudest possession, the land.

Family farms which depend little upon supplementary non-agricultural income are generally larger, but two types are distinguishable. The most commercialised farms, averaging 4–6 ha. and providing 85 per cent. of their owner's income from the sale of agricultural produce (40 per cent. from arable crops), are most intensively cultivated, with proportionately more industrial crops, vegetables and fodder than other farm types. These farms dominate in the more favourable agri-cultural regions A and B (Figure 13), where urban markets are more developed. In contrast, somewhat smaller farms (2–4 ha.), deriving 55–80 per cent. of their income from the sale of farm produce (33 per cent. arable and tree crops), characterise poorer, less accessible, more overpopulated, often upland regions, chiefly in regions C and D but also in regions B and E; they are more truly subsistence farms, with most arable in bread grains and little in other crops.

Everywhere 'peasant-industrial workers' realise the highest income from combined farm surpluses and non-agricultural employment. 'Subsistence' farmers realise the lowest incomes. However, the highest *farm* incomes are earned in the northern agricultural regions A and B, where average farms are largest (3·9 ha.), overpopulation and fragmentation are least, com-mercial farms are most important (47 per cent. of all farms), where greater socialisation offers additional farm assistance (seed, fertilisers, mechanical aids) and where larger urban markets stimulate more commercial dairying and market-gardening.[27] Farm incomes, gross and per head, here average 70 per cent. more than farm incomes in regions C and D, where farms are smallest (2·6 ha.), overpopulation and fragmentation are greatest, commercial farms are least important (31 per cent.) and where more limited socialisation and urban market demand mean less intensive farming. Region E occupies an intermediate position.

Despite improvements in peasant farming, the basic problems of low productivity and irrational land use that result from small farm size, acute fragmentation and limited income, still hinder progress. The government has put its faith in socialised farming to overcome these problems.[28]

THE SOCIALIST FARM SECTOR

Socialist farms are the vanguard of government land policies and aim at raising agricultural yields and improving land uses through the wider application of modern practices. Two complementary approaches have been used to achieve these aims: the direct expansion of the socialist farm area and the indirect extension of government influence on to peasant farms through co-operation. Today, over four million hectares of land are state-owned. Half, however, comprises poor Karst pasture which is protected for future reclamation or afforestation, though some of it is potentially cultivable lowland marsh and common pasture. The remainder, 2·2 million ha., 15 per cent. of all farmland, is farmed by 285,000 workers on 2,570 state and co-operative enterprises. These yield 30 per cent. of all farm output and net marketable surpluses, indicating above-average productivity and commercial pre-eminence.

Socialised farming was initiated in 1945 and maintained for a decade on land expropriated from private landlords by agrarian reform. State farms, or *Poljoprivredna Dobra*, were formed on 388,000 ha.[29] as model farms resembling Russian *sovkhozy*. Settlers from upland regions revived their traditional *zadruga*[30] organisation to pool scarce implements in Peasant Working Co-operatives, called *Seljačke Radničke Zadruge* (S.R.Z.), in order to work 216,000 ha. lowland expropriated in Pannonia. A nominal 41,000 ha. was allocated to General

Agricultural Co-operatives, or *Opšte Zemljoradničke Zadruge*, (O.Z.Z.), which were established as marketing organisations in rural centres throughout the federation.

The Communist Party decision in 1948 to extend socialised agriculture initiated forced collectivisation involving coercion of the peasantry to join the S.R.Z. These were collectives, of four types, in which peasants pooled their land, tools and live-stock, received a wage for their labour and could retain their own garden plot of up to one hectare. By 1951 419,000 peasant families, formed into 6,976 collectives, were working 2,330,000 ha. out of a maximum socialised area of 2·8 million ha. (22 per cent. of all farmland), mostly in the north. Many weak-nesses pervaded the movement. Peasants joined collectives to evade compulsory deliveries and state taxation. In-efficiences in the S.R.Z. alienated the peasantry, depressed production and remuneration and induced resistance, which even prevented land consolidation. Farm managers were novices who lacked knowledge of agronomy and experience of large-scale farming. Where successful, land consolidation and the rationalised use of production factors converted high labour:land ratios—on average 60 families per 330 ha. farm—into high rates of unemployed labour. The government starved agriculture and its supporting industries of capital; it failed to provide the fertiliser, machinery, improved seed and livestock that were essential for successful large-scale farming. Moreover, the Federal Planning Commission 'delegated sowing plans which frequently ignored the suitability of physical and economic conditions on farms for producing particular crops'.[31] A localisation of state and collective farms in the more fertile northern lowlands alone enabled them to achieve yields 20–30 per cent. above those of peasant farms; within relatively uniform environments such as Vojvodina or Montenegro average yields were the same on socialist and private farms.[32]

After 1951 a freer, more remunerative market replaced compulsory deliveries. Peasants removed their property *en masse* from the collectives, except dwarf-farm owners who had least to gain from a free market and least to lose from co-operation, and settlers in Pannonia who had least 'attachment' to their soil. The socialised area was stabilised around 900,000 ha., or one-third of the 1951 maximum, only with the transfer of 227,000 ha. expropriated from larger landowners under the 1953 National Agricultural Property Law.

Major policy changes followed. Since 1955 the nationalised land area has been expanded by 1·3 million ha. by new methods: by buying and leasing 590,000 ha. from peasants, by reclaiming 190,000 ha. of marshland and by cultivating 520,000 ha. of state or common pasture.[33] Land purchases by socialist farms increased from 5,000 ha. in 1957 to over 125,000 ha. in 1964, as banks made more credit available for this purpose and as leasing, which provides 25 per cent. of land in the O.Z.Z., became expensive. The supply of peasant farmland substantially exceeds the demand of socialist farms for, as credit is still scarce, farm councils increasingly buy only land of better quality, land adjacent of their farms, land blocks for easier consolidation, and cheaper land. The present socialist farm area should be doubled by these means[34] by 1970.

Intensification of agriculture replaced land nationalisation as first priority in 1954. The government assigned this task to the O.Z.Z., replacing the S.R.Z. which were reorganised, mainly into state farms, and lost importance (Table 17). The O.Z.Z. assumed a wide range of functions to *attract* peasant membership:[35] (1) improvement of their own production by leasing land from, and by co-operative contract farming with, the peasantry, to whom the O.Z.Z. conceded the retention of land ownership; (2) marketing of produce for the peasantry; purchasing of fertilisers, seed, young trees and livestock with bank credits and their own profits to raise their own productivity and to enable the peasants to raise theirs; (3) demonstration to the peasants that modern methods yield higher incomes; (4) maintenance of agricultural machinery to service its own land and to hire out to co-operating peasants; and (5) development of food-and-fodder-processing facilities on the farm.

Today, 2,000 General Agricultural Co-operatives farm 1 million ha., own half the farm machinery and dispose of one-third of all fertiliser consumed in Yugoslavia. Rarely, however, are they consolidated farms, but comprise scattered strips and blocks reflecting the complex patterns of peasant land lease and sale. Four hundred O.Z.Z. remain marketing organisations only, chiefly in overpopulated areas of Croatia, Bosnia

N

TABLE 17

THE NUMBER, AREA AND AVERAGE SIZE OF FARMS
in the Social Sector 1950 and 1965

	State Farms		Collectives (SRZ)		Co-operatives (OZZ)	
	1950	1965	1950	1965	1950	1965
Number	279	356	6,964	30	9,060	2,424
Total Area (ha.)	424,000	1,100,000	2,300,000	23,000	95,000	903,000
Av. Farm Size (ha.)	1,520	3,085	330	765	10	370

Sources: B. Stružek, *op. cit.,* pp. 123–5; J. Zmaić, *op. cit.,* p. 33
Statistički Godišnjak SFRJ, 1966.

and Macedonia. Since 1956 the O.Z.Z., in particular have extended their influence, through co-operative production, to an additional million hectares of ploughland on 1,250,000 peasant farms. Co-operation[36] ranges from periodic services from the O.Z.Z. to the peasant to contract-farming for the cultivation of certain crops—most commonly for wheat, maize, sugar beet and oilseeds and locally for tobacco, hops, fruits and vegetables—or the rearing and fattening of livestock and poultry. Peasants provide the land, labour for weeding or spreading fertiliser, and buildings for livestock. The O.Z.Z. supplies high-yielding seeds, improved livestock, fertilisers and mechanised services on credit and its experts define production methods. The peasant refunds the costs from his earnings after selling the contracted produce through the O.Z.Z. Such co-operation in 1965 yielded a third of the cereal and industrial crop output, one-tenth of the potato crop and 15 per cent. of livestock production.

Co-operation is advantageous. Peasants co-operate primarily to raise their net income per ha. from higher yields and secondarily to obviate shortages of labour, draft power and implements by having access to the Co-operatives' machinery.[37] The O.Z.Z. gain economies from employing their machinery more fully over larger areas, from increasing their turnover and from increasing the volume and certainty of supplies of crops and meat to their processing plants. The state encourages co-operation to ensure greater reinvestment in agriculture and less spending on consumption than is traditional among peasants.[38] It also provided the persuasion: the Law on Agricultural Land Use (1959) which obliges every peasant landowner to use certain basic techniques in cultivating his land.

Co-operation solves some problems and creates others. As some peasants terminate and others begin co-operation each year, causing changes in the size, distribution and quality of land to be farmed, the O.Z.Z. management must devise flexible production and land-use plans. Advantages of better machine utilisation are offset by tractor time and fuel wasted in movement between scattered plots. More O.Z.Z., therefore, are offering discounts on supplies and services to induce groups of peasants with adjacent plots to sign 3–7 year contracts or leases to permit field 'enclosure' and to cultivate intervening access paths in order to introduce rational crop rotation and integrated arable fodder-livestock farming. By extending mechanisation, co-operation has aggravated the problem of surplus labour on peasant farms. Co-operatives, therefore, have recently increased contracting for livestock-farming, for the cultivation of vegetables and industrial crops, and for irrigated farming to increase and to even-out the number of man days' labour required per hectare annually in addition to mechanised services.[39]

State farms failed to stimulate progress before 1955 because, in addition to the handicaps of the S.R.Z., they suffered also acute shortages of labour, improved seed and livestock to act as model farms. Averaging 1,500 ha. (Table 17) 'state farms were large-scale only in area; the other elements of large-scale farming—mechanisation, livestock, roads and consolidated fields—were often lacking'.[40] In 1954 economic reforms introduced cost-accounting, encouraging production for the market. Subsequently, farms have been amalgamated (Table 17) to obtain economies through the fuller use of pooled machinery, transport equipment and buildings and through better integration of arable and livestock production and of farm output and industrial processing. The reorganisation of co-operatives has followed similar lines. State farms have had more access to imported high-yielding seeds and livestock. For example, numbers of imported Frisian, Simmental and Jersey cows, Hereford cattle and Yorkshire pigs soared from

TABLE 18

YIELDS OF WHEAT, MAIZE AND SUGAR BEET
in Different Sectors of Agriculture, 1963–65
(quintals per ha.)

	Wheat	Maize	Sugar Beet
State Farms	34	46	346
Collectives	34	44	348
Co-operatives	28	37	284
Peasants in Co-operation	21	31	226
Peasants outside Co-operation	16	17	206
Prewar Average 1930–39, all farms	11·5	16·4	176

Source: Statistički Godišnjak SFRJ, 1966, pp. 137–154.

3,000 annually before 1957 to 114,000 since 1961. State farms are now able, therefore, to stimulate progress directly by higher productivity (as Table 18 shows for three leading crops) and indirectly by diffusing the fruits of experimentation and improved seed and livestock throughout the hierarchy from the collectives to the peasants. At present all the wheat and three-quarters of the maize grown by peasants under contract (70 per cent. of all wheat and 35 per cent. of all maize grown anywhere in Yugoslavia) is of high-yielding varieties. Lower yields on co-operative farms stem largely from fragmentation, which makes crop-rotation, rational land use and standardised methods almost impossible. Higher yields resulting from co-operation (Table 18), however, demonstrate the advantages of using modern methods even on tiny, fragmented and tiny peasant farms.

(1) Land Use in the Social Sector

State and co-operative farms are responsible for postwar improvements in land use. Commercial industrial crops (sugar beet, sunflower) and arable fodder crops (lucerne) are far more important on socialist farms (accounting for 19 per cent. of all crops) than on peasant farms (6 per cent.). The opposite is true of food grains, potatoes and vegetables (59 per cent. cf. 70 per cent.). Arable land uses on peasant farms have changed little since 1955, reflecting conservatism in thought and practice. Co-operation, alone, has extended cultivation of sunflower, lucerne and potatoes. By contrast, a certain dynamism characterises socialist farms, where wheat has replaced maize as the major cereal to meet home market deficiencies, industrial crops have been extended to meet the expanding demand of processing industries, while the fodder area also increased to meet livestock requirements. The stable importance of maize conceals a reorientation from human food to livestock feed. A marked contraction of 'other crops' expresses greater specialisation. These trends are stronger on state farms than on the O.Z.Z., which, as a result of fragmentation and their 'bridge' function between state and peasant, have intermediate land use patterns.

Changes have been uneven spatially. Socialist farms manage one-third of all farmland in Vojvodina (650,000 ha.) and

Macedonia (450,000 ha.) and one-fifth in Slavonia (250,000 ha.) and Kosmet (100,000 ha.), i.e. in lowlands and reclaimed basins, where overpopulation is limited, where larger average farms and one-time landed estates made consolidation easier, where resettled peoples offered less resistance and where physical and social conditions favour large-scale mechanised agriculture. Elsewhere under 6 per cent. of agricultural land is socialised as broken relief and walled fields restrict mechanisation, land use and ownership patterns with highly fragmented farms are complex, forest frequently occurs and peasant attachment to the soil is strong. Here socialist farms are localised in larger *polja* and depressions: Medjumurje, Doljensko (Slovenia); Lika, Sinj *polje*, Ravni Kotari (Croatia); Livno, the lower Neretva (Herzegovina); Mačva and the Morava valleylands (Serbia); or in areas of marked rural depopulation and economic change around larger towns: Rijeka, Pula, Sarajevo, Banja Luka and Titograd.

Increases in the socialist farm area have been achieved in different ways in different areas. In overpopulated Macedonia and Kosmet irrigation and land reclamation have been the major means. In Slavonia and Vojvodina, where peasants are offering land for sale and numerous existing socialist farms have the finance to buy more land, land purchase has been the dominant element. In Serbia co-operative farms chiefly lease land. Continued overpopulation and increased demand for land by peasants and state afforestation schemes have restricted expansion of the socialised farm area in Bosnia-Herzegovina, while afforestation and high land prices have actually reduced it in Slovenia since 1957. Peasant co-operation, too, has developed in the more advanced areas; Vojvodina localises 40 per cent. of contracted arable and livestock farming, followed by Slavonia, Croatia-Slavonia and Serbia. Co-operation has advanced little in the areas of most severe overpopulation and least peasant responsiveness: Bosnia-Herzegovina, Sandjak and Macedonia.

In consequence, regional progress towards specialisation within the ecological framework of the agricultural planning regions has been varied. A marked reorientation of farming from traditional cereal cultivation with some industrial crops and extensive livestock grazing in region A to cereals with more industrial crops, and fodder for intensive dairying, cattle-rearing for baby-beef and pig-rearing, has been achieved through substantial commercial large-scale and co-operative farming where transport is good to major urban centres. Success has been limited in developing new orchards and vineyards in region B: only 8 per cent. of the land is socialised and complex land tenures on slopes prevent proper terracing. Nevertheless, some socialist farms have developed specialised dairying and market-gardening, notably in Slovenia, around Zagreb and major Serbian towns, or livestock-fattening near meat-processing works at Petrinja, Sesvete (Zagreb) and Kragujevac. Least change has occurred in the upland pastoral region (C). Here *potential* for change lies in extensive state-owned pastures which can be improved and several *polja* which can be reclaimed. The *stimulus* to change lies in expanding markets in the densely populated and developing Jesenice-Sarajevo-Niš zone to the north-east and in the food-deficient Mediterranean zone with a marked tourist season peak demand to the south-west. State farms in Lika, Livno and Sjenica *polja* are beginning to replace the traditional potato—winter rye or oats—natural pasture economy oriented to sheep rearing for meat and wool by a fodder grains—permanent sown grassland-clover economy for meat and dairy cattle, with pigs fed on potatoes and skimmed milk. Such changes, however, presuppose radically improved road links with coastal and interior towns as well as skilled agronomists, especially in Sandjak and Kosmet, who could introduce rational crop rotation and better use of fixed capital generally.[41] Change in the Mediterranean economy of maize-rough pasture-livestock rearing with olives, vines and fruits is hampered by insufficient funds for essential irrigation. Nevertheless, mixed dairy and fatstock farming is developing on state farms in Istria and the inland *polja* while early fruit and vegetable crops and poultry farming are encouraged by contract farming on small, fragmented farms. The opening of new international airports at Dubrovnik and Split should stimulate further change.

(2) A Case Study: The Belje State Farm

Located in Baranija (region A) north of Osijek (Figure 14), this farm was founded in 1921 on former Austro-Hungarian crown land. It has been expanded since 1945 to its present area of 52,181 ha. by expropriating land, by purchasing adjacent peasant farms and by absorbing land of the O.Z.Z. at Darda, Čeminac, Bilje and Bijeli Manastir. The original estate was an integrated agricultural-industrial combine

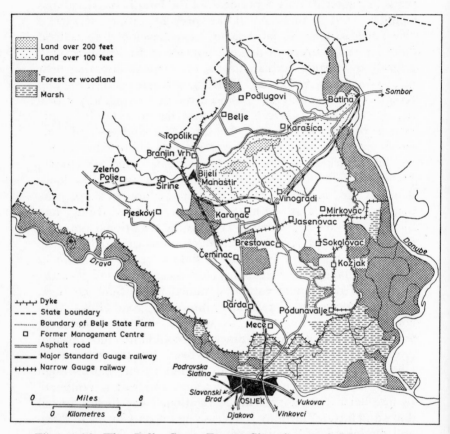

Figure 14. The Belje State Farm: Situation and Management Sections

growing sugar beet for the Branjin Vrh refinery, founded in 1911 (Figure 15). Today farm production and processing are diverse, but highly integrated. Before 1952 individual sections of the farm, e.g. Karašica, were directed to produce as many as 24 crops. Subsequent economic reforms encouraged greater specialisation throughout the farm (Figure 15). About 78 per cent. of the land is arable, growing wheat, maize, sugar beet, lucerne and clover, with some hemp, flax and oilseeds. Nearly 20 per cent is meadow and pasture, the remainder forest and vineyards. Over 40,000 head of livestock are kept for rearing, fattening, and producing milk, along with 1,000,000 poultry.

Only wheat and flax are sold directly off the farm to mills in Osijek; all other crops are processed, or consumed by livestock, on the farm. Silage maize, grass, lucerne and clover are fed to livestock. Oilseeds are processed locally and the by-products

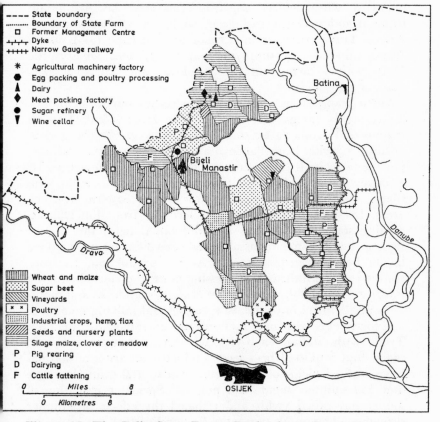

Figure 15. The Belje State Farm: Predominant Land Uses and Integrated Processing Plants

fed as concentrates to cattle. Milk is processed into butter and cheese at Belje, skimmed milk from the dairy being fed to pigs. Meat is canned at Kneževo (Figure 15). Sugar beet is milled at Branjin Vrh, the by-products being returned as livestock feed. The farm is thus self-sufficient in livestock feed throughout the year. Perishable final products—milk, eggs and poultry—are sent to Pannonian towns, while durable produce—canned meat, dried milk, cheese and sugar—are distributed throughout central and western Yugoslavia.

Figure 15 indicates the predominant land uses on various sections of the farm. Areal specialisation is characteristic although careful rotations are practised. Cereal-growing areas follow a wheat-maize, wheat-lucerne-sugar beet/flax/hemp rotation, fodder areas a silage maize-lucerne-clover-wheat rotation. Three areas are in permanent land uses: the Kneževi Vinogradi vineyards (supplying grapes to the local winery), the Mece poultry farm, and the Sokolovac and Mirkovac permanent grasslands.

Good transport is vital to the successful operation of this large, highly integrated concern. The farm is linked to all regions of Yugoslavia by road and railway via Osijek, and to fertiliser supplies from Pančevo and Prahovo via the Danube. On the farm itself the main road network is supplemented by a narrow-gauge railway for transporting beet to Branjin Vrh, silage and industrial concentrates to the eastern livestock areas, livestock to slaughter and fertiliser from the Danube loading stage. Cart-tracks link individual fields but in wet seasons they become impassable and caterpillar tractor haulage incurs heavy transport costs. Arable production, livestock conversion and industrial processing must, therefore, be highly integrated spatially. A factory at Kneževo produces and maintains agricultural implements, spraying and milking machines.

Experiments with new methods are an important function. Trials with Italian high-yielding wheat, American hybrid maize and imported beet seed conducted on areas of 400 ha. have realised yields of 87 quintals wheat, 100 quintals maize and 550 quintals sugar beet per ha. Sprinkler irrigation of fodder has raised yields and reduced the effects of summer droughts. Thousands of quality foreign livestock are imported for breeding, rearing and fattening and for supplying state and

co-operative farms throughout the federation: in 1959 17,270
head of cattle were purchased and 12,605 were later sold.

ECONOMIC POLICIES

In common with agrarian reforms, economic measures depressed agriculture before 1953 and stimulated it after that
date. Heavy progressive taxation, introduced in 1945, pena-
lised producers of larger farm surpluses. High compulsory
delivery quotas at low prices discouraged increased output of
cereals, dairy produce, meat and industrial crops. Peasants
reacted by slaughtering livestock. Resulting food scarcities
permitted peasants to earn as much money from selling one
fifth of their output in the *seljačka pijaca* (open peasant market)
as from selling four-fifths to the state.

Compulsory deliveries were abandoned after 1951 in favour
of relatively free, 'stimulative' market prices. In 1954 new,
mildly progressive taxes were introduced on a 'cadastral income
norm' calculated for each farm as the average income reasonably to be expected from selling average farm output, an
assessed figure based on farm size, soil fertility, production
composition and average crop and livestock yields *minus*
average costs of seed, fertiliser, livestock, mechanised services and depreciation. As net income above the norm is
not taxable, the system encourages higher productivity. Since
1957 additional measures have induced changes in peasant
agricultural methods and greater co-operation with socialist
farms: tax rebates or exemptions for land improvement, for
increasing the area of industrial crops or vegetables (near
urban markets) or planted with fruit trees and vines, for leasing
land to co-operatives. Increased taxes have been levied on
draft animals, farm implements and hired private labour.[43]

Restrictions on progress have resulted from inadequate
capital inputs, rarely exceeding 7 per cent. of total investment
before 1956 or 10 per cent. since 1962. Real investment per
hectare, it is true, has trebled since the war, but its effectiveness has often been low. Before 1953 the limited funds available from federal and republic sources were channelled into
cereal and industrial-crop farming on collectives in Pannonia
and Macedonia and into buildings and drainage which yielded
few short-term results. Investment in machinery, livestock and

tree-crops was negligible. Policy de-capitalised and extensified agriculture by transferring funds from the peasant sector, which owned 95 per cent. of all livestock, to the economy at large and to arable collectives, so almost closing the door to integrated mixed farming. From 1953 the National Bank had more regard for broad agricultural needs and for the economic potential of the agricultural planning regions in allocating money from the General and the Republic Investment Funds by competition. By 1958 livestock farming was receiving more investment than arable farming. Between 1957 and 1961 co-operation channelled the increased flow of capital (amounting to 12–16 per cent. of total investment) to peasant farms, so raising the productivity of under-utilised land, labour, and livestock.

Yet output still lags behind demand, as credit supplies are both insufficient and insufficiently effective. Decentralisation scatters capital resources among many farms and communal banks, although state and co-operative farm amalgamation attempts to concentrate capital in fewer units. Unequal regional opportunities for capital accumulation arise as socialist farms are localised on better soils and produce cereals and industrial crops which prices favour. Thus half the communes in Vojvodina can invest 5,500 dinars per ha. farmland whereas two-thirds in Serbia Proper and Kosmet have only 1,400 dinars per ha. to invest.[44] Agricultural progress is thus inhibited in the critical hilly agricultural regions B, C and D (Figure 13), except in Slovenia, where greater advancement and more intensive dairying and horticulture yield (and require) greater investment per ha. than in Pannonia and Macedonia.

Investment allocation by competition, operative for a decade, was unco-ordinated, dispersing finance among many farms for specific links in the farm production chain rather than concentrating capital on equipping fully integrated facilities on individual farms. Bank experts lacked time and skill to assess hundreds of demands. Decisions tended to favour state farms,[45] stunting the principle of equal competition based on the profitability of co-operative and state farms alike. Thus not only are state farms highly capitalised, but one-third, mostly in Vojvodina and Slavonia, are overcapitalised, incur losses and tie up funds in loan repayment.[46] Their managements often lack the ingenuity to change cropping and land-use patterns and to stimulate peasant co-operation to fuller utilisation of fixed assets. Adjacent farms on similar land and producing similar outputs, therefore, may yield totally different financial results. That they can do so reflects food shortages and inflationary food prices.

Pricing policies have not always encouraged progress. Subsidies made fertilisers after 1952 available to a far wider farming public with beneficial effects on yields, yet they also 'encouraged incorrect fertiliser usage and a tolerance of continuing low yields on some farms.'[47] On mixed farms wheat subsidies disguised losses arising from low fodder yields and low livestock productivity; this explains why the largest state farm deficits occur in fertile Pannonia. High subsidies and price support for wheat, industrial crops (up to 35 per cent. of guaranteed prices), lean pork and baby beef (20 per cent.) explain the persistence of traditional cereal farming but with increased industrial-crop cultivation and livestock-fattening. The virtual lack of subsidies for dairy produce (until 1965) and high-priced fodder, and of price support for relatively low-priced grapes, fruit and vegetables has slowed the adoption of mixed farming and the emergence of distinctive dairying and horticultural zones around cities. Generally, however, prices far exceed pre-war levels, stimulating increased production; recent reforms, fixing agricultural prices at parity with other prices should accelerate improvement.

Subsistence agriculture yielded its traditional dominance to commercial farming only in 1963. Even when collectivisation and compulsory deliveries achieved their 1951 maximum 65 per cent. of farm output was consumed by the farmers themselves. Now 55 per cent. is marketed, although 5 million peasants still work the land. Four factors explain this change: rising non-farm populations: increasing specialisation of farm production by peasant families who can buy with their off-farm incomes what they do not produce; an expanding socialist sector, which contributes one-third of marketable surpluses (cf. only 8 per cent. in 1955); and increasing production of cash crops and livestock by peasants under contract to the O.Z.Z.

Changing market demand, following industrialisation and rising living standards, has induced some re-orientation of farming activities. Sugar consumption has risen since 1950 from 3 to 6 per cent. of total average calorie intake and meat, fats and dairy produce from 16 to 22 per cent., stimulated by and stimulating beet and livestock production. Nevertheless, diets remain strongly traditional. Cereals account for 58 per cent. of calorie intake (69 per cent. in 1950), a cause of wheat imports and of rigidity in domestic agriculture. Small fruit and vegetable intakes (11–12 per cent.) combine with rising retail costs and with poor packing, marketing and road transport facilities to retard horticulture. Regional differences in food consumption stress the continuity of traditional cultures and ecological conditions and underline the inadequacy of interregional marketing and transport facilities. Cereals remain most dominant in the diets of people living in regions of backward Moslem culture and subsistence agriculture, just where cereal deficiencies are greatest: Kosmet, Macedonia and Bosnia-Herzegovina. Livestock products, vegetables and fruit are consumed in greatest quantities in northern Yugoslavia and Montenegro. Marketing involves supplying flour, fruit and industrial crops from the north-eastern quadrant to the remainder of Yugoslavia, of potatoes and dairy produce from the north and west to the east, centre and coast, of special fruits and vegetables from the coast to interior. Such marketing is only partially effective because of poor transport links between the north-east, centre and coast and between the west and south-east. Intra-regionally, cityward movements of produce are increasing as growing urban demand for fresh food and industrial crops induces greater specialisation, usually by villages and not simply by producers. Thus Danube-bank villages near Belgrade produce vegetables and hillside villages overlooking the Danube produce soft fruits for the city market.

LAND IMPROVEMENT & MECHANISATION

Agrarian reform, socialisation and economic stimuli would be ineffective in improving agriculture without land improvement and mechanisation. Over 3 million ha. of farmland are liable to periodic flooding and 4 million ha. are subject to degradation by erosion. Over 5 million ha. of arable land cannot contribute higher crop yields without physical and chemical soil improvement, 1·5 million ha. require fertilisers simply to maintain yields and another 1·5 million ha. are exhausted enough to warrant fallowing.[48] Recently prolonged summer drought (1964), followed by heavy autumn floods (1964) and summer floods (1965) prevented the sowing or ripening of crops on 550,000 ha., causing estimated agricultural losses to over $300 million.

Since 1945 1,200,000 ha. have been drained and protected from flood and 100,000 ha. have been irrigated, bringing the drained and irrigated areas respectively to 3,110,000 ha. and 150,000 ha. These improvements, though noteworthy, are not enough. Capital scarcity is to blame, especially for shifting priorities from long-term capital-intensive construction to cheaper fertilisation and mechanisation which would yield short-term results. Progress has been much greater in draining land than in irrigation, because drainage costs per ha. (12–54,000 dinars at 1960 prices) are far below those for irrigation (350–410,000 dinars). Material shortages and complex peasant landownership patterns also hinder progress. At present land drainage is localised (Figure 16) in river floodplains in Vojvodina (1·5 million ha.), Slavonia (1·1 million ha), north Serbia (330,000 ha.), north Bosnia (150,000 ha.) and Prekomurje (30,000 ha.), the remainder being in Metohija, Pelagonia and Zeta. Irrigation is confined to Macedonia (60,000 ha.), Kosmet (60,000 ha.) and Vojvodina (30,000 ha.).

Work began in earnest after 1956 on several projects aimed at improving 3·6 million ha. of agricultural land by 1980. The main multi-purpose project comprises a 163 mile-long navigable Danube-Tisa-Danube canal (A in Figure 16) and 240 miles of canals for accommodating flood water, draining 1 million ha. in Bačka and Banat more efficiently and irrigating 360,000–550,000 ha. in areas where average annual deficiencies of 10″ (250 mm.) rainfall in the growing season cause substantial shortfalls in crop yields. Another scheme, in Macedonia, aims at: protecting 90,000 ha. overgrazed hill land from further erosion by controlling torrential runoff; protecting 150,000 ha. from seasonal floods by regulating rivers; draining 66,000 ha. of salt marsh in Pelagonia, Struga and Skopje *polja*; and irrigating 220,000 ha. in fourteen

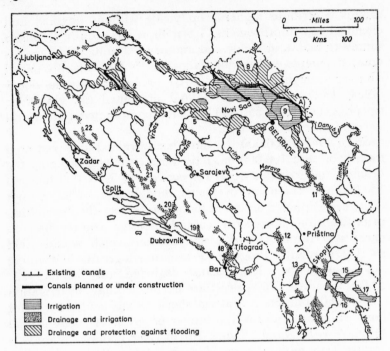

Figure 16. Actual or Potential Farmland in need of Flood Protection, Drainage and Irrigation

CANALS: A – Danube/Tisa/Danube; B – Sisak-Zagreb; C – Skadar-Bar.
LAND IMPROVEMENT SCHEMES: 1 – Medjumurje/Prekomurje; 2 – Lonjsko Polje; 3 – Lijevce Polje; 4 – Posavina; 5 – Bosanska Posavina; 6 – Macva; 7 – Podravina; 8 – Bačka; 9 – Banat; 10 – Lower Morava; 11 – Middle Morava; 12 – Metohija; 13 – Polog; 14 – Pelagonia; 15 – Kočani and Ovče Polje; 16 – Tikveš; 17 – Strumica; 18 – Skadar/Zeta; 19 – Popovo Polje; 20 – Neretva; 21 – Livno/Glamoč Polja; 22 – Lika.

polja where rainfall deficiencies in the growing season average 25″ (625 mm.)[49] So far irrigation is confined to Kočani, Ovče (Štip), Tikveš (Kavadarci) and Strumica *polja* (Figure 16). Irrigation is extending double-cropping, in Vojvodina primarily of maize and lucerne fodder, which is quadrupling the livestock carrying capacities of mixed farms, and in Macedonia of cotton, rice, tobacco, fruits and early vegetables. High crop yields in Vojvodina are being doubled, low yields in Macedonia quadrupled.

In the Sava, Morava and Neretva basins 860 miles of river

are being regulated, 760,000 ha. protected from flood, 960,000 ha. protected from erosion, 1,130,000 ha. drained and 130,000 ha. irrigated.[50] Former marshlands already produce crops in Lonjsko and Jelas *polja* (Posavina), Pomoravlje and Herzegovina (Figure 16). Agricultural incomes in the Karst may be trebled by the improvement of 650,000 ha. of state pastureland to support more cattle and the summer irrigation of 461,100 ha. *polja* and *uvala* land, lying mainly below 2,200 feet from storage lakes located in seasonably flooded parts of the same *polja*. Higher productivity, more diversified output and savings on imported food and cotton would repay the costs within five years.[51]

By doubling the number of man-days per hectare required to tend maize, cotton, vegetables, tree crops and pasture, such irrigation is essential for 'absorbing' indirectly immigrants into Pannonia from, and for reducing rural labour surpluses in, overpopulated regions.

Simple provision of improved land, however, has been no guarantee of better use. Kardelj complained[52] in 1959 that only 10–45 per cent. of costly irrigation facilities were being used in Yugoslavia through inefficient farm management or peasant inability. The Law on Agricultural Land Use (1959) was introduced to enforce the use of minimal modern farming norms by all farmers according to local conditions. Commune councils defined the minimum area to be cultivated and the norms of fertiliser input (150–300 Kg. per ha.) and ploughing depth (20–33 cm.). These minima were adopted quickly in the more developed, more socialised north.

The law increased the use of fertilisers and machinery. In 1939 peasants applied only 46,673 tons fertiliser, or 3 Kg. per ha., to Yugoslav soils. Increasing domestic supplies, government subsidies, education and co-operation expanded fertiliser use from only 79,000 tons in 1952 to 2·3 million tons, or 200 Kg. per cultivated ha., in 1965, so raising and stabilising yields despite climatic fluctuations. Inputs, however, remain among the lowest in Europe. Peasants rarely apply 150 Kg. per ha. and in 1965 inputs on peasant farms averaged only 63 Kg. per ha. Only on socialist farms is as much fertiliser applied as on western European farms (c. 800–1200 Kg. per ha.). Fertiliser effectiveness is reduced by the application of incorrect amounts

o

or unsuitable mixtures, reflecting insufficient knowledge of soil requirements. Inputs are higher in Vojvodina (415 Kg. per ha.), Croatia (255 Kg.), Kosmet (230 Kg.) and Slovenia (190 Kg.) where socialised and co-operative farming are most developed, farmers' purchasing power is higher, peasant ability to innovate is greater, and rail-or-waterborne supplies of bulky fertiliser are available cheaply. Consequently agricultural progress is greatest in these areas. Inputs are far lower where these conditions are less operative, in Serbia Proper (112 Kg.), Macedonia (104 Kg.), Bosnia-Herzegovina (70 Kg.) and Montenegro (33 Kg.). In northern areas, however, where mainly nitrogen and phosphates are applied, lime applications are deficient on 4 million ha. of acid soils. The abundance of lime in Dinaric Yugoslavia is little exploited for this purpose, chiefly because of poor transport for such a bulky low-value product.

Until the advent of co-operation mechanisation was restricted by small, fragmented farms. In 1939 only one tractor was available per 3,200 ha. of arable, but some estates in Pannonia were completely mechanised. After 1945, with the help of subsidies and credit, machinery became available from UNRRA supplies (2,000 tractors in 1945–46), imports and domestic factories. Today there is one tractor for every 166 ha. of arable, a ratio well above the European average. The socialist sector monopolised machinery until 1956 so that numbers of draft animals on peasant farms continued to increase. Agricultural-machine stations, *Poljoprivredno-mašinska stanica*, founded in 1945, were closed in 1950 to make machinery deployment a matter of farm economics and to eliminate heavy deficits which the P.M.S. had incurred through inefficient seasonal operation, high overhead and operational costs, and below-cost pricing of services to collectives. Mechanisation has been extended to peasant farms since 1956 following increased co-operation, taxes on draft animals, obligatory agro-technical norms, and increases in numbers of tractors from 14,696 to 46,000 and of combine-harvesters from 658 to 9,500. Machines have displaced 400,000 draft cattle by replacing horses in northern areas, which in turn replaced cattle in more overpopulated central regions. In 1965, nevertheless, 700,000 oxen, 675,000 cows and 525,000 horses provided power on peasant farms, for few peasants outside Slovenia and Vojvodina can afford machinery.

More powerful socialisation has facilitated above-average mechanisation in Vojvodina (one tractor per 90 ha. arable), Kosmet (100 ha.), Slovenia (130 ha.), Croatia and Macedonia (165 ha.), as compared with one tractor per 225 ha., 240 ha. and 560 ha. in Montenegro, Serbia Proper and Bosnia-Herzegovina respectively. Mechanisation, by speeding operations and so stabilising production (despite climatic fluctuations), yields greater benefits in the north and south-east than elsewhere. The cultivation of high-yielding wheats has made mechanisation essential here since these require more rapid harvesting once ripe than do older varieties. Mechanisation has reduced the areas of barley and oats, which peasants formerly grew with wheat to 'cushion' peak harvest-time labour demands by lengthening the harvest period. It has facilitated greater specialisation, but has discouraged the extension, especially on socialist farms, of crops for which mechanised methods are inappropriate. Nevertheless, much farmwork can still be mechanised.

REFERENCES

1 During harvest-time over 5 million people work on the land. The 500,000 or more 'seasonal' agricultural workers comprise peasant family members who normally work in industry, transport and commerce, and women who live on the farm but do not normally engage in farm work.

2 An authoritative work on the nature of agricultural problems before the Second World War is: J. Tomašević, *Peasants, Politics and Economic Change in Yugoslavia*, Stanford, 1956.

3 Population growth accounts on average for an increase of only 0·6 per cent. per annum in food demand, whereas rising per capita income accounts for 5·8 per cent. per annum.

4 *Changes in Agriculture in Twenty-Six Developing Nations 1948–1963*, U.S. Department of Agriculture, Economic Research Service, Foreign Agricultural Economic Report No. 27, 1966, p. 19.

5 S. Tosović, 'Neki Pokazatelje Prinosa Glavnih Poljoprivrednih Kultura', *Economika Poljoprivrede*, 12 (4), 1965, pp. 281–7.

6 Petar J. Marković, *Strukturne Promene na Selu kao Rezultat Ekonomskog Razvitku: period 1900–1960*, Belgrade 1963, pp. 129–39.

7 These points have emerged during fieldwork undertaken by the author in Hrvatsko Zagorje and Dalmatia in 1960 and 1966. For further

reading the following works should be consulted: (1) W. B. Johnston and K. Crkvenčić, 'Changing Peasant Agriculture in Northwestern Hrvatsko Primorje, Yugoslavia', *Geographical Review*, 45, 1954, pp. 352–72. (2) M. Jeršić, J. Lojk, L. Olas and M. Vojvoda, 'The Village of Sebeborci on the Slovenian Fringes of the Great Pannonian Plain', *Geographia Polonica*, Warsaw, 5, 1965, pp. 215–34.

8   Stjepan Lovrenović, *Ekonomska Politika Jugoslavije*, Sarajevo, 1963, pp. 352–3.

9   Svetozar Ilešić, 'L'état actuel et les problemes des recherches sur l'utilisation du sol en Yougoslavie' and I. Crkvenčić, 'Land Use Mapping Under Yugoslav Conditions', *Land Utilisation Methods and Problems of Research*, Geographical Studies, 31, P.A.N. Institute of Geography, Warsaw, 1962, pp. 181–95.

10 B. Petrović and S. Žuljić, editors, *Kotar Krapina: Regionalni Prostorni Plan*, Urbanistički Institut N. R. Hrvatske, Zagreb, 1958, pp. 79, 87.

11 *Ibid.*, p. 86.

12 F.A.O. *Mediterranean Development Project: The Integrated Development of Mediterranean Agriculture and Forestry in Relation to Economic Growth. A Study and Proposals for Action.* F.A.O., Rome, 1959, p. 90.

13 V. Stipetić, *Agrarna Reforma i Kolonizacija u F.N.R.J. godine 1945–48*, Jugoslovenska Akademija Znanosti i Umjetnosti, Zagreb, 1954, 444 pp. Also: B. Bukurov, *Poreklo Stanovništva Vojvodine*, Matica Srpska, Novi Sad, 1957, p. 69.

14 Jovan F. Trifunoski, *O Posleratnom Naseljavanju Stanovništva iz N.R. Makedonije u Tri Banatska Naselja—Jabuka, Kačerevo i Glogonj*, Matica Srpska, Novi Sad, 1958, pp. 19–25.

15 'Sladak je šećer ali je glibava repa'. M. Vasović, *Najnovije Naseljavanje Crnogoraca u Nekim Bačkim Selima*, Matica Srpska, 1959, p. 156.

16 E. Kardelj, *Problemi Socijalističke Politike na Selu*, Belgrade, 1959, p. 133.

17 D. Jelić, M. Jeršić, J. Lojk and M. Vojvoda, 'Cadastrian Commune of Trebijovi in the Karstland of Herzegovina', *Geographia Polonica*, Warsaw, 5, 1965, pp. 267–84.

18 Marković, *op. cit.*, p. 127.

19 *Ibid.*, pp. 46–49.

20 *Popis Individualnih-Poljoprivrednih Gadzinstava*, Belgrade, 1960.

21 E. Kardelj, *op. cit.*, p. 146.

22 D. Jelić, *op. cit.*, pp. 275–6; M. Jeršić., p. 222.

23 Svetozar Ilešić, *Sistemi Poljske Razdelitve na Slovenskim*, Slovenska Akademija Znanosti in Umjetnosti, Ljubljana 1950, pp. 103–4. This work analyses in detail the origins and patterns of different types and degrees of fragmentation in Slovenian villages in 32 maps and text.

24 C. Malovrh, 'Die Bodenfragmentation als betriebsformende Kraft der Kleinbäuerlichen Betriebe. Bespiele aus dem slowenischen Alpenvorland', *Festschrift Leopold G. Scheidl zum 60. Geburtstag*, 1., Vienna, 1965, pp. 257–67.

25 P. Marković, 'Vučna snaga u Jugoslovenskoj poljoprivredi', *Ekonomist*, Belgrade, 12 (3), 1959, pp. 303–24.

26 Marković, *op. cit.*, p. 92, 106.

27 Examples of these kinds of land use are analysed in detail, for dairying, in: V. Klemenčić, 'The Village of Podgorje in the Slovenian Sub-Alpine Region', *Geographia Polonica*, 5, 1965, pp. 195–214, and for market-gardening (fruits) in: M. Lutovac, 'The Village of Ritopek on the Danube in the Suburban Zone of Belgrade', *Geographia Polonica*, 5, 1965, pp. 235–65.

28 B. Strużek, *Rolnictwo Europejskich Krajów Socjalistycznych*, Warsaw, 1963, pp. 117–34; Jack C. Fisher, 'Political Decision: A Factor in the Changing Agricultural Geography of Yugoslavia', *Journal of Geography*, 58(8), 1959, pp. 399–406.

29 This figure includes 290,000 ha. allocated directly to new state farms, 60,000 ha. allocated to farms of government institutes later reorganised as state farms, and 38,000 ha. belonging to state farms which had been established in 1921 on former Austro-Hungarian crown land.

30 A traditional *zadruga* was a single-family or multiple-family household collectively owning and managing farm property.

31 J. Zmaić, editor, *Razvoj i Perspektiva Poljoprivrednih Dobara Hrvatske*, Zagreb, 1961, p. 35.

32 *Statistički Bilten*, 95, 1958, pp. 10–25.

33 '*Proširenje Površina Društvenih Poljoprivrednih Gadzinstava*', *Jugoslovenski Pregled*, 8(1), 1964, pp. 7–13.

34 N. Suljmanac, 'Intenziviranje Proizvodnje—Uslov Napretka Poljo-privrede', *Ekonomist*, 16 (3–4), 1963, p. 740.

35 V. Popović, 'Zemljoradničke Zadruge u Aktuelnim Društvenim i Privrednim Kretanjima', *Agronomski Glasnik*, 3(6), 1963, pp. 5–9.

36 Useful descriptions, with examples, may be found in: M. Ilijin, *Kooperacija na Selu*, Medjunarodna Politika, Belgrade, 7, 1965, 38 pp., and 'Rezultati Proizvodnje Saradnje u Ratarstvu', *Jugoslovenski Pregled*, 7(5), 1963, pp. 228–33.

37 P. Milenković, 'Stepen Podruštvljenosti Proizvodnje Preko Ko-operacije na Području nekoliko Razvijenih Zadruge Vojvodine', *Ekonomika Poljoprivrede*, 12(5), 1965, pp. 325–70.

38 Kardelj, *op. cit.*, pp. 123–4.

39 S. Cukanović, 'Uslovi i Rezultati Kooperacije Dvuštvenih i Indivi-dualnih Gadzinstava u 1964 godini', *Ekonomika Poljoprivrede*, 12 (9), 1965, pp. 614–23.

40 J. Zmaić, *op. cit.*, p. 51.

41 *Economic Management of State Farms in Kosmet*, O.E.C.D., Paris, 1966, 93 pp.

42 S. Lovrenović, *op. cit.*, p. 316.

43 'Oporezivanje Individualnih Poljoprivrednih Proizvodjača, *Jugoslo-venski Pregled*, 8(3), 1964, pp. 125–9. Increased taxes on draft animals, farm implements and hired labour were intended to force peasants into greater dependence upon the O.Z.Z.

44 S. Popović, 'Problemi Akumulacije i Koncentracije u Poljoprivredi', *Ekonomist*, 3/4, 1963, p. 716.

45 E. Kardelj, *op. cit.*, p. 198.

46 V. Stipetić, *op. cit.*, p. 158.

47 *Ibid.*, p. 146.

48 P. Jakovljević and S. Popović, *Melioracije*, Belgrade, 1964.

49 'Melioracija u Makedoniji', *Jugoslovenski Pregled*, 2(10), 1958, pp. 400–2.

50 *Tehnika*, 3, 1960, p. 407.

51 'Proširenje Površina Društvenih Poljoprivrednih Gadzinstava', *Jugoslovenski Pregled*, 8(1), 1964, p. 9 and S. Sinanović, *Melioracije Nikšićkog i Grahovskog Polja i Značaj Melioracija Kraških Polja za Unapredjenje Poljoprivredne Proizvodnje Dinarske Karsne Oblasti*, Belgrade, 1959, pp. 17, 113, 153, 198, 222–6.

52 E. Kardelj, *op. cit.*, pp. 307–8.

CHAPTER 10

Crops and Livestock

GRAIN CROPS

Cereals are the mainstay of Yugoslav agriculture and one key to general prosperity. Improved methods of cultivating maize and wheat have raised average grain output from 7·6 million tons (1930–39, with a record 8·8 million tons in 1938) to 10·5 million tons (1957–66, and a record 13·4 million tons in 1966). The sown area, however, has contracted from 6·2 million ha. to 5·4 million ha. Maize is the leading arable crop (Table 12) because of its greater utility as a subsistence food, as animal fodder and as an industrial raw material, its greater spatial adaptability to climatic conditions, its greater tolerance of widespread podsolic soils, and its higher average yields at altitudes up to 3,000 feet (900 m.) than other cereals. Maize, therefore, is the main subsistence cereal throughout the over-populated upland and Karst regions, although inadequate summer rain puts it second in importance to wheat in dry southern Serbia, Kosmet and Macedonia. Three-quarters of the maize output, however, comes from the fertile Pannonian lowlands, where yields average 35 quintals per ha., and north Serbia, where summer rainfall is adequate and most reliable. Although this region continues to export maize abroad, off-farm sales are declining as more maize is fed as silage to livestock, chiefly pigs, on a growing number of mixed farms. Planning has concentrated more maize production in the north-east than formerly and has achieved much higher yields through the sowing of hybrid varieties, but more irrigation and fertiliser are required to reduce the annual fluctuations in yield that result from uncertain summer weather.

Postwar wheat production has increased faster than maize production (Table 12). Higher prices for wheat, substantial subsidies to growers on fertilisers and on high-yielding seed, and more growing of wheat by peasants on contract have stimulated greater increases in wheat yields in an effort to reduce imports. On socialist farms this has changed crop-production economics enough to induce some substitution of wheat for maize in the drier east, from Posavina to Macedonia, where maize yield margins over wheat yields are small or negative. Wheat is also preferred on newly-drained and ir-rigated land. Being more sensitive than maize, however, wheat is more confined to areas of richer soils (e.g. chernozems), of lower altitudes (below 1650'), of greater warmth and of less moisture. Two-thirds is produced north-east of a line from Varaždin to Niš. Here yields average 24 q. per ha. (35 bushels per acre) and, with low agricultural population densities and high socialisation, farm surpluses may reach 40 per cent. of output. Little wheat is cultivated in highland Yugoslavia where physical environments are unfavourable, yields are below 15 q. per ha., agricultural overpopulation is widespread, and farm deficiencies exceed 25 per cent.

Barley, oats and rye are essentially fodder crops and are unimportant except in wetter, colder upland districts with poor soils where maize and wheat cannot ripen. They are almost absent from the 'maize-wheat belt', where they cannot compete in yield and return for the best soils. Their cultivation has contracted sharply since 1945 in Slavonia, Srem and Šumadija. Oats and rye are now largely localised in the Dinaric lands. Barley cultivation continues in a broad belt from central Slovenia through central Bosnia and the Karstlands to the Upper Vardar. Recently, however, barley cultivation has expanded in Vojvodina, which now produces 37 per cent. of Yugoslav output compared with 13 per cent. in 1930–39. This follows resettlement of peasants from Dinaric areas, the growth of brewing and the need for more fodder from sandy soils in drier areas for extending mixed farming. Rice cultiva-tion, although still small, has been extended, and yields greatly increased, on irrigated lands in Macedonia (region E) and, more recently, in Pannonia.

INDUSTRIAL CROPS

The expansion in production of these crops is a central object of the postwar government's commitment to 'complex regional

development' of integrated farm production for industrial processing wherever ecological conditions permit. Increased prices,
substantial subsidies, expanding factory capacity and ultimate
consumer demand have sustained large increases in the production of sugar beet, sunflowers (Table 12), tobacco, cotton
and hops, mainly through expanding the sown area rather than
through raising yields. Increasing use of artificial fibres at
home and abroad, however, is causing stagnation in hemp and
contraction in flax cultivation.

Eighty-five per cent. of the chief crop, sugar beet, is grown on
the best 'wheat belt' soils in Pannonia, Šumadija and Pomoravlje and near sugar refineries. More beet comes now from state
farms cultivating reclaimed land in Pelagonia, Metohija and
Semberija, where new refineries commenced operation between
1958 and 1964. Sunflowers have replaced rapeseed throughout
the federation and poppies in Macedonia as the major oilseed,
although most are produced by socialist farms and co-operating
peasants in the north and east for processing into industrial
oils or into cattle cake. Tobacco-growing has been stimulated
by higher prices and contract-farming to increase vital exports
and to generate greater employment of surplus labour and
greater income mainly in underdeveloped regions: areas of
summer drought with well-drained lowland soils in south-
central Macedonia producing 50 per cent. of total output, the
upper Morava region 18 per cent., and Herzegovina 12 per cent.
Most tobacco is 'Turkish', but since 1961 'Virginian' tobacco
with a higher export value has been cultivated, chiefly in
Vojvodina. Hemp and flax, once grown widely by peasants
for making clothes, are being localised in the most suitable
areas—hemp in Bačka and flax in Posavina—because competition from man-made fibres has necessitated rationalised
mill location. Cotton cultivation has been forced, to economise
imports for a relatively large industry, in areas with a long
growing season, a warm dry late summer and autumn, and with
irrigation facilities, namely in agricultural region E. Trial
production in similar conditions near new cotton mills in
Herzegovina, Dalmatia and Montenegro was largely abandoned after 1960. Minor crops of local importance include
hops in the Celje basin and Bačka (where Germanic culture
has been strong), paprika near Subotica (where Hungarian

culture has been important) and various special crops (e.g. pyrethrum, lavender) on Dalmatian islands, especially Hvar.

HORTICULTURE

Physical conditions are exceptionally favourable for horticulture 'for with only minor exceptions there are no fruits (or vegetables) grown elsewhere in Europe which cannot be produced in Yugoslavia'.[1] Yet horticulture remains very backward, with little specialisation, as cultivation and marketing are largely subsidiary to or a by-product of subsistence agriculture. Yugoslavs have no tradition of market-gardening as do the Bulgars. Peasants are unable or unwilling to make long-term investments in glasshouses and in developing new or in replacing old orchards and vineyards, for lack of knowledge, capital and of sufficient labour to tend trees, and for fear of socialisation. Unfavourable prices discouraged fruit and vegetable cultivation on socialist farms, too, investment being channelled into more profitable wheat and livestock production. Poor and costly transport and marketing facilities have restricted the emergence of specialised suburban horticultural zones although some peasants and state farms are adjusting production to market needs.

Sixty per cent. of the potato crop, the chief vegetable, comes from cooler, wetter, podsolic northwestern districts. Postwar urbanisation, the growth of restaurant catering, and the realisation of the nutritive value of potatoes for man and beast alike, have extended cultivation throughout the federation. Cabbages, cultivated on alluvial soils, and beans, inter-cropped with maize, are grown everywhere, but most off-farm sales come from Croatian Zagorje, Bačka, Pomoravlje and Polog. Tomatoes are cultivated under contract for city markets in Pannonia and, on reclaimed land, in Herzegovina and Macedonia for canneries. Serious shortages of spring and winter vegetables can be eliminated by developing a glasshouse industry and by expanding vegetable cultivation on irrigated land in the Adriatic and the Vardar lowlands.

Fruit- and vine-growing are characterised by low and uncertain yields from poorly tended, rarely-sprayed and ageing trees on peasant farms. Socialist farms manage only 18 per cent. of all trees, including those on peasant holdings that co-operatives tend. However, large orchards (averaging 115 ha.) on state farms account for expanded fruit cultivation since 1958. Temperate fruits are widely grown in the Danube drainage basin, although production is localised in agricultural region B. (Figure 13). 'Mediterranean' fruits are grown in regions D and E. Plums cover half the total fruit area, furnishing the peasantry throughout the temperate zone with prunes, brandy (*rakija* or *šljivovica*) and preserves. Two-thirds of plum production comes from cool, moist but well-drained hill areas in northern Bosnia, northern and central Serbia. Only here do peasants own specialised orchards; other fruits are confined to the *okućnica*. Nevertheless, plums are declining in importance because stagnant demand has depressed prices. By contrast, buoyant urban demand for more nutritive fruits has made more profitable the cultivation of apples, pears, peaches, apricots and cherries. Although grown widely, these fruits are substituting plums, especially near towns. Apples and pears thrive on lower sheltered slopes throughout regions B and C. (Figure 13). Peaches, apricots and cherries are more sensitive to late spring frosts, require warm summers and well-drained soils, and may be grown wherever there are vines. Good transport to urban markets, however, localises production in the Vipava-Soča valleys (east Slovenia), central Dalmatia, Bosnian Posavina, Fruška Gora, and around Belgrade and Subotica. Maraschino cherries from Dalmatia are processed into liqueurs. Olives demarcate the Mediterranean region. Figs are grown everywhere from the Soča valley to Ulcinj (Montenegro) and the lower Vardar, while citrus fruits are confined to the warmer coasts southward of Split.

Since 1961 state and co-operative farms, particularly in Bosnia and Macedonia, have obtained cheap credit to develop large specialised non-plum orchards in the best microlocations. Before 1961 farm managements favoured small, diversified orchards but these offered no economies of scale. Contracted fruit-farming has been unsuccessful because peasants can get higher prices by supplying the retail market direct and can do that at less cost than can the co-operatives.[2]

Unlike fruit cultivation, which continues to expand steadily, viticulture is now declining. The cause is not *phylloxera*, which devastated vines earlier in this century and induced the substitution of resistant American stocks for domestic vines. Today, poor quality, unstandardised grape and wine supplies by 1,500,000 peasant producers are uncompetitive in glutted home and foreign markets. Labour shortages cause neglect of inconveniently distant vineyards on peasant holdings, especially in Dalmatia. Another factor is state taxation on home wine-making to divert production into new co-operative wineries where better quality can be achieved. Viticulture is widespread in Yugoslavia, being well adapted to the warm moist growing period, sandy and limey soils and hilly terrain (with or without terracing) where overpopulation demands maximum land use. Vineyards occupy over 5 per cent. of all farmland in three areas: the northeast, on sands around Subotica and on the slopes of Fruška Gora, the Banat hills (Vršac), Šumadija, the Morava and the Timok valleys (40 per cent. of all vines); the north-west in Slovenske Gorice (around Maribor), which produces export dry wines and Croatian Zagorje (16 per cent.); and the Mediterranean region, particularly the Vipava-Soča valleys, Istria and Dalmatia (25 per cent.). Vines are absent only from the cooler, frostier Alpine and Dinaric mountain areas. Viticulture has expanded only in Kosmet and Macedonia, where state farms have planted vineyards in highly suitable environments which the peasants, because of their Moslemism, could not exploit for this purpose. State farms generally have increased vineyard productivity by substituting wide-row systems (for double-storey cordon pruning) for narrow-row cultivation.[3]

LIVESTOCK HUSBANDRY

With production now 45 per cent. above the pre-war level, progress in livestock-farming compares unfavourably with that in arable farming where production is 80 per cent. higher. The reasons are many. Livestock have remained around 21 million head, although numbers of pigs and cattle have increased while latterly numbers of sheep have decreased. Peasant management is more dominant than in arable farming. State and co-operative farms rear only 8 per cent. of all livestock (13 per cent. of the pigs) and co-operate with peasants in rearing another 5 per cent. (18 per cent. of the pigs). Fodder supply is uncertain outside Slovenia and frequent summer droughts decrease livestock numbers in the subsequent months. The economics of peasant farming result in the cultivation of the better soils to the maximum for food, reduction of fodder acreages to the minimum and relegation of grazing from meadows to poorer upland soils, along with rough pasture, and to periodically flooded valleys and *polja*. Except on a few progressive state farms ley farming is rare, so that two-thirds of Yugoslav arable fodder (lucerne, clover, silage maize and turnips) is produced in Vojvodina, Slavonia and Šumadija despite favourable conditions for meadows, whereas three-quarters of meadows and pasture hay is produced in highland Yugoslavia, where more arable fodder could be grown. Thus hay shortages decrease livestock numbers in the northern plains in summer and autumn and arable fodder shortages in the highland zone in winter and early spring. Such scarcities are regular and they may lead, as for example in 1961–62, to the slaughter of as many as 1,100,000 underfed pigs.[4]

Increased livestock production has been achieved through cross-breeding with better quality imported animals and through better feeding. Average annual fodder supplies have been raised from 6·5 million tons (1930–39) to 8·5 million tons (1957–65), following the expansion of arable fodder output from 1·4 million tons to 3·4 million tons. The use of concentrates has improved quality, too. Consequently, yields per head of livestock have been raised from 78 Kg. to 150 Kg. in beef, 530 Kg. to 635 Kg. in pork, 11 Kg. to 14 Kg. in lamb and from 980 to 1,100 litres of milk per annum (2,300 litres on state farms). Such yields are still low, being only two-thirds of those in Bulgaria and half of those in Poland, Austria and Hungary, and result from low fodder yields per ha. which restrict both the quantity and the quality of livestock rearing.

Between the decades 1947–56 and 1957–66 numbers of cattle increased from 5·1 to 5·5 million. This trend, stimulated by a doubling of prices for beef and milk to satisfy growing demand was slowed after 1962 by the trebling of prices and scarce fodder. Cattle are more evenly distributed than other livestock because of their prime subsistence rôle for meat, milk and draft power. There is, nevertheless, a clear concentration in a north-west–south-east belt from east-central Slovenia to the Šar Planina which corresponds with both the belts of densest population and of the best fodder supplies of arable fodder from hillside plots, grass from valley meadows and upland summer pastures which are accessible in the central Dinaric zone by transhumance. The highest cattle densities occur in the north-west, where higher rainfall gives higher-yielding pastures (25 quintals hay per ha. per annum), where population is densest and where the stimuli to commercial meat and milk production —good transport, large urban markets and factory-processing—are greatest. Southwards, the Karst, coastal regions and Macedonia are too dry for more than rough pasture, which is too poor for much cattle-rearing or dairying. Recently, expanded arable fodder supplies have permitted a substantial increase in cattle densities in Slovenia and Pannonia. Poor hay supplies have decreased cattle numbers in central, eastern and southern Yugoslavia. Contrasts in rates of progress be-tween areas to the north and to the south of the Sava-Danube are indeed striking. Artificial insemination, for example, is applied to 60 per cent. of the cows in the north compared with only 12 per cent. of those in the south. Foreign cattle, it is true, are imported into all regions, but the higher-yielding types depending for successful results upon arable fodder and scienti-fic management, are almost inevitably localised in Pannonia and Pomoravlje. Domestic 'buša' cattle, small and poorly productive, are grazed on pasture in central and southern districts. General improvements are more advanced in the north as a result of higher cultural and economic development and more socialisation.

Dairying displays similar features. Milk production has increased by only 25 per cent. since 1930–39; annual per capita consumption decreased from 124 to 119 litres. Pro-duction became increasingly unprofitable after 1959. Fodder shortages pushed up fodder costs (accounting for 43–58 per cent. of milk costs) and until 1963 raised production costs to almost 50 per cent. above the fixed selling price.[5] Hardest hit were producers living everywhere southward of the Sava-Danube in the areas of the least certain fodder supply, which were also the areas of lowest milk production and, because of rapidly increasing population, of greatest decline in per capita output. Milk production remained stable or actually increased where arable fodder supplies were most easily available: in the north. For these reasons well-marked dairying zones have not emerged. Production exceeds 200 litres per head of population per annum everywhere northward of the Danube-Sava, including Lika but excluding Istria. Except for areas around Sarajevo, Mostar and Štip, and in Pomoravlje (between Kruševac and Smederevo) per capita milk production everywhere in the south is below 100 litres. Despite favourable physical conditions and poor transport access, important industrial centres in west and north-east Bosnia and around Skopje completely lack dairy zones within 40 miles.

Progress has been spasmodic in raising cattle productivity in the socialist sector. Until 1957 cattle-rearing and dairying were restricted to state farms (e.g. Belje) with their own fodder-concentrate supplies from processing industries. The intensive use of silage maize, lucerne and clover began only in 1955, but farm managements continued to consider livestock-farming unprofitable until 1957, when experiments demonstrated that high yields of arable fodder could be obtained.

Pig-rearing for Central-European markets has a long tradition in Yugoslavia. Exports continue to encourage a broad upward trend in numbers, from 4·4 million (1947–56) to 5·2 million (1957–65); in 1964, for the first time, there were more pigs than cattle in the state. The shift to lean pork for export, however, has been hampered by deficiencies in quality fodders—oil-seed cake, fish meal and concentrates—which must be imported. Pig-rearing is now more localised in the maize-wheat belt, where factory by-products augment substantial grain surpluses, so stabilising pig numbers. Fodder scarcities have caused a marked decline in pig-rearing in drier areas elsewhere. However, pig-rearing is underdeveloped in Bosnia, Sandjak, Kosmet and Macedonia not so much because of insufficient fodder as of prohibition by Moslemism.

Poultry-farming, with production of meat and eggs 60 per cent. above the pre-war level, has recently displaced sheep-farming as the third largest source of meat. Ninety per cent. of all poultry are kept by peasants as supplementary sources of subsistence. Recently, however, state farms have introduced factory farming methods particularly for broiler chicken in Slovenia. Numbers of sheep have declined from 12 million in the 1950s to 9·7 million in 1965. Sheep are few in Slovenia or Pannonia but are widespread in highland Yugoslavia, most grazing on poor rough pasture where surface water is scarce as in the Karst, the Carpathians and Macedonia and where transhumance is necessary. Herein lies one cause of decline: the control of grazing on 2 million ha. of state pastures in the main sheep-rearing region (C). Another cause is that demand and prices for poor quality wool and for lamb are declining, so depressing the main occupation in poor regions. The government has refused to support prices for these commodities in order to stimulate rural depopulation of the uplands and begin land-use improvement.

REFERENCES

1 *Jugoslavia*, Vol. III, Geographical Handbook Series, Naval Intelligence Division, 1945, p. 92.
2 A. Mišev, 'Neki Problemi Potrošnje i Proizvodnje Pojedinih Vrsti Voća', *Poljoprivredni Pregled*, 13 (9–10), 1964, pp. 445–54; A.Tomin, 'Marža Voća i Stonog Grožda kao Faktor Prometa i Potrošnje', *Ekonomika Poljoprivrede*, 12(9), 1964, p. 640–53. R. Hadžiomerspahić, 'Putevi Razvoja i Organizaciono-ekonomska Problematika Voćarske Proizvodnje na Društvenim Gadzinstvima S. R. Bosne i Hercegovine', *Poljoprivredni Pregled*, 13 (9–10), 1964, pp. 433–43.
3 B. Colić, L. Avramov and R. Lovrić, 'Efekat Rekonstrukcije Uskoredih Vinograda', *Ekonomika Poljoprivrede*, 12(6), 1964, pp. 403–13.
4 *Politika*, 14 September, 1962, p. 6.
5 'Mlekarstvo', *Jugoslovenski Pregled*, 8(9), 1964, p. 344.

CHAPTER 11

Forestry and Fishing

Yugoslavia possesses extensive forests, covering 8·6 million ha. or 34 per cent. of the state area—a higher proportion than in any other European country outside Scandinavia and Austria. About 3 million ha., however, support degraded woodland, coppices or shelter belts that are unsuitable for commercial exploitation. Over 70 per cent. of the reserves, which are estimated at 740 million cu.m., are deciduous hardwoods, chiefly beech and oak, which are less suitable than conifers (softwoods) for industrial processing. Only in Slovenia are the softwood reserves greater than the hardwood reserves. Forests occur widely throughout upland Yugoslavia, yet five areas, where forests occupy 50–55 per cent. of the land, are of outstanding importance (Figure 17). Nearly one half of the reserves lie in east-central Bosnia and west Serbia between the rivers Vrbas-Neretva (west), Spreča-Kolubara (north), Ibar-White Drim (east) and the southern Adriatic littoral (south). Other important forest regions are: Alpine, inner (Notranjsko) and lower (Dolenjsko) Slovenia; the Gorski Kotar-Velebit-Kapela-Grmeč uplands of south-west Croatia and north-west Bosnia; central Slavonia; and the Carpathians in east Serbia.

Forestry is an important activity. It employs 90,000 workers, provides valuable exports and is becoming an integral part of land-use management and resource conservation. For centuries the forest area declined at the hands of peasants who sought land, fuel or building materials, and of foreign enterprises that cut timber to serve markets in Hungary and Mediterranean Europe where wood was scarce. Statistics after 1920 showed that the annual cut regularly exceeded the annual increment of timber (18–20 million cu.m.) by 1–10 million cu.m. For example, between 1947 and 1952 the annual cut averaged 28·7 million cu.m. More valuable conifers were being depleted

P   213

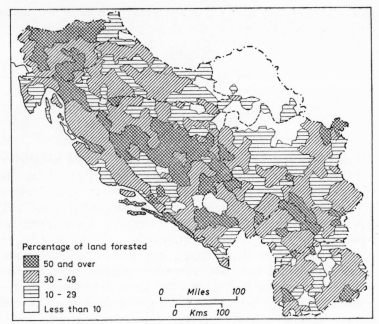

Figure 17. The Distribution of Forested Land

more rapidly as they contributed 35 per cent. of timber supply compared with only 28 per cent. of timber reserves. Rapidly depleted were the more accessible pure stands of conifers in Slovenia and Gorski Kotar, of oaks in Slavonia and Srem, and of conifers and oaks of mixed forests along the narrow-gauge forest railways of Bosnia.[1] Large stands of primeval forest remained untouched, however, in the Drina basin and Sandjak.

Despite high timber production before 1952, more rational forest management has been achieved progressively since 1945. Land reforms have increased the forest area in State administration from 50 to 70 per cent., thus extending the area subject to scientific management, restricting the area liable to cutting by peasants and eliminating exploitation by foreign firms. State ownership is highest in Bosnia (79 per cent.) and lowest in Serbia, the only region with less state owned (47 per cent.) than privately owned forest. Four trends indicate the success achieved so far in rationalising forest management. First, the annual cut has been substantially reduced, to 13–16 million

cu.m. (1960–65) or somewhat below the annual timber increment, following the decreased use of wood for fuel in industry,
on railways, in homes and as pitprops in mines. Second, the
cutting of softwoods has been reduced drastically, from 35 per
cent. of the total in 1947–52 to 27 per cent. in 1960–65, to stabilise
coniferous reserves; hardwoods are substituting softwoods in
some industrial processes, notably cellulose manufacture. Third,
afforestation policies have succeeded in planting 500,000 ha.
chiefly in areas of rapid deforestation or of insufficient forest
cover, since 1947, with quick-growing conifers and poplars to increase future forest reserves and to protect land against erosion.
Another million hectares are being prepared for planting
especially in agricultural region C where reduced grazing of
sheep, cattle and goats (which numbered 3 million in 1956) in
forests has opened the way for improvement, especially of areas
of *šikara* (thickets). Fourth, these measures have been applied
also to rationalise the geography of timber exploitation. This
has involved: (1) decreased production especially of coniferous
and oak timber and increased afforestation in Slovenia and
Croatia (particularly in the Karst); (2) greatly increased output
from recently opened primeval forests in east-central Bosnia
and Sandjak; and (3) afforestation, chiefly to increase poplar,
conifer and oak reserves in western and northern Bosnia and in
drier eastern Yugoslavia. Nevertheless, timber-cutting still
exceeds timber increments in Slavonia, while insufficient
forest communications mean that nine underdeveloped districts
(Čačak, Kraljevo, Niš, Požarevac, Vranje, Doboj, Livno,
Mostar and Štip), with 22·7 per cent. of total forest reserves,
yield only 8·5 per cent. of total timber output.[3] The location of
timber industries in part explains these features (Chapter 13).

Like most other branches of the economy, the fishing industry
is under-developed. Although the Yugoslav coastline is long
and indented, and large rivers and lakes are numerous, fishing
is of minor importance. It provides only a useful source of
livelihood on the coast and islands where agriculture and forestry are restricted. About 18,000 men are engaged in the industry, but fewer than 3,000 are active all year. Landings of
fish, averaging 21,000 tons per annum in the last decade, are
still small, but show a marked improvement over landings

before the war (8,000 tons) and between 1947 and 1956 (17,000 tons). A commonly accepted explanation for the smallness of the industry has been that the Adriatic fishing grounds are very poor. The narrowness of the continental shelf and the great depth of the sea off southern Yugoslavia, it has been thought, restricted the development of plankton. Observers also considered that inshore fishing is hampered all year by the rockiness of the coast and islands and often is made impossible in winter by the suddenness and duration of the *bora*. Srdar,[4] however, in an exhaustive study, argues that although the resources and movements of fish in the Adriatic are insufficiently known, the landings of Italian fishermen on the western Adriatic shore of 70–75,000 tons of fish per annum indicate in comparison with landings on other Mediterranean coasts, that the Adriatic has above average resources for the Mediterranean. This also suggests that the Yugoslav fishing industry has much scope for expansion.

Social and economic factors help to limit the size of the fishing industry. Centuries of foreign domination and instability had stifled the emergence of a sea-faring and fishing tradition among the coastal peoples so that the labour force had always been small. After the war many Italian fishermen on the Kvarner and Istrian coasts migrated to Italian towns; today youth migrates to urban centres, where more renumerative employment is on offer, so that numbers are still declining and personnel are ageing. Postwar re-equipment with better ships and fishing gear explains the increased catch, despite the declining labour force. The industry, however, is over-capitalised. Ships and tackle are used only seasonally and insufficiently in the open sea, and production costs are therefore high.

Yet the most serious problem is the restricted market for fish. Transport from the Adriatic coast even today is slow and expensive and in the past was much more so. Fish therefore never became part of the traditional diet inland, and high prices and inadequate refrigeration facilities now give no help towards overcoming this traditional reluctance and developing a significant inland market. Between 30 and 60 per cent. of the catch is consumed as fresh fish in coastal towns and villages, where only 7 per cent. of the population live; in contrast only

10 per cent. of the fresh fish is consumed in towns in the interior although fish salted or canned on the coast (amounting to 32 per cent.) is marketed inland. Figures of fish consumption per head of population in major urban centres in 1955 clearly illustrate this: 20·5 kg. in Pula, 12 kg. in Rijeka and Zadar, 9·5 kg. in Split, 7·5 kg. in Šibenik and 5 kg. in Dubrovnik, as compared with 2·5 kg. in Zagreb, 1·2 kg. in Ljubljana, 0·8 kg. in Belgrade and 0·3 kg. in Sarajevo. This pattern illustrates two further points as well: consumption is greatest in those coastal towns in which landings of fish from the nearby continental shelf are greatest, notably in Kvarner, Istria and north Dalmatia; consumption in inland towns is greatest where accessibility from more important fishing ports is greatest, notably at Zagreb and Ljubljana. Consumption per capita in Zagreb, however, is much higher than in other inland towns and in absolute terms is greater than in any coastal town, even Rijeka or Split. No doubt the presence of many Dalmatians in Zagreb is very relevant to the greater demand there.

A substantial increase in capacity for canning fish and for producing fish meal has promoted total demand for fish since the war and has, in part at any rate, offset generally stagnant or declining per capita consumption of fresh fish. In recent years, however, high production costs and insufficient markets for canned fish have made these outlets less reliable, too, causing some hardship to communities on Dalmatian islands where canning is located.

Most fishing is localised in the northern Adriatic off the Istrian coast, the Kvarner Bay islands, and Kornat and Vis in north and central Dalmatia. Sardines, caught mainly in spring and autumn in the north-west, tunny from the Velebit coast, mackerel, shellfish and oysters form the bulk of the catch. Freshwater fishing yields some 10,000 tons of fish a year, chiefly in Croatia-Slavonia from state-farm fishponds, from Lake Vrana in Dalmatia, from the Danube and from the lakes Skadar, Ohrid and Dojran.

REFERENCES

1 *Razvoj Privrede F.N.R. Jugoslavije*, Belgrade, 1957, pp. 287–97.
2 Stjepan Surić, *Razvoj Šumarstva i Drvne Industrije Jugoslavije 1945–1956*, Belgrade, 1959, 46 pp.
3 'Šumsko Bogatstvo i Njegovo Iskorišćavanje', *Jugoslovenski Pregled*, 4(9), 1961, pp. 364–73.
4 Srdjan Srdar, *Morsko Bogatstvo Jadrana i Njegovo Iskorišćavanje*, Zagreb, 1960, 502 pp.

CHAPTER 12

Industry: Patterns of Growth
and Changing Location

Yugoslav industry in 1938 was only in its infancy. Mines and quarries had capacity for only 60,000 and manufacturing industries for only 300,600 workers in that year.[1] The economic depression, however, still left its mark in substantial surplus capacity, so that actual employment was only 41,200 in mining and only 196,900 in manufacturing.[2] Most enterprises comprised one or several workshops or primitive mines and quarries, where artisan methods, simple equipment and little mechanical or electrical power were characteristic. There were few factories in the true sense. Indeed nearly three-quarters of the 4,257 establishments had fewer than '50 working places' each. Only 120 mines and factories employed more than 500 workers. Most of these were owned by the State, as for example, coal mines and metallurgical plants in Bosnia, railway vehicle works and tobacco factories in Serbia, or by foreign companies as, for example, non-ferrous metal mines and smelters in Serbia and cement in Dalmatia.

In 1945 the postwar government proposed industrialisation as the main vehicle of economic development. Nationalisation of the economy concentrated capital in the hands of the government which was then free to channel more investment into mining, energy and manufacturing than into any other sector. In all, between 1947 and 1965, more than $7000 million (at 1962 prices) were invested in fixed capital in industry, or 41 per cent. of gross investment in fixed capital. Consequently industrial production has expanded on average by 10·4 per annum, so conditioning the speed of general economic development. Production is now six times as great as in 1938 and employment in mining and manufacturing has risen from 238,115 in 1938 to 1,362,000 in 1964 (Table 19). War damage, and the postwar concentration of workshop industries into larger units, reduced the number of enterprises by well over half, so that, including the 625 new factories constructed since 1946, only 2700 enterprises are now in operation as compared with 4257 in 1938. The scale of industrial activity has increased greatly: the average Yugoslav mine or factory now employs over 500 workers as compared with only 45 in 1938.

Parallel with the growth of industry there have been significant changes in its structure. Two indices, employment and production, demonstrate, in Table 19, the absolute and the relative trends. Employment statistics suggest the size and relative importance of each industry in the years 1938 and 1964, though they tend to undervalue capital-intensive industries and to overvalue labour-intensive industries. Production indices, which relate to changes in physical output, avoid the pitfalls of comparing values of production, which until 1965 were subject to arbitrary manipulation. Table 19 also presents indices showing the long-term trends, 1939–64, and the intervening short-term trends.

Clearly, the most rapidly expanding industries in postwar Yugoslavia have been, in descending order, the electrical, oil-drilling and refining, metal-working and engineering, electric power, chemicals, cellulose and paper, iron and steel, and rubber industries. These activities in 1964 accounted for 42·6 per cent. of total industrial employment and production, compared with 26·3 per cent. in 1938, and may justly be termed *the* growth industries. Such trends reflect broadly the priority given to investment over consumption and to investment in industry and transport over investment in agriculture or forestry, as well as the pattern of capital allocation among industries themselves. Over two-thirds of all postwar industrial investment has in fact gone into these eight growth industries in an effort to satisfy the markets for energy and capital goods.

Electrification, absorbing 21 per cent. of all capital allocated to industry since 1947, has been the cornerstone of industrialisation; in turn, it demanded the expansion of the electrical industry to supply cables, transformers and other equipment. Metal-working and engineering consumed nearly 12 per cent. of industrial investment in order to supply the boilers, turbines and pylons for electrification, and metal products, machinery and vehicles required by the expansion of mining, manufacturing, building, transport, forestry and agriculture generally; it therefore became *the* key manufacturing industry. Priority for investment in engineering also aimed at substituting home production for imports or increasing exports (e.g. shipbuilding) to improve the trade balance. Such growth has called forth the expansion of steel industries to supply metal and rolled products, and of non-metallic mineral industries to meet demands from steel plants for refractories, from engineering works for abrasives and from electricity installations for insulators. The need for new chemicals in a growing economy and the increasing availability of chemical raw materials—gases from various refineries, natural gas and salt—have stimulated and facilitated progress in heavy chemicals.

Rates of expansion, while still rapid, have been much slower in industries producing materials or manufactures for markets which, over the postwar period, have been less expansive, i.e. 'non-productive' building, including housing, and personal consumption. These industries are food-processing, leather-shoe, building materials, timber-processing, textiles and tobacco. Two exceptions are coal and non-ferrous metals, heavy industries in which growth has also been much below average. This reflects, first, the problem of mining poor quality coal and the general trend of substituting hydro-electricity, oil and natural gas for coal as an energy source, and, second, the large pre-war capacity in non-ferrous metal industries that required less expansion.

Nevertheless, the decline in the relative importance of light industries—despite great absolute growth—has resulted less from restricted markets than from restricted investment in new capacity, only 19 per cent. of industrial investment since 1947 being allocated to the light industries as compared with 81 per cent. to the basic industries. The strong inflationary pressures characteristic of the postwar economy have therefore been most apparent in the de-controlled consumer market, where supply has been unable to meet demand. Other factors, are however, also important. Foreign capital controlled 51·4 per cent. of all Yugoslav mining and manufacturing[3] in 1938 and the greatest profit to foreign companies lay in exploiting raw materials with cheap labour to feed their home manufacturing industries.

They had invested most heavily in light manufacturing industries such as textiles and leather-shoe, which were more or less dependent upon imported materials. While causing 'growing pains' in the Yugoslav economy, the faster postwar growth of basic industries, to insert important 'missing links' between extraction of raw materials and marketing of finished products, and the slower growth of light industries, already relatively large, were necessary measures for achieving a better integrated industrial structure. The large expansion of employment and production shown in Table 19 indicates, however, that light industries have not been neglected. Indeed, these structural changes have brought Yugoslav industry[4] very close to the United Nations' 'model of manufacturing industry'.[5] The only significant deviations from the model include the food, drink and tobacco industries, which are under-represented, largely through backwardness in agriculture, and timber-processing, metallurgy and metalworking, which are over-represented but reflect the nation's resource endowment. Balance of payments deficits also contributed to slower expansion of light industries by impairing the ability of the country to import cotton, wool, natural rubber and cattle hides for their respective industries. This was particularly noticeable after the Cominform break, when imports of capital goods were given urgent priority.

Table 19 indicates also changes in industrial growth patterns from period to period. They reflect changes in emphasis in investment policy from plan to plan, themselves expressing short-term advantages in opportunity cost or the need to achieve better inter-industry balances in material and product flows. Heavy war damage limited the expansion of oil, metal, timber and paper industries up to 1947, while highly effective investment, rationalisation and more shift work permitted substantial expansion in both basic and light manufacturing industries. Between 1947 and 1956 basic industries expanded more rapidly[6] and light industries less rapidly. During the second Five Year Plan, electricity and steel industries lagged, causing serious power and metal shortages, but timber, leather and rubber industries expanded relatively fast to meet the government's insistence upon more exports. Although electricity output has again forged ahead since 1960, there has still

TABLE 19

INDICES OF CHANGES IN THE STRUCTURE OF YUGOSLAV INDUSTRY, 1938-64

Activity	Changes in Employment				Indices of Production					
	1938		1964		1939-47 (1939 = 100)	1947-52 (1947 = 100)	1952-57 (1952 = 100)	1957-60 (1957 = 100)	1960-64 (1960 = 100)	1939-64 (1939 = 100)
	Numbers	%	Numbers	%						
ALL INDUSTRY	238,115	100	1,218,645	100	120	137	189	145	136	600
Electric Power	10,950	4·3	31,198	2·5	126	185	231	143	155	1165
Coal-mining and processing	32,450	13·6	82,217	6·7	115	125	152	121	115	300
Oil production and refining	2,500	1·1	11,753	0·9	88	476	247	178	169	3016
Ferrous Metallurgy	7,550	3·1	47,165	3·9	123	143	277	140	113	755
Non-Ferrous Metallurgy	8,500	3·5	45,028	3·7	90	161	162	128	143	413
Non-Metallic Minerals	4,200	1·7	39,026	3·2	150	175	242	146	139	1285
Metalworking and Engineering	19,310	8·3	245,186	20·1	152	172	200	164	121	1315
Electrical	1,300	0·4	62,715	5·1	233	357	310	186	160	7608
Chemicals	12,845	5·3	52,200	4·3	120	137	256	177	155	1130
Building materials	12,700	5·3	56,222	4·8	129	127	152	139	119	396
Timber-processing	28,725	11·6	131,977	10·8	106	116	139	150	142	354
Paper and Cellulose	5,005	2·1	17,028	1·4	117	120	233	140	180	809
Textiles	54,000	22·7	184,544	15·1	123	97	167	134	136	351
Leather-Shoe	6,760	2·8	36,912	3·0	132	97	157	153	136	407
Rubber	1,160	0·5	17,228	1·4	138	120	184	150	140	628
Food Processing	24,275	10·2	85,734	7·0	131	87	226	142	136	482
Printing	4,100	1·7	38,843	3·2	no data available			145	130	—
Tobacco-manufacture	2,150	0·9	19,543	1·6	111	113	127	111	105	186

Sources Statistika Industrije Kraljevine Jugoslavije, Belgrade, 1941, p. 26.
Statistički Godišnjak SFRJ, 1964, p. 178.
Statistički Kalendar Jugoslavije, 1965, pp. 54 and 59.

been insufficient investment to eliminate power shortages. The continued lag in steel production has retarded expansion in engineering. The decentralised economic system, by partially controlling prices for basic products (which thus were less 'remunerative' investments), discouraged adequate investment in building-materials industries, especially cement, which is thus in short supply. For the opposite reasons (apparently highly remunerative investment) textiles, leather, rubber and food, have continued to expand to meet inflationary demand and are now generally faced with a problem of surplus capacity.

One postwar trend, however, has been both continuous and common to all Yugoslav industries, namely the more rapid expansion of the production of finished products than of raw and semi-processed materials. This trend results from government measures to use domestic resources to a maximum to ensure the greatest value of production, accumulation and employment at home.[7] The major postwar expansion of industry has occurred, therefore, in plants producing many new products: finished metal articles, including machinery; complex chemicals, which include both materials (e.g. plastics) and products (e.g. fertilisers); furniture; clothing; tobacco manufactures. Other manufacturing activities, however, have also risen greatly, particularly electrical products, refractory, ceramic and glass products, shoes, rubber products and canned foods. Sometimes the development of new capacity has eliminated illogical bottlenecks in earlier stages of manufacture. The iron and steel industry provides an example. Before the war iron ore was being exported while simultaneously pig iron had to be imported to feed the steel mills that the domestic blast furnaces were unable to satisfy. More blast furnace capacity has remedied this situation[8].

Broad success in industrialisation should not mask the existence of important problems both old and new. First, despite the trebling of average per capita consumption since 1939, the Yugoslav market remains small. The economy is still the least-developed in Europe except for those of Albania and Portugal. Half the consumers gain a precarious livelihood from backward agriculture. Indeed, the emergence of nearly a million 'peasant-industrial workers' since 1945 has reduced the per capita purchasing power of the rural population because their agricultural productivity has diminished so much that they use most of their income from industry to buy food or to pay taxes on their land.[9] Expansion of the market is closely linked, therefore, with radical improvements in agriculture.

Secondly, poor interregional transport and marketing organization hampers flows of goods between producers and consumers, permitting the local operation of monopoly conditions and the survival of inefficient producers. Third, the unfavourable balance of payments has stimulated the development of industries to reduce imports or to increase exports. This has had its advantages, yet 'an insistence upon increasing exports at all costs, not taking sufficient account of the rentability and general economic effect of such exports'[10] was sometimes evident. Exports of ships, for example, involve increased imports of components. Fourthly, the manufacture of finished products under licence from West-European firms, while helping to produce a supply of skilled labour and to raise the standing of Yugoslav products in world markets, has sometimes led to restrictions on exports wherever the parent firm competes for markets.

Many factors adversely affect internal industrial efficiency. Productivity is low, averaging one-third of that in the developed countries of western Europe. Since also postwar industrial growth owes more to the growth of employment (7·4 per cent. p.a.) than to the rise in productivity (4·7 per cent. p.a.) production costs are relatively high and place Yugoslav industry at a serious disadvantage now that the economy (since 1965) is more openly linked with the world economy. Low productivity results from: insufficiently high technical and organisational standards associated with a shortage of skilled labour; high rates of absenteeism, especially among 'peasant-industrial workers' during harvest-time and their low output at any time; and a surplus of workers actually employed in industry which exceeds 10 per cent. of all industrial workers and which in some plants attains 20 per cent.[11] This fact justifies recent attempts to slow down city-ward migration. Decentralisation and localism have encouraged the growth of many small and medium-sized plants which realise few economies of scale. For example, four electrical factories produce only 25,000 refrigerators each and seven produce 50,000 irons each. Enterprise managements have been slow to change their policy of producing large ranges of products in small quantities, which was possible in a protected and under-developed market, with further loss of possible economies of scale. The formation of local or regional 'associations' (*Zadrvženja*) within the same industry to promote co-operation and specialisation, i.e. through the evolution of various types of linkage, have met so far with only limited success, because associations tried to delegate lines of production to enterprises or workers' councils considered that to change in function from producing complete finished articles to manufacturing components was a form of 'degradation'. Specialisation and effective linkages are as yet in embryo.

CHANGES IN INDUSTRIAL DISTRIBUTION, 1938-65[12]

The location of industry in 1938 underlines the spatial dualism of the pre-war Yugoslav economy. More than three-quarters of all industry in the Kingdom, numbering 321,653 'working places' and employing 186,650 workers, was localised north of the Danube-Sava line, mainly in two districts and equally important 'zones with industry', one in the north-west, the other in the north-east. Industries in the north-west were dispersed along valleys in central Slovenia, with concentrations of metalworking, chemical and textile activities in and around Ljubljana, Maribor, Kranj and Celje; and in west Croatia where, apart from scattered sawmills in Gorski Kotar, chiefly textile, leather, metalworking and chemicals were localised in Karlovac, Varaždin and notably Zagreb which, with 14,671 industrial workers, was the largest manufacturing centre in the region. In the north-east, an unparalled position in relation to land and water communications had attracted a wide variety of industries to Belgrade, which with neighbouring Zemun and Pančevo, localised 11 per cent. of all Yugoslav and 60 per cent. of all Serbian industry (about 24,000 workers) making it the largest single industrial centre of the Kingdom. Elsewhere, factory industries in the main towns of Osijek, Novi Sad and Subotica were interspersed with scattered mills processing agricultural produce.

Industries southward of the great fluvial divide provided

69,159 'working places' but only 52,465 jobs. Three 'zones with industry' were significant here: first, central Bosnia, where manufacturing was localised in Sarajevo and mining, sawmilling and metallurgy were dispersed along the railways linking the town with the Sava valley and with central Serbia; secondly, central Serbia, where metalworking, textiles and tobacco were located in the main transport centres of Niš, Leskovac and Kragujevac; and Dalmatia centred on Split and Šibenik, where port facilities, access to Italian markets, and proximity to raw materials and hydro-electricity had encouraged the growth of cement, aluminium, chemicals and shipbuilding. Large areas of Bosnia-Herzegovina, Serbia, Montenegro and Macedonia virtually lacked industry because of poor accessibility and poverty; even larger towns like Banja Luka, Mostar, Vranje and Bitola were without anything but handicrafts.

Broad indications of the regional distribution of industry today and of the change from the 1938 pattern that this represents are evident from statistics of employment in mining and manufacturing given in Table 20. Clearly the north is still

TABLE 20

CHANGES IN REGIONAL INDUSTRIAL EMPLOYMENT, 1938–64

	1938		1964	
	Nos.	%	Nos.	%
NORTHERN YUGOSLAVIA	186,650	77·7	708,554	56·8
Slovenia	51,494	21·5	211,964	17·0
Croatia-Slavonia	68,945	28·7	292,725	23·4
Vojvodina	40,265	16·7	120,858	9·7
Belgrade	25,946	10·8	83,007	6·7
SOUTHERN YUGOSLAVIA	52,465	23·2	538,275	43·2
Bosnia-Herzegovina	24,526	10·5	179,654	14·4
Dalmatia	7,620	3·4	39,250	3·1
Serbia Proper*	12,620	5·5	201,370	16·1
Kosovo-Metohija	1,892	0·1	26,728	2·1
Macedonia	5,715	2·6	67,954	5·5
Montenegro	295	0·01	23,769	1·9
TOTAL YUGOSLAVIA	238,115	100	1,247,279	100

Sources: Statistika Industrije Kraljevine Jugoslavije, Belgrade, 1941.
　　　Statistika Radničkog Osiguranja, Zagreb, 1940.
　　　Statistički Godišnjak SFRJ, 1964, pp. 562–85.
* Excluding Belgrade.

the more important zone, with over 708,000 industrial workers in 1964—nearly four times the number so employed in 1938. Equally evident, is the uneven geographical distribution of industrial growth, for industries southward of the Danube—Sava employed over 538,000 workers or ten times the pre-war number. Contrasting growth rates caused, therefore, a radical change in the relative importance of the north and the south. The spatial dichotomy of industry has tended to fade. Today the north accounts for 56·8 per cent. of industry, compared with nearly 78 per cent. in 1938, while the share of the south has been increased from 22·2 per cent. to 43·2 per cent.

Growth has been slowest in Vojvodina: it lacks materials for basic growth industries, its output of agricultural produce for industrial processing has expanded relatively slowly and its strategic position became vulnerable after the Cominform break. Somewhat quicker industrial expansion in Belgrade, Slovenia and Croatia has followed from the responsibility of manufacturing industries in these areas for supplying plant and chemicals for new industries elsewhere in the federation. Except for Dalmatia (where industry is of long-standing), all regions of southern Yugoslavia have experienced rapid industrialisation; growth rates here have been far above average because the policy of developing these areas was aided by the availability of vital raw materials and energy, and reinforced by their strategic isolation. Employment in Bosnian industries expanded less rapidly than in the other backward regions because of the dominance there of heavy, capital-intensive activities. Indeed the increased industrial importance of the south since 1938 owes more to industrialisation in the east and south-east, in Serbia, Macedonia and Montenegro where 300,000 new jobs (30 per cent of all new federal jobs) have been provided. Their combined share has consequently risen from 8·2 per cent. in 1938 to 25·6 per cent. in 1964. While this 'shift' in industrial location towards the centre, south and east does considerable credit to the government's efforts to develop the backward regions, nevertheless, the *absolute* increases of employment, and the intensity of new jobs in mines and factories per 1,000 population, have been greater in the north (521,900 new jobs or 68 per 1,000) than in the south (485,800 jobs or 45 per 1,000).

The more detailed current geographical pattern of industrial employment is given in Figure 18. Two distinct features emerge: first, the wide dispersion of mining and manufacturing and second, the continued concentration of industry in the main centres of pre-war industry.

Dispersion increased as new manufacturing plants were opened in areas which lacked industry thirty years ago. Whole areas have received their first factories since 1945: the inland Karst, western Bosnia, Herzegovina, Sandjak, south Serbia, Kosmet, Montenegro and much of Macedonia. In these regions, medium-sized and even small towns have gained their first factory industries as a consequence.

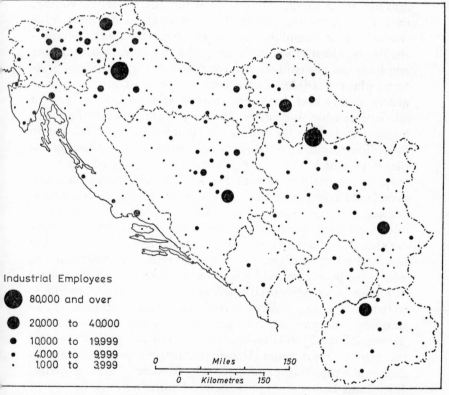

Industrial Employees

- 80,000 and over
- 20,000 to 40,000
- 10,000 to 19,999
- 4,000 to 9,999
- 1,000 to 3,999

0   Miles   150

0   Kilometres   150

Figure 18. The Location of Employment in Mining and Manufacturing

Q

Examples are: Banja Luka and Bihać (Bosnia), Mostar (Herzegovina), Nikšić and Titograd (formerly Podgorica) in Montenegro, Valjevo and Vranje (Serbia) and Bitola, Titov Veles and Tetovo (Macedonia). The opportunity for increased dispersion given by the construction of several hundred new industrial plants, i.e. by the 'spatial elasticity' of postwar industrial development programmes, was reinforced by several considerations. In part it was appropriate to the establishment of new industries with new locational needs processing hitherto unexploited or exported raw materials: refractories and insulators, cellulose, chemicals (using natural gas), electricity and processed foods. Widely scattered sources of bulky, low-in-value raw materials have also contributed to dispersal. So, too, has the fact that two-thirds of postwar investment has gone into industries which usually process raw materials near source: energy, metallurgy, non-metallic minerals and timber-processing. The 'mobility' of major energy supplies—hydro-electricity, electricity from lignite, oil and natural gas—and the emphasis on electrification have made the operation of scattered plants feasible. Large regional pools of surplus labour nearly everywhere have encouraged widespread location of labour-intensive industries (textiles, light engineering and leather) to reduce the total socio-economic costs of labour by providing employment where people already live rather than in places to which they must migrate and be housed. Political pressure on the government has stimulated interregional dispersal of factories as equitably as possible among the republics. Strategic circumstances after 1948 strengthened that pressure and weakened government resistance to it: federal unity depended on dispersion. Nevertheless, industrialisation has involved selective dispersion, avoiding remote mountain areas, which are poorly served by communications and which appear in Figure 18 as substantial blank areas, but clearly spreading to settlements along valleys served by major railways. Outstanding, for example, is dispersion along the following lines: Trieste/Rijeka-Ljubljana-Maribor; Rijeka-Zagreb-Varaždin; the international route Jesenice (Austrian frontier)-Zagreb-Belgrade-Skopje-Gevgelija (Greek frontier); and Prijedor-Jajce (and Doboj)-Sarajevo-Mostar-Dubrovnik.

Nevertheless, thirteen towns (with over 15,000 industrial

workers each) contain one-third of all Yugoslav industry (Figure 18). The wide spacing of most centres, however, means that there are in fact no zones of highly concentrated urban-industrial activity. This results largely from the scattering of postwar establishments, since the thirteen towns in question received only one-fifth of all new industrial plants, though the average size of those they did receive was larger. The near lack of reliable and detailed statistics of the industrial importance of towns before 1953 makes analysis of postwar change almost impossible. It is certain, however, that Zagreb, with 96,000 industrial workers in 1964, has replaced Belgrade (now shorn administratively of Pančevo), with 83,000 workers (or 90,000 including Pančevo), as the largest manufacturing centre. While the share of Belgrade in Yugoslav industry has declined from 10·8 per cent. to 6·6 per cent. since 1938, that of Zagreb has increased from 5·1 per cent. to 7·7 per cent. Whereas administration and services have taken pride of place in Belgrade as federal capital, industrial expansion in Zagreb results from its existing manufacturing capacity, its excellent communications with all regions, its proximity to the ports (Rijeka and Split) and from its pool of labour skilled in crafts which have become the major growth industries of postwar Yugoslavia: engineering, electrical products and chemicals. Latterly, too, continued expansion of textile, shoe and food industries has been stimulated by the greater funds available in the city since decentralisation. Belgrade has enjoyed similar advantages. So, too, have other centres where capital-goods industries have expanded: Ljubljana and Maribor (35,000 industrial workers each); Sarajevo, Niš, Novi Sad and Skopje (20–30,000); and Rijeka, Osijek, Zenica, Kragujevac and Subotica (15–20,000). Bosnian and Croatian towns in particular have increased their share of Yugoslav industry. Only four of the thirteen centres mentioned, however, lie south of the Danube and Sava. This underlines a basic interregional difference in the geographical impact of industrialisation: in the north the expansion of existing centres of manufacturing has been dominant, in the south the multiplication of new mining, processing and manufacturing centres. In short, the growth of employment has been more dispersed in southern Yugoslavia.

GOVERNMENT POLICY AND INDUSTRIAL LOCATION
(1) Principles of Socialist Location[13]

These changes in distribution result from the interplay
between the location principles that the government applied to
industrial growth on the one hand and the spatial elasticity of
that growth, a concept which consists in the possibilities
offered by the nature and extent of new industrial development
for fashioning new distribution patterns on the other. Industry
had been selected as *the* vector of economic progress, the major
weapon for fulfilling the aims of policy discussed in Chapter 6,
and specific socialist principles were regarded as essential to the
correcting of the contrasts, left by previous capitalist development, between 'growth' regions of increasing industrial agglomeration and 'problem' regions of contracting or over-special-
ised industry, and between natural resource regions which
lacked industries and developed industrial areas which lacked
natural resources. The first Five-Year Plan established three
principles of location: the 'even' spatial distribution of industry;
location near sources of materials and fuel; and the 'correct
distribution' of new plants.[14] These concepts have never been
officially defined or clearly explained, but a good deal can be
gleaned from works by socialist economists and deduced from
location in practice.

The ambiguous principle of 'even' location demands the
long-term allocation of proportionally more new industrial
capacity to the backward, lower-income, unindustrialised
areas to permit their more rapid development and progressively
greater interregional equality. This produces wider dispersal
of industry—to all regions of the country and to an increasing
number of centres within each region and tends to reduce the
extreme pre-war inter-areal differences in employment structure
and national income. Industrial dispersion *has* been increased
and backward areas *have* been considerably developed since
1945 by applying this principle. Without it, the pre-war
dichtomy between north and south would inevitably have been
intensified as the sharp inequalities in economic and social
environments (existing industry, transport, infrastructure,
literacy and productivity) would have more strongly favoured
northern areas. Dispersion was in fact demanded by political
considerations: the creation of more nuclei of proletariat labour

sympathetic to communism in the peasant countryside, the nationalist pressures from the republics and autonomous areas, and the strategic needs of federal defence. Government control of the allocation of investment made it possible.

The second principle, the development of industries near the sources of materials and the fuel they use, may appear to stem from the Weberian concept of material-orientation when industries process weight-losing, bulky, low-value materials. This is true in so far as the socialist concept of increasing productivity includes decreasing the 'social effort' involved in the process of production (including transport) from the material source to the market. Rather in the light of the writings of Marx and Lenin, the Yugoslav government saw in the development of processing and manufacturing industries near the material and energy resources localised in backward areas a major weapon for creating greater wealth and employment there. These industries could utilise much of the increased material output though some still had to be sent to the developed north for processing in existing industries. Lenin's concept of the industrial *Kombinat* or 'combine' as an integrated complex of plants processing materials into high-value finished products in one location, was invoked to give practical force to this principle. Although the location of such combines in backward areas could result in higher transport costs on finished articles, it is argued that these costs are offset in the long-run by greater plant efficiency, greater utilisation of waste and by the very creation of markets merely with the process of developing backward areas, i.e. by creating high added-value in manufacture in those areas, so that transport costs on products are eventually reduced.

The third principle, the 'correct distribution of new plants' is vague. Research[15] has shown, however, that it includes the following. Industries should be dispersed singly or in groups to form centres of adequate labour-supply regions so that populations from villages and small towns do not have to seek employment in distant centres. The aim here is to avoid or to reduce two types of social cost: commuting, which congests scarce transport facilities and reduces productivity, and urban housing which raises investment costs and lowers investment efficiency. Industries should be located where raw materials and social capital (e.g. transport facilities) are under-utilised, providing that alternative locations are no better. Industries which process light 'imported' materials, which produce high-value products and which are labour-intensive should be located in overpopulated areas which lack local natural resources. Industries which employ women should be located in areas of heavy industry to diversify employment and production and to use local labour resources rationally. Finally, every location decision should involve the 'complex' planning approach to dovetail plant location into the whole system of spatial linkages between that plant and other plants, settlement, transport networks and land uses.

In summary, industrial location in Yugoslavia has been guided by the application of the three basic principles of economic policy in their spatial guise: to achieve rapid economic development by choosing locations giving the greatest effectiveness of investment and the least 'social' effort in plant operation (i.e. including transport); to use resources fully by locating plants where materials, energy and labour can be harnessed most effectively; and to achieve greater interregional equality by allocating proportionally more industry to backward areas.

(2) The Course of Locational Change, 1945–48

Already during the reconstruction period, 1945–47, the government began re-shaping industrial distribution patterns. War-destroyed plants in the northern periphery were not rebuilt. In contrast, areas transferred from Italy—Istria, west Slovenia, Rijeka and Zadar—and scheduled as backward areas received 36 new factories between 1945 and 1955. These processed local materials (non-metallic minerals, timber, food) or served local shipbuilding markets; their purpose was to provide greater prosperity locally to stabilise a politically unstable area.

More radical changes, however, resulted from the physical concentration of many workshops in northern Yugoslavia into fewer, larger factories, particularly within 'mobile' industries, metalworking and textiles. In Serbia[16] 305 works were concentrated into 116 factories by 1951, in Belgrade alone 97 into 21. Such concentration provided larger nuclei of scarce skilled labour, better and cheaper opportunities for future expansion, larger-scale and better integration to expand production immediately. Complex plant re-location movements accompanied concentration. Re-location of scattered rural plants increased industrial concentration in larger towns. The transfer of equipment led to greater specialisation of towns on a narrower range of larger industries, with a tendency to concentrate engineering in larger towns, which could attract skills, and textiles and leather industries in smaller towns. As republic governments managed small industries, there was little inter-republic re-location of industry. The largest interregional movement involved the net migration of 63 works from Vojvodina to Serbia Proper, which increased industrial concentration in Belgrade but also provided 'ready-made' employment in backward Sandjak and south Serbia during the Cominform blockade, just when the need to develop backward areas to counter Soviet propaganda was greatest and the ability to do so, for lack of capital, was least.

The first Five-Year Plan proved to be the most fundamental document in postwar industrial development. It established basic location principles and suggested many projects which, although abandoned during the Cominform blockade, were revived after 1956. The original plan stressed the growth of heavy industry and, while over-ambitious in scope, was realistic in three broad aims: first in expanding regrouped engineering industries in the chief towns of the north and east to provide nuclei of projected industrial 'cores' in each republic and to supply equipment for industrialisation in backward republics; secondly, in achieving, on the model of Soviet economic regions, certain balances in each republic between self-sufficiency in engineering and in industries processing dispersed resources (energy, timber, minerals and food) and specialisation in heavy industries according to local resources and comparative advantages—lead, aluminium and heavy engineering in Slovenia; oil-processing, chemicals, electrical and lighter engineering in Croatia; copper, lead, non-metallic minerals and heavy engineering in Serbia; and ferrous metallurgy, fuels, chemicals and aluminium in Bosnia-Herzegovina; thirdly, in developing light industries (textiles, food and leather) in Macedonia and Montenegro until resources for heavy industries had been investigated there.

Progress in fulfilling the plan before the Cominform resolution of June 1948 indicates an overwhelming concentration of new engineering, electrical, chemicals, textile and rubber-manufacturing capacity in the north-west (in Ljubljana, Maribor, Rijeka and especially Zagreb), in the north-east (Belgrade-Zemun and Novi Sad) and along the Morava (Kragujevac, Kruševac, Kraljevo and Niš). Clearly high priority had been accorded to expansion, as the pre-condition of industrialisation elsewhere, in areas where existing plant, skilled labour and better infrastructure made growth cheaper and quicker. Economic co-operation between Yugoslavia and the Soviet bloc at this time also encouraged such localisation, as nodes along the Drava/Sava-Morava axis offer excellent locations for industries processing materials from, and manufacturing products for, East-Central Europe and the mineralised mountain regions of Yugoslavia. The location of the aluminium industry near Maribor to process Hungarian bauxite using Slovenian hydro-electricity provides an example.

(3) The Cominform Blockade, 1948–54

By terminating supplies of 95 per cent. of all capital equipment required by the Five-Year Plan and by applying military pressure, the Cominform countries in 1948 forced the Yugoslav government and Federal Planning Commission to revise radically industrial development strategy to reflect the realities of the new situation. Enforced dependence upon restricted domestic capital compelled planners: (1) to abandon 'unessential' projects in consumer food, textiles and leather industries, which virtually stopped industrial construction in Pannonia and backward south-eastern Yugoslavia, and (2) to change locations planned for essential heavy industries from underdeveloped areas where costly infrastructural facilities were lacking to developed areas where, as additions to existing plants, projects would incur the lowest investment costs in plant and ancillary services. Thus the steel project for Doboj (Bosnia), a virgin location, was abandoned in favour of extensions to plant at Zenica (Bosnia).

Threats of Soviet attack resulted, too, in the hasty development in 1949–50 of defence industries which had not been planned before. Their location, dictated by the strategic needs of the new situation, radically modified the distribution of engineering in particular: all defence factories were dispersed from each other and from existing industrial centres throughout the less accessible backward, mountain regions of central Bosnia, central Serbia and the Karst. The locational disadvantages of this general area were offset as far as possible by locating all plants (1) along the narrow-gauge railway system between Karlovac, Sarajevo, Dubrovnik, Belgrade and Bor to give mutual interlinkage for supplies of copper, steel, components and explosives; (2) near existing fuel and power supplies; and (3) along with new towns which could attract from the northern towns the skilled labour that was lacking locally.

The blockade also compelled Yugoslavia to depend entirely upon indigenous natural resources. The Planning Commission responded to these circumstances with a programme of 90 'key industrial projects' for construction between 1949 and 1952 financed entirely centrally and vetted by the Defence Ministry. This programme specified 75 new projects designed to satisfy domestic demand in energy, minerals, metals, timber and their products from domestic resources and to increase exports of manufactures. Two-thirds of the key projects were part of the original five-year plan. Their dispersal, chiefly[17] in the mountainous central, eastern and southern Yugoslavia, results from the prevalence of raw material-oriented activities: mines, power stations on major rivers and in major coal basins, and factories processing bulky, but varied and scattered materials (iron in Bosnia, non-metallic minerals in Serbia and Macedonia, timber and cellulose in Bosnia). Textile mills were located in Herzegovina and Macedonia, first to process locally-grown cotton, wool and silk in overpopulated areas to create the maximum possible local employment, production and income, and, secondly to encourage peasants in those areas to increase their supplies of textile fibres to replace imports. Construction of these plants went ahead as originally planned, except that the Defence Ministry required the dispersed *siting* of factories. Thus, three refractory and ceramics factories using clays from Arandjelovac (Šumadija), for example, were allocated among three settlements—Bukovik, Arandjelovac and Mladenovac—a few miles apart. Such siting placed the industries centrally in adequate labour-supply areas.

Most remaining projects (metallurgical, engineering and electrical) had been revised following the Defence Ministry's prohibition of new development in exposed Vojvodina and Slavonia, in large towns or in high concentrations. Thus the great Doboj iron and steel project was replaced by scattered capacities located at Zenica and Ilijaš (Bosnia), Sisak (Croatia) and Nikšić (Montenegro). Here strategic factors had economic support, for the change enabled the steel industry to make more effective use of domestic resources, using oil fuel at Sisak, and hydro-electricity in electro-iron production at Ilijaš and electro-steel production at Zenica and Nikšić, with a saving of bituminous and coking-coal imports. A similar instance was that of a cable factory, originally planned for location in Belgrade,[18] which was in fact developed at Svetozarevo 80 miles further south, nearer to sources of copper, lead and fuel in Serbia and no further from major cable markets.

The same cannot be said for other plants. Economic factors in location choice were ignored, in the face of strategic demands, by centralised and administrative planning, which fixed prices uniformly for the whole federal market area and thus made transport costs appear to be zero. Two projects, for instance, the Sevojno copper-rolling mill (Serbia) and the Nikšić steelworks, were located at great distances from their materials; these have to be brought over 150 costly miles of tortuous narrow-gauge railway and substantial backhauls are necessary to take metal products to engineering plants. Administrative haste led also to the location of the coke plant at Lukavac (Bosnia) and a ceramics factory in Zagorje (Croatia) near materials which later proved useless for manufacture.

The dispersal of key projects was not only a response to federal strategic needs in exploiting scattered resources. It was a response to a political situation in which latent instability, exploited by Cominform propaganda, among the peoples of Yugoslavia, demanded the relatively equal dispersal of projects among the republics, especially those whose backwardness justified genuine discontent. This explains the allocation of steel and ceramic industries among three republics, of eight textile, five electrical and five metal-working industries among five republics (including Kosovo-Metohija) in southern Yugoslavia. The Nikšić steelworks, built to provide a heavy industry for a backward republic with few natural resources but powerful Parliamentary representatives, is the best example. Although, then, the backward areas lost many light industries, they gained many strategic and key industries during the Cominform blockade; their share of gross investment[19] in mining and manufacturing consequently increased from 19·6 per cent. in 1947 to 35·1 per cent. in 1952.

(4) Transition to the New Economic System, 1952–56

The system of uniform prices, in disregarding transport costs, encouraged many inefficiencies in the centralised allocation of flows before 1952, as, for example, in the 400 mile two-way exchange of lead concentrate between Slovenia and Kosovo. Introduction of the new economic system in 1952 led to some rationalisation of flows since transport costs and demand now influenced selling prices, sales revenues affected workers' pockets and workers had power to improve production and locational efficiency. 'Political' factories, like the Nikšić steelworks, were destined for a subsidised life even before production commenced. Workers' councils began to influence the location of industrial growth as increasing funds were left in the enterprise and at their disposal. This gave them power to re-invest those funds in expanding the enterprise itself *without* federal control or to invest in a branch plant located elsewhere if this were approved by the Investment Bank.

Decentralization began as early as 1950 when textile and leather industries, followed subsequently by other consumer-goods' industries, coal, electrical and chemical industries, were transferred from federal to republic control. *Effective* decentralised decision-taking, by workers' councils and local and republic authorities backed by their own funds, became a reality in 1952. The federation, however, retained far more control over investment decisions in industrial development than in any economic sector. In 1957 it was still financing 50·3 per cent. of all industrial investment (cf. only 34 per cent. of all economic investment) and in 1964, 25 per cent. The slowness of this decline reflects the twin facts that 'key projects' continued to be financed from the General Investment Fund in the mid-fifties and that large 'guaranteed investments' were allocated to backward areas, 1954–64, for plant construction to give some compensation for the disadvantages to them of decentralisation. Federal control over investment and location, however, was greater (50–80 per cent.) in basic industries, while republics and local authorities (communes after 1957) had greater control over light industries, the federation providing 25–40 per cent. of investment in food-processing, non-metallic minerals, building materials, textiles and timber industries, and under 15 per cent. in leather and printing industries.[20]

Such decentralisation has had four important consequences. First, increasingly, new 'mobile' industries have been duplicated between republics, where growing demand, especially for consumer products, went unsatisfied. For example, until 1951 only one factory, located in Belgrade, manufactured radios; by 1958 eight were doing so, two of them 'key projects' in Serbia and Montenegro, the others financed by local funds and located in Ljubljana and Koper (Slovenia), Zagreb (Croatia) and Kragujevac (Serbia). Generally, plants financed by local (commune, factory or republic) investors were developed in the more advanced areas.

Second, far greater absolute growth of industrial employment along the Sava-Morava axis than in the backward regions has resulted from local investments in labour-intensive textile, leather, printing and electrical industries, which were already localised along that axis. These industries could be cheaply expanded without federal control but at the same time the requirement of plans after 1953 was for more consumer industries. This fact is not invalidated by the localisation of key projects in southern Yugoslavia for, while, between 1952 and 1957, the key projects provided 56,000 jobs, the extension of existing industry and the growth of new plants with decentralised funds provided 322,000 new jobs.[21] Thus industrial employment has been increasingly localised in developed regions, industry in Slovenia, Croatia and Serbia providing 484,927 jobs between 1952 and 1965 while industry in Bosnia-Herzegovina, Sandjak, Macedonia and Montenegro provided only 132,792 jobs.[22] Guaranteed investments have aided the substantial growth in Serbia (by 226,100 jobs), Macedonia (47,170) and Montenegro (19,181); their lack has exposed Bosnia-Herzegovina (66,450), with its heavy industry, to the full disadvantages of decentralization. Meanwhile growth in

Slovenia (100,000) has become greater. The third and fourth effects of decentralisation, the emergence of the commune as the basic government unit and the financing of branch plants by large concerns and their effects on industrial location are discussed later.

Characteristic of the period 1952–56 was the evolution of a system of location choice which compared alternative locations for given projects using cost analyses or 'rentabilities'. These analyses were still of limited utility, as subsidies and semi-controlled prices were common. Open competitions, organised in 1955 as 'trials' for allocating new capacity in food-processing industries, were still methods of the future. Major industrial plants financed from the General Investment Fund were still planned centrally by the Federal Planning Institute and located according to the 'rentabilities' of areas selected by the Institute anywhere within the federation, or within the region specified if guaranteed projects for backward areas were in question. Between 1954 and 1956 this system was applied to viscose, cellulose and fertiliser factories for general allocation and to guaranteed projects already designated for Northern Istria (Zone 'B' of Trieste—motor vehicles and cement), Kosovo (fertilisers) and Macedonia (electro-chemicals, steel and sugar-refining).

An analysis of one project of the first type and one of the second is given here as an example of the method; it may be compared with that of open competition (see pp. 244–251). The first example is the Viscose Factory located at Loznica, Serbia (Figure 19). Federal planners compared four areas where water supplies were sufficient for such a plant: the river valleys of the middle Sava (Croatia), the Sana and the Bosna (Bosnia) and the lower Drina (Serbo-Bosnian border). To compare their 'rentabilities', calculations were made of costs of plant and workers' housing, material-transport, labour and depreciation; these are given in Table 21. Clearly, a location in the Sana valley offered lowest economic and social investment costs whereas a location in the Drina valley offered lowest production costs, primarily through lower transport costs. Since the continued production-cost advantage (174 million dinars annually) of the Drina would offset the initial investment-cost advantage (1,010 million dinars) of the Sana area in under six years,

TABLE 21

COSTS OF LOCATION OF A VISCOSE FACTORY
of 20,000 tons capacity in Four Alternative Areas, 1954
(in million dinars)

	Sava Valley	Sana Valley	Bosna Valley	Drina Valley
INVESTMENT				
Plant	11,600	10,800	11,800	11,690
Housing	710	1,030	1,150	1,150
TOTAL	12,310	11,830	12,950	12,840
ANNUAL PRODUCTION COSTS				
Raw materials (at source)	4,500	4,500	4,500	4,500
Transport of materials	220	320	180	130
Lignite or Brown Coal	392	392	400	354
Wages	204	204	204	204
Depreciation	971	927	984	981
Management costs	375	375	375	375
TOTAL	6,662	6,718	6,643	6,544

Sources: P. Gustavson, 'Problemi Izgradnje Tvornice Viskoze u Hrvatskoj',
    Ekonomski Pregled, 1952, p. 143.
    Ekonomska Politika, March 1954, p. 738.

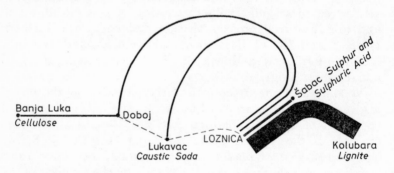

Figure 19. Patterns of how Material Supply to the Viscose Factory
of Loznica

the choice of the former area was obviously the most economic.
   Figure 19, showing the location of the Drina plant in relation
to sources of materials and to transport lines, suggests, however,
that Loznica was not the obvious location choice. High
transport costs on heavy, low-value sulphuric acid from Šabac,
compared with low costs of hauling cellulose from Banja Luka,

required a location near Šabac; a location between cellulose and soda producers in the Bosna valley would have involved higher costs of sulphuric acid. Transport costs alone, however, show Šabac to be the least-cost location since such a location would clearly eliminate the additional costs of (1) hauling sulphuric acid, sulphur and zinc sulphite from Šabac to Loznica, (2) hauling cellulose, soda and fuel which must pass through Šabac anyway to reach Loznica and of (3) back-hauling viscose fibres from Loznica. Several factors favoured Loznica, not Šabac. The priority for developing backward areas when such a location is highly economic was important as no industry existed at Loznica to employ labour in an over-populated area. Several industries exist at Šabac; construction of another plant would have necessitated much greater housing provision there than at Loznica. Viscose production requires pure environments; these were lacking at Šabac where air and water are polluted by sulphuric acid, zinc-electrolysis and fertiliser factories. Greater proximity to hydro-electricity supplies from Zvornik was desirable. The 'dynamic' or long-term socialist approach was also important, namely, that Loznica will *become* the least-cost assembly-point for materials from Banja Luka, Lukavac-Šabac and Kolubara when railways, planned to link Tuzla and Valjevo, are completed (Figure 19).[23]

Guaranteed investments were introduced in 1954 to finance plants designated by the Federation for development in backward areas. The plants, chosen according to the *potentialities* of the areas concerned, may be as economic in backward regions as elsewhere: for example, aluminium and timber-processing in Montenegro, non-metallic minerals and chemicals in Kosovo and Macedonia, all based on local resources. Nevertheless, the guarantee restricted comparative locational analysis and provided the Federation between 1954 and 1964 with an opportunity to develop large industries in under-developed areas for socio-political purposes.

An example will illustrate the point. The Annual Plan, 1953, scheduled an integrated steelworks for construction in Macedonia to provide the heavy industrial basis for a 'take-off' there in metal-fabricating industries. Delays in constructing the plant were lengthy (more than five years before the site was cleared) chiefly because technological and economic problems of producing iron and sheet steel from the only local resources, low-grade phosphoric ores from west Macedonia and semi-coke from Kosovo lignite, were formidable. Undoubtedly Skopje is the best location for assembly and distribution in south-eastern Yugoslavia, but it is an economic location only within this area; costs of expanding steel production in Bosnia would have been far lower. These considerations were subordinated to the need of utilising resources and providing employment locally in the one republic without a steel industry, to lengthen the life of Bosnian ore resources and to make more effective use of spare transport capacity on railways in south-eastern Yugoslavia rather than to overburden already congested lines in Bosnia. Cost-benefit analysis was thus invoked to justify what was basically a political decision. Economic reforms since 1965 with their emphasis on economic profitability, however, would make the construction of such a plant far less likely today.

(5) The Period of Open Competition, 1957–65

The system of open competition for loans from the General Investment Fund became the major means of deciding the location of the industrial growth broadly outlined by the Second Five-Year Plan (1957–61). This system shifted responsibility for location planning to the local authorities and workers' councils who wished to compete, while retaining sufficient Federal control of investment allocation to ensure fulfilment of broad goals. While, however, only 42 per cent. of industrial investment came from federal sources between 1957 and 1963, the very fact that new plants or significant extensions to old plants were beyond the resources of most enterprises and communes meant that they had to compete for loans from federal sources. In this way the federation actually controlled the use of 70–75 per cent. of all industrial investment.

The system is analysed here with reference to the competition, run in 1958–59, for the construction of new sugar-processing factories. The Plan required an increase in domestic sugar-processing capacity from 1,350,000 tons in 1962, with a longer-term plan to attain 3,700,000 tons by 1966. Existing works were to have their mean capacity for daily processing (assuming a normal season's activity of 100 days) increased from 13,500 tons to 17,500 tons and new factories with mean daily capacity of 19,500 tons established. The competition related only to *new* factories. Nineteen would-be investors sought loans to construct plants in specified locations. Details of investors, of the location and size of plant they proposed, and of loans required to cover construction costs of plant, housing and infrastructure are given in Table 22.

The Investment Bank calculated that the most economic scales of sugar-processing plant were from 1,000 to 2,000 tons daily capacity; this requirement was a condition of competition. Loans were to be allocated to those applicants who could satisfy the following criteria:[24] first, the best sugar-beet supply conditions, in volume, in beet-procurement costs (i.e. production costs and transport) and hence the lowest production costs per unit processed sugar; second, the largest sugar output per unit of capital cost input, i.e. the lowest capital costs per unit sugar output; third, the offer of the largest contribution to investment costs from the investors' own budget; fourth, the shortest period of plant gestation to full production; and fifth, the offer of the shortest period for repayment of the loan without interest.

Clearly, investors (e.g. the workers' council of the food combine at Zrenjanin) could propose to develop several plants if they possessed sufficient funds of their own to cover almost entirely the costs of most plants (as at Sećanj and Novi Bečej). Investors could propose to locate plants as additions to existing works (e.g. the workers' councils of the Županja and Crvenka refineries), or in their own communes, especially by peoples' committees of sizeable market towns (15–30,000 population) which have little manufacturing industry (e.g. Požarevac, Virovitica, Peć and Bijeljina). Yet investors could also propose to develop plants in other locations, workers' councils favouring areas with better material-supply conditions and peoples' committees, especially of more developed communes, favouring development in backward, purely rural areas of the same district or republic (e.g. proposals for plants at Sivac, Jasenovac, Ludbreg and Ormož).

Having analysed the voluminous documentation submitted for each project with information on plant costs and material-supply and labour costs, Investment Bank experts chose

R

TABLE 22

The Sources of Demands for Grants for Constructing New Sugar Factories, the Size and Location of Projects Proposed and the Investment Loans Required, 1958

INVESTOR	Location of Proposed Plant	Capacity (tons beet per day)	Loan required million dinars	Loan per Ton capacity (million dinars)
WORKERS' COUNCILS OF:				
Food Combine, Zrenjanin	Sečanj (Vojvodina)	1,000	276·7	0·276
Food Combine, Zrenjanin	Senta (Vojvodina)	2,000	4,149·5	2·075
Food Combine, Zrenjanin	Novi Bečej (Vojvodina)	1,000	304·8	0·304
Sugar Refinery, Belgrade	Kovin (Vojvodina)	1,500	3,607·6	2·40
Sugar Refinery, Vrbas	Bačka Palanka (Vojvodina)	1,000	1,939·3	1·94
Sugar Refinery, Vrbas	Stari Bečej (Vojvodina)	1,000	1,883·1	1·88
Sugar Refinery, Županja	Županja (Croatia)	1,500	2,305·3	1·53
Sugar Refinery, Crvenka	Crvenka (Vojvodina)	1,500	2,635·9	1·75
PEOPLE'S COMMITTEE OF COMMUNES				
Novi Sad	Novi Sad (Vojvodina)	1,500	2,630·3	1·73
Sombor	Sivac (Vojvodina)*	800*	1,121·7	1·00
Sremska Mitrovica	Sremska Mitrovica (Vojvodina)	2,000	4,711·2	2·35
Požarevac	Požarevac (Serbia)	1,500	3,570·3	2·38
Šabac	Šabac (Serbia)	1,500	3,525·1	2·35
Nova Gradiška	Jasenovac (Croatia)	2,500	4,875	1·95
Varaždin	Ludbreg (Croatia)	1,500	2,020·8	1·35
Virovitica	Virovitica (Croatia)	1,500	2,344·0	1·56
Maribor	Ormož (Slovenia)	1,500	2,878·0	1·92
Bijeljina	Bijeljina (Bosnia)	1,500	unspecified	—
Peć	Peć (Kosovo-Metonija)	1,500	2,785·2	1·85

Source: Vesnik Investicione Banke, December 1958, p. 20.

* Later altered to a project for a 1,500 ton capacity plant at Sombor to qualify for competition.

fourteen of the nineteen projects as suitable for development.[25] Their construction was scheduled in three phases: first, at Senta, Kovin, Sremska Mitrovica, Županja and Peć by 1963; secondly at Požarevac, Virovitica and Bijeljina by 1964; and third, at Sećanj, Novi Bečej, Novi Sad, Sombor (instead of Sivac), Ludberg and Ormož by 1966. Demands for loans to build capacities at Bačka Palanka, Stari Bečej, Crvenka, Šabac and Jasenovac were not approved.

Low investment costs per unit capacity were decisive in approving sugar-refining development at Sećanj, Novi Bečej, Novi Sad and Sombor. High investment costs and size too big to permit supply from within the economic transport limit for low-value, bulky beets excluded the Jasenovac project. Plants chosen for Požarevac, Kovin, Sremska Mitrovica and Senta required greater federal loans than those which were not approved for development at Stari Bečej, Šabac and Bačka Palanka. There were several reasons for this choice. The former factories were to be developed in high yield beet-growing areas, where refineries were lacking, or in areas which did not have direct rail connection with existing refineries. The latter were at least as costly to finance as factories approved for Novi Bečej, Sremska Mitrovica and Novi Sad respectively, which draw supplies from similar areas. The three plants not approved could obtain beet only at higher cost because of poorer communications, supply-areas overlapping with those of existing refineries at Vrbas and Crvenka, and less intense beet cultivation by area (and hence longer hauls), especially around Šabac. Further development at Vrbas and Crvenka would have also required extension of supply areas beyond the economic transport limit and was therefore not approved.

Unfortunately no figures are available of the costs of supplying beet, coal and lime to the proposed factories. The major cost item, however, is beet, and the volume of beet, within a given radius of a plant as determined by sown area and yield, and the transport network density are important indices of possible regional transport cost variations. Such indices point to undoubtedly lower beet-procurement costs in north-eastern Yugoslavia, whence the allocation of ten of the new refineries to this region. Lower yields or poorer transport facilities, or both, placed five factories, approved for Ormož,

Virovitica, Ludbreg, Bijeljina and Peć, at some production cost disadvantage. The large increase in sugar production, however, was far beyond the capabilities of agriculture in the north-east alone despite the localisation there of better soils and larger socialist farms, where it is easier to extend beet-cultivation. Expansion had to be achieved partly, therefore, in areas where some beet is grown or where environmental conditions are suitable. The government saw that the development of factories in these areas—Kosmet, the Drava valley and north-east Bosnia—would encourage peasant farmers there to change traditional farming methods and to substitute beet for other crops. Provision of refineries in these underdeveloped areas had the advantages of intensifying agriculture and of eliminating the haulage of beet to distant refineries in the north-east or in Bitola. Moreover, their more dispersed location brought them nearer to markets, so reducing transport costs on refined sugar to major markets in the western half of Yugoslavia and in the south-east, including Montenegro, which could be supplied from Peć. These five plants and those at Kovin and Požarevac also provided increased industrial, if seasonal, employment in backward areas. One further feature of the spatial allocation of new sugar factories is their dispersion among six administrative areas (Slovenia, Croatia, Bosnia, Vojvodina, Serbia Proper and Kosmet) in response to a multi-national federal structure.

Potentially this ingenious system of competition provided the Investment Bank with the opportunity of choosing *the* optimum location of different industries. In practice, however, the system suffered from many deficiencies.[26] Although the plans from which they originated contained integrated inter-sector and inter-industry balances, the competitions themselves, partly due to their variable character and to the voluminous analyses that they generated, were often treated in isolation, with important consequences. The time between initiation of competitions and the activation of plants varied greatly, frequently causing temporary bottlenecks in supply. Co-ordination in executing interlinked projects which were being analysed in different competitions was very poor. A three-year delay (1960–62), for example, in deciding the development and location of electric power stations and transmission lines, because of insufficient response by investors or poor documenta-tion of projects, caused serious power shortages in processing industries developed in Montenegro and Macedonia under competitions similarly dated 1959. The sulphate-cellulose and paper factory at Ivangrad, Montenegro, due for completion in 1964, was not in fact activated until 1966 because of delays in allocating funds under other competitions for expanding coal-production and coal-processing at the Ivangrad mine and for developing new roads in primeval forests.

More serious, however, has been insufficient co-ordination on the spatial level. The Bank's experts in deciding upon proposals in three separate competitions, for example, allocated grants for developing slaughtering facilities and meat-canning capacities in area 'A', greater livestock rearing in area 'B' and cattle-feed factories in area 'C'.[27] This underlines several problems. Unless the Federal Planning Institute provided the Bank with some guidance as to the best areas for particular projects then locational optima would be missed simply be-cause a commune which either had no initiative or no money did not apply for a loan, or alternatively because a commune had submitted an inadequately documented project which the Bank rejected. Local authorities have often failed to analyse their long-term development *possibilities* or to co-ordinate such analyses and applications for loans with those of neighbouring districts. Problems arose also even within the same commune when investors from different areas proposed projects for the one commune. Two glass-manufacturing plants were approved for location in Pula (Istria) to process local sands, the one initiated by Pula people's committee, the other by the workers' council of a firm in Zagreb. Both investors operated indepen-dently and, for lack of a local master urban land-use plan, sited their plants differently, wasting investment in duplicated separation and washing installations, communications and powerlines. Lack of co-ordination, human failures, and diffi-culties in comparing semi-artificial prices and costs[28] led, with weakened central control, to the abandonment of a fascinating experiment in controlling industrial locations.

The commune became an initiator of industrial development proposals when, in 1957, the commune was constituted the kernel of local social 'self-management'. Decentralisation to this level gives small areas, which might have been ignored under a centralised planning system, a chance to attract industries. The commune council is stimulated to attract as much new employment opportunity and productive activity as possible, since this means greater income for its own budget to improve local facilities and services. The communal system thus encourages wider dispersion of industrial plants. The political strengthening of communes has generated greater awareness in republic, district and developed-town administrations of the socio-economic problems of underdeveloped areas. Capital has thus been put aside in the budgets of more-developed republics and districts to finance small industries in backward communes. For example, in 1960, Tuzla district council (Bosnia) allotted most of its budget for the developing of textile factories in underdeveloped communes within the district, in Kladanj, Zvornik, and Bratunac.[29]

This trend towards intra-regional plant dispersion has been intensified by a further result of effective decentralisation: the greater availability of investment funds in the largest firms. That availability, sometimes sufficient to finance substantial capacity expansion, has enabled workers' councils to consider the possibility of building branch plants rather than expanding *in situ*. Branch plants have become important since 1958 in those industries which use varied materials, and components and which use processes that can be operated without physical plant integration: metalworking, electrical, textile, shoe and printing industries. Branch plants are usually developed in backward areas to provide employment where raw materials for processing industry are scarce but labour abundant, such provision also reducing labour migration to the parent enterprise in a developed centre and so reducing the burden of housing investment on the budget of the enterprise.[30] For example, in 1960 the workers' council of the 'Iskra' electrical factory in Kranj (Slovenia) decided that expansion of the size and range of production could be made more economically by constructing four branch plants in Nova Gorica, Otoče, Lipnica and Novo Mesto (also in Slovenia), where unemployed male and female labour was available, rather than expanding at Kranj, where labour was scarce and new housing for workers would be necessary. In selecting types and locations of branch plants, parent firms have ignored opportunities for reducing the costs of supplying markets distant from the parent plant. Nonetheless, small investments from large firms or developed communes have brought industries to many backward communes since 1957 and have provided an important means, additional to the 'guaranteed investments' of spreading both the means (capital, training labour, services) and the benefits of industrial growth.

The recent economic reforms have slowed new industrial building, at least temporarily. The system of open competition for capital from federal sources (the General Investment Fund) has been swept away. Federal Planning and Banking authorities retain investment initiative only for developing energy, chemicals, metallurgical and cement industries. Management of three-quarters of finance in these industries and of all finance in all other industries is now in the hands of the workers' councils of industrial enterprises or of republic and communal banks. Capital mobility has been greatly increased by inter-enterprise and inter-area investment loans. Larger manufacturing firms are increasingly investing in smaller enterprises to induce greater specialised component manufacture or in suppliers of raw materials. For example, textile-manufacturing enterprises are investing in expansion of artificial fibre production at the Viscose Plant, Loznica. A Zagreb textile firm has invested in expanded cotton-thread output at the Sinj cotton mill to guarantee material supplies. The Šabac zinc-electrolysis firm and Trepča lead-zinc firm have loaned capital to lead-zinc mine enterprises in Montenegro and Macedonia to ensure increased metal supplies. This development aims at overcoming two legacies of the 'new economic system': unco-ordinated decisions by the Investment Bank under separate competitions for essentially linked projects and unremunerative investment in raw material and basic industries which caused material shortages and excess manufacturing capacity after 1962.

By achieving parity prices and costs, the economic reform uncovered the full inefficiencies of Yugoslav industry. These resulted from semi-arbitrary prices and from small-scale plants producing many products with poorly-productive labour and equipment at high costs which, ultimately restricted sales outlets. The reform exposed that nearly half the Yugoslav industrial labour force, 600,000 workers, were employed in enterprises which operated at a loss which amounted, in aggregate, to $60 million annually. Part of the deficit originated in some 684 enterprises employing over 200 workers which were operating in 1965 below three-quarters capacity because of poor management, materials shortages, high costs and unstandardised production lines. On the other hand, the Nikšić steelworks operated at a loss of up to $3 million, or $20 per ton output, per annum because of its uneconomic location. Losses from excess transport and production costs in 'some 40 other such political factories',[31] which stand as monuments to earlier periods of greater centralisation, account for a substantial part of the total industrial deficit. The economic reform is thus causing radical changes in factory production lines and even factory and mine closures. Some of these have resulted, e.g. coal mines, from the cheapness of imports now that home prices have reached parity with world prices. Most significant of all, however, it is leading to integration of firms, e.g. for building ships.

Greater capital mobility and greater investment by manufacturing firms should certainly encourage substantial transfer from developed to less developed areas, without Federal assistance, mainly because raw materials and energy sources are localised in less developed areas. Federal funds for backward areas are being retained, however, in an effort to prevent polarisation, to the disadvantage of underdeveloped areas, between high-value manufacturing and finishing in developed areas and low-value raw material production and processing in backward areas.

REFERENCES

1 These figures are taken from *Statistika Industrije Kraljevine Jugoslavije*, Belgrade, 1941, p. 10 which quotes them as 'working places', i.e. the number of workers that could be employed if all enterprises were operating to full capacity. The total of 360,600 'working places' should be compared with a total population in 1938 of 15,384,000.

2 *Ibid*, p. 24.

3 S. Dimitrijević, *Strani Kapital u Privredi Bivše Jugoslavije*, Belgrade, 1952, p. 10.

INDUSTRY: PATTERNS OF GROWTH 253

4 Dragomir Vojnić, 'Problemi Razvoja Industrije i Industrijska Politika', in J. Sirotković, ed., *Suvremeni Problemi Jugoslovenske Privrede i Ekonomska Politika*, Zagreb 1965, pp. 107–9.

5 This 'normal model' is derived in the United Nations' publication *A study of Industrial Growth*, New York, 1963, from studies of the relation between national income, social product and the structure of manufacturing industry for 53 countries (1953) and 42 countries (1958).

6 Indeed the heavy industries, especially engineering, expanded more rapidly still since the figures given in Table 19 do not include the growth of strategic industries.

7 This is borne out by the following. While the production of iron ore in 1964 had increased by an index of 335 over production in 1939 (= 100), the corresponding indices for the production of iron, steel, rolled and drawn steel products were 1150, 660, 985 and 760 respectively. Comparative indices in other industries are: non-ferrous metals (smelted copper 120, refined copper 396; bauxite 173, aluminium 4300), metalworking (foundry metal 924, vehicles 7655); chemicals (sulphuric acid 1700, fertilisers 3125); textiles (fibre and cloth 360, clothing 885); timber-processing (logs and sawn timber 144, veneers 1900, furniture 2143, cellulose 750).

8 F. E. Ian Hamilton, 'Location Factors in Yugoslavia's Iron and Steel Industry', *Economic Geography*, 1964, pp. 51–53.

9 D. Krndija, *Industrializacije Jugoslavije*, Sarajevo, 1961, p. 135.

10 D. Vojnić, *op. cit.*, p. 134.

11 Vojnić, *op. cit.*, p. 128 and *Politika*, 24 July, 1960, p. 10.

12 Much of the following analysis of changes in the distribution and location of industry in postwar Yugoslavia is drawn from the author's unpublished doctoral thesis entitled *Recent Changes in Industrial Location in Yugoslavia*, London University, 1962, 321 p., and 53 maps. Some of the broad findings are published in the following articles: F. E. Ian Hamilton, 'The Changing Pattern of Yugoslavia's Manufacturing Industry, 1938–1961', *Tijdschrift voor Economische en Sociale Geografie*, 54 (4), 1963, pp. 96–106. F. E. Ian Hamilton, *op. cit.*, pp. 46–64. F. E. Ian Hamilton, 'The Skopje Disaster', *Tijdschrift voor Economische en Sociale Geografie*, 55 (4), 1964, pp. 76–79.

13 A survey of concepts relating to industrial location in general and to capitalism and socialism in particular may be found in F. E. Ian Hamilton, 'Models of Industrial Location', Chapter 10, in R. J. Chorley and P. Haggett, eds., *Models in Geography*, 1967, pp. 362–425. Comments made there are in part complementary to ideas stated here.

14 *Petogodišnji Plan Razvitka Privrede Jugoslavije*, 1947–51, Sections 2 and 3.

15 Hamilton, *op. cit.*, pp. 128–32.

16 *Proizvodne Snage Srbije*, Ekonomski Institut N. R. Srbije, Belgrade, 1953, pp. 369–558.

17 The 75 projects in the basic industries comprised 16 hydro-electric power stations, 9 thermal power stations (coal-fired), 2 coke plants, 1 oil-refinery, 4 iron and steelworks, 5 non-ferrous metal refineries, 15 non-metallic minerals mines, 6 non-metallic minerals processing plants, 4 cement works, 5 engineering works, 5 electrical factories and 3 chemical combines. The remaining 'light' industries included 3 key timber-processing factories, 3 cellulose-paper works, 8 textile mills and 1 leather factory. The key projects were allocated among the regions in the following numbers: Northern Yugoslavia 14 (Slovenia

9, Croatia-Slavonia 5, Vojvodina and Belgrade 0); southern Yugoslavia 76 (Serbia Proper 26, Bosnia-Herzegovina 21, Macedonia 19,
Dalmatia 4, Kosovo-Metolija 3 and Montenegro 3). The 41 factories
(excluding power stations) are located on a map in Hamilton, 1962,
op. cit., p. 82.

18 *Petogodišnji Plan*, Article 10, section 41.

19 *Investicije u Razdoblju 1947–56*, Belgrade, 1958.

20 Between 1962 and 1964 the General Investment Fund was used to
finance projects only in power, metallurgy, chemicals and paper
industries. The Fund was abolished in 1964.

21 *Osnovni Podaci o Udelu Novih Preduzeća u Industrijii*, 1952–57, Belgrade
1959, p. 13.

22 *Statistički Godišnjak FNRJ.*, 1954, 1957, 1961 and *Statistički Godišnjak
SFRJ.*, 1964, 1966.

23 A similar situation exists in Montenegro and Sandjak where a number
of strategic 'key' or 'guaranteed' projects at present poorly served by
only road or narrow-gauge railway transport are expected to become
economic when the Belgrade-Bar railway is completed, probably in
1969.

24 *Vesnik Investicione Banke*, December, 1958, p. 19.

25 *Ibid.* August, 1959, p. 4.

26 There are numerous sources on this topic. The more important are:
D. Gorupić, *Problemi Sistema Investiranja u Industriji*, Ekonomski Institut
N. R. Hrvatske, 47 (1), 1962; S. Blagojević, *Investicije i Razvoj Industrijske
Proizvodnje* Belgrade, 1961; *Vesnik Investicione Banke* 1960–64, monthly
articles; *Ekonomska Politika*, 1956–65, weekly.

27 B. Srebić, 'Nužnost Potpunijeg Obuhvatanja Teritorijalnog Aspekta
Razvoja', *Ekonomist*, 3–4, 1963, p. 689. The exact areas are not specified.

28 These points are supported by the observations of Vladimir Bakarić in
Aktuelni Problemi Izgradnje Našeg Privrednog Sistema, Zagreb, 1963.
He finds three particular aspects of the economic system reduced
its utility prior to 1965: (1) the lack of relationship between many
prices and the value and the costs of production, (2) the lack of relationship between the profits of enterprises and the incomes of workers, so
restricting the impact of competition and profitibility upon the decisions
of the workers' council and (3) the tendency for both investors and
Bank experts to consider the rentability of projects in isolation. As
regards the last point Bakarić emphasises that the oil industry only
appears to be highly profitable because investors have not included the
overhead costs of oil exploitation in calculations of investment in oil-
production.

29 *Vjesnik*, 8 March 1960, p. 5. Further details are given in Hamilton,
op. cit., pp. 167–71.

30 This holds even if the commune undertakes to finance housing since
in this case the firm will pay higher rates into the commune budget for
covering this expense on the assumption that communal housing will
benefit workers wishing to work in the firm in question.

31 Zoran Pjanić, quoted in *Życie Warszawy*, 6 September 1966, pp. 3, 5.
See also: Djordje Vrcelj, 'Potpunije Korišćenje Proizvodnih Kapaciteta
Jedna od Osnovnih Preokupacija Preduceća, U Novim Uslovima
Privredjivanja', *Ekonomika Preduzeća*, 14 (8), 1966, pp. 559–65. *Yugo-
slav Life*, 6, 1966, pp. 6 and 11, 1966, p. 6.

CHAPTER 13

The Major Manufacturing Industries

References to particular industries have been made hitherto only by way of illustrating the methods of location selection and the trends in industrial distribution in different postwar periods. Attention here is turned to developments in the major branches of manufacturing. Such a study should help a deeper understanding of the operation of industrial location *factors* in the Yugoslav economy.

ELECTRICITY GENERATION

Marxists have deemed electrification the key to progress ever since Engels noted its potentialities for bringing industry and a proletariat to rural areas—implying its utility for dispersing industry, for developing backward areas, for achieving greater 'evenness' in industrial distributions. That the chief Yugoslav energy resources—water and low-calorie coals—are eminently suited to electricity generation provided an added stimulus to Tito's government to expand output rapidly—from 1,181 million KWh (1939) to 14,182 million KWh (1964). Such growth permitted important changes in the power industry. Five-hundred tiny generating units averaging under 250 KWh installed capacity were closed and over 100 new larger stations, averaging 40,000 KW capacity, were brought into operation and linked to a grid. Hydro-electric power stations (installed capacity 3,070 MW) have replaced coal-fired stations (2,570 MW) as the more important source of power because of the abundance of water power and running costs of only a fifth to a third of those of coal-fired stations. Yugoslav thermal electricity-generating stations are relatively high-cost producers because they burn, on average, 4,900 Kilocalories coal per KWh electricity compared with a world average of under 3,900 K.calories.[1]

Other factors account for a substantial expansion of thermal electricity-generating capacity. Lower capital costs and shorter periods of construction were vital considerations while capital was scarce and power demands growing rapidly. Coal-fired stations were indispensable in the Alpine and Dinaric upland areas where loads are great and where hydro-electricity supplies suffer from extreme seasonal fluctuations. Moreover, most of the larger brown-coal and lignite basins, with their poorly transportable coal, offered good locations for thermal power stations because of their proximity to major urban-industrial load centres in the 'white coal-deficient' areas of Pannonia, Serbia and Macedonia. Certain new stations, burning better brown coal from Kakanj and Banovići (Bosnia), have been constructed, however, in the load centres of these areas (e.g. Subotica, Zrenjanin).

Nevertheless, the lack of an interregional 110 KVA grid network until 1960, and the continued lack of *adequate* links, has demanded the location of most new stations near new load centres of power-intensive heavy and 'key-project' industries, especially in underdeveloped areas. The spatial dispersal of suitable water-power and coalfield sites in these areas was initially an important permissive factor, but the construction of a better 220 KVA grid network is encouraging greater localisation of generating capacity in larger stations on rivers with greater power potentials (e.g. Cetina, Zeta, Drina and Danube) and in larger low-cost coal basins (Velenje, Zenica-Sarajevo, Kreka, Kolubara, Kostolac and Kosovo) to reduce electricity-supply costs.[2]

The pre-war dominance of generating capacity in northern load centres (Maribor, Zagreb, Rijeka, Osijek, and Belgrade) has been reduced by the growth of most new capacity in all mountain and coalfield areas of the centre and south. This 'migration' represents the response both to the need to utilise resources more fully and to serve changing spatial patterns of power demand more satisfactorily. Nevertheless, in practice, power shortages in Slovenia and Croatia have been serious because of priority for expanded generating capacity elsewhere. No plans foresee the generation of electricity from hydrocarbon fuels since these scarce resources are more valuable for chemical-processing, while water and coal have little alternative utility; nevertheless, one station, at Sisak, is fired by oil-refinery and blast-furnace gases.

Power-availability has been a decisive locating factor only with electro-chemical and electro-metallurgical plants. These have been developed near large suppliers of cheap hydro-electricity from the Drava, Cetina, Drina, Zeta and Vardar rivers. After 1957, electricity rates, which had formerly varied between republics, were fixed uniformly for the whole federation, with the result that power costs, played little, if any, role in the location of power-generating and power-using industries.[3]

METALLURGY[4]

Over 92,200 people were working in Yugoslav metallurgical industries in 1965, compared with only 16,050 in 1939. Such substantial growth has resulted from priority investment to develop metal-smelting from domestic resources and especially metal-rolling and finishing for domestic and foreign demand.

The pre-war steel industry was neither balanced nor integrated. High-grade Ljubija ores were exported and low-grade Vareš ores were virtually unutilised, while pig iron was imported to meet the requirements of steelworks in Bosnia, Slovenia and Serbia. Heat economies were lost and high transport costs were incurred in hauling pig iron by railway from ironworks at Vareš, Sisak and Topusko to steelworks at Zenica, Jesenice (the largest and only 'integrated' plant) and elsewhere. Growth in steel capacity, from 315,000 tons in 1939 to 2 million tons in 1966, has facilitated important adjustments in the industry. Central Bosnia, with 55 per cent. of all coke, iron, steel and rolling capacity localised in Zenica (1965), has replaced Slovenia as the major steel-producing area. This reflects the location of resources of ore, non-coking fuel, and power and an economic advantage derived from moving imported coking-coal to low-grade ore and not vice-versa. Clearly the industry has become more raw material-oriented, in line with the government's location principles. High-cost peripheral plants in Slovenia and Serbia have been reorganised rather than expanded by integrating iron and steel production, by substituting electric processes for traditional methods to save on coking-coal imports, and by expanding quality-steel output to offset inherited cost disadvantages.[5] New steel plants developed at Sisak and Ilijaš, following the Soviet blockade, were too small, but their locations near resources and served by good transport were economically sound. Plants located at Nikšić and Skopje, however, are high-cost producers because of isolation from materials and markets in the former and problems of using low-grade ores and fuels in the latter. Their construction was undertaken in response to strategic needs, socio-economic advantages of providing 'location-leaders' for backward areas of surplus labour and transport capacity, and political pressure from 'have-not' republics for heavy industries.[6]

In 1958 a fifteen-year development plan was adopted to increase steel output to 3·2 million tons by 1972, localising nearly all new capacity at Zenica (to reach 1·7 million tons) and at Skopje (to reach 900,000 tons). Although in 1963 this target was brought[8] forward to 1969, the present rate of development is not encouraging, there being a 500,000 short-fall of both iron and steel production in 1965. That steel is cheaper to import (450,000 tons of steel products were imported in 1964) than to produce underlines other problems within the industry. Costs are high. Diseconomies of small scale raise costs substantially in all but the Zenica plant. Zenica, however, suffers from high-ore and coke inputs which resulted, until 1966, from the lack of ore-enrichment facilities at Vareš. The mixing of imported coking coals with Ibar bituminous and best Bosnian brown coals increases coke costs by raising coal inputs and lowering coke quality. Moreover, the Lukavac (Tuzla) coke-plant, having failed to produce metallurgical coke from local brown coal in 1951, consumes imported coal and burdens the industry with the costs of non-integration (lost gases) and of coke transport over 310 miles to Jesenice, 190 miles to Sisak and 80 miles to Zenica. Finally, imports of scrap are substantial and costly, waste has risen and the expansion of quality-steel output has been hindered by the difficulties of training unskilled, often illiterate, peasant labour, which daily commutes up to 30 miles to work.[9] One result of these difficulties in the light of the 1965 economic reform is the changed long-term plan, involving the expansion of existing capacity at Smederevo (Serbia)[11] to produce 500,000 tons of iron using Banat natural gas to supplement coke by 1968. This may mark the beginning of a reorientation of growth from interior areas to the Sava–Danube–Morava axis (see Chapter 16) and to the coast.

Unlike steel, non-ferrous metallurgical industries are major export industries; between 1946 and 1957 they supplied 20 per cent. of all exports by value. Pre-war smelters, located near expanding mines and flotation plants to reduce bulky ore transport, have been increased in size and integrated with new refineries since 1947. These are located at Bor (copper), Trepča and Mežica (lead-zinc), Celje (zinc) and Zajača (antimony). Copper, formerly exported as blister (30,000 tons) or rolled in Slovenia (10,000 tons), is now almost entirely processed in modern American-equipped plants in Serbia, being refined at Bor (50,000 tons), rolled and alloyed at Sevojno (50,000 tons) and manufactured into cables at Svetozarevo (45,000 tons). Such 'regionalisation' of the industry could have achieved greater economies had strategic considerations not ruled out integration of rolling with refining at Bor or with cable manufacture at Svetozarevo.[11] Increased production from existing lead-zinc refineries is absorbed by a new zinc-electrolysis plant at Šabac using cheap power from Zvornik (Drina) and gaining integration economies by supplying by-product gases and zinc for sulphuric-acid production in an adjacent chemical combine. Similarly, chrome is now refined and processed in an electro-metallurgical/chemical combine located near Tetovo (Macedonia) near chrome mines and cheap electricity from Mavrovo (Vardar).

These are highly localised activities. For aluminium industries on the other hand the main inputs—bauxite, coal, caustic soda and electricity—are available throughout the underdeveloped Karst of three republics, Croatia, Bosnia-Herzegovina and Montenegro. Capital shortages, however, have meant that, despite great potential, aluminium production is still small, even though it increased from 1,800 tons (1939) to 36,000 tons (1965). Locational planning has been poor, partly at any rate because of competing political pressures. In 1947 most of the planned capacity (50,000 tons alumina and 30,000 tons aluminium) was allocated to a new plant at Strnišče (Ptuj, Slovenia) near cheap hydro-electricity from the Drava stations but 170 miles from Istrian bauxite. Later, an existing integrated plant located at Šibenik (Dalmatia), within 20 miles of bauxite (Drniš), coal (Siverić) and hydro-electric power (Krka river) was somewhat expanded to produce 4,100 tons alumina, 8,200 tons aluminium and 16,000 tons rolled aluminium products—thus making it dependent upon costly alumina and aluminium supplies from Strnišće! Various circumstances explain this pattern, clearly uneconomic as it now is. First, there was at Strnišće a partially-constructed German wartime plant which could be completed relatively quickly and cheaply, and in 1947, nearby Hungarian bauxite was available. Second, Dalmatia, which was not connected to the grid till 1955, had not then sufficient power to cater for a large aluminium industry in addition to the power-intensive industries it already had.[12] However, that Boris Kidrič, then chief federal planner, clinched the issue in favour of his native Slovenia cannot be ruled out: later Strnišće was renamed Kidričevo! Capital shortages have persistently held up plans for further expansion of the industry. For socio-political reasons, supported by purely economic considerations, priority goes to the integrated plants at Titograd (Montenegro) and Mostar (Herzegovina) for producing 100,000 tons alumina and 50,000 tons aluminium each.

NON-METALLIC MINERALS MANUFACTURING

This broad group of activities is located close to the sources of the materials processed. Building-materials industries, using widespread ('ubiquitous') materials and producing bulky low-value products, however, are *market-oriented* and located near those material sources which are best situated in relation to markets. Other industries (e.g. refractory materials) are *material-oriented*, using localised materials and producing higher-value products. Being among the oldest industries in Yugoslavia, some of them originally export-oriented, the cement, glass and brick industries[13] have required adjustment since 1945 both to greatly increased, and to changing spatial patterns of, demand. Localisation of pre-war cement producers in Dalmatia and Istria (to supply Italy) and in Trbovlje, Zagreb and Beočin meant costly transport to distant, yet major postwar growth centres in Bosnia, Serbia and Macedonia. New plants, increasing output from 900,000 tons (1939) to 3,200,000 tons (1965), are located, therefore, near Paraćin,

Čačak, Skopje and Kakanj to serve regional markets[14] and at Split and Umag (Istria) to maintain exports. Similarly brick and glass outputs have increased most in Bosnia, Serbia and Macedonia.

Many new activities are located in backward areas. Non-metallic minerals in Šumadija, unused in 1941, are now manufactured into refractory, porcelain, asbestos and ceramic products in an important industrial complex around Arand-jelovac and Mladenovac. Chrome-magnesite refractories have been produced at Kraljevo since 1954 using west Serbian magnesite and Macedonian chrome. Silica bricks and insulating materials have been manufactured at Gostivar and Prilep (west Macedonia) since 1957.

FOREST PRODUCTS INDUSTRY

Substantial forest resources and vital timber export markets explain why timber-processing and paper-manufacturing rank third among Yugoslav industries by value of output and employment. Far-reaching changes since 1939 have enabled the industry to maintain its importance. Wartime destruction and postwar rationalisation by the republic planning authorities have reduced the number of sawmills from 401 (1939) to 253 (1965), removing substantial excess processing capacity. Sawmills located in areas of inadequate local timber-supply, especially those mills in 'developed' Pannonia which consumed timber floated down Bosnian rivers from 'backward' areas, were closed, removed and concentrated in better supply-areas. New mills were developed to tap primeval forests in Montenegro and Macedonia. Federal investment has expanded most substantially secondary manufacturing, especially of veneers, plywood and furniture, and chiefly in central Yugoslavia. Integration of fifty new timber-manufacturing plants with sawmills in Bosnia (as at Bihać, Zavidovići, Blažuj-Sarajevo, Foča) and northern Montenegro (Mojkovac, Rožaje) has reduced the importance of Slovenia and Croatia (30 plants). Despite the construction of furniture factories in backward, material-source regions in line with government principles, furniture manufacture is still localised in major centres of consumption, skill and better transport in Serbia, Croatia and Slovenia.

S

The introduction to Yugoslavia (1952) of the sulphate-cellulose process, permitting the use of beechwood and pine in cellulose manufacture, gave Bosnia and Montenegro, with large deciduous and coniferous forests, decisive locational advantages for cellulose-paper industries over Slovenia and Croatia where spruce and fir supplies, required by the sulphite-cellulose process, are diminishing and beechwood is scarcer. The sulphite-cellulose newsprint factory developed in 1951 at Videm-Krško (Slovenia) thus imports Bosnian coniferous timber and cellulose, raising costs substantially. Later combines, therefore, ate localised in Bosnia at Prijedor, Drvar[15] (sulphite-cellulose), Banja Luka and Maglaj (sulphate-cellulose) and in Montenegro, at Ivangrad.

FOOD, DRINK & TOBACCO INDUSTRIES

These industries, in contrast, have declined in importance: investment has been low in agricultural production, in manufactured-foods production and in the road transport and refrigeration facilities that would permit areas distant from processing-plants to supply perishable produce. Seventy per cent of production is localised in northern Yugoslavia, food-processing and canning in major supply areas of bulky or perishable grains, fruits, vegetables, oilseeds and sugar-beet, industries producing weight-gaining drinks, bread and confectionery in major city markets. In the light of regional demand and supply there is excess capacity in the north and insufficient capacity in the south, a legacy of the former dominance of Austro-Hungarian capital. Steps have been taken to remedy this situation. Through rationalisation, the present 330 factories produce five times the output of 1,374 factories[16] in 1939. New processing plants have been developed, especially in Serbia and Macedonia, but also in Bosnia-Herzegovina, Slavonia and Vojvodina. These are sometimes integrated with co-operative farms to guarantee sufficient supplies of produce, especially of crops new to backward areas, as, for example, tobacco-manufacturing at Skopje and Titograd, tomato-processing at Negotin (Serbia) and Opuzen (Herzegovina), sugar refining at Bitola and Peć. Tobacco-processing is still underdeveloped in Macedonia. Market-oriented industries are underdeveloped in the Dinaric and coastal region, beer, for example, being supplied more cheaply by sea from Trieste than by railway from Pannonian breweries.

CHEMICALS

Foreign entrepreneurs had already developed heavy chemicals before 1918 to process resources locally—salt, limestone, water-power, non-ferrous metal by-products—into soda (Lukavac), carbide and cyanamide (Jajce, Maribor, Omiš), sulphuric acid and fertilisers (Hrastnik, Celje, Subotica) for Austro-Hungarian markets. Between 1918 and 1938 Yugoslavia developed light chemicals industries. producing soaps, dyes and paints, chiefly in larger urban markets. Output of heavy chemicals, including new products, has been expanded rapidly since 1938 to substitute domestic production for imports in growing home markets. Expansion has been concentrated in a few regions, often in existing plants (e.g. at Šabac, Kruševac and Celje) to save capital, and in new integrated plants to exploit efficiently the complex interlinkages and numerous by-products arising from multiple division and synthesis of gases and liquids effected during chemical processes. Thus, nitrogen-fertiliser and sulphuric-acid plants have been integrated respectively with the Lukavac coke-plant, the Bor and Trepča metal-smelters to use their formerly wasted by-product gases. Electro-chemical plants have been located near both raw-materials and hydro-electricity supplies; 'Jugovinil', Split, producing plastics from carbide and chlorine, and 'Jugohrom', Tetovo, producing carbide and cyanamide from chrome by-products. Good transport facilities for assembly and distribution decided the development of superphosphate-fertilisers at Prahovo and Kosovska Mitrovica (using sulphuric acid from Bor and Trepča respectively), nitrogen-fertilisers at Pančevo and Kutina (using local natural gas), and petro-chemicals at Zagreb using Slavonian gas and oil-derivatives from expanded refineries at Sisak, Brod (consuming Slavonian oil) and Rijeka (consuming imported oil). Plans made in 1952 for nitrogen-fertiliser factories using coal from the major lignite basins still await approval, with the exception of the plant at Velenje (Slovenia) which is now under construction. The presence of skilled labour, good labour-training facilities and a chemical tradition have encouraged the growth in

Zagreb of industries producing tars, dyes and film, and in Ljubljana of the first artificial silk factory in Yugoslavia. Pharmaceuticals for similar reasons are localised in Zagreb, Ljubljana, Belgrade and Skopje.

METAL-WORKING, ENGINEERING & ELECTRICAL INDUSTRIES

These industries evolved, chiefly after 1918, from repair workshops in northern and coastal towns. In 1939 engineering and electrical industries were still very tiny; only simple metal-manufacturing of wire and tools was more developed. By comparison, postwar growth, especially of engineering and electronics, is spectacular. The fifth largest industrial group in 1939, employing 20,610 workers, it now occupies first place, employing 310,000 workers. Growth has been achieved in three ways. First, pre-war workshops were amalgamated to increase scale and specialisation. Thus, seven workshops previously manufacturing metal castings, structures, chains, boxes and machinery were amalgamated into one plant at Sombor (Vojvodina) to produce building machinery.[17] Second, selected workshops were expanded into large factories: the 'Rade Končar' electrical engineering plant in Zagreb, which today employs 8,000 workers, for example, grew from a Siemens workshop where, in 1939, 60 men assembled radios. Third, over 150 completely new plants were built to manufacture new products: roller-bearings, machines, motor-vehicles, tractors and electronic products.

The availability of skills and better labour-training and transport facilities encouraged planners to localise *both* workshop expansion *and* new factories in medium- and large-sized towns in a crescent from Trieste through Belgrade to Leskovac. This ensured the continued dominance in engineering of the Sava-Morava axis and the significant spread of only simpler metal-manufacturing to the backward republics, except for machinery to Sarajevo and to strategic plants located in Bosnia. Pre-war experience often determined post-war speciali-sation in expanded factories supplying federal markets, e.g. earth-moving equipment at Kruševac, railway vehicles at Brod and Kraljevo. Research shows,[18] however, that plants were usually planned to meet the needs of markets which they were well located to serve. Linkage is well exemplified by the localisation in Rijeka, the major port and shipbuilding centre, of factories producing dockyard cranes, marine engines, telegraph equipment, pumps and welding gear. Factories producing industrial, building and mining machines and consumer goods are scattered, each to serve a specific regional market. Most metal and electrical consumer-goods factories are located in Ljubljana, Maribor, Zagreb, Subotica, Belgrade-Zemun-Pančevo, Kragujevac, Niš, Sarajevo and Skopje. Exceptions to this rule include isolated strategic factories and light metal and electrical industries located in overpopulated areas to provide employment and to create high-value products (as in Karst areas) or to reduce commuting to large towns (as in villages near Zagreb and Belgrade).

TEXTILE, LEATHER & RUBBER INDUSTRIES

These became the largest pre-war Yugoslav industries, employing one-third (62,000) of the industrial workforce in 1939, as a result of the introduction of high tariffs on imported manufactures (1920–32), the abundance of cheap labour and the willingness of large foreign firms (e.g. 'Bata', from Czechoslovakia) to enter Yugoslav markets. Despite low investment priorities since 1945 textile, leather and rubber-manufacturing has provided more *new* jobs (183,000) than any other group except engineering.

Important structural readjustments have been made by expanding: first, cotton-spinning to supply thread to formerly idle weaving mills; second, cotton-cloth output to reduce the market dominance of woollens; third, clothing and rubber-manufactures to reduce costly imports; and fourth, leather-manufacturing to substitute exports of finished goods for exports of hides and skins. The dominance of traditional producing areas—the north-west (Kranj, Zagreb, Varaždin and Maribor) and the north-east (Osijek, Subotica, Belgrade and Vinkovci)—continues as a result of early postwar plant rationalisation, expansion after 1952 which was financed from local city and enterprise sources, and existing skills, for example, in clothing manufacture at Varaždin and in shoes at the largest combine (formerly 'Bata') at Borovo-Vukovar. Nevertheless, many new plants have been located to provide labour-intensive and rapid capital-accumulating activities in backward areas. In 1965, therefore, the pre-1878 Turkish areas produced 19 per cent. of the textile thread, 10 per cent. cloth, 25 per cent. clothing, leather products and 20 per cent. rubber manufactures produced in Yugoslavia as compared with 0 per cent. in 1939. Certain new textile mills at Mostar, Štip, Tetovo and Veles, are located near cotton, wool and silk supply resources. Recently the workers' councils of these mills established branch plants in nearby labour-surplus rural areas. While much expansion in rubber-manufacturing has been allocated to Pirot (east Serbia) where general unemployment is high, textile and leather factories have been located chiefly to employ female labour in underdeveloped areas where existing mining, forestry and heavy industries employ male labour.[19] Although it was not a factor originally in the choice of location of these plants, lower wage rates today give south-eastern Yugoslavia an important advantage for the development of light manufacturing.

Clearly, in conclusion, raw materials have been the most important industrial location factor in post-war Yugoslavia, since the dispersion of varied resources nicely matched the government's location principles. Metallurgical, non-metallic minerals manufacturing, timber-processing, food and tobacco, and chemicals industries have become more raw-material oriented. Where highly-localised materials would normally encourage localised processing, however, the need to reduce the costs of social investment and commuting encouraged dispersed *siting* of plants to different labour-supply areas in proximity to resources. Coal, because of its wide dispersion and poor quality, has not influenced location, except of thermal power stations and then only as regional power demands required. Similarly, hydro-electricity influenced the location only of power-intensive industries while the federal grid remained incomplete. Although markets are limited, the market *areas* for particular engineering manufactures have determined the spatial pattern of production lines in finishing and assembly industries, although skilled labour encouraged the expansion of existing engineering plants. As labour surpluses are widespread outside northern Yugoslavia, labour has been a permissive location factor, except for localised skills. No mention has been made of *cheap* labour as a location factor before 1964 as the principle of equal pay for equal work tended to make labour in the backward areas expensive. No mention has been made either of transport as an important location factor: the reasons why must now be examined.

REFERENCES

1 *Materijal o Privrednim Razvitku Hrvatske—Industrija, Rudarstvo, Gradjevinarstvo i Zanatstvo*, Ekonomski Institut N. R. Hrvatske, Zagreb, 1959, pp. 9–11.

2 Smaller stations on minor rivers or in high-cost coal-producing areas such as Croatian Zagorje are being developed only to augment regional supply in the absence of adequate alternative local sources and grid supplies.

3 Aleksej Šermazanov, *Razvoj tarif za Prodajo Električne Energije v Sloveniji 1945–60*, Ljubljana, 1961, p. 26.

4 See Ivan Avsenek, *The Yugoslav Metallurgical Industry*, New York, 1955, for a general analysis of historical evolution and early postwar development.

5 F. E. I. Hamilton: 'Location Factors in the Yugoslav Iron and Steel Industry,' *Economic Geography*, 40 (I), 1964, pp. 46–64. This article includes details of production costs.

6 All other republics possessed heavy metallurgical industries when the decisions were taken to build the Niksić and Skopje plants (1952 and 1954 respectively). At that time Montenegro lacked known metal resources for a major industry. Had bauxite (discovered 1953–54) been found earlier, it is doubtful whether the Niksić project would have been carried through.

7 *Metalurg*, Jan., 1960, pp. 2–5.

8 *Jugoslovenski Pregled*, 7 (9), 1963, p. 337.

9 *Statistički Bilten 101: Dnevna Migracija Zaposlenog Osoblja*, 1957, pp. 21, 22 and 32.

10 *Yugoslav Life*, 12, 1966, p. 5.

11 According to calculations given in N. Perić, *Tarifski Sistem i Tarifska Politika Jugoslovenske Željeznice u Periodu 1945–54*, (Unpublished Doctoral Thesis, Ekonomski Fakultjet, Zagreb, 1957, p. 184–5) average rolled copper delivery costs per ton to any part of Yugoslavia from Sevojno amounted to 10,875 dinars compared with 6,448 dinars from Svetozarevo-Paraćin and 5,812 dinars from Bor, the least-cost point. Copper transport from Bor to Sevojno (150 miles by narrow-gauge railway) adds (at 1956 prices), therefore, 5,063 dinars or $20·25 per ton to rolled copper delivery prices compared with costs at Bor.

12 *Problemi Privrednog Razvoja Sjeverne i Srednje Dalmacije i Dijela Zapadne Bosne, II: Rudno Bogatstvo, Energetski Izvori i Industrija*, 1953, Zagreb, pp. 129–38.

13 The oldest surviving operating plants are the glass factory Rogaška Slatina (Slovenian/Croatian border) established in 1840 and the cement works at Beočin (near Novi Sad, Vojvodina) established in 1869.

14 The locations of these new plants correspond quite closely to the least transport-cost location at the centre of Löschian-type market areas (which vary size according to plant scale) covering western and central Serbia Proper, Macedonia and Kosmet, and Bosnia. See Ivan Krešić, *Prilog Izgradnje Perspektivnog Lokacionog Modela Cementne Industrije Jugoslavije*, Ekonomski Institut N. R. Hrvatske, 1961 and Ivan Krešić, *Lokacija i Problemi Razmještaja Naše Cementne Industrije*, Zagreb, 1962.

15 A cellulose factory located at Drvar produced all Bosnian cellulose output until 1941. The plant was totally destroyed during the Second World War and not rebuilt. Bosnia did not produce cellulose again until the Prijedor plant was completed in 1952. The new cellulose factory at Drvar began production only in 1964.

16 *Statistika Industrije Kraljevine Jugoslavije*, 1941, p. 11. *Statistički Godišnjak SFRJ*, pp. 176, 424.

17 *Proizvodne Snage Srbije*, *op. cit.*, pp. 411.

18 F. E. Ian Hamilton, *Recent Changes in Industrial Location in Yugoslavia*, Unpublished Ph.D. Thesis, University of London, 1963, pp. 228–49.

19 *Ibid.*, pp. 250–70.

CHAPTER 14

Transport

Modern Yugoslavia inherited an inadequate, poorly-equipped, poorly-integrated and regionally unbalanced transport system. Even today, with less than 5 km. each of railway and asphalt road per 100 sq. km. area, Yugoslavia possesses the thinnest network in Europe outside Fenno-scandia[1] and Albania. Transport provision in relation to population density, as expressed in lengths of railway and road per 1,000 population, is also lower than elsewhere in the continent except Albania. Transport, then, severely restricts the number of locations suitable for successful commercial production, especially for secondary and tertiary activities. This is particularly true, however, in the Dinaric 'mountain core' where communications are sparse (Figures 20 and 21). It is far less true in the peripheral 'axial belts', the Sava/Drava–Danube valleylands, the Morava–Vardar corridor and the Adriatic coast, in which most of the facilities are localised (Figures 20 and 21). Conceptually, these three belts form the sides of a triangle, with the Belgrade region at the apex, the centre of transport 'gravitation' from the Sava, Danube and Morava directions. By contrast, the Dinaric–Pindus ranges prevent contact between the north-western Sava axis and the south-eastern Vardar axis on the one hand and the coastal axis on the other. Linkage of the axial routes via the best transverse routeways was hindered before 1945 in the north-west by Italian control of the Soča valley and the Postojna *vrata* ('gate') and is still hindered in the south-east by Albanian control of the Drin valley.

The three axes, however, are of unequal importance. On average there are more than 7 km. each of railway and good road per 100 sq. km. area and nearly 0·9 km. each per 1,000 population along the Sava/Drava–Danube axis in contrast with less than 3·5 km. each per 100 sq. km. area and 0·5 km. per

269

1,000 population along the other axes. Northern Yugoslavia also monopolises inland waterway facilities. It is not surprising, then, that the northern routes, serving areas of greater economic and urban development, handle 65 per cent. of the combined value of rail, road and river traffic carried in Yugoslavia or 55 per cent. of all traffic, including shipping in Adriatic ports (compare Figures 21 and 22). Until recently, the coastal axis had limited importance because the dearth of good transport lines across the Dinaric system and of good coastal roads reduced the utility of port facilities south of Rijeka. The coastal and Morava–Vardar routes each handle one-sixth of all traffic in Yugoslavia.

Economic development and transport provision are closely interrelated. Greater accessibility to area and population in northern Yugoslavia, where junctions are more frequent, distances between locations are shorter and hence transport costs are lower, stimulates the more vigorous development there of a wider range of commercial activities. Moreover, locations in the north, and also along the Morava axis, gain further cost advantages from the ease of communications along broad, gently-graded valleys and across plains. Locations in highland Yugoslavia, excluding only those in Alpine Slovenia but including those on the coast which depend on land communications, suffer the disadvantages of high transport costs which result from fewer junctions, longer distances between locations, circuitous and often steeply-graded routes, 'bottleneck' passes and lower carrying capacity. Initially, too, transport lines are far cheaper to construct in the north because of simpler engineering. Throughout highland Yugoslavia, except in the Morava valleylands, road and railway construction costs may be trebled per mile by the need for frequent tunnelling, embanking, bridging and for longer stretches of graded route per given horizontal distance covered. The new standard-gauge Sarajevo-Ploče railway, for example, threads 106 tunnels and crosses 71 viaducts along its 194 km. route. It took eight years to build and it cost $35 million supplied by the American Overseas Development Bank.

Contrasts in physique between highland and lowland do not explain, although they influence, the sharp interregional disparities in transport facilities. After all, Slovenia (19 km. of combined railway and modern road per 100 sq. km. area) has the densest network despite the dominance there of Alpine and Dinaric highlands. Vojvodina (15 km.) is second, followed by Croatia (12 km.), Serbia Proper (7 km.), Kosmet (6 km.), Bosnia-Herzegovina (5 km.), Macedonia (5 km.) and Montenegro (4·5 km.). Divided and dominantly foreign administration of the South Slav lands before 1918 (Chapter 2) is the root cause. Political frontiers terminated transport facilities abruptly at rivers or in longitudinal NW–SE through valleys, especially near the Serbo-Bosnian frontier, e.g. at Han Pijesak, Priboj and Loznica. Austro-Hungarian strategy bequeathed: first, the present north-south alignment of most communications in Slovenia and Pannonia, i.e. *across* rather than *along* the transport axis; second, the narrow gauge railway system of Bosnia-Herzegovina; third, the lack of railways in large, but no more difficult, areas of west Serbia, Sandjak and Montenegro; fourth, the lack of direct communications between eastern Yugoslavia and the Dalmatian-Montenegrin coasts; and, fifth, the lack of interregional lines across major rivers to connect Slavonia with Vojvodina, Bačka with Banat and Srem, Banat with Serbia, Bosnia with Dalmatia and Serbia, Croatia with Dalmatia and Serbia with Kosmet.

Few improvements were made between 1919 and 1941. Fifteen alternative projects had been proposed by 1927 for providing the vital direct railway link between Belgrade and the coast south of Split, but strong regional and local interests prevented its construction.[2] Instead, the State invested foreign loans in two railways, one connecting Kragujevac with Kosovska Mitrovica to give Belgrade a direct Serbian route, additional to that via Niš, to the free port in Salonika, the other connecting Zagreb via Serb-inhabited Lika with Split and Šibenik to enable Yugoslavia to import and export independently of the most accessible ports, Fiume (Rijeka) and Zara (Zadar), which were then under Italian administration. The modern growth of the port of Split dates from these years. Apart from building a short rail connection between Užice (Serbia) and Višegrad (Bosnia), the government made no attempt to construct the other 'missing interregional links' noted. Such inaction undoubtedly maintained the agglomerating influences of the inherited centripetal transport pattern around Belgrade, the new Yugoslav capital. Scarcities of capital and the lack of definitive development goals for the whole Kingdom perpetuated the *status-quo* in the economy. Existing transport routes carrying food, timber and minerals to Central European markets in exchange for manufactures continued to be adequate. There was no feeling of *need* for improvement. Indeed, by stimulating some industrialisation, the localisation of transport facilities in the north merely confirmed the utility of the existing network.

By contrast, transport improvements since 1945 have had to be on a large-scale to meet the needs of a defined policy of widespread and comprehensive economic development. These improvements have had to 'telescope' development stages by continuing railway-building to complete the basic network while also building up a network of modern roads, a shipping fleet and air transport facilities from scratch. Several inter-related factors have influenced the nature of postwar transport improvement. Broad economic development has generated more freight and passenger traffic, demanding increased capacities on most forms of transport. Thus 15 per cent. of all investment between 1947 and 1966—more than in any other sector except industry—has financed the construction of 2,200 km. of railways, some 14,000 km. of modern roads, more port facilities and supplies of modern transport vehicles. As progress depends upon harnessing domestic resources, new routes link formerly inaccessible sources of coal, ore and timber in central and southern areas with the main transport arteries, which have also been improved. Better access to overseas markets has become necessary, whence efforts to develop new Adriatic ports served by adequate communications from the interior. The tourist boom motivated the construction of the Adriatic Highway and of new airports. The quest for better economic and social integration and the opportunity to tap international traffic in transit from western Europe to Greece and Turkey inspired the building of the 'Brotherhood and Unity Highway' (*Autoput Bratstva i Jedinstva*), from Jesenice to Gevgelija via Ljubljana, Zagreb, Belgrade and Skopje. Serious capital shortages, especially after the Cominform resolution, however, have caused long delays in starting large-scale projects such as the Belgrade-Bar railway and the regulation

of the Sava river for navigation as well as in commencing
transport improvements in backward highland areas where
marginal costs are high. Foreign loans have thus financed major
projects latterly, although before 1956 extensive use was made
of large-scale 'voluntary' labour to replace capital equipment
in building key railways in Bosnia and the 'Brotherhood and
Unity Highway'.

The volume of traffic carried by Yugoslav transport systems
has quadrupled since 1939. Freight and passenger traffic has
increased on all forms of transport, except for a decline in
passenger movements by river steamer. Until 1956, the railways monopolised most traffic. Since 1956, however, expansion
has been rapid in goods' haulage by road, in inter-city coach
travel and in river freight transport. In consequence, the
proportion of total ton-miles and passenger-miles performed
by the railways has decreased from 90 per cent. (for both) in
1939 to 74 per cent. (freight) and 65 per cent. (passenger) in
1966. Absolute traffic, however, has increased from 21 million
tons and 4,784 million ton kms. and 58 million passengers
and 3,191 million passenger kms. (1939) to 77 million tons
and 18,258 million ton kms. and 225 million passengers and
12,308 million passenger kms. (1966). The growth of road
transport has been remarkable. Motor vehicles in 1939
executed only 0·05 per cent. of total ton-miles and 0·3 per cent.
of total passenger miles; today, they execute 15 and 33 per cent.
respectively. The railways have retained their dominant
rôle mainly because of their advantages for bulk transport in
the earlier stages of industrialisation, when heavy industries
expand rapidly, and because of their advantages over lorry
transport for lighter products while Yugoslavia still lacks in
any real sense a network of modern roads. Even as such a
network takes shape, however, the greater comfort and convenience of coach travel, especially where railway facilities
are poor, enabled the roads already in 1966 to carry more
passengers (280 million) than the railways (220 million).

THE RAILWAYS[3]

Yugoslav Railways (*Jugoslovenske Železnice*) operate 11,850
km. (7,365 miles) of track, which is less, for instance, than
Belgian Railways operate.[4] Not only is the length of railways

short, their carrying capacity is extremely low. Only 9,265
km. of line are standard gauge (4' 8½" or 1·5 m.); the remaining
2,585 km., or more than one-fifth, are narrow-gauge railways,
the carrying capacity of which for a given distance is barely one-
third of that of standard-gauge lines. Only 6 per cent. of the
total network is double-tracked, the remainder, including all
narrow-gauge railways, being single track upon which trains
may pass only at stations. Only a third of all lines is horizontal,
two-thirds are inclined, with 15 per cent. inclined at more than
1 in 100. Although more than 67 per cent. of line is straight,
some 22 per cent., mainly narrow gauge, is sharply curved
with radii of less than 500 metres. In consequence, train speeds
are substantially reduced. Indeed, until 1964, commercial
train speeds on the main Jesenice–Belgrade–Gevgelija line
averaged only 40 km.p.h. (25 m.p.h.), on other standard-gauge
railways, 30 km.p.h. (19 m.p.h.) and on narrow-gauge railways
only 20 km.p.h. (12 m.p.h.).[5] Only 2,300 km. permanent way
is fit for speeds of 80 km.p.h. (50 m.p.h.) and only 3,000 km.
can sustain axle loads of 18 tons. In addition, over half the
railway traffic is hauled by steam traction and half the rolling
stock and locomotives are more than 40 years old.[6] These
factors combine to raise operating costs markedly; they are
increased further by costs of transferring freight between gauges.

Differential carrying capacities have geographical significance. The transport contrasts between lowland and highland
earlier outlined are accentuated by the localisation of higher-
capacity standard-gauge railways along the northern and
eastern transport axes, while low-capacity narrow-gauge
railways are largely confined (Figure 20) to the mountain core
bounded by the rivers Una, Krka, Sava, Kolubara, Ibar and
Vardar and by the coast. Double-tracked railways link
Ljubljana and Belgrade and 'parallel' single-track railways
via Niš and Kraljevo link Belgrade and Skopje; elsewhere
railways are single-track. Tariffs, for hauling freight over given
distances in the 'core' region, as fixed since 1 January 1966 by
regional railway administrations,[7] exceed those for the main
transport axes by up to 25 per cent.[8] Costs of transferring
freight between standard 1·5 m. and narrow 0·76 m. gauge
lines at Prijedor, Slavonski Brod (until 1948), Sarajevo, Metković (since 1966), Belgrade, Kraljevo and Gostivar (0·60 m.

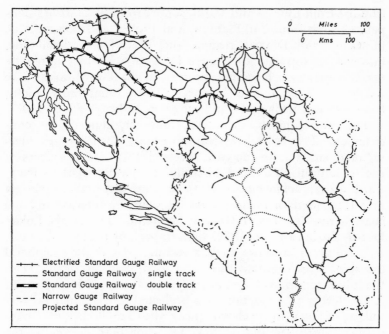

Figure 20. The Railway Network

gauge) form a spatial 'tariff frontier' which accentuates the economic disadvantages of the 'core' region. Yugoslavia, in effect, then, is divided between two poorly-integrated railway systems, giving highly unequal competitive ability to the areas they serve.

By 1949 voluntary labour had largely made good 6,000 km. of war-destroyed permanent way and 1,600 bridges. Further railway improvement also began with massive assistance from youth, who built nearly 300 miles (500 km.) of *Omladinske Pruge* (Youth railways), chiefly in Bosnia.[9] Apart from double-tracking parts of the busiest, 'spinal' Belgrade-Ljubljana railway, all new lines were constructed southward of the Danube-Sava. There, too, standard-gauge railways are gradually replacing narrow-gauge railways. New feeder lines to trunk railways have facilitated the development of the mining and processing of resources in isolated areas to serve federal markets: coal from Raša, Kreka, Banovići, Kolubara and Despotovac, iron-ore from Ljubija and Vareš, copper from Bor and Majdan-pek, chrome from Šar Planina, and timber and non-metallic minerals from Dinaric regions and Macedonia. Lead-zinc, however, is supplied to Trepča from new Kosmet mines by aerial ropeway. Regional centres in backward areas like Titograd, Prizren and Zadar (30,000 inhabitants each), have received their first standard gauge railways since 1960.

The most important changes, however, concern the con-struction of new railway-transport axes to improve inter-regional contact, to increase accessibility to the resources of the 'mountain core', and to stimulate development in back-ward areas; achievement of these aims depends chiefly on providing modern railway links between the interior and the coast across the broad Dinaric highland. The Banja Luka–Doboj–Tuzla railway (1952) links important towns and indus-trial resources (iron-ore, fuels, salt, timber) with the peripheral transport axes (manufactures and food) and Sarajevo. With the standardisation of the Čačak–Kruševac line (1963), however, it also forms a key section of a projected longitudinal railway linking Rijeka to Prahovo (near the Timok–Danube con-fluence) via Bihać and Valjevo, i.e. a southern parallel of the Ljubljana–Belgrade trunk route. As other links (Ogulin–Bihać, Tuzla–Valjevo) do not yet exist, freight en route from eastern Yugoslavia to the ports has been hauled usually via Belgrade, Brod and Zagreb to Rijeka; narrow-gauge routes to Dubrovnik and Ploče have been avoided as far as possible because of high transport and transfer costs. This explains the concentration of freight along the Sava axis and northward to the Sava axis from the highland Yugoslavia (Figure 21). To rectify the situation the government ordered the construction of the Una railway (Bihać–Knin) in 1949 to give Croatia-Slavonia shorter and faster connections with Split than the Lika railway which heavy snowfall often closes in winter. A second standard-gauge railway, Vrpolje–Sarajevo–Ploče, replacing narrow-gauge lines, was also built to give north-eastern Yugoslavia a shorter route to the coast. Completed only as far as Sarajevo (1947) this line did not begin to relieve the roundabout Brod–Zagreb–Rijeka route until the standard-gauge Sarajevo–Ploče railway was completed in 1966. Both this and the Brčko–Banovići line facilitated interregional exchanges of timber, minerals and fuel from Bosnia with foods and manufactures from northern Yugoslavia.

The main gap in the network is still a direct railway from the Morava–Vardar corridor lands through Sandjak to the Montenegrin coast (Figure 20). The Belgrade–Bar railway (c 492 km. long) will shorten the haul of goods for export from, or import to, Belgrade by 150 km. as compared with the Rijeka route. Planned two decades ago, however, its construction has been delayed by shortages of capital, materials and skilled engineers, by the costs of tunnelling one-sixth of its length (80 km.),[10] and by the uncertainties of long-term hydro-electric power barrage plans along the route. When complete and linked by new or improved railways with Tuzla from Valjevo, Prahovo from Titovo Užice, Sarajevo from Priboj, and Macedonia and Kosmet from Bijelo Polje (Figure 20), the railway will become a trunk route, a 'zonal multiplier' for the economy of the eastern two-fifths of the federation. This new network, by integrating industrial resource and food-producing areas more effectively, will assist in eliminating a loss to the Serbian economy caused by the poor transport system of around $5 million a year.[11]

Some authors hint that the Belgrade–Bar project is supported only by Serbian national whim, not by sound cost analysis since, it is argued, transport costs of freight access to Bar are higher per mile than those to Rijeka.[12] Such an argument is unacceptable if one weights up the macro-economics against the micro-economics of the project. When the railway is operational (probably in 1970) higher mile for mile transport costs should be more than offset by savings of $20–$30 million annually in federal transport costs from eliminating (1) 1,000 million net ton-kilometres freight haulage to Rijeka; (2) costly hauls of heavy goods by road transport throughout west Serbia, Sandjak and Montenegro to and from distant railheads; (3) costly narrow-gauge railway transport between Belgrade, Titovo Užice and Priboj; (4) excess idle wagon time (averaging 4 days) in marshalling yards at Rijeka because of port congestion and slow loading; (5) deficits on the short, presently isolated Titograd–Bar railway; (6) deficits of factories located along the line of the railway at Priboj, Bijelo Polje, Ivangrad and Titograd which are caused by dependence on costly road transport; and from alleviating (7) costly bottlenecks on the

T

steeply-inclined railways that mount the Dinaric 'wall' from Rijeka, Split, Šibenik and Dubrovnik. Profits expected from carrying produce of the gravitational area of the railway (greater commercial quantities of livestock produce, fruits, cereals, ores, timber, coal, manufactures) should repay construction costs in 30 years.[13] Finally, by stimulating industrialisation in some of the most backward regions of Yugoslavia, the railway should save the federation certain social costs of agglomeration, particularly around Belgrade.

Economic development after 1947 generated such increased volumes of traffic that by 1958 there were serious bottlenecks on the key 'coal railway' Brčko–Banovići, the heavy industrial line Doboj–Zenica, and on steeply-inclined sections of the Sarajevo–Mostar, Knin–Split and Zagreb–Rijeka lines. For instance, with inclines of 1 in 35 and 1 in 60 the Split–Knin railway could carry a maximum of 1,600 net tons freight daily with steam traction before 1958 and 2,200 net tons with diesel traction after 1958[14] to or from the second port and eighth town of Yugoslavia! The government, therefore, has adopted three measures to increase technical railway capacity. First, electric signalling is replacing station-by-station hand signalling to speed train movements. Second, diesel traction was introduced in 1959 on a major scale to replace the steam locomotive especially on heavily-graded railways across the Dinaric system to the ports and to Sarajevo. At present, one-third of all traffic is diesel-hauled. Third, electrification began in earnest in 1962; previously only the Rijeka–Pivka–Sežana railway inherited from Italy had been electrified. The cost of electrifying up to 3,500 km. railway is estimated at over $200 million. A loan of $70 million from the World Bank in 1965 has speeded electrification to double the carrying capacity of the key, and overburdened, Jesenice–Belgrade–Gevgelija and Vrpolje–Sarajevo–Ploče axes by 1970. It is planned to electrify other routes linking the interior with the coast after 1970 (e.g. Zagreb–Split, Belgrade–Bar) in order to attract more transit traffic through Rijeka to and from Central Europe (via Maribor and Koprivnica) and to make way for that traffic by steering more Yugoslav import and export traffic through Split, Ploče and Bar.

Problems still face the railways, however. Narrow-gauge

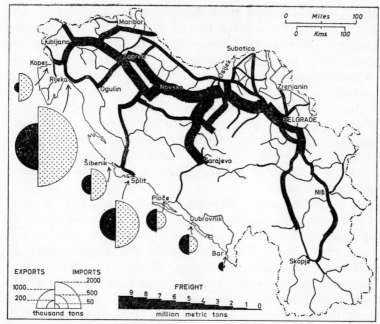

Figure 21. Flows of Freight on the Railways and Cargo Tonnages
handled by the Chief Ports, 1965

railways still form serious bottlenecks between Drvar, Jajce,
Sarajevo, Višegrad and Belgrade and between Metkovic,
Dubrovnik and Titograd. Transport costs on the 0·60 m.
gauge Gostivar–Ohrid railway are five times the Yugoslav
average,[15] virtually isolating western Macedonia from the rest
of the economy. Replacement by standard permanent-way
is essential. Meanwhile the growth of road transport has
caused financial losses on some railways in Vojvodina and
Slovenia, where lines almost duplicate each other and where
agriculture and light industry produce articles more suited
to road haulage. At present the railways carry some 80 million
tons of freight annually, mainly coal (30 per cent of all freight),
building materials (16 per cent), metal ores (10 per cent), metal
products, timber, grain and oil.

PORTS

When in 1924 the Free City of Fiume (Rijeka) was divided
between Italy (the main port, Fiume) and Yugoslavia (the

suburb, Sušak, with a small harbour), the Yugoslav government financed the construction of the Lika railway to foster commerce in particular through Split. By 1938 Split and Šibenik were handling 28 and 9 per cent. respectively of the 2·6 million tons annual Yugoslav seaborne cargo. Greater accessibility to northern industries and commercial agriculture via Karlovac–Metlika and Zagreb, however, still ensured that Sušak handled 23 per cent. Nearly 20 per cent., mainly Bosnian raw materials, passed through Dubrovnik. Lacking competitiveness with Trieste in west Slovenia and Istria, and avoided by Yugoslav traffic, Fiume, within Italy became a *città morta*.

Since 1945 commerce through Yugoslav ports has expanded to more than 15 million tons annually, following increased domestic requirements especially in oil, solid fuel, cereals, scrap, machinery and fertilisers, and increased opportunities for marketing manufactures outside Europe and for tapping Central European transit traffic. Ships now carry 10 million passengers annually as compared with 3 million in 1939. Recently, however, motor transport, using the new Adriatic Highway, has begun to make inroads into coastwise freight and passenger movements. It is thus easing the severe strain which increased traffic has imposed upon port facilities.

Changes in the Italo-Yugoslav frontier in 1945 gave Yugoslavia Rijeka in its entirety, as well as Pula (Istria). While passenger traffic trebled though Rijeka, freight movements reached the pre-war level, 2·3 million tons,[16] only in 1951, as continued neglect of war-damaged wharfage restricted port capacity and as Soviet occupation of eastern Austria together with Hungarian and Czechoslovak militancy towards Yugoslavia had effectively stifled sources of transit traffic. After 1954 trade through Rijeka expanded rapidly to reach 6·5 million tons in 1966, transit traffic accounting for 2·8 million tons and domestic traffic 1·4 million of the increase.[17] This marked change is attributable to: (1) the Soviet withdrawal from Austria (1954) and the resumption of trade with Hungary and Czechoslovakia (1955), which opened the hinterland; (2) the solution of the Trieste problem (1954), which, in allocating Trieste to Italy, effectively put an additional tariff barrier across the path of transit traffic between the hinterland and the Adriatic, and thus clinched the traffic for Rijeka; (3) tariff rebates of up to 40 per cent. for transit freight on Yugoslav Railways via Maribor or Koprivnica to Rijeka which encouraged the transfer of some Austrian commerce from Trieste and of Hungarian and Czechoslovak commerce from Hamburg. The Yugoslav port also scored an 'ideological' advantage, as well as a geographical advantage of better access to 'Third World' markets, over Hamburg.[18]

Nevertheless, the Dinaric mountains crowd in around Rijeka and severely restrict expansion of the port. It has thus been specialising more on Central European transit traffic which is seen as its optimum and maximum function,[19] a trend which has accelerated since the declaration of Rijeka as a free port in 1964. Clearly this has necessitated expansion at alternative ports to handle increasing volumes of *Yugoslav* imports and exports (Figure 21). Between 1948 and 1950 federal planning and railway experts devised a long-term idealised division of Yugoslavia into five port hinterlands[20] centring on new or improved rail communications with Rijeka, Split (with Šibenik), two new ports, Ploče and Bar, and Salonika. Rapidly changing administrative and economic circumstances after 1949, however, prevented the translation of the scheme into practice.

In fact, the federal authorities have had to face not only a technical and economic, but also a political, choice as to *which* ports other than Rijeka should be developed and modernized. Deep harbour entrances, sheltered bays, and virtually no tides or silting especially favoured low-cost expansion of such fine natural ports as Šibenik, Split (the Solun-Kaštel basin or 'North Port'), Dubrovnik and Kotor. Paradoxically, Rijeka is an artificial port, but it is by far the largest, the best equipped, and the most accessible by road and electrified railway from northern Yugoslavia. It alone transships transit freight, but poor communications with other ports mean that it still must handle 25 per cent. of Yugoslav commerce. Significantly most of the increased commerce has been channelled through Split (2 million tons more) and Šibenik (700,000 tons) because of their better inland access (Figure 21).

Elsewhere along the coast, however, each republic has been seeking to develop its own port, with an extensive hinterland

and overseas connections, in rivalry with its neighbours. Political pressure upon the central authorities at first, followed by decentralisation of investment later, has made piecemeal development feasible. Slovenia is financing entirely the development of Koper to exploit the overseas trading potential of her 'proud toehold on the sea'[21] in relieving Rijeka of 'excess' Slovenian and transit traffic. However, the project has involved financing new railway construction which could have had greater economic effectiveness as part of the Belgrade–Bar railway in a region where resources are under-utilised. In addition, certain tariff 'manipulations' by the Slovenian railway administration, which controls the branch railways to Rovinj and Pula in Croatian Istria, have been applied to make Pula with a fine harbour and existing infrastructure facilities, a less attractive outlet for relieving Rijeka than is Koper.[22] Such tactics are reminiscent of Austro-Hungarian discriminatory practice. Koper now handles 700,000 tons cargo annually, having replaced under-utilised Pula (200,000 tons) as the main port of Istria. Bosnia-Herzegovina has successfully supported the development of Ploče as a new port replacing Metković at the mouth of the Neretva river and, although requiring investment in piles in mud flats in constructing a harbour, it already had rail links (since 1966 direct standard-gauge links) with central and eastern Bosnia and eastern Slavonia. For this reason the development of Ploče, although in Croatia, was preferred to Croatian pressure for constructing an expensive new railway from Zenica to Split via Duvno and Livno to make Split the major outlet for central Bosnian traffic.[23] Ploče is already trans-shipping 750,000 tons annually, although it now handles some trade which formerly passed through Dubrovnik. The latter, poorly served by an incredibly tortuous narrow-gauge railway, handles only 500,000 tons annually (cf. 389,000 tons in 1939). Finally, Serbian, Kosovo-Metohijan and Macedonian interests support Montenegrin efforts to convert Bar into a new artificial port[24] to provide eastern Yugoslavia with 'Serbian' access to overseas resources and markets in competition with Ploče. Non-completion of the Belgrade–Bar railway, however, leaves much of the $5 million sunk in Bar largely unproductive; the port, with an annual capacity of 600,000 tons, handles only 150,000 tons at present.

From Figure 21 it will be seen that imports exceed exports at all ports, except Ploče which handles export timber and bauxite. This reflects trade patterns, the dependence of Yugoslavia on seaborne imports of grain, fertilisers, oil and scrap in contrast to greater exports of raw materials and manufactures by railway to European markets.

Inter-republic rivalry, therefore, has succeeded in reducing the dominance of Rijeka in trans-shipping *Yugoslav* freight, from 51 per cent. in 1951 to 25 per cent. in 1965, and in increasing regional accessibility to a port. The price has been a fairly equal allocation of postwar investment (c. $42 million) between Rijeka (27 per cent.) Ploče (21), Bar (18), Koper (13), Split (12) and Šibenik (9), involving a certain amount of waste.

OTHER TRANSPORT MEANS
(1) Road Transport

After reconstruction in 1947 Yugoslavia could boast a mere 1,800 km. of modern asphalt, concrete or *pavé* road which

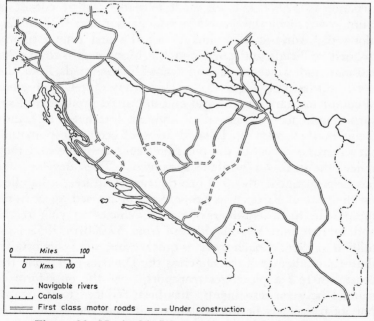

Figure 22. Navigable Waterways and Modern Roads

formed a skeleton network only in Slovenia. There were no modern inter-republic roads. Most (70,000 km.) were pot-holed macadamised or rutted dirt tracks fit only for transport by animals or carts. Fewer than 25,000 motor vehicles (including 15,000 UNRRA lorries) were available, although this compared favourably with 17,000 (mainly saloon cars) in 1939! Little changed for a decade, as road transport, except for some inter-city traffic along the new Ljubljana–Belgrade *autoput* (literally 'motorway') was restricted functionally as a feeder to, and not a competitor with, the railways.

Road transport has become a competitor since 1956, numbers of vehicles rising from 39,000 (one-third private cars) to 300,000 (two-thirds private cars), and haulage of passengers and freight respectively on public transport from 5 million tons (200 million ton-kms.) to 45 million tons (4,000 million ton-kms.) and from 37 million passengers (966 million passenger-kms.) to 280 million (2,500 million passenger-kms.). The reasons are manifold. An interregional network is taking shape since substantial World Bank loans assisted the construction of 12,000 kms. of modern road.[25] These consist of trunk roads along the Sava–Morava–Vardar axes (Figure 22), along the Adriatic coast linking for the first time formerly isolated railheads and ports and the Montenegrin coast with Kosmet and Macedonia, and trans-Dinaric roads from the north to the coast (Figure 22). These routes integrate regions of complementary agricultural and industrial produce, of food surplus and food deficit, they improve international transit facilities, they open up isolated areas of economic potential, they increase access to the ports and coastal resorts and they relieve the strain on 'bottleneck' railways. Their development has been justified. By 1959 one quarter of all freight handled by the port of Rijeka was brought to, or carried away from, the port by road. Numbers of foreign vehicles carrying freight and tourists into Yugoslavia rose from 59,000 in 1955 to 4 million in 1966. Coach travel is quicker and more comfortable than roundabout rail travel across the Dinarics and along the coast, where sea passenger transport, once the only form of contact between settlements, 'has been reduced to the transport of passengers between islands and from the mainland to the islands, to the transport of tourists during the season and tourist cruises.'[26] Along routes in east-central Yugoslavia, indeed, road transport is likely to provide serious competition for the Belgrade-Bar railway as Starivlah (T. Užice), Sandjak, Kosmet and Macedonia have received road connections with Bar in advance of the railway. Vital as both are, unco-ordinated planning of different types of transport gives road transport an important 'initial advantage' in this region. Little effort has been made in Yugoslavia to create effective division of labour, with road transport specialising in hauling loads of less than 1,000 tons daily on routes of up to 200 kms., the margin at which railway transport is more economic.[27]

Increased crediting by communal banks and industrial enterprises of the 250 road transport enterprises enabled them to expand vehicle fleets, in some cases to more than 50 lorries and coaches. Between 1957 and 1964, for example, the number of enterprises operating more than 20 vehicles increased from 99 to 155.[28] More vehicles became available, with savings in foreign currency, following the conversion of strategic factories in 1954 (e.g. 'Crvena Zastava', Kragujevac, and 'Fabrika Automobila Priboja') to the production of vehicles and components, often manufactured under foreign licences (e.g. Citroen, Fiat, Saurer). Higher priorities for agricultural progress after 1956 encouraged the people's committees of districts and communes to replace dirt tracks by macadamised roads (50,000 km.) and to improve existing macadam to increase rural accessibility as the pre-condition for commercialising farming. Still 20,000 kms. of dirt track, however, await improvement. Nevertheless, larger local credit sources, better roads, more manufacturing, commercial agriculture and urbanisation facilitated more rapid motorisation in Slovenia, where there is now 1 vehicle: 30 inhabitants, Croatia (1:90), Vojvodina and Serbia (1:125) than in Macedonia (1:175), Montenegro (1:210), Bosnia (1:240) and Kosmet (1:575).

(2) River Transport

Inland waterways (1,770 km.) are localised largely in north-eastern Yugoslavia. The Danube, the major waterway (Figure 22), carries 6 million tons of Yugoslav traffic annually, primarily sand, coal and fertiliser, and 4 million tons of transit traffic, mainly to and from the Soviet Union, Rumania, Austria and West Germany. Craft of 1,500 tons carry more than 4 million tons of cargo on the Sava river below Sisak, primarily oil products, non-metallic minerals and fertilisers. The Tisa, which can carry 1,500 ton vessels, and short sections of the Drava and Begej rivers, which 650 ton vessels can navigate, are unimportant. Upon completion, the Danube–Tisa–Danube canal will be able to handle 1,000 ton craft.

Waterway transport showed little upward trend before 1956, when 3·2 million tons domestic and 2·2 million tons transit cargo were carried. Stagnation resulted from general economic stagnation in Vojvodina–Slavonia following the Cominform blockade and the neglect of agriculture, from a tariff policy which gave railways advantages in carrying bulky, low-value goods, and from the dilapidation of river-port facilities, which made transfers between rail and river costly. General economic development at home and abroad has caused a steady rise in waterway traffic to 10 million tons domestic and 4 million tons transit traffic; movements of oil, coal, building materials and fertilisers have grown most. This has partly resulted also from the introduction of more favourable river tariffs, drawing, for instance, the transport of sand for the Belgrade building industry away from the railways, and of combined rail-river tariffs for moving products from interior regions throughout Pannonia and the Danubian lands. Modernisation has facilitated marked expansion of port traffic, first, at Belgrade which handling 2·5 million tons annually, rivals Split as the second largest port of Yugoslavia, and second, at Osijek, Sisak, Bosanski Brod, Novi Sad, Smederevo and Prahovo which handle more than 500,000 tons. Navigation is still hindered, however, by the unregulated nature of the rivers which are characterised by numerous shoals, sandbanks, sharp bends, shifting channels as well as by spring and autumn flood, summer low water and winter ice. The greatest hindrance, nevertheless, remains the dangerous Iron Gates gorge. Work now in progress on the Djerdap hydro-electric power station, however, will provide, it is hoped by 1970, locks and a deep 'lake' as far upstream as Belgrade, making navigation safe twenty-four hours a day for vessels of up to 5,000 tons. This will reduce transport costs by speeding cargo movements since these are primarily upstream (4 million tons of raw materials

compared with 1 million tons of manufactures downstream)
and at present require assistance from locomotives at the Sip
Canal against a river current which averages 18 km.p.h.[29]
Waterway traffic is expected to increase also when the Sisak
canal (B in Figure 16) links Zagreb to the navigable Sava; in
addition, a Vukovar–Šamac canal has been suggested to shorten
waterway links between Posavina, Sisak and Vojvodina.

(3) *Air Transport*

Unlike river transport, which is losing passenger business to
the buses, air transport has continually gained traffic on
account of speed. Nearly 1 million passengers now pass through
Yugoslav airports compared with 13,000 in 1939, and 93,000
in 1956. This growth is a result of greater movement of business-
men and planners between republic capitals following increased economic decentralisation and of tourists from interior
Yugoslavia and abroad to the Adriatic coast. Cheap, subsidised
fares on domestic J.A.T. (*Jugoslavenski Aerotransport*) lines
stimulated passenger flights until the economic reform substantially raised fares in 1965. Replacement of the old DC-3
planes by modern jets has permitted J.A.T. to serve more
international centres, while conversely the opening of large
modern airports at Belgrade, Ćilipi Polje (for Dubrovnik and
Hercegnovi) and Split since 1962 has encouraged more foreign
companies to use Yugoslav airports. The number of air routes
operated by J.A.T. has risen from 13 in 1939 to 70 in 1966.
Figure 23 shows the pattern of main domestic lines and airport
traffic. Two features are outstanding. First, the large number
of lines crossing the Dinaric upland from Zagreb and Belgrade
to the coast and to Titograd. Second, the fact that Titograd
handles more passengers and freight annually than any other
airport, except Belgrade. There could be no more eloquent
expression of the relative inaccessibility of the coast and of
Titograd from the north interior than this. The reason is
simple. Until 1966, a rail journey from Belgrade to Dubrovnik
and Titograd took 22 and 26 hours respectively, and by road at
least ten hours. The journey by air is less than one hour.

Rapid expansion of air and road transport, of shipping and
of railway dieselisation has greatly increased the demand for oil
and oil derivatives in Yugoslavia in recent years and far

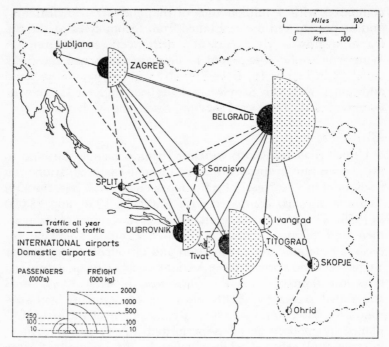

Figure 23. Domestic Airlines and Traffic at Major Yugoslav Airports 1965

beyond the capacity of domestic sources. Imports, chiefly from the Middle East and the Soviet Union, have become necessary. To cope with the increasing quantities that have been congesting railways between Rijeka and refineries at Sisak and Brod, as well as the Danube and Sava navigation to the same places, a 36″ pipeline is under construction to link a new deepwater oil port at Bakar, near Rijeka, for 100,000 ton tankers with refineries at Sisak, Brod and Pančevo. When complete in 1970 its capacity will be 20 million tons.[30] Existing gas and oil pipelines are of local importance only.

TRANSPORT & THE LOCATION OF ECONOMIC ACTIVITIES

The foregoing stresses that regional differences in transport facilities, carrying capacity and costs have favoured location, especially of manufacturing industry, marketing and servicing establishments, along the three, though especially the northern, transport axes. Federal government policy acknowledged this, among other things, in developing most manufacturing industry along these belts before 1949. Between 1950 and 1964 it actively encouraged further expansion in the north by double-tracking the Ljubljana–Zagreb railway, by electrifying railways between Rijeka, Jesenice, Ljubljana and Zagreb, and by building the Ljubljana–Belgrade motorway *before* such improvements were made along the Morava–Vardar and coastal axes or across the backward regions to the coast. This endowed northern enterprises, which could expand production or services more easily with their own funds, the additional advantage of lower transport costs in their main northern markets, enabling them to extend their market areas even more easily into the backward areas in competition with, or to the exclusion of, similar enterprises in those areas. Improved coastal and trans-Dinaric communications since 1963 have given enterprises located in central and eastern Yugoslavia also cheaper transport, but this has not necessarily enabled them to break the initial advantages of the northern firms. Yet it is difficult to conceive that the federal government could have done otherwise, for had it neglected communications along the northern 'spinal' axis, bottlenecks there would have slowed economic development everywhere, including central and eastern Yugoslavia.

A high degree of federal influence in the location of industry before 1960, however, permitted much development of industries, especially strategic, 'key' and 'guaranteed' industries, processing minerals and fuels, in central and southern districts despite the thin transport network, low carrying capacity and high haulage costs, and even where only poor roads offered transport facilities (as in parts of Slovenia and Montenegro). The general ignorance of transport tariffs before 1952, and continued subsidisation of tariffs (especially railway and shipping tariffs) out of the federal budget at least until 1960, encouraged such locational decisions by apparently 'reducing' haulage costs on narrow-gauge railways and of transfers between gauges. Nevertheless, location decisions were not taken in ignorance of transport facilities, for if the cost of transport was not decisive, the *availability* of transport facilities at all *was* decisive. Many strategic and 'key' industrial plants were chosen for location within the zone served by narrow-gauge railways, so that the assembly of raw materials and the distribution of products (in some cases between those plants) was possible without involving transfers on to standard-gauge lines.[31] Furthermore, limited capacity on sections of narrow-gauge railway encouraged the government to disperse industry in central and southern regions in order to avoid, as far as possible, heavy localisations of traffic. Plants assembling materials from sources or distributing products to consumers located along both narrow and standard-gauge railways were located almost invariably in inter-gauge junction towns: Banja Luka, Prijedor, Zenica, Sarajevo, Mladenovac, Kraljevo and Svetozarevo. Where localised resources demanded economic and technical localisations of industry in limited areas, money and labour were channelled into replacing or duplicating narrow-gauge by standard-gauge railways to increase capacity and to reduce transfers, as along the Bosna valley, where single-line railways have to carry, in opposite directions, large quantities of coal, iron-ore, coke, limestone, timber, metal and metal manufactures for consumers located both inside and outside the valley. On other lines, such as the Sarajevo–Višegrad–Belgrade and Skopje–Gostivar railways, industrial location was intended to use railway capacity more fully.

The significance of transport tariffs has not always been appreciated nor their effect fully realised as economic instruments. Railway tariffs have been of particular importance in view of the decisiveness of railway transport upon location as compared with the influence of other forms of transport. Before 1960, 25 classes of freight tariffs were differentiated on Yugoslav railways with a ratio of the lowest tariff (for class 25) to that of the highest tariff (for class 1) of no less than 1:14! Manufactures (classes 1–6) bore high tariffs to subsidise the haulage of raw materials (classes 16–25) and coal at low ordinary, or after 1953 'exceptional' tariffs, which were below cost—indeed, for lignite, below variable transport costs.[32] Semi-manufactures (classes 7–15) bore intermediate tariffs. All tariffs were uniform for the whole railway system; individual factories could be subsidised, therefore, only from the federal budget, not by the railways.

To reduce production costs, enterprise managements, especially workers' councils after 1950, responded to the tariff system by arranging for supplies of bulky, low-value materials (coal, or, timber, sand and gravel) to be brought by railway, and not by river transport, on which tariffs were higher for those goods,[33] or for distribution of light or high-value manufactures (chemicals, electrical products, furniture, machines) to markets by lorry at lower tariffs than by railway. For many years, therefore, factories located beside the Danube and Sava relied entirely on rail transport even when direct water transport was a simple matter. On the other hand, decentralised investment after 1952 enabled republics and enterprises to finance the development of industries to produce high-value manufactures in locations where only road transport facilities existed, as in parts of Slovenia and Montenegro. In addition, railway fares, subsidised to the tune of 34 per cent. of passenger transport costs (c $23 million annually),[34] enabled the railways to retain their monopoly of passenger movements until 1958.

Large differentials in tariffs between materials and products were accentuated by the greater proportional decrease in tariffs per mile with increasing distance for lower, than for higher tariff classes. Theoretically this favoured transport of materials and coal, encouraging market–rather than material-orientation of industry. Since backward areas were major sources of materials and more advanced areas were major markets, this operated contrary to the government's efforts to develop backward areas. In fact, reduced tariffs were designed to cheapen production generally, so that in 1954 transport costs to enterprises were 39 per cent. below those of 1939[35] relatively strict control of investment by the federal government ensured the location of manufacturing near raw-materials and energy sources and in backward areas, despite tariffs, to reduce unnecessary overburdening of the railways with bulky material. Indeed, before 1952, tariffs had no influence whatsoever on location decisions. Prices, fixed equal for each good for the whole federation, made transport *costs* as part of the price seem to be zero to location planners. Some normally market-oriented plants, therefore, were developed in isolated, backward regions (e.g. metal-working in the Karst) while some plants processing bulky materials were similarly isolated from both materials and markets (e.g. copper-processing in Serbia, iron and steel in Montenegro). After 1952 transport tariffs formed an increasingly important part of production-cost calculations, and, while undoubtedly decentralisation and the 'new economic system' rationalised transport movements, the unchanged tariff structure encouraged, and decentralised finance permitted, the expansion of manufacturing industry (e.g. furniture, paper-cellulose) in northern Yugoslavia, using raw or semi-processed materials from underdeveloped areas. For instance, it resulted in Zagreb industry being supplied with coal from Banović (304 km.) in Bosnia rather than from Croatian Zagorje mines (between 65 and 128 km.), which were unfavourably placed because of high short-haul tariffs.[36]

Changes in tariffs since 1960 have been far-reaching. Tariffs have been reorganised into 8 freight classes and differentials between the lowest and the highest tariffs reduced to 1:3 (in 1960) and 1:2 (in 1966). Tariffs, therefore, now express real transport costs more closely. While this has meant a sharp rise in tariffs for materials and semi-manufactures, it also means that tariff policy is now more in line with the objectives of regional economic development policy. Once again inland waterways have become important carriers of bulky goods and cheapness has encouraged federal authorities since 1959 to invest in fertiliser and petrochemical plants depending upon waterborne facilities on the Danube. The introduction of special combined rail-river tariffs has offset the former diseconomies of high-cost short rail hauls of materials from northern Dinaric sources to the Sava valley for trans-shipment. A great rise in passenger fares to real-cost levels has been an important factor in the recent boom in road passenger transport; accessibility by road is becoming a far more important location factor, therefore, in service and tourist provision.

The railway tariff reform of 1966, however, has made other important changes. Now tariffs increase at uniform rates with distance for all classes of freight. This measure aims at reducing hauls, especially of lower-value goods which are unremunerative to the railways. For the first time uniform tariffs have been replaced by differences in tariffs between railway administration regions, a change which does make activity in central and eastern Yugoslavia subject to higher tariffs, expressing higher operational costs in Montenegro, Macedonia and Bosnia-Herzegovina than elsewhere. But whereas these rates are fixed uniformly for all lines within each region, the new 'liberalism' has permitted the Slovenian railway administration, *Ž.T.P. Ljubljana–Postojna–Maribor*, which also supervises Istrian railways, to have its own tariff system. This is unique in introducing differential tariff scales for different railways. It also seems to represent a serious attempt to use economic instruments through decentralisation for 'chauvinistic' ends of national betterment at the expense of non-Slovene areas. Tariffs sharply decrease proportionately for the routes Kotoriba–Ormož–Zidani Most–Ljubljana–Pivka–Rijeka and Zagreb–Ljubljana–Rijeka in order to channel Hungarian transit traffic en route for Rijeka along *longer* railways through Slovenia than along shorter routes, entirely within Croatia (Kotoriba–Varaždin–Zagreb–Delnice–Rijeka), on which tariffs, following the Yugoslav norm, are less sharply regressive. Conversely, tariffs *increase* proportionately for lines from Slovenia to the Croatian ports, Pula and Rovinj, in Istria.[37]

In the past easier access to Rijeka from the interior has made it the only port at which produce from the interior is processed for export and at which imports are processed to serve interior markets. Poor access to other ports until recently meant that industries located on the coast depended largely on coastwise supplies or distribution of bulky goods by sea or simply processed local materials mainly for export as high costs of transport over 'bottleneck' passes restricted their market areas towards the interior.

Increased transport tariffs since 1966 have made transport costs a far more important element in production, and hence location, costs than hitherto. They make efficiency essential if Yugoslav industry is to compete successfully on the international market, for it has been stated that:

'The underveloped transport network and its technical obsolescence are the principal causes of high transport costs, which burden the Yugoslav economy. According to a study of the Transport Institute in Belgrade entitled *Uticaj Transportnih Troskova na Privreda*, made in 1963, transport costs in

U

Yugoslavia are relatively higher than in other countries. Thus the proportion of rail, river and road transport haulage in the total value of industrial and agricultural production amounts to 7·7 per cent in Yugoslavia, as compared with 4·7 per cent. in France, 5·9 per cent. in Austria, 6·4 per cent. in Italy, 2·4 per cent. in Poland, 3·3 per cent. in Belgium and 4·0 per cent. in Federal Germany. If the costs of loading and unloading, which amount to 3·1 per cent., are added to haulage costs, then the total costs of transport amount to 10·8 per cent. of the total value of industrial and agricultural production.'[38]

REFERENCES

1   Fenno-scandia in this context includes Norway, Sweden and Finland.

2   Mijo Mirković, *Ekonomska Struktura Jugoslavije 1918–1941*, Zagreb, 1950, pp. 121–3.

3   A very detailed analysis of the Yugoslav railway system before the Second World War is given in *Jugoslavia, III: Economic Geography, Ports and Communications*, Naval Intelligence Division, London, 1945, pp. 416–50.

4   The comparable figure for Belgium is 8200 miles of railway, despite the fact that Belgium has only one-ninth of the area of Yugoslavia (11,775 sq. miles cf. 99,000 sq. miles) and half the population of Yugoslavia (10 million cf. 20 million).

5   Milan Stevanović, *Ekonomsko Saobraćajna Geografija*, Zemun, 1957, pp. 76–77 and *Jugoslavija 1945–1964: Statistički Pregled*, Belgrade, 1965, p. 175.

6   *Yugoslav Survey*, 7 (26), 1966, p. 3813.

7   Between 1950 and 1953 the Yugoslav railways were administered by regional directorates with central offices in Ljubljana, Zagreb, Belgrade, Novi Sad, Sarajevo and Skopje; Montenegrin lines were administered from Sarajevo (in fact only one significant railway, the continuation of the Sarajevo-Trebinje line to Titograd). Since 1953 the railways have been slightly reorganised into Railway Transport Enterprises (*Železnička Transportna Preduzeća*) for the republics, including a new one for Montenegro. Before 1966 all tariffs were the same for all administrations.

8   *Tarife za Prevoz Robe*, 4, Belgrade, pp. 9–59.

9   These were the standard-gauge railways, Vrpolje (east of Slavonski Brod)-Sarajevo, Banja Luka-Doboj and Brčko-Banovići, and the narrow-gauge Nikšić-Titograd railway (Montenegro). Some 70,000 youths and schoolchildren, for example, completed the 56 mile-long Brčko-Banovići railway in six months in 1946. The other railways had began operation by 1953.

10 *Yugoslav Survey*, 3, 1962, p. 1163.

11   C. Popović and D. Miljković, 'Problemi Akumulativnosti u Privredi Srbije', *Ekonomika Preduzeća*, 12 (3), 1964, p. 159.

12   Jack C. Fisher, *Yugoslavia—A Multinational State*, San Francisco, 1966, p. 59 and also Dennison I. Rusinow, *Ports and Politics in Yugoslavia*, New York, American Universities Field Staff Report, Southeast European Series, 11 (3), 1964, pp. 8–11.

13   Mirko Dokić, 'Pruga Beograd-Bar: Osnovne Postavke i Efekti', *Ekonomika Preduzeća*, 14 (4), 1966, pp. 222–7.

14   Martin Dobrincić, *Razvitak Glavnijih Luka u N.R. Hrvatskoj*, Zagreb, 1959, pp. 113–14.

15   Dokić, *op. cit.*, p. 222.

16   Dobrincić, *op. cit.*, p. 93 and 'Development of Yugoslav Seaports', *Survey*, 3 (9), 1962, p. 1295.

17   'Saobraćaj i Veze, 1965', *Statisticki Bilten*, 1966, pp. 67–71.

18   By 1958 for example Rijeka was handling 420,000 tons of transit freight for Czechoslovakia as compared with only 40,000 tons in 1938; by contrast Hamburg handled 800,000 tons in 1958 as compared with 955,000 tons in 1938. Similarly the volume of Czech transit traffic passing through Trieste had declined from 374,000 tons (1938) to 36,000 tons (1958). Sources: *Verkehr*, Vienna, 5, 1959, p. 142 and *Internationale Transport Zeitschrift*, Basle, 4, 1959, p. 253.

19   Dobrincić, *op. cit.*, p. 84.

20   This scheme is referred to in *Željeznička Veza Srednje Bosne s Morem*, Trgovinska Komora, Split, 1957, p. 232.

21   Rusinow, *op. cit.*, p. 10 and Toussaint Hočevar, *The Structure of the Slovenian Economy 1848–1963*, New York, 1965, pp. 243–51 who gives the Slovenian view point.

22   Dobrincić, *op. cit.*, p. 22 and also Zvonimir Jelinović, 'Nove Željeznicke Tarife i Njihove Ekonomske Posljedice', *Ekonomski Pregled*, 4–5, 1966, pp. 275–7.

23   *Željeznicka Veza Srednje Bosne s Morem*, *op. cit.*, 416 pp.

24   Despite its magnificent fjord-like natural harbour, Kotor cannot become a port on account of poor site conditions and the impossibility of linking the town economically with anything but tortuous roads. The coast road to Dubrovnik and Ulcinj is difficult, but the one road inland, to Cetinje and Titograd, climbs the slopes of Mount Lovčen from sea level to about 4,500 ft. in about 30 hairpin bends. From here, too, an economic hinterland is less accessible than from Bar.

25   Capital would have been forthcoming from Shell Petroleum Co. to build the Adriatic Highway had the Yugoslav government agreed to allow Shell to sell its petrol and oil products from its own stations en route. This scheme was rejected on principle since socialist management is seen as being incompatible with capitalist enterprise, let alone *foreign* capitalist enterprise, within the federation. That the Yugoslav government, nevertheless, realises that such agreements could open the doors to more foreign investment to stimulate economic growth is shown by the fact that in 1967 discussions will take place in the Executive Council on the question of allowing foreign concerns to operate on Yugoslav soil. It has been rumoured also, however, that Shell Petroleum has been allowed to finance construction of the Plitvice-Split road on terms outlined above.

26 'Development of the Transport System', *Yugoslav Survey*, 7 (7), p. 3806.

27 Dokić, *op. cit.* p. 222.

28 'Saobraćaj i Veze', *Statisticki Bilten*, nos. 121, 1958, p. 125 and 324, 1964, p. 116.

29 Hitherto all shipping has been allowed to navigate the Iron Gates channel only in daylight hours to avoid wreckage on numerous rocks. Ships spend the night at Golubac and Sip. The author recalls an excursion, through the Iron Gates from Belgrade to Prahovo (c 275 km.) and back again, which well illustrates the problem. Leaving Belgrade at 18.00 hours, the ship reached Golubac by 22·00. It left Golubac the next day at 5·00 and, navigating the Iron Gates, arrived at Prahovo at 14·00. The return journey began at 15·00 for Sip where the ship arrived at 21,00 hours for the overnight stop. Having left Sip at 5·00 the following day the ship arrived at Belgrade at 21·00 hours. In other words travelling time downstream was 15 hours and upstream 21 hours. Statistics of inland waterway transport are drawn from 'Saobracaj i Veze', *op. cit.*, 1958, pp. 87–98 and 1964, pp. 74–94. See also D. Dukić, 'Djerdapska Hidroelektrana', *Glasnik Srpskog Geografskog Društva*, 44 (2), 1964, pp. 91–117.

30 *L'Usine Nouvelle*, 46, 17 November 1966, p. 19.

31 For further details on this and subsequent points, readers are referred to the author's unpublished doctoral thesis entitled *Recent Changes in Industrial Location in Yugoslavia*, University of London, 1962, Chapter IX, 'The Transportation Factor', pp. 202–27.

32 *Tarifska Politika Jugoslovenske Železnice u Periodu od 1945 do 1954 godine*, Ekonomski Institut N. R. Srbije, Belgrade, p. 93 and *Tarifa za Prevoz Robe u Prugama J. Ž.*, Belgrade, annually. Indeed, in 1957 it was estimated that while 37 per cent. of the freight hauled by rail was rated at above-cost tariffs, 50 per cent. was rated at below-cost tariffs and 13 per cent. was rated at below variable-cost tariffs. See *Jugoslovenski Pregled*, 5, 1958, p. 217.

33 For instance, in 1957 haulage of lignite 278 km. by rail cost 390 dinars while the same journey by river cost 530 dinars. *Ibid, p.* 217.

34 *Ibid.*, p. 217.

35 *Tarifska Politika*, *op. cit.*, p. 193.

36 Ivan Jelen, 'Prostorna Komponenta u Valorizacija Malih Ugljenokopa S.F.R.J.', *Ekonomski Pregled*, 17 (4–5), 1966, pp. 245–61.

37 Zvonimir Jelinović, *op. cit.*, pp. 263–85.

38 'Development of the Transport System', *Yugoslav Survey*, 7 (26), 1966, p. 3814.

CHAPTER 15

Tourism and Trade

TOURISM

Improvements in transport have been both a cause and an effect of the growth of tourism. Better transport facilities expanded capacities for conveying domestic and foreign tourists, the sources of demand, to the coast and interior mountains, the main sources of supply of touristic phenomena. Tourism grew steadily after the Second World War, having stagnated during the 1930s. The total number of tourists rose from 940,000 in 1939 (and 1 million in 1946) to more than 6·5 million in 1963, primarily as a result of the growth of domestic tourism. The influx of foreign visitors remained modest, although it did raise the supply of valuable hard foreign currency from $3 million in 1952 to $18 million in 1961. Since 1964, however, dramatic changes have converted tourism into the fastest-growing sector of the Yugoslav economy. Numbers quadrupled in three years, with a startling increase in the number of foreign visitors from 1·5 million (1963) to 16 million in 1966. In consequence, foreign tourism, which brought in $160 million in 1966, has replaced agriculture as the second largest foreign currency earner after industry and is challenging transport as the leading source of invisible exports. This amount was sufficient to offset 77 per cent. of the trade deficit last year. Moreover, the expansion of tourism, stimulating transport, catering and trade, has come at a critical time when employment, following the economic reforms, has been hard to find in manufacturing and administration. What factors, then, account for the prominence of tourism in Yugoslavia?

The federation abounds in assets of touristic significance. Regional and interregional variety in both natural and cultural attractions draws foreign tourists and stimulates interregional movement of domestic tourists in search of environmental change for rest and recreation.

Undoubtedly the greatest natural assets are located in the Adriatic region. Here, a large number of clear days with high insolation, yielding 2,400–2,725 hours of sunshine annually (6·6–7·5 hours daily), provide a long season of up to eight months of fine, warm weather. This is greatly enhanced by contact with the sea along 1,000 miles of rocky coastline with many sheltered bays clothed in olives, vines and Aleppo pines; by the presence of many offshore islands with luxuriant vegetation; and by the imposing scenery of high mountains close to the sea. Here, indeed, the proximity of two entirely different natural worlds even yields the possibility in early Spring of combining winter sports with a 'Mediterranean' holiday at centres only a few miles apart. The scarcity of sandy beaches, however, is a handicap. Highland Yugoslavia is generally forested, and offers opportunities for hunting (e.g. bear), while swift rivers offer scope for canoeing and fishing. A number of national parks have been created in this region, of which the largest are Mavrovo, 65,000 ha., Galičica, 23,000 ha. Durmitor 32,000 ha. and Plitvice, 15,000 ha. Climate is more invigorating and, while cloudier, nevertheless provides mostly 1,800–2,400 hours of sunshine annually (5–6·6 hours daily). Scenic variety is great. Alpine landscapes, including the lakes of Bled and Bohinj, in Slovenia, are matched in central Yugoslavia by magnificanet gorges along the rivers Vrbas, Neretva, Drina and Tara, in the Karst by fine underground caves as at Postojna (16 miles long) and by the unique Plitvice lakes in the wooded Karst, in eastern Yugoslavia by the Iron Gates gorge and by the impressive mountains of the Nišava region, Kopaonik, Prokletije and Šar, and in the south-east by the beautiful mountain-girt lake Ohrid. Snow and ice provide excellent conditions for winter sports on plateaux and slopes, especially around Kranjska Gora (Jesenice), Jahorina (Sarajevo), Durmitor and Kopaonik. Mineral springs, with medicinal properties, located along major fault lines or in formerly active volcanic areas, are an additional asset in central-east Slovenia, Croatian Zagorje, central Slavonia, central Bosnia and central Serbia.

Yugoslavia boasts a cultural heritage which is unsurpassed

for variety in Europe. Easily accessible is a Balkan and old
world culture which, for political and economic reasons, has
been less accessible in other countries in east-central Europe or
Asia Minor. Town and country in central and south-eastern
Yugoslavia abound in mosques and other living symbols of
Moslem culture. Sarajevo, however, with 80 mosques and with
whole streets of specialised oriental handicrafts, or *esnafi*, is
unsurpassed in this respect. Slovene towns and villages, on the
other hand, show close affinities to Austrian settlements, and
those in Slavonia and Vojvodina to Hungarian. Byzantine art
and architecture distinguish ancient buildings, especially
churches and monasteries, in Serbia and Macedonia, while
Ohrid is a gem of Macedonian building. Coastal settlements, by
contrast, owe their character in large measure to Venetian
influence, including the unique walled city of Dubrovnik.
In addition, ancient Greek remains may be seen at Stobi
(Macedonia) and fine Roman monuments at Pula, Split and
Solun (Split). Throughout Yugoslavia, traditional regional
folklore adds even more colour and variety.

Postwar government policies have been instrumental in
developing tourism on a large scale to exploit these resources,
both by increasing the propensity of the Yugoslavs to 'consume'
tourism and by tapping progressively more of the large European tourist market. In pre-war times a poverty-stricken
peasantry and a small, underemployed proletariat lacked the
finance and the inclination for tourism. In 1939 only 4 per
cent. of the population—primarily wealthier merchants,
landowners and officials—took holidays. Since 1946 domestic
tourism has developed steadily, and by 1966 over 30 per cent.
of the population engaged in tourism. Economic development,
subsidised housing, and guaranteed holidays with pay for
workers in the social sector, have been factors in multiplying
the number of people with money enough for tourism. The
construction of *odmaralište*, rest homes, and sanatoria by trade
unions, enterprises and ministries has provided cheap holiday
facilities for over one million adults and children. Heavily
subsidised railway transport for one holiday journey annually
has increased the tourist mobility of lower social strata.
Nevertheless, the average sojourn of Yugoslav tourists declined
from one week in 1948 to four days in 1965. This reflects the

more limited propensity to consume of lower social strata as well as the general effect on demand of postwar wage restraint; both factors have induced the substitution of day excursions for strict tourism.

Foreign tourism did not regain its pre-war importance until 1955. Europe was still recovering from war, political tensions restricted international movement and the Cominform blockade prevented visits to Yugoslavia by would-be tourists from east-central Europe. The government appreciated even so, first, that foreign tourism could yield vital hard currency to cover mounting trade deficits, and, second, that within two days' land journey was concentrated a very large and rapidly expanding tourist market of some 450 million people, a market which increasingly 'gravitated' annually towards the Mediterranean region within which Yugoslavia lay. Tourist offices were opened in many European countries to propagate tourist interest in Yugoslavia. Visa and other documentary formalities—an inconvenience and a psychological, if not an economic, discouragement to tourists—were simplified or abolished. As Yugoslavia became a clearly non-aligned country with a unique internal political economy which drew visitors out of curiosity, so the government made agreements by 1966 with 18 countries in western, northern and east-central Europe, as well as the 'third world', for reciprocal tourist movements without visas. As International Tourist Year 1967 dawned, Yugoslavia unilaterally abolished visas for all tourists; every artificial barrier to tourism has gone.

Moreover, the economic competitiveness of the federation in the international tourist market has improved. Tourist exchange rate bonuses of 33·3 per cent. before 1962 and devaluation of the dinar more recently have trebled foreign currency values in Yugoslavia—from 400 dinars for $1 (including the bonus) in 1956 to 1,200 dinars (12 new dinars) in 1965. Simultaneously, hotel and catering prices have doubled, while most retail prices have not yet doubled. Already one of Europe's cheapest tourist countries, Yugoslavia, therefore, has become relatively cheaper still. This has enabled the federation, first, to entice overseas tourists to substitute Yugoslavia for more expensive countries with similar assets, second, to draw tourists from a larger market area as visitors, by saving money in Yugoslavia, can spend it on lengthier air or land journeys to reach Yugoslavia, and third, to encourage visitors to stay longer in Yugoslavia. Additional inducements have been the organisation of festivals in July–August in Rijeka, Pula, Split and Dubrovnik. These factors explain the phenomenal increase in foreign tourist traffic.

Yet tourist assets are still under-utilised, not so much in relation to the restricted domestic market as in relation to the large existing international market. Income from foreign tourists in 1966 was barely one sixth of that from similar sources in Italy and Spain. Moreover, an income of only $10 per foreign visitor is equivalent, at best, to three days' sojourn. The brevity of foreign visits is explained not by a lack of currency, but by inadequate transport and accommodation. Until 1964 access to the coast, the islands and the interior was poor, and time-consuming. The dearth of airports for modern aircraft and of modern roads to and along the coast channelled most tourist traffic on to slow, infrequent and often uncomfortable services on railways to Rijeka, Split and Dubrovnik, on coastwise steamers, or on coaches which gave punishing rides over pot-holed roads. These factors outweighed the advantages of very cheap transport with second-class railway and inter-city bus fares (1967) standing at only 1d. (1 U.S. c) per mile and petrol the cheapest in Europe (including U.S.S.R.). Since 1964 improvements have facilitated the large-scale movement of foreign tourists to and around Yugoslavia: new airports for jet airliners at Dubrovnik, Split and now Pula (1967); completion of the Adriatic Highway and other trans-Dinaric routes; the new Sarajevo–Ploče railway; a 25 per cent. increase in railway carrying capacity with new rolling stock; new international coach services; the Zadar–Pesaro car-ferry; and a fast hydrofoil service between Split and the Dalmatian islands. Nevertheless, more interior roads and duplication of the Adriatic Highway may soon be necessary.

If improved access has permitted foreign tourists to spend longer in Yugoslavia, the meagre increase in accommodation, especially to cope with the peak July–August demand, has not. Whereas in 1956 accommodation in hotels, guest houses, camps and rest houses could cater for all domestic and foreign tourists for ten days each, in 1966 it could cater for all tourists for only three days each. During the decade the number of tourists has increased seven-fold whereas the provision of tourist accommodation has not even trebled. The main reason is the lack of capital. A low priority for tourism necessitated the channelling of limited funds from local sources into low-cost accommodation, mainly private households and camping grounds to supplement republic or federal investment in hotels. Emphasis on low-cost accommodation, however, also meant some loss of foreign currency. Sometimes, scarce funds have been misused and, at one time, it was even suggested that federal funds should be equally apportioned among the republics despite the localisation of most foreign tourist potential along the coasts of Croatia and Montenegro. Provision of adequate hotel accommodation has proved to be the biggest problem. For years the Yugoslav government refused to allow foreign enterprise to build hotels in the federation, although offers were frequent. The need has become so great recently, however, that, besides receiving substantial loans from western Europe and America for hotel construction, the Yugoslav government is willing to permit foreign hotel or chalet developments, providing that the land remains in Yugoslav ownership and that profits are shared.[1] Tourist organisations offer reduced terms for off-season accommodation in an effort to cater for more tourists and to make more efficient use of capital. Under United Nations' auspices, 14 countries will now take part in planning recreational and hotel facilities for southern Dalmatia.

The supply of adequate food to meet July–August peak demand has become a serious problem of late. Increasing amounts of exportable surplus food have been transferred to tourist resorts, especially meat and fruit, while more imports have become necessary. Far from reducing the value of foreign tourism, it seems that this can actually *improve* the balance of payments for it is estimated that tourists pay at least twice the export or import prices for such foods so that they are really re-exports.[2]

The number of nights spent by tourists in the more important centres of tourism is shown in Figure 24. This indicates clearly that the coast attracts most visitors. Nearly two-thirds of all tourist nights are spent along the coast, which forms an almost

continuous zone of tourist activity. Three sub-regions, however, are notable. The Istrian-Kvarner area is the foremost
tourist region of Yugoslavia (28 per cent. of all tourist nights) by
reason of its good road and railway access from the main Yugoslav tourist markets of the north and from abroad. Leading
centres here are Opatija, Crikvenica, Pula, Rovinj, Poreč,
Rab and Portorož. A second area in central Dalmatia (16 per
cent.) is developed around Biograd, Split, Hvar and Makarska
and is accessible through Split, Šibenik and Zadar. A third
area, southern Dalmatia and Montenegro (18 per cent.) offers
outstanding resorts in Dubrovnik, Hercegnovi, Budva and
Ulcinj, which are accessible through the port (Gruž) and airport (Ćilipi) at Dubrovnik and through Titograd airport.
Spa towns, accounting for 10 per cent. of all tourist nights, are
popular only with Yugoslav tourists. By far the most important
spas are Vrnjačka Banja, Niška Banja and Sokobanja (Serbia)

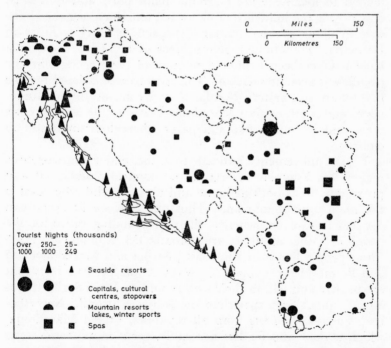

Figure 24. Numbers of Nights spent by Visitors at leading Tourist
Centres 1965

and Rogaška Slatina (Croatia). Another 10 per cent. of tourist nights is spent in the republic capitals, partly as centres of interest in their own right and partly as convenient stopovers. Belgrade, however, is the main tourist centre, largely because, as the federal capital, it draws many Yugoslavs for business and culture. Zagreb has many visitors to its international fairs (*Zagrebački Velesajam*). Of least importance in aggregate are mountain-region resorts, but Alpine Slovenia (Bled, Bohinj and Kranjska Gora) and Ohrid in Macedonia are of outstanding popularity.

Nevertheless, the pattern stresses a certain regional under-development of tourism. Many more centres in Dalmatia could become important in the way in which the north-west Adriatic resorts have done so. Greater localisation of tourism in fewer centres in Dalmatia reflects the situation before completion of the Adriatic Highway when accommodation and transport tended to localise visitors around main ports and railheads; only now is the influence of motorised tourism along the High-way invoking greater spatial dispersion of hotel facilities in Dalmatia. Potentials in many areas of highland Yugoslavia have not yet been exploited because of poor accessibility or insufficient accommodation. This is as true of isolated regions in western and eastern Bosnia, west Serbia, northern Monte-negro and south-eastern Macedonia as it is of the winter sports areas and the main national parks where tourism is still in embryo.

Tourist movements indicate that the major tourist-source regions for Yugoslav resorts are economically advanced and proximate areas both at home and abroad, while the coast is the main aim of tourism.[3] Thus one Slovene in every two engages in tourism, whereas the corresponding ratios for the peoples of other republics are: Croatia 1:3, Montenegro 1:3·5 (most people live near the coast), Serbia and Macedonia 1:5 and Bosnia-Herzegovina 1:6. Most people prefer resorts that are nearby and within their own republic. More Serbs, there-fore, frequent Serb spas than the Adriatic littoral. Neverthe-less, Yugoslav tourists from all republics, except Macedonia, which is poor and far less accessible, spent more *tourist nights* on the coast than anywhere else. Foreign tourists, however, far outnumber Yugoslavs on the coast and recently, by increasing prices, the influx of overseas visitors has displaced Yugoslav tourists from the larger resorts to the smaller, less accessible, resorts. Elsewhere foreign tourists are in the minority. The 'pull' of the sea on foreign visitors is clear and reflects the fact that the majority come from 'continental' source regions in Germany, Austria, Czechoslavakia and Hungary. The importance of different source regions of foreign tourists, however, has also been influenced strongly by Yugoslav international relations. Before 1948 most visitors came from Czechoslovakia and Hungary. Between 1948 and 1955 there were no visitors from Cominform countries, all foreign tourists coming from 'western' countries, chiefly Austria, Germany, Italy and Britain. From 1955 tourists were again allowed to visit Yugoslavia from the Cominform states, but in the decade to 1964 they accounted for less than 8 per cent. of all visitors and 0·5 per cent. of tourist nights. Arrangements for travel without visas for tourists from these states (except the U.S.S.R.) in 1964–65, however, raised their share of foreign tourism in Yugoslavia in 1965 to 17 per cent of all visitors and 12 per cent. of all tourist nights. Now tourists come to Yugoslavia in the largest numbers (in decreasing order of importance) from West Germany, Italy, Austria, France, Britain, Czechoslovakia, Hungary, U.S.A. and Poland.

INTERNAL TRADE

Already references have been made to regional and inter-regional movements of agricultural produce and industrial raw materials. Attention here focusses on internal trade as an indicator of spatial market demand. Wartime destruction and subsequent socialisation reduced the number of retail shops and wholesale establishments by more than half by 1950, chiefly as a means of eliminating excessive 'unproductive' middlemen in the economy, removing duplicate and 'unnecessarily competitive' trading facilities, and achieving economies of scale in turnover. Employment today in commerce is little more than 30 per cent. above what it was thirty years ago. Yet the volume of goods handled has quadrupled since then. Significant changes in the composition of trade flows reflect the general course of postwar Yugoslav economic development. Manufactured, and higher-value, articles are far more important objects of trade; and raw or semi-processed produce far less important than formerly. Most growth has been recorded in the marketing of finished electrical, oil, metal, textile and timber products, and least growth in the flows of tobacco, food, coal, building materials, leather and rubber products.

Wholesaling is localised in larger cities. Eighteen urban settlements, each with more than 50,000 inhabitants, are media through which two-thirds' of the federal wholesale business passes. Establishments in Belgrade alone handle 21 per cent. and supply goods to retail markets and enterprises not only in Serbia and Vojvodina but also in parts of Slavonia, Bosnia and Montenegro. Zagreb wholesalers distribute articles to Croatia-Slavonia, Dalmatia and western Bosnia, areas which are also supplied from Rijeka and Split. Ljubljana is a major centre for wholesaling manufactures from European sources over western Yugoslavia. Important interior regional whole-saling centres are Sarajevo, Novi Sad and Skopje.

Retail trade patterns express consumer demand more closely, and hence, regional productivity. Per capita sales turnover in Slovenia far exceeds that in any other region, while that in northern and coastal regions substantially exceeds that in central and south-eastern Yugoslavia (Figure 25). Thus in 1965 annual per capita retail sales turnover ranged from 164,000 dinars ($136) in Slovenia through 114,000 dinars in Croatia, 108,000 dinars in Vojvodina, 86,000 dinars in Serbia Proper (including Belgrade) and 76,000 dinars in Macedonia and Montenegro, to only 64,000 dinars in Bosnia-Herzegovina and 36,000 dinars ($30) in Kosovo-Metohija. This sharp downward gradient from north-north-west to centre and south-east correlates with, first, a decrease in the importance of employment in secondary and tertiary activities, second, a decrease in the proportion of the population that is employed, third, a decrease in labour productivity, and fourth, an increase in labour surpluses along that gradient. The third and fourth factors are manifest in a marked decline, from north-west to south-east, in average monthly personal income levels of workers in socialised activities (state and collective agriculture, manufacturing and services) in 1965 from[4] 64,000 dinars (in Slovenia) through 54,000 dinars (Croatia), 50,200 dinars (Bosnia-Herzegovina), 49,400 dinars (Serbia Proper), 47,800

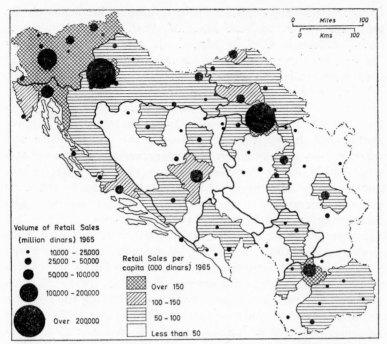

Figure 25. Retail Trade Turnover 1965: Per Capita Sales Turnover
by Districts and Volume of Sales Turnover by Cities

dinars (Vojvodina and Montenegro), to 44,000 dinars in
Kosmet and only 41,500 dinars in Macedonia.[5] The effects are
clearly demonstrated by a comparison of aggregate monthly
incomes of workers in the social sector in Slovenia and in
Macedonia, the two republics that have almost equal populations (1·5 million in 1961). In 1965 some 505,350 workers outside peasant agriculture earned 32,900 million dinars in
Slovenia whereas 237,030 such workers earned only 9,900
million dinars in Macedonia.

Such variations in regional purchasing power find expression
not only in the volume, but also in the composition of demand,
and hence in retail trade.[6] Where per capita purchasing power
is low, as in Bosnia-Herzegovina, Kosmet and Macedonia in
particular, expenditures result in greater sales turnover in
foodstuffs and household goods than in other products—despite
a prevalence of subsistence-type agriculture in those areas.

In more backward areas, too, sales of tobacco are relatively far more important, as 'semi-luxuries', than in northern Yugoslavia, although sales in Macedonia are small since many people grow their own tobacco. Kerosene for rural lighting and textiles generally also figure prominently in trade. By contrast, sales turnover in Slovenia, Croatia and Vojvodina is much higher for metal, electrical and textile products and shoes than for foodstuffs, reflecting higher living standards. The proportionately higher turnover in meat and in chemicals and machinery in these republics, moreover, reflects greater urbanisation and greater commercialisation of agriculture. These differences between more advanced and more backward areas are also discernible in the different character of retail sales between urban settlements and rural communes.

Figure 25 attempts to summarise the broad spatial patterns of market demand and trading by means of per capita retail sales turnover by districts and volumes of retail sales in 70 towns in 1965. Clearly the most developed markets are in Slovenia and west Croatia, extending into Istria and along the Adriatic littoral, where seasonal tourism, transferring purchasing power from abroad and from interior Yugoslavia to these regions, is an important contributory factor. Six of the fourteen leading Yugoslav commercial centres, each with a turnover of more than 25,000 million dinars (c $20 million) in 1965, are located in these regions: Zagreb, Ljubljana, Rijeka, Maribor, Split and Celje. A second more developed market area is discernible in the north-east, where Belgrade, with the highest turnover in the federation (256,000 million dinars), is supported by Novi Sad, Osijek and Subotica, where sales exceed 25,000 million dinars annually. Economically more advanced areas around Sarajevo and Skopje fall into the same sales categories as important regional centres. Elsewhere in Slavonia, the Dinaric regions, Serbia, Kosmet and Macedonia, retail sales are well below the Yugoslav average (92,000 dinars per head), expressing economic backwardness. The only important qualification concerns the very low per capita sales values for the districts and towns of Sisak, Karlovac, Varaždin and Bjelovar around Zagreb, of Sremska Mitrovica, Pančevo, Smederevo and Valjevo around Belgrade, and of Kumanovo near Skopje. Their values are low because they come within the sphere of influence in retail sales of the large cities which, as regional centres, and as employers of commuting labour, draw in purchasing power earned by people living in surrounding districts.

Indeed, as Figure 25 shows, a hierarchy of urban trading centres may be partially ascertained from the volume of urban retail sales turnover—partially because central place hierarchies can be determined fully only by examining retailing in conjunction with wholesaling, transport, professional services and administrative functions. Belgrade is closely rivalled in retailing by Zagreb (241,000 million dinars sales), their widest retail sales area dividing east and west of Sarajevo. Ljubljana is in a class of its own, serving the richest market, if confined market *area*, in the federation. Important regional retail centres are Sarajevo, Skopje, Novi Sad, Rijeka, Maribor and Split. Smaller market areas, approximately of district size, are served by some 50 towns with annual retail sales turnover ranging from 5 to 20,000 million dinars. A major reason why retail sales volumes in Yugoslavia are not a good guide to the urban hierarchy is that marked interregional differences in levels of economic development mean that cities of more or less equal regional functional importance and size may have rather different per capita, and hence total, sales turnovers. Zagreb rivals Belgrade in turnover, for example, and Ljubljana far excels Sarajevo or Skopje through serving populations with higher purchasing power. The contrast is still more clearly seen if one compares two centres with similar volumes of retail trade from two different areas. Celje (Slovenia) and Kragujevac (Serbia), for example, both sold 24,000 million dinars' worth of goods through their shops in 1965, but whereas Celje has a population of 26,000 and serves a district population of 275,000 people, Kragujevac has a population of 52,000 and serves a district population of 500,000 people.

FOREIGN TRADE

In tonnage, imports have increased ninefold since 1939, from 1·1 million tons to 10 million tons (1965) whereas the volume of exports has scarcely doubled, rising from 3·5 million tons (1939) to 6·6 million tons (1965). Three factors account for the radical change. First, rapid economic development at home multiplied needs for imports while simultaneously absorbing

x

increasing proportions of formerly exported material. Second, government subsidies on imports to reduce home production costs and a shift to lower-value imported materials encouraged decentralised enterprise managements to import their inputs (industrial raw materials, semi-manufactures, livestock fodder) rather than to produce these requirements themselves—and this despite the control of imports through quotas, bi-lateral trade agreements and tariffs. Third, industrialisation at home has progressively substituted imports of raw materials, food and semi-manufactures (55 per cent. of all imports by volume in 1965 as compared with 42 per cent. in 1939) for imports of finished products (45 per cent. and 58 per cent. respectively). Textile materials and clothing, the major imports in 1939, have been surpassed in importance in recent years by metal and engineering components and products, food, fodder, chemicals (mainly materials for fertilisers) and steel. Most significant is the change of agriculture from a net exporting to a net importing branch of the economy since 1945. Conversely, exports of manufactures, especially finished products, (46 per cent. in 1965, cf. 34 per cent. in 1939) have progressively substituted for exports of raw materials (54 per cent. and 66 per cent. respectively). The dominant exports in 1939—livestock, sawn timber, fresh and processed foods, non-ferrous metal ores and cloth—have declined sharply in importance as exports of engineering products, metal manufactures, ships, electrical products, leather and tobacco products grew far more quickly. Only exports of textile manufactures retained their former position. By and large these industries have become more dependent on export markets, whereas basic industries (including most semi-processing activities) and chemicals have oriented production more to domestic markets.

Rising levels of economic development and changing patterns of market demand and production at home have induced significant changes in the international spatial links of the Yugoslav economy with sources of imports and with markets for exports. Political considerations, too, have played their part as have also postwar economic trends in the major regions of the world. Yugoslav overseas trade in the late 'thirties was conducted overwhelmingly with European nations. In 1939 some 80 per cent. of Yugoslav exports, mainly primary products, went to and 87

TABLE 23

Changes in the Geographical Distribution of Yugoslav Trade as indicated by Sample Patterns in the Years 1939, 1948, 1952 and 1965 (percentages)

	Western Europe[1]		Eastern Europe and U.S.S.R.		Asia		Africa		North America		Latin America		Oceania		Total Value (thousand million dinars)
	a	b	a	b	a	b	a	b	a	b	a	b	a	b	
1939	72	66	15	23	2	1·5	2	3	5	5	4	1·5	0	0	10·3
1948	33	39	57	52	2	1	2	4	4	3	2	1	0	0	181·0
1952	63	77	—	—	10	3	1	3	25	15	1	2	0	0	185·9
1965	37	43	33	35	7	9	4	5	14	6	3	2	2	0	663·8

a = Imports; b = exports.

[1] This includes all countries of Europe not belonging to the Cominform; it excludes Albania.

Source: Jugoslavija 1945–64: Statistički Pregled, Belgrade, 1965, pp. 202–5.

per cent. of imports, mainly manufacturers, came from European countries (Table 23) and chiefly from the Axis states, Germany, Italy and, by virtue of annexation, Austria and Czechoslovakia. Except for exchanges with the U.S.A., commerce with the rest of the world, which was under-developed like Yugoslavia, was negligible.

Table 23, giving percentage figures of the geographical distribution of Yugoslav imports and exports in three sample postwar years, 1948, 1952 and 1965, elucidates the periodic readjustments of trade patterns since the war. Integration of the Yugoslav economy with the Soviet bloc till 1949 is clearly expressed in the high proportion of trade with member countries which far exceeded trade with western Europe. With the exception of former links with Czechoslovakia, integration with the socialist countries resulted in a marked geographical re-orientation of trade in comparison with the pre-war years. Of necessity, however, trade *composition* remained similar, for Yugoslavia supplied the Cominform nations with non-ferrous metal concentrates, timber and food in exchange for machinery, equipment and fuel. Except for vigorous trade with Italy, ideology and German reparations resulted in restricted trade with Western Europe. For similar reasons, trade with the rest of the world was of even less consequence than it had been in 1939.

The Cominform blockade of Yugoslavia completely disrupted the new interregional commercial ties that were being forged. From early 1949 to mid-1953 no trade whatsoever was carried on with the U.S.S.R. and the East-Central European states. Tito's quest for market outlets for Yugoslav raw materials and semi-manufactures and for securing supplies of vital fuel and capital goods led to the re-establishment of western Europe as the major trading partner. A resumption of economic ties with West Germany quickly led to the resumption of pre-war trade patterns, while Italy and Britain also became more important trading partners. The Cominform break, however, led to the introduction of a new element in Yugoslav foreign trade patterns, the growth of large-scale trading with the U.S.A. which has remained a major source of fuel and machinery for Yugoslavia and a major market for Yugoslav non-ferrous metals and luxuries until the present day.

Table 23 shows clearly that there has been a marked geographical redistribution of Yugoslav overseas trade since 1952. The U.S.S.R. and the East-Central European countries have re-established themselves as trading partners of the first order almost on a par with western Europe. A far less prominent, though less significant, trend has been the growing importance of trade with the developing nations in Asia, Africa and Latin America. These trends are associated with certain major factors. They are the logical outcome of Yugoslavian progress to a higher stage of economic development. Increasing home needs have led to increased imports, therefore, of coffee from Brazil and Colombia, rubber from Malaysia and Indonesia, wool from Argentina and Australia, cotton from India and U.A.R., oil from Iraq and phosphates from Algeria. Yet imports from these countries are limited because Yugoslavia, too, possesses varied raw materials and her industries often now require more components and semi-processed materials which must be obtained primarily from the developed world.

Of prime importance has been the rôle that Tito has forged for Yugoslavia since 1955 as the leader of non-alignment, a stroke of genius which has won the respect of the Cominform countries and of the developing nations, so opening the door to closer economic co-operation. Increasingly the Cominform countries have seen the virtue of trading with Yugoslavia as a means of furthering their own international division of labour to advantage, especially in manufacturing. The U.S.S.R. is now Yugoslavia's second largest export market, primarily for non-ferrous metals, cables and transport vehicles, and fourth largest source of imports, primarily of coal, oil, steel products and machinery. Czechoslovakia, East Germany and Poland are among the first ten trading partners, exchanging manufactures and fuels for foods, timber, machinery and cables. The developing countries have offered Yugoslavia vital potential market outlets for her growing output of finished products, especially timber (to the Middle East), ships, cement, chemicals and machinery. The exploitation of those markets, however, has depended upon certain 'anti-imperialist' attitudes in new countries which preferred inferior Yugoslav products to superior 'western' ones, but particularly upon the link of

Yugoslav credit supplies with investment projects in the developing countries. In this way, for instance, outlets were found between 1959 and 1963 for cement, machinery, equipment and vehicles destined for some 150 construction projects (power stations, factories, ports and irrigation works) valued at $252 million and located in some 25 countries in Asia, Africa and Latin America; most were financed by credit since, between 1957 and 1964, Yugoslavia gave credit to the value of $400 million to these same countries.[8] Although trade has greatly increased with these nations since the war, it is still very small by comparison with trade with either western or East-Central Europe, and accounted for 14 per cent. of Yugoslav imports and 16 per cent. of exports in 1964. Only India finds its way into the first ten Yugoslav trading partners—as a market for machinery. Four of the ten leading trading partners are west European countries. Italy is the largest market for Yugoslav exports (food, timber and non-ferrous metals) and the largest source of Yugoslav imports (chemicals, textiles and engineering products). West Germany is the third largest trading partner, Britain the fifth, while Austria and France occupy ninth place for exports and imports respectively: all exchange mainly manufactures for Yugoslav semi-manufactures. In recent years the growth of trade with Western Europe has slowed, partly because Yugoslav manufactures are less competitive there than in the less discriminating markets of East-Central Europe and the U.S.S.R. Part of the slowing, however, is a result of the unfavourable terms upon which Yugoslavia has been trading increasingly with members of E.E.C. across tariff barriers. The corollary has been for Yugoslav traders to turn more towards East-Central Europe in search of markets or opportunities for economic co-operation which would give them a market for components. Another factor has been the continued trade deficits of Yugoslavia with E.E.C. and E.F.T.A. countries with resulting currency difficulties.

REFERENCES

1 It has been reported, for instance, that an American company, Lloyd Pacific, has put shares in two new luxury hotels from which it will derive profits from American tourists only, profits from other tourists going to Yugoslav budgets. *Yugoslavia: Quarterly Economic Review*, Economist Intelligence Unit, 4, 1966, p. 6.

2 Zdenka Devčić, 'Značenje Inozemnog Turizam za Platnu Bilancu Jugoslavije', *Ekonomski Pregled*, Zagreb, 11–12, 1965, pp. 813–19; also Regina Bienfeld, 'Značenje Inostranog Turističkog Prometa za Platni Bilans i Njegov Uticaj na Trgovinski Bilans Jugoslavije,' *Ekonomski Pregled*, 7–8, 1965, pp. 525–65.

3 Conclusions given here have been deduced from the following statistical sources: *Statistički Godišnjak F.N.R.J: 1960*, pp. 222–3, 418–19 and 542–3; *Statistički Godišnjak S.F.R.J.:* pp. 130–41, 260–7, 390–1, 395, 397, 470, 476–9 and 643; and from: 'Ugostiteljstvo i Turizam 1965', *Statistički Bilten*, 413, Belgrade, 1966, 64 pp.

4 'Zaposleno Osoblje i Lični Dohodak 1965', *Statistički Bilten*, Belgrade, 1966.

5 The factors implicated here for differences in personal incomes, however, should not be considered in isolation. Higher rates for workers in heavy industries (fuel, power, ore-mining and metallurgy) in Bosnia-Herzegovina raise the average for that republic, while the greater importance of state and collective farm workers earning lower wages depress the averages for Vojvodina and Macedonia. A further factor, which has inflated Slovene wages and depressed Macedonian wages, has been the ethnic limitation to outmigration from Macedonia where there is a labour surplus and to in-migration to Slovenia where there is a labour shortage. Migration is studied in Chapter 3.

6 The following broad conclusions are based on statistics in: 'Unutrašnja Trgovina 1965', *Statistički Bilten*, 000, 1966.

7 L. Rip, 'Ekonomski Odnosi s Inostranstvom', in J. Sirotković, ed., *Suvremeni Problemi Jugoslavenske Privrede i Ekonomiska Politika*, Zagreb, 1965, p. 194.

8 'Investiciona Saradnja Jugoslavije sa Zemljama u Razvoju', *Jugoslovenski Pregled*, 9, 1964, pp. 333–40; also, L. Rip, *op. cit.*, p. 193.

PART IV

ECONOMIC REGIONS
AND
PLANNING

CHAPTER 16

A Regional Synthesis

The foregoing pages attempt to trace the historical origins of marked economic backwardness and spatial economic differentiation in Yugoslavia and to examine the ways in which the postwar government has harnessed and redeployed natural, demographic and financial resources to modernise, expand and alter the locational patterns of manufacturing, agricultural production, transport facilities, trade and tourism as means of achieving federal development and interregional equality. The aim, then, has been to erase, progressively, the legacies of former foreign domination.

Several broad conclusions emerge from the attempts made to realise that aim. Yugoslavia no longer ranks as an underdeveloped state on the global scale, economic progress having raised average per capita national income above the $200 level more than a decade ago. Yet by European standards the economy remains backward, per capita income being lower in 1965 than in all other European countries except Albania and Portugal. Considerable reserves of minerals and energy, substantial labour surpluses and some unworked land await engagement in production. A good deal of labour, capital equipment and poorly productive land awaits more *effective* utilisation. Contrary to the intentions of the government however, this has become even more a regional than a federal problem than it was two decades ago. Regional economic contrasts continue as sharply as ever. All regional economies have progressed some way along the path of development, but Yugoslavia continues to be divided among the same more advanced, the same less developed and the same very backward areas as it was in 1945. Continuity in regional development differentiation has resulted not from the lack of will, nor indeed from the lack of the effort, to accelerate progress in backward areas. Rather it is consequential upon the complex—and sometimes unpredicted—interaction of a set of factors which operated to make the major disadvantages of the backward areas that are the legacy of history, the very inferior quality of their demographic resources and the very inferior quantity and quality of their infrastructure facilities, diminish their prime advantage, the localisation of natural resources, in the location of 'growth' activities, manufacturing and services. Those factors are: capital scarcity, patterns of investment allocation, the lack of parity in pricing between as well as within different economic sectors, differing degrees of decentralisation in the management of various productive activities, decreasing capital mobility with increasing decentralisation before 1964, increasing attention to the 'rentabilities' of individual projects, the consequences of the Cominform Blockade and regional or 'national' pressures. Conversely, superior labour resources and infrastructure outweighed inferior resource endowment in favouring the expansion of secondary and tertiary activities in the more developed north.

Industrialisation has been the main agent of economic development, and rightly so in view of the availability of resources. However, the Cominform Blockade led to distortions in the scale of priority for, and to tying-up excessive capital in, factory building to the detriment of progress in agriculture, transport and services, and hence of balanced growth. Lacking sufficient finance, and in agriculture lacking positive social response as well, these activities were unable to exploit adequately the multiplier 'effects', or more appropriately 'opportunities', opened by industrialisation. Trends in most economic sectors have stimulated, on balance, greater absolute, and sometimes even relative, growth in per capita income in the north than in the centre and south-east. Broadly speaking, despite the introduction of many new industries to the backward regions, the north has shared to a greater extent in the expansion of industries manufacturing higher-value finished products and employing relatively more skilled labour, whereas the centre and east have shared to a larger extent in the growth of extractive and basic processing industries which not only produce lower-value products and employ fewer skilled workers, but which are expanding generally less rapidly than manufacturing. In addition, a more favourable physical environment has encouraged, and the existence of better infra-structural facilities and more commercially viable production units (which often pre-date 1939) has facilitated, greater expansion in agricultural output, transport, trade and services along the Danube–Sava–Kupa axis than elsewhere. Even tourism, until recently, yielded the highest financial rewards in the north-west and today its importance along the remainder of the Adriatic coast still leaves it peripheral to the backward southern regions. In the last analysis, however, the rates of growth in per capita wealth in the backward areas are being continually prevented from rising by the higher rates of population growth there. These maintain a higher proportion of child dependents in the population than elsewhere, while the general migration of more productive youthful labour to more developed areas, although not usually decreasing population, distorts the age/sex structure of the remaining working population in favour of the less productive, less adaptable members of the community.

These broad findings are an oversimplification, fundamental though they are to an understanding of the spatial structure of the Yugoslav economy. The interplay of marked spatial variations in physical environment, natural resource endowment, demographic characteristics and in the levels of economic development inherited from the past, make for a spatial complexity which demands a regional approach. This chapter, then, attempts to synthesise the patterns of economic activity through an analysis of economic regions, of postwar regional development processes and of regional planning policy.

ECONOMIC REGIONS

Yugoslavs consider these three facets under the umbrella term 'regional aspects of economic growth'.[1] An 'economic region' is broadly considered to be a 'human region' since it denotes a spatial complex of phenomena 'which are not only economic in the proper sense, but also include other features of the community, such as habitat, settlement or administrative organisation, which are indirectly conditioned by economic life.'[2] To geographers and economists alike this 'complex economic region' is a planning tool for the guidance of the initiators and executors of economic and social policy at all levels from the federation to the enterprise. Thus regionalisation is intended to delimit areas with similarities and linkages in their economic development *potentials*, rather than in existing structure. Two decades ago economic regions were conceived on the Soviet pattern as 'largely self-sufficient units disposing of their own energy, building materials, metals, machines, fertiliser, food and consumer goods to restrict interregional exchange to a minimum'.[3] Resulting from the realisation of the non-comparable spatial, resource and man/land characteristics of the two states, and also from the radical changes in Yugoslav socio-economic theory and practice, concepts today stress the need for economic regions to focus attention on the comparative advantages of developing potential types of specialised, and sets of linked, productive and consumptive activities. These, according to regional natural, demographic and infrastructure resources and federal needs, may optimise each region's contribution to federal progress, maximise investment efficiency, optimise interregional flows and minimise production costs. Regional divisions should define (1) areas requiring immigration where growth potentials exceed local labour resources, (2) areas requiring emigration where labour surpluses exceed growth potentials, and (3) areas where better long-term balances between primary, secondary and tertiary activities may be achieved with local resources to meet local demand.[4] 'Complex' economic regions are delimited, therefore, 'for the application of particular economic policies which are aimed at specific economic and social goals.'[5]

Boris Kidrič, who tried to improve planning practice by original conceptualisation, conceived of economic regions which were defined according to: (1) the degree to which the traditional economy was subject to change under the impact of commercialisation and of socialisation, especially in agriculture; (2) the level of industrial development in relation to mineral and energy resources; (3) the extent of transport facilities and the degree of interregional and intra-regional interconnection that they offer and (4) the possibilities for future economic development.[6]

Views conflict over the utility of 'uniform' and 'nodal'

regionalisation. The general opinion seems to be, however, that 'uniform' regions are useful for the analysis and description of the spatial incidence of specific economic patterns, of growth potentials, of growth factors and of socio-economic problems as a prelude to the definition of regional policy, while the 'gravitational' principle is of value for defining sub-regions and growth points where the policy defined will take effect within the complex economic regions but not for delimiting the regions themselves.[7] It is generally agreed, however, that regional boundaries should not divide areas with social cohesion, similar problems, functional linkages, diurnal labour movements, or divide river basins, but that they should follow well-marked watersheds.[8]

In Yugoslavia, as in any socialist state where the achievement of interregional equality is a long-term goal, economic regions are indispensible for the formulation of the character and the tempo of growth and change in each region. Yet Yugoslavia still lacks any official system of economic planning divisions. The causes are basically six: first, the priority given since 1945 to *federal* development, and hence, to sector planning; second, the lack of data on regional input-output balances, regional potentials and interregional flows of capital, labour, goods and services;[9] third, the preoccupation with continued radical change in methods of regulating the economy; fourth, uncertain international relations and hence foreign trade patterns, which generated uncertainties about the comparative regional advantages of developing the North-east (for river-borne trade with COMECON), the North-west (for rail-carriage of trade with E.E.C. and E.F.T.A.) and the coast (for sea-borne trade overseas); fifth, the instabilities in the size and functions of local administrative units (districts, communes) which might execute the details of regional policy; and sixth, the strength of the 'national' interests that identify themselves by the six republics and two autonomous areas.

MAJOR 'UNIFORM' REGIONS

Emphasis in postwar regional research has shifted from 'homogeneous' to 'nodal' regions as the dominance of the traditional rural economy declined and man's immediate ties with physical environment loosened under the impact of

spheres of influence of towns with rapidly expanding com-
merical and industrial functions.[10] Early on 'natural-geographical regions' were delimited to establish areas in which similar
possibilities were on offer by physique, soils, climate, vegetation,
minerals and water for the development of particular activities.[11] Six main natural-geographical regions are readily distinguishable (Figure 26). The *Pannonian plain* boasts first class
quality soils and water supplies for highly productive arable
and mixed farming, which itself provides raw materials and
markets for manufactured products; oil and natural gas can
support specialised chemical industries. *Alpine Slovenia* has
advantages in livestock-farming, forestry, power and related
manufacturing and for summer tourism and winter sports.

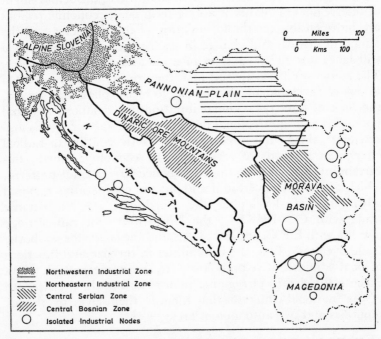

Figure 26. 'Natural-Geographical' Regions and Industrial Regions

The *Dinaric 'ore' mountains* localise resources for extractive and
heavy processing industries (coal-mining, power, metallurgy,
chemicals and timber-processing) and offer some opportunities

for fruit and livestock farming. The *Adriatic coast*, with its tributary Karst mountain region, offers limited potentials for
irrigated horticulture, mixed farming and hill sheep-farming,
but provides far more scope for the development of tourism
(coastal and mountain), sea-borne trade and a variety of
industries based on bauxite, hydro-electricity, non-metallic
minerals, timber and shipping demands. The fifth region,
comprising the *Morava basin*, Kosmet and east Serbia, is distinguished for its arable, fruit and mixed farming potentials
as well as for extractive and mineral-manufacturing industries.
Macedonia, the last region, is characterised by its sub-Mediter-
ranean crops for food and tobacco processing, and by its metal
and non-metallic mineral industries.[12] Most similar analyses
stress the importance of the anthropogenic factor and the broad
coincidence of an advantageous legacy of greater cultural and
economic advancement with Pannonian, Alpine and partially
also Mediterranean Yugoslavia.[13] The 'natural-geographic'
approach formed the basis of the division of the federation into
the five agricultural planning regions analysed in Chapter 9.

Although Melik (1950) noted the emergence of industrial
zones around existing and new centres, industrial regionalisation
was not attempted until 1960.[14] The reason is simple. Even
today only areas with greater, lesser or no industrial development may be discerned on account of the late start in industrialisation, the dominant use of electricity, the scatter of
industrial resources and the active discouragement of agglomeration. Indeed, employment in mining and manufacturing
exceeds 35 per cent. of the working population only between
Jesenice, Ljubljana, Celje and Velenje (Slovenia) and between
Sarajevo, Zenica and Travnik (Bosnia); in most 'industrial'
areas it does not exceed 20 per cent. Four 'industrial regions'
are outstanding. The first, Slovenia and west Croatia (Figure
26), comprises diverse engineering, electrical, textile, timber-
processing, chemical, food and metallurgical industries, which
depend primarily on supplies of materials and fuels (except oil)
from other regions and from abroad and which produce
finished and special articles requiring generally higher labour
skills than elsewhere. The second area lies in the north-east
(east Slavonia, Vojvodina and north Serbia), where varied
industries process local agricultural and livestock products, serve

Y

agriculture with machines and fertilisers, manufacture textiles, shoes, engineering and electrical products for purchase in markets which are easily accessible from the excellent Belgrade distribution area. Central Bosnia is the third area; here, within a triangular zone between Prijedor, Sarajevo and Tuzla, heavy industries based on local resources (coal, water-power, ores, timber) dominate. Finally, a diverse, if less marked, industrial area in the central Morava valleys between Titovo Užice, Leskovac, Svetozarevo and Kragujevac boasts food-processing, textiles, non-metallic minerals with skilled engineering and electrical industries in the main towns. Isolated and specialised industrial areas occur in Dalmatia, centring on Split (cement, chemicals, shipbuilding, aluminium), around Brod in Posavina (food, timber, engineering), the lower Timok valley (copper-smelting, chemicals, glass, food, textiles), Kosovo (lead/zinc, chemicals and coal) and north-central Macedonia (non-ferrous and alloy metals, non-metallic minerals, food-tobacco, leather and metallurgy); all these industries process local resources.

Increasing commercialisation and specialisation in the Yugoslav economy of late have prompted the delimitation of transport regions.[15] The Sava–Danube region, covering nearly half of Yugoslavia contains the best and cheapest transport facilities, combines river with road and rail transport and through its three main nodes, Belgrade, Zagreb and Ljubljana, links all regions of the federation. The Morava–Vardar area, however, requires improved facilities to exploit its internationally important location and its several nodes (e.g. Skopje, Niš, Kraljevo) for local economic development. The Adriatic Sea endows the coastal region with unique transport potentialities, but the area is partly isolated from its economic hinterland, the Sava 'spine', by the Dinaric mountains, which form a transit region between plain and coast. Transport access is very poor here and transit is confined to the central Bosna–Neretva and western Una–Krka, Kupa–Rijeka and Postojna routes; transit potentials are least favourable in the east. Here, at last, is recognition that transport provision conditions regional development potentials and that the *type* of transport available conditions the location of activities depending mainly on water, rail or road transport facilities.

Economists have concentrated their efforts upon the assessment of regional differences in the levels of economic development in order to define, for planning purposes, the location of 'backward areas'. Most commonly, per capita income is used to do this, as in Figure 27, which presents data by communes for 1962. In interpreting Figure 27, however, three points need to be borne in mind. First, national income levels in northern Yugoslavia do not reflect adequately the higher labour skill and higher intensity of service activity which yield higher productivity (and hence, real income) per unit fixed assets there.[16] Second, per capita national income relates to income generated by productive activities in the commune divided by *resident* population of the commune[17] so that where large-scale inter-communal commuting to work occurs, as around Zagreb or Zenica, for example, actual income levels are depressed in the commuter-source communes (where non-agricultural activities are limited) and exaggerated in town communes (where ratios of jobs : total population are high). Third, low prices for agricultural produce before 1964 depressed income levels, chiefly in Slavonia, Vojvodina, Serbia and Macedonia. Complementary social and economic indices must be invoked, therefore, to support and to interpret the income variations shown in Figure 27: data for each commune on population age structure, levels of population literacy and educational training, sources of household income (whether agricultural, mixed or non-agricultural) and on fourteen occupations of the population.[18]

On this basis Figure 27 may be interpreted in the following way. Communes with more than 300,000 dinars per head (c $400 in 1962) are mainly urban areas in which there are: first, higher proportions of active and more highly educated or skilled members in the population; second, a greater proportion of households which derive incomes from non-agricultural sources; and third, a localisation of transport, trade and other tertiary service functions which support important and varied manufacturing industries. These comprise a belt from Jesenice and Ljubljana to Pivka, Celje and Velenje, and Maribor (Slovenia); areas around Pula, Rijeka, Split, Zagreb, Sisak-Kutina, Osijek and Vukovar (Croatia); Novi Sad and Zrenjanin (Vojvodina); Belgrade, Niš and Titovo Užice

(Serbia); and Sarajevo and Zenica(Bosnia). Skopje (290,000 dinars) almost attained this level. Tertiary and secondary activities are less important, but still dominant, and primary activities (with less skilled labour) are more important in communes with 226,000–300,000 dinars per head of population: the remainder of Slovenia (except the Mura region); the Istrian coast, Dubrovnik, Gorski Kotar, Karlovac, suburban Zagreb, Varaždin and Požega; central and northern Bačka including Subotica; Tuzla, Banoviči, Vareš; and Smederevo, Kraljevo, Bor-Majdanpek.

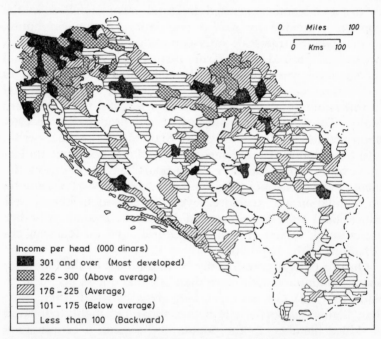

Figure 27. Patterns of Per Capita National Income 1963

Average income levels characterise communes where agriculture, forestry, fishing and mining are somewhat more important than industry and services: north-eastern Pannonia, 'tourist' Dalmatia and southern Montenegro, 'industrial pockets' in Bosnia-Herzegovina (e.g. Mostar, Drvar), Serbia (e.g. Kragujevac, Leskovac), Montenegro (Nikšić, Titograd), Kosmet

(Kosovska Mitrovica) and Macedonia (Titov Veles, Štip). Where income is below 175,000 dinars demographic resources are of poor quality, and agriculture, forestry and often handicrafts provide dominant sources of livelihood, while mining, manufacturing and services are limited and in embryo: central Slavonia, much of Banat, Lika, west and central ('industrial'!) Bosnia and north-central Serbia, and pockets in the South-east. Areas with less than 100,000 dinars per capita were officially designated 'backward areas' by the Federal Planning Commission in 1961 for purposes of allocating guaranteed investments, for there poor agriculture supports up to 90 per cent. of the people while extractive activities (water power, forestry, quarrying) are very limited. These communities lack industry and services, except handicrafts, and are often rather isolated. Illiteracy is high, population growth is rapid and the proportion of active people low. Such backward areas comprise Banija, Kordun, certain islands, most of west and east Bosnia, Herzegovina, Sandjak, northern Montenegro, south and south-east Serbia, Kosmet and west and central Macedonia.[19]

Figure 27 suggests moreover that postwar development, beginning on marked different levels in different regions, has enabled every region to proceed to a higher level of economic development, but largely *en échelon*. Clearly the 'backward areas' today are those of longest Turkish domination, where postwar changes have produced 'islands' of more varied economic activities. Development is more widespread, continuous and intense in former Austro-Hungarian areas and in the former Pashalik of Belgrade (free Serbia after 1830). This broad conclusion should not, however, disguise marked spatial differentiation within each of these 'cultural spheres'. The striking advancement of Slovenia, with Rijeka and its immediate hinterland, has been built on the benefits of industrial and commercial integration with the Austrian economy and of Hungarian commercial patronage. East Slavonia and Bačka shared similar, if less marked, benefits from their former integration, via the Danube and by railway, with Budapest. By contrast, Slavonia, Lika, Dalmatia and Banat have much lower income levels. These areas were isolated between or outside the north-western and north-

eastern commercial arteries, besides suffering economic discrimination or 'frontier' vulnerability, and their activities were
far more 'primary' in 1945 than elsewhere in the north or west.
Most of the 'developed' areas today in central and eastern
Yugoslavia have been built up on the infrastructure legacies of
Austrian occupation in Bosnia-Herzegovina (the railway network, mine and forestry facilities) and of national independence
in Serbia (the Morava, Ibar and Vardar railways and some
industries). It is significant that the more developed communes
in every republic (with more than 300,000 dinars per capita in
Slovenia, 226,000 dinars in Croatia and Vojvodina, and 101,000
dinars elsewhere) lie along main transport arteries and at
transport nodes.

A crude summary index of relative development has been
worked out on a republic basis using data other than national
income. The index is for the average percentage of all communes in each republic which fulfilled the following fourteen[20]
criteria in 1962: (1) more than 80 per cent. literacy among the
adult population, (2) less than 50 per cent. of the population
dependent for a livelihood on agriculture, (3) more than 40 per
cent. of employment in the socialist sector in industry, (4) more
than 30 per cent. of total income (from social and private
sectors) generated by industry, (5) more than 50 per cent. of
income generated by the social sector, (6) more than 10,000
million dinars ($13·3 million in 1962) of fixed assets in pro-
ductive activities, (7) more than 4,000 million dinars annual
income, (8) more than 2,000 million dinars annual total investment, (9) more than 500 million dinars annual investment
in construction, (10) more than 75,000 dinars per capita trade
turnover, (11) the existence of railway facilities—communes
with one passenger and freight station, (12) the annual construction of 200 flats or more, (13) financial autonomy in
managing commune affairs as indicated by the lack of grants
from federal and republic sources, and (14) more than 2,000
radio-subscribers. It is very striking that 73 per cent. of all
communes in Slovenia fulfilled these criteria, followed a long
way behind by Vojvodina (53 per cent.) and Croatia (51 per
cent.), and then by Serbia Proper (38 per cent.), Montenegro
(35 per cent.), Bosnia-Herzegovina (28 per cent.), Macedonia
(24 per cent.) and, lastly, Kosmet (17 per cent.).[21]

GRAVITATIONAL REGIONS & CENTRAL PLACES

As early as 1946, Boris Kidrič proposed a division of Yugoslavia into four 'complex macro-economic regions'[22] according to criteria set out on page 322. The key concept, however, was 'dual gravitation' to an intra-regional node and to an overseas trade outlet. A Western region, comprising Slovenia, Croatia-Slavonia, Istria, Lika and the Croatian Littoral, centred on Zagreb as the intra-regional node and on Rijeka as the gravitational centre for the foreign trade flows to and from the region. A Central region, embracing Bosnia-Herzegovina, Montenegro and Dalmatia, focussed on Sarajevo and gravitated partly to central Dalmatian ports (Split and Šibenik) and Bar and partly to the Sava-Danube. An Eastern region, including Vojvodina and Serbia Proper, clearly centred on Belgrade as the transport node for the region and for overseas trade by the Danube. Finally, a Southern region, comprising Kosmet and Macedonia, 'gravitated' to Skopje, but for trade (artificial barriers excepted) to Salonika. This concept was supported broadly by railway experts who, after the commencement of the Cominform blockade, drew up a scheme of 'gravitational regions of main Yugoslav ports' as a master plan for constructing trans-Dinaric railway lines.[23] As they left international river transport out of account for strategic reasons, however, their scheme allocated Bačka and Srem to the trade 'hinterland' of Ploče and Banat and Serbia Proper to that of Bar.

In 1954 Serbia was divided for planning and statistical purposes, into a hierarchy of economic regions drawn according to economic and social linkages around a hierarchy of central places. Table 24 sets out the regions and centres concerned: Broadly, nowadays, gravitational regions on this pattern are considered valuable as a framework for the formulation of policies for urbanisation, food and labour supplies, and the location of market-oriented or other industries in centres of the appropriate hierarchical scale.[24]

Figure 28 is an attempt to construct the central place hierarchy for the whole of Yugoslavia. The hierarchy is based on an analysis of four sets of complementary data. First, the importance of the tertiary functions of 70 towns in 1963 was established in relation to their districts by using eight indicators. These were: employment in services, handicrafts and

TABLE 24

CENTRAL PLACE HIERARCHY, PEOPLE'S REPUBLIC OF SERBIA, 1954

Centres (Names of Regions in *Brackets*)

FIRST ORDER

Belgrade (*Serbian Republic*)

SECOND ORDER

Novi Sad (*Vojvodina*); Belgrade (*Šumadija*); Kraljevo (*West-Morava*); Svetozarevo (*East Serbia*); Niš (*South Morava*); Priština (*Kosmet*).

THIRD ORDER

Vojvodina: Novi Sad, Subotica, Zrenjanin, Pančevo, Sremska Mitrovica.
Šumadija: Belgrade, Smederevo, Kragujevac, Šabac, Valjevo.
West Morava: Kraljevo, Titovo Užice, Kruševac, Novi Pazar
East Serbia: Svetozarevo, Požarevac, Zaječar, Negotin
South Morava: Niš, Pirot, Prokuplje, Leskovac, Vranje.
Kosovo-Metohija: Priština, Kosovska Mitrovica, Peč, Prizren.

Sources: *Rejoni N.R. Srbije,* Zavod za Statistiku i Evidenciju N.R. Srbije, Series B (9), Belgrade, 1954, 46 pp.
S. Obradović, 'Ekonomski Rejoni Jugoslavije i Problem Rejoniranja', *Ekonomski Anali,* 1955, pp. 47–64; and M. Sentić, 'Problemi Rejoniranja u Regionalnim i Istoriskim Istraživanjima', *III Godišnji Sastanak Jugoslovenskog Statističkog Društva,* Zagreb, 1955.

administration,[25] retail trade turnover, wholesale trade turnover, and numbers of secondary and high schools, of cinemas, of doctors and of hospitals in absolute figures and in proportions of district activities; and, finally, the size of open markets.[26] Second, use was also made of a method of ranking towns according to the percentage of their working population engaged in each economic activity, as a gauge of urban functional specialisation.[27] Third, the alignment and density of transport facilities between towns and their surroundings was studied in order to delimit broadly the urban spheres of influence.[28] This was supported, fourthly, by an analysis of the journey to work in 70 towns as a measure of the labour supply areas to those towns.[29]

From Figure 28 it is apparent that Yugoslavia has a somewhat irregular central place hierarchy. The first significant irregularity is rivalry between *two* first-order centres, Belgrade and Zagreb. The former city is much larger in population and in administrative functions but has only a very slight superiority over Zagreb in commerce and crafts; indeed, Zagreb is more

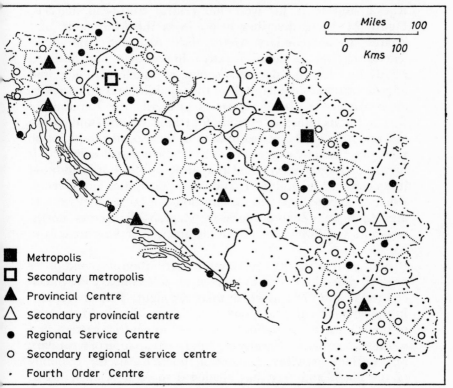

Figure 28. A Hierarchy of Central Places

The *continuous solid lines* represent the approximate extent of the spheres of influence of the metropolis, secondary metropolis and provincial centres except in Serbia. The *dashed lines* represent the approximate extent of the spheres of influence of the provincial centres and the regional service centres in Serbia and Montenegro. The *dotted lines* represent the approximate extent of the spheres of influence of all other regional and secondary regional service centres

important than Belgrade as a transport and industrial centre. The root cause is the unique historical evolution of the Yugoslav state from two 'political core areas', one Croat and one Serb, which, following political division and contrasted economic experience before 1914, made Belgrade the capital of a politically more mature area but also the focus of a poorer continental economic area and Zagreb the centre of a more advanced economic region with easy access to the main port,

Rijeka, and to major west and central European markets. Figure 28, then, describes Belgrade as the Metropolis, and Zagreb as 'a secondary Metropolis'. Although Belgrade is federal capital its administrative importance has declined relatively with the decentralisation of much planning and administration to the capitals of the republics and autonomous areas. Belgrade, therefore, serves primarily the Republic of Serbia, but its influence extends, for ethnic, cultural and economic reasons, over Montenegro as well; the federal capital is also more accessible by rail and road from north-east Bosnia than is Sarajevo. Zagreb serves the Croatian Republic, but in addition it is a commercial and international airport centre for Slovenia, which 'gravitates' towards the city along the Sava valley railway and Ljubljana–Zagreb highway; Zagreb also serves north-west and west Bosnia because of the isolation of these areas from Sarajevo.

Another irregularity concerns the distribution of second-order centres, called here 'Provincial centres' or 'secondary Provincial centres' (Figure 28), of which there are eight. Five are located in Slovenia, Croatia and Vojvodina (areas with only 40 per cent. of the Yugoslav population) and three in central, eastern and south-eastern areas. Greater regional participation of secondary and tertiary activities, i.e. urban functions, in the economy of the north and west has yielded a more developed urban network with a regular rank-size city distribution, and hence, a regular central place hierarchy. Here, then, six towns exceed 75,000 population (excluding Zagreb). By contrast, the city distribution in one-time Turkish Yugoslavia is primate where, excluding Belgrade, only two large centres (Sarajevo and Skopje) and only one with more than 75,000 people (Niš) dominate many much smaller towns. These intermediate cities are the 'provincial centres' (Figure 28); Ljubljana (serving Slovenia), Rijeka (serving Istria, Kvarner and Hrvatsko Primorje), Split (Dalmatia and Livno *polje*), Sarajevo (Bosnia-Herzegovina), Novi Sad (Bačka and Banat), and Skopje (southern Kosmet and Macedonia). According to the indices noted above, however, four towns with more than 75,000 people do not qualify as 'provincial centres', on account of their poor service functions. Niš and Osijek are classified as 'secondary provincial centres' because, as Christaller has recognised,[30] they are clearly potential provincial centres. However, like the 'secondary regional centres' discussed below, they have suffered from the postwar emphasis on industrialisation often to the neglect of seemingly 'unproductive' tertiary facilities, the lack of which has caused serious bottlenecks in the urban and regional economy (e.g. insufficient transport, housing, water supply, trade facilities, maintenance services) and so held in check the growth of urban 'centrality' functions.[31] Both Niš and Osijek, however, inherited poor service provisions, having been located in areas of nineteenth-century political upheaval (Niš Pashalik, 1878) and relative economic neglect (Slavonia).[32] Neither Maribor nor Subotica ranks as a second-order centre: Maribor is primarily a factory town, and Subotica is a large 'village-town' of the Hungarian plain which specialises on industry and agriculture, not services. Both suffer from hinterlands truncated on the north by the state boundary and by proximity to major service centres to the south (Zagreb and Novi Sad), while Subotica has suffered since 1948 from a vulnerable frontier position with a Cominform member country, Hungary.

Third order centres, 'Regional' or 'secondary Regional' centres, of which there are 62 (Figure 28), are spaced more regularly. Particularly striking is the relatively even distribution of such centres within a radius of 60 miles around Zagreb and Belgrade, expressing clearly the impact of higher levels of economic development. Several features demand comment, however. Third order centres are few and far between in the mountains of southern Yugoslavia, to the south of a hypothetical line joining Rijeka and Niš. This is the region of the Karst or forested mountain, of thinnest population, of extensive agriculture and forestry, of isolation or limited access to central places, and of rural poverty which restricts urban functions. Throughout Yugoslavia, though, the predominance of poorer 'secondary' regional centres indicates broad underdevelopment, even in Slavonia, which for historical reasons, lacks any real regional centre. Many 'secondary regional centres' are, for reasons noted above, largely expanded 'factory towns' with low percentages of their labour force engaged in tertiary activities. This is characteristic in central and southern areas: Slavonski Brod; Tuzla, Zenica; Smederevo, Titovo Užice, Kragujevac,

Svetozarevo, Kruševac; Tetovo, Prilep, Štip and Titov Veles, for example. Others are quite agricultural, especially towns in Podravina and Vojvodina. Some are too near to major tertiary centres to become significant service towns, as, for example, Kranj (near Ljubljana), Novo Mesto (between Ljubljana and Zagreb) and Pančevo (near Belgrade). West Slovenia, on the other hand, lacks a regional centre because historically, Trieste fulfilled this function, while today Nova Gorica and Koper are no more than secondary centres. The true regional centres are those with long traditions in tertiary functions, especially commerce (Dubrovnik, Kosovska Mitrovica, Čačak, Požarevac and Zadar), transport (Zaječar, Šibenik and Kraljevo), handicraft services (Šabac, Valjevo, Banja Luka, Peć, Prizren and Pula), while Titograd and Priština have a high proportion of their active labour forces engaged in administration (for the Republic of Montenegro and the Autonomous Kosovo-Metohija District respectively).

Below the regional centres there are some 500 commune centres some of which are potential regional centres; in Figure 28, however, these are undifferentiated as fourth-order centres.

Despite the irregularities consequent upon interregional differentiation in levels of economic development, the emerging pattern comes fairly close to Christaller's observation that 'the ninefold (or 8 or 10) division occurs frequently, as in ... Yugoslavia.'[33] If Zagreb is treated as an extraordinarily important centre of a separate order and all other 'secondary' centres are treated as 'full' centres of each order, then there emerges a 1–1–8–62–500 hierarchy which is remarkably close to Christaller's scheme, 1–8–64–512.

ADMINISTRATIVE REGIONS

In Chapter 8 it was hinted that the six republics and the two autonomous areas could form planning regions on account of their size and varied resources. Opinion, however, is divided between those who believe that republic boundaries are inviolable and those who consider that, as politico-administrative, historical and ethnic areas, the republics and autonomous units are unsuitable as economic planning regions.[34] It is particularly felt that the basins of the Middle Sava and the

Drina rivers, which form Bosnian frontiers with Croatia and Serbia respectively, ought to be planned as whole units linked, not divided, by the rivers concerned. Whatever the views, decentralisation of economic and social management and initiative—first to workers' councils (1950) which were elected in socialist farms, factories, stores and offices, and second, to the communes (1955) as basic 'territorial-administrative units'— eroded the power of the republics, partly in order to weaken republic, and hence 'national', consciousness and so weaken the clash of republic interests. The New Constitution of 1963 saw a further step in this direction, in devolving greater powers to the communes and in encouraging inter-communal co-operation. Here were the makings, it seemed, of an opportunity for grouping communes into economic regions according to economic criteria. Unfortunately, in late 1964 the communes were shorn of many economic functions and some of their power became the preserve of the republic authorities, so hardening the republic frontiers.

Between 1955 and 1965, however, the communes played an important role in economic development. Before 1955 more than 3,900 rural and urban authorities, of which the most important was the district (*srez*), performed relatively simple administrative tasks. The Law on the Organisation of the Communes (1955) eliminated urban-rural distinctions and enlarged the area of all communes (*opština*) to enable them to take on new responsibilities: the initiation of taxation on all fixed assets on their own territories in order to form a commune budget with which to finance the provision of water supply, electricity, roads, municipal transport, other public services and to initiate, with their own funds or in competitions for federal and republic investment funds, also productive activities.[35] Small size, and sharp inter-communal differences in levels of economic development, and thus in taxable fixed assets, restricted or made inequitable the ability of the communes to improve infrastructure and social facilities from their own sources. This threw the commune councils into substantial dependence on Republic and Federal funds, and hence permission for investment, to the detriment of local autonomy or 'self-management'.

Two steps have been taken since 1955 to reduce the gap

between political motivation and economic realisation. First the number of communes has been reduced from 1,479 (associated in 107 districts) in 1955 to 577 communes (40 districts) in 1964 giving a corresponding increase in average size of area and population respectively from 172·9 sq.km. and 11,890 people to 443·3 sq.km. and 32.320 people. Amalgamation often linked less developed communes to more developed communes as a means of increasing communal economic viability in providing services more efficiently in selected places, using larger funds to the benefit of all parts of the commune. Even so, in 1964, 316 communes depended on federal or republic grants for providing public services or for developing new economic projects. Although 260 of these were located in central and south-eastern Yugoslavia, the communal system was unable to eliminate marked interregional differences in infrastructure facilities. To some extent it even increased those differences in so far as 'localism' prevented intercommunal capital mobility. Thus, second, the 1963 Constitution, supported by the economic reform, encouraged inter-communal co-operation in the provision of basic services. The result has been the pooling of budgetary funds between 'associations' of communes as, for example, the three adjacent towns of Svetozarevo, Ćuprija and Paraćin (Morava valley), or the eight communes of Braničevo (Mlava valley, Serbia), to provide water, electricity, transport, special education facilities, agronomic and land protection facilities more efficiently or, indeed, to provide them at all.

Continual changes in local administrative units have created an unfavourable environment for spatial planning of any sort. Moreover, while the amalgamation of some communes has taken into account the increasing spatial extent of gravitational influences that follows from economic development and urbanisation, the amalgamation of others has occurred mechanically, following existing boundaries, without regard for actual or emergent patterns of central places. Communes remain too small for long-term planning purposes since most productive projects, wherever they are located, generate spatially extensive or dispersed multiplier effects on the use of resources and infrastructure. Sizes, however, do vary inversely with population density and levels of economic development in an attempt to achieve minimal budgetary funds, a 'threshold', for the provision of infrastructure as the basis of future development.[36]

REGIONAL DEVELOPMENT PROCESSES

The broad lines of federal economic progress have conditioned postwar regional development processes. Stress is laid upon 'complex' (i.e. integrated) development in each region. Investment priority supports the construction and expansion of industries in every republic, and in greater or lesser measure in every region of every republic, to extract *and* to process the natural resources into semi-finished and finished products in integrated plants located within the region, and to manufacture products for regional markets. Such industrialisation attempts, first, to absorb surplus labour directly from agriculture as a means of breaking the vicious circle of poverty in the countryside; second, to stimulate increased productivity from agricultural land and labour by providing a local (and remunerative) market in industrial capacities for processing and canning agricultural produce and by providing cheap chemical fertilities, farm machinery, and construction equipment (for drainage, for example); third, to expand existing and to create new markets for capital and consumer goods and so to form a threshold for the location of further industries within each region; and fourth, to generate local capital accumulation for re-investment in the improvement of regional infrastructure. Success in achieving each of these aims, as we have seen, has largely depended on the levels of regional economic and social development inherited from the past.

Comparative cost advantages now influence regional trends. Until 1960, however, Soviet concepts shaped development through projects which, although planned in 1947, were still under construction. Economic progress in each republic has been centred on some kind of 'heavy industrial core' area in which energy production, metallurgy, engineering and usually chemicals are interlinked in varying degrees. Core areas include central Slovenia, Zagreb-Sisak (Croatia), northern Serbia including Belgrade-Pančevo, central and east Bosnia, Nikšić (Montenegro), Priština-Kosovska Mitrovica (Kosmet) and Skopje-Tetovo (Macedonia). Metal-working and engineering have been dispersed within, and in areas tributary to, the core for strategic reasons. There has been some attempt to make the republics 'self-sufficient' or 'closed' regions, especially by duplicating metal and consumer goods industries, but this is now considered to be impractical on account of losses in economies of scale. Here, selected regions will be examined briefly as examples of regional development processes.

THE DEVELOPMENT OF 'BACKWARD REGIONS'

The underdeveloped regions are those that have received financial and technical assistance from federal or republic sources as a means of exploiting their resources to meet federal needs and of raising their levels of development towards the federal average: Bosnia-Herzegovina until 1952 but only for selected industries since 1952, Macedonia, Montenegro and Kosmet[37] since 1947; and within the other republics, south and south-west Slovenia until 1956 and the Croatian Karst, Banija, Kordun, and the Sandjak and Upper Morava regions of Serbia since 1947. Before 1960 guaranteed investments were allocated for essentially centrally-determined projects in these regions, primarily for large, heavy, capital-intensive, energy and basic industries processing local resources, leaving only limited funds for other activities. Since 1960 more finance has been available, on the basis of comparative competitive advantage, for the development of smaller and lighter manufacturing industries, infrastructure, services and education.

(1) The Karst

This unique region covers 23 per cent. of the federation. Once the area was thickly forested. As a result of forest clearance and restrictions imposed on nomadic pastoralism by political frontiers,[38] causing overpopulation and soil erosion, today 41 per cent. of the karst surface supports poor pasture, 35 per cent. forest and only 12 per cent. arable land. The remainder (12 per cent.), barren limestone, accounts for one-third of all unproductive land in Yugoslavia. Not surprisingly, only 2·6 million people, 12 per cent. of the total population, inhabit the region, 1·2 million of them living in the narrow coastal belt where more can gain a livelihood from secondary and tertiary activities.

Except in the north-west near Rijeka, the interior 'high Karst' and the Velebit coast remain very backward, over-populated (Figure 6) and highly dependent on agriculture (55–88 per cent. of the population); per capita income is everywhere below 150,000 dinars. The region contributes only 4 per cent. of the Yugoslav national income in contrast to 10 per cent. by the coastal region.[39] The chief regional problems—economic development, land-use improvement and prevention of further extension of the barren Karst—are far from being solved. Excepting federal grants to Montenegro, investment in the region has been restricted because it is not treated as a federal problem area but as a part of four separate republics. A 10 per cent. reduction in population since 1948 has relieved pressure on pastureland, permitting afforestation on abandoned land acquired by the state. Continued poverty and farm fragmentation have maintained the traditional pattern of subsistence agriculture and extensive sheep-rearing, although destructive grazing by goats is now illegal. Proper use of regional water resources is vital to the improvement of agriculture as well as to the growth of industries, towns and tourist facilities throughout the interior and the coast. Hitherto, however, storage basins have been constructed to serve hydro-electric power installations, but not with a view to the regulation of rivers for purposes of the drainage and the irrigation of the Karst *polja* that is basic to agricultural progress. Outside Gorski Kotar, industrial development is confined to widely scattered 'oases' of secondary activity—at Gospić, Drvar, Knin, Sinj, Mostar, Trebinje, Nikšić and Titograd—which provide limited employment opportunities. Most Karst communities are too isolated from these centres, or from the coast towns, for people to commute to work. Dispersed timber-processing and bauxite-mining have been joined since 1949 by a series of metal-working and engineering industries for which the Karst offered strategic isolation. The Nikšić steelworks was located in this region as the 'location leader' and source of metal supply. Most plants employ plentiful labour in the production of light or high-value articles (tools, aircraft parts, screws, razor blades, electrical appliances, cotton thread and cotton cloth), which can stand high transport costs to and from isolated plants and which can raise local income levels more effectively. Labour has proved

z

to be rather adept in these industries. Shortages of electricity and of capital, and a disregard for comparative advantage have prevented the significant development of aluminium and electrochemical industries which could make the greatest contributions to industrialisation in the Karst.[40] Until now the major handicap of the region has been its inaccessibility, for even after construction of the Bihać-Knin and modernisation of the Sarajevo–Ploče railways, transport facilities remain extremely poor between the interior and the coast. The most serious deficiency, however, is a major longitudinal highway which could not only induce more commercial food production but also more tourism. Only in Montenegro has per capita income been raised towards the Yugoslav average: high rates of investment in steel, in road improvement and in the new town of Titograd is the prime reason.

By contrast, economic development in the coast region has been dynamic, with rapid urban growth associated with expanding secondary and tertiary functions, in and near Pula, Rijeka, Šibenik, Split, Ploče and Dubrovnik, which employ generally more than 45 per cent. of the population. Development consists in the expansion of overseas trade, stimulating growth in transport and services in the ports and in industries processing local resources for export (e.g. cement, timber, aluminium and glass). The availability of hydro-electricity and limestone has encouraged the development of electrochemicals and plastics industries which have provided the raw materials for a proliferation of labour-intensive factories manufacturing finished plastic products along the Dalmatian coast and on most Dalmatian islands. Today, the major growth activity is tourism, and with the increase in investment in this branch, in the construction of the Adriatic Highway and of new airports, this is spreading the benefits of economic development to smaller communities which, hitherto, have remained isolated and poor. Such communities are situated in: first, Ravni Kotari (Zadar region) which suffered from economic isolation in the interwar years from the regional focus, Zadar, which was an Italian enclave, and from the lack of railway communications until 1965 (Knin-Zadar railway), and second, the islands. Except for these areas, per capita income in the coast region is around or above the Yugoslav average.[41]

(2) Macedonia

Five hundred years of Turkish occupation left Macedonia extremely poverty-stricken in 1913. Several factors operated between the two World Wars, moreover, to reduce the chances for beginning the economic development process. Further pauperisation of the population, virtually eliminating local capital accumulation, resulted from increasing rural over-population and the fixing of very low prices for tobacco and opium—two major commercial crops—by the State monopoly. Unemployment rose to nearly 25 per cent. in the towns, as industry (which could employ only 3,000 workers, or 10,000 workers if tobacco preparation is included, out of a total population of one million!) was 'steered' by the Serbian nationalist government to locations in Serbia Proper. That government was also largely responsible for the closure of most secondary schools after 1927 so that Macedonia lost a generation of scarce, educated personnel.[42]

Economic development began in 1947 and has been sustained only by the transfer of large sums of capital from northern Yugoslavia through the federal budget for investment in projects in the republic. Between 1955 and 1963 alone this amounted to more than $200 million or one quarter of all federal capital inputs in backward areas, including the Croatian Karst, while in any one year such grants (dotacije) formed up to 65 per cent. of the republic budget. Seventy new industrial plants have been constructed with the money and substantial improvements made in agriculture. Income per capita has doubled, and in 1962 reached the level of per capita income in Slovenia in 1947. Yet the rate of investment has been insufficient to provide employment enough to prevent absolute increases in the agricultural population, even though labour-intensive activities have gained more support here than in other backward regions. Fifty-two per cent. of the population still depend on agriculture. Macedonia, nevertheless, provides a good case study of the way in which the concept of an 'integrated' regional development process has been applied in practice.

Investment in Macedonian agriculture has exceeded the Yugoslav average, being third in the volume of investment after Serbia (including Vojvodina) and Croatia. This reflects the appreciation by the federal authorities that the rapid extension of socialised agriculture on to newly reclaimed low-land or pasture in the republic offered a major opportunity to exploit the physical environment for the production of crops, first, to save expenditure on imports (e.g. sugar beet, rice, cotton, silk, fruits, wool, hides), and, second, to boost exports (tobacco). The cultivated area under these crops has quadrupled since 1939, but hides and wool are still in short supply because of the low productivity in an essentially unchanging form of livelihood. Peasants have sometimes readily agreed to co-operate with the socialist farms, especially in the production of the more labour-intensive or higher-yielding crops (tobacco, sugar beet). The extension of the cultivation of these crops, however, has been closely interrelated with the location of modern processing plants since 1950 in the areas where they are produced: sugar-refining (Bitola), tobacco-processing (Skopje, Titov Veles, Prilep, Kumanovo), cotton textiles (Štip), silk textiles (Titov Veles), woollen textiles (Tetovo), leather products (Bitola, Skopje), fruit-processing and canning (Skopje, Tetovo, Kumanovo, Kočani, Štip, Resen) and wine production (Kavadarci). These industries, whether processing bulky or perishable materials or not, nevertheless represent an attempt to manufacture into a high-value finished product the raw materials of the region as a means of employing local labour and of increasing national income more effectively. In addition, the recent economic reforms, stimulating the interplay of demand and supply and local living costs, have made Macedonian labour the cheapest in the federation, at least according to wage levels.

Investment in agriculture and land drainage created a new market in Macedonia for agricultural machinery, which is now manufactured at Štip, and for ceramic products, which are manufactured from clays near Titov Veles. Other industries have been developed to utilise mineral resources for the federal market: lead-zinc smelting (Zletovo), chrome-refining (Skopje), electro-chrome and electro-chemical products (Jegunovci), non-metallic minerals for insulating materials (Gostivar, Prilep), and timber. Growth of the republic market for building materials and fixtures encouraged the planners to develop cement, glass, brick and ceramics manufacture (Skopje,

Strumica, Titov Veles, Vinica) using local materials, as well as metal products (Štip, Titov Veles). Textile manufacturing at Skopje and electrical appliance production at Bitola were designed for the local market, although the production of refrigerators at Bitola was intended to boost exports of high-value manufactures to Greece and Middle Eastern countries. The limitation of consumer goods' production chiefly to textiles expresses the restricted markets in dominantly poor rural areas.

The basis of Macedonian economic development has been the production of electricity, chiefly from the Mavrovo (Vardar) hydro-electric power station and from the Skopje lignite-burning plant. Electricity supply shortages, however, are causing frequent shut-downs in Skopje industries since large new plants (steel, chemicals) commenced production. Local fuel resources are very meagre and 98 per cent. of needs must be supplied from Kosovo and Banovići. For this reason leading Macedonian industries—tobacco, textile, food and timber— are consumers of electricity; fuel-using industries, metal-working and non-metallic minerals are of less importance. However, the steelworks now under construction at Skopje is intended to provide the local stimulus to the growth of metal-working and engineering industries in south-eastern Yugoslavia. More skilled labour will be required if these activities are to develop. Hitherto, most Macedonian industries have required only the unskilled or semi-skilled labour appropriate in a land with high illiteracy rates. Industries requiring higher skills (pharmaceuticals, oxygen, rubber and artificial fibres) are localised in Skopje, where training facilities and an attractive urban environment are important factors in the availability of such labour.

The dispersion of industries to the more important towns of the Republic has reduced the relative concentration of Macedonian industry in Skopje from 70 per cent. (1939) to 37 per cent. (1964). Skopje, on the other hand, localises much administration and tertiary employment. Most other towns had populations of 15,000–30,000 in 1946, but, except for handicrafts, were entirely without industry. Much of this dispersion, however, was achieved before 1960. Since then, major projects have been located in Skopje, largely because of its superb nodal situation in south-eastern Yugoslavia. The economic reform has thrown into sharp focus the extremely poor transport access to important potential agricultural and industrial areas (Kičevo, Ohrid, Strumica, Kriva Palanka) and the consequently poor competitive position of centres located away from Skopje and away from the international Vardar route. Unemployment in some towns, such as Bitola, has again become serious. Improved infrastructure and modernisation throughout the economy are essential, for in 1964, Macedonia, with 10 per cent. of the federal area and 8 per cent. of its population, contributed only 4 per cent. of the national product.

PROGRESS IN 'ADVANCED AREAS'
(1) Vojvodina, Slavonia and Croatia

If one excludes the highly concentrated growth of interlocking industries and services in Belgrade and Zagreb, postwar economic progress has been slower in northern and north-eastern lowland region than anywhere else in Yugoslavia, except Kosmet. Indeed Vojvodina is the only 'advanced' region in which per capita income has declined[43] from well above the Yugoslav average in 1947 (index 124·9) to about the average in the early 'sixties (104 in 1962). The same trend certainly applies, too, in Slavonia, although no separate statistics are available for this area. The reasons are manifold. Poverty in industrial resources, except some oil, gas, building materials and timber, inevitably meant a low priority for the region in the allocation of investment for heavy industry; in part that priority went to Zagreb and Belgrade, especially for engineering, optical glass and chemical industries. Regional economic development has depended primarily upon increased agricultural productivity as a means of broadening the regional raw material basis for food-processing and leather industries— as in Macedonia.

Unlike Macedonia, however, the Pannonian region has a metal-working and engineering industry which is second in importance only to food-processing. Even if low agricultural prices restricted local markets for manufactures, the question arises as to why engineering, the key Yugoslav growth industry, has not expanded quickly in this region and has not contributed to faster regional economic growth by serving federal markets, including Belgrade and Zagreb nearby. Engineering in this region has received a low priority, except for farm and building machinery. Existing plants were amalgamated and expanded to some degree, but very few new factories were built. There were two reasons. First, the agricultural towns—really over-grown villages—of the region, excepting Novi Sad, Osijek and Slavonski Brod, could not compete with Belgrade or Zagreb in training or in attracting the necessary skilled labour. Second, after 1948, many factories (in the metal-working, textile and leather industries) were dismantled and re-located in central and southern Yugoslavia, depressing building activity, and incomes generally for several years. Handicrafts, however, were stimulated by shortages of farm implements and by willing labour which had been displaced by the factory closures.

New problems emerged with the extension of the new economic system and the introduction of the commune as a factor in economic management (after 1955). Factories in Vojvodina and Slavonia are old, their equipment often out-dated. Workers' councils soon found themselves operating with thin profit margins and on far less competitive grounds with more modern plants in other regions. Indeed, still today, the northern lowlands are the only region of Yugoslavia where agriculture contributes substantially more to the regional gross social product than does industry. This being so, the under-privileged position of agriculture restricted taxable assets, and hence, the budgets of the communes in the region, impairing their ability to compete for grants for the development of industries other than food-processing. Recent industrial developments, therefore, have been confined to the growth of sugar refineries, cattle-feed factories and chemical-fertiliser plants. This 'advanced' area, then, has seen two decades of considerable neglect on account of its agrarian character, and its vulnerable exposure to the north. Planners now realise that economic development has largely by-passed a region with at least three major assets: land with the greatest potential popula-tion carrying-capacity; the greatest concentration of water for productive purposes; and the greatest spare transport capacities in Yugoslavia, with the rivers Sava, Danube and Tisa sub-stantially under-utilised and with the railways (apart from the Sava valley line) utilised to only 30 per cent. of their capacity. One root cause of neglect is undoubtedly the localisation of economic activities in Belgrade and Zagreb. The dominance of these two cities is clearly summed up in their percentage contributions to the federal social product: Belgrade 8·5 per cent., Zagreb 8·5 per cent., as compared with Croatia-Slavonia (without Zagreb) 7·8 per cent., and Vojvodina 11·4 per cent.

(2) Slovenia

This small republic, with less than 9 per cent. of the Yugoslav population, contributes almost 17 per cent. of the gross federal social product. Quite contrary to the intentions of the federal planners, the rate of economic growth in this, the most developed republic in Yugoslavia, has outstripped that in every other republic, causing an increase and not a decrease in interregional levels of development. Publicity of this fact after 1962 has stimulated the recent rise of nationalism. This simply underlines the political and social necessity for a realistic economic policy, more purposefully pursued than hitherto, towards greater interregional equality within a multinational state where interregional ethnic differences are clearly indentifiable with sharp interregional economic differences. What is all the more remarkable is that the Slovenes have achieved an average annual economic growth rate of 9 per cent. since 1947, 2 per cent. above the Yugoslav average, while simultaneously transferring as much as one third of their income to the federal budget for redistribution to other republics.[44] Before 1964, the Slovenian contribution often equalled two-fifths of total federal revenue.

How has such growth been achieved? Once reconstruction of wartime damage was complete, Slovenia began her postwar development with two great advantages; both permitted the use of most of the capital investment for direct production. First, the railway network was complete and facilities were enhanced by the only electrified railway in Yugoslavia, linking Rijeka with Trieste via Pivka on territory that had been acquired from Italy in 1945. Second, many industrial plants were in operation and could be expanded cheaply; in addition, a number of important factories, begun or completed near Maribor by the Germans during the war, were quickly turned into major textile, motor vehicle and aluminium plants. Moreover, the republic already had a heavy industrial base and the availability of resources—coal, limestone, lead, zinc and hydro-electric power—simply encouraged the expansion of steel, non-ferrous metals and integrated chemical fertilisers, as well as ubiquitous timber-processing. Industrial traditions combined with the needs of the federal economy to encourage the planned development of varied engineering and electrical industries in Ljubljana, Kranj, Maribor and smaller towns. By the early 1950s, therefore, the Slovene economy began to become more diversified with major growth industries manufacturing high-value finished machinery, vehicles, electrical equipment and aluminium. These were supported by a substantial growth, financed locally, to meet inflationary demand, in traditional textile, leather, furniture and paper industries. Production, even in steel industries, is becoming specialised mainly because Slovenia is becoming more dependent upon raw materials and fuel transported from central Yugoslavia; high-value output is required to offset higher transport costs. There is little doubt, however, that the costs of a peripheral position within Yugoslavia are offset by a highly nodal position in relation to European markets, and via Rijeka, overseas; export-oriented industries (e.g. furniture at Nova Gorica) have accordingly prospered. 'Nodality' also brings the Slovene railways substantial revenue from transit traffic moving north-south and east-west. It will be recalled that services generally are more highly developed in Slovenia than elsewhere, giving a well-balanced employment structure between primary, secondary and tertiary activities. Slovene enterprises—for instance, road-haulage and wholesale enterprises in Koper and in Ljubljana—trade all over the federation, bringing in high returns on relatively limited capital investment. In the last analysis, however, the major factor of growth in Slovenia has been the educated, hard-working, conscientious and relatively efficient Slovene himself.

Agriculture, too, has played its part. Greater employment of labour off the farm has reduced overpopulation. Dispersed settlement and industry and good communications permit more people to live in the village and to work outside agriculture. In this way more money and effort is yielding results in farm production by the increased use of fertiliser and improved mixed farming.

Dispersion of much new industry and services is characteristic in Slovenia and has been a response to widespread infrastructure facilities, and made possible by the use of hydroelectric power. Many of the social costs of congestion, which are associated with the large cities of Zagreb and Belgrade, have been avoided. The lessons of Slovene experience are important. They underline the exceptional significance of infrastructure, of inherited productive capacity, of trained labour and of a well-balanced regional economic structure in stimulating a high rate of economic progress, and they point clearly to lines of action needed today in the underdeveloped regions of the federation.

REGIONAL POLICY

The absence of official economic regions which are supervised by planning authorities explains why in Yugoslavia there is no comprehensive regional planning in the form of projections of long-term developments in economic and social activities and their spatial interlinkages within, and according to the potentials of, a defined area. Regional plans do exist for the former districts of Krapina and Split in Croatia.[45] Problems encountered by the Zagreb city council in devising a regional plan, however, indicate reasons why very few regional plans have been made. The acute shortage of trained planners and specialised survey institutions is a major handicap everywhere.[46] The lack of long-term federal and regional guiding policies for development retarded plan formulation as assessments of the likely interrelationships of the Zagreb city region with neighbouring areas of Croatia, Bosnia and Slovenia were highly subjective. A further obstacle was the lack of interest shown by councils of districts within the city region in assisting the planning work of a 'foreign' council, although those districts are clearly affected by all developments in or near Zagreb. Plan formulation, moreover, is no guarantee of plan fulfilment. The Krapina and Split plans became plans for 'collections of communes' once the districts were amalgamated (1963) into a Zagreb and a 'Dalmatian' district respectively.[47] Plans then lacked authoritative support. Moreover, the increasing power of the communes for the initiation of projects, their direct liaison with Investment Banks for securing loans for other projects by the competition system, and their frequent 'self-interest' permitted developments and locational patterns which were not envisaged in the regional plans. The transfer of economic investment initiative from the communes to the enterprises since 1964 has made it imperative for regional planning authorities to be formed to co-ordinate spatially piecemeal decision-taking by 'sector-oriented' interests.

Throughout the postwar years, regional policy has been confined to the development of underdeveloped areas, largely because these areas were most dependent upon the federation for capital investment. As Čolanović states, 'the following premises were indispensible for any policy of developing backward regions: (1) a policy of growth for the country as a whole, (2) an underdeveloped area officially determined, and (3) a definite economic policy concerning that area.'[48] Any region which was not officially 'backward' was left to the spontaneous sector and spatial effects of separate investment decisions taken, on separate projects, by the republics, enterprises and later by the communes and investment banks. Federal territory was never viewed as a *whole* for locational purposes, except possibly in the late 'forties by Kidrič.[49] Preoccupation with the problems of underdeveloped regions led to an absence of concepts relating to the possible functions of the advanced areas in solving the problems of less developed areas. Fundamentally, the policy 'to develop the backward areas' involved a substantial transfer of capital from the Sava–Danube–Šumadija axis to the remainder of the country (1947–51) or to large areas of the south and south-east (after 1951) for the development of local industry, construction and some services in proportion to the population. People began to expect 'the right to work' where they lived and, in effect, the policy was an acceptance of a population distribution which was more the result of political history and social experience than of the exploitation of economic possibilities.

The motives for the policy were, first, to restrict interregional migration because of ethnic barriers and job scarcities in most regions, second, to restrict expenditure on 'non-productive' housing and communal facilities which would be necessary if people migrated, and third, to save investment on transport improvements so long as railways and roads, however poor, lay under-utilised in overpopulated areas. Little investment in infrastructure in these areas was later to prove a great competitive disadvantage. Widespread factory dispersion resulted, often diffusing investment effectiveness and tying-up scarce capital in plants which, because of their location where transport was poor, operated at high, uncompetitive, costs. Factories of this nature were located, for example, at Mrkonjić Grad (Bosnia), Nikšić, Mojkovac, Ivangrad, Cetinje (Montenegro), Berovo and Pehčevo (Macedonia). Investments were more effective in some backward areas with transport facilities and comparative advantages (e.g. metallurgy in Bosnia) and in manufacturing in more 'advanced' areas.

After 1955 the commune system perpetuated these trends. Every commune attempted to share in federal development, irrespective of regional or local potentials. Underdeveloped communes, moreover, have been delimited according to the criterion of 'uniformity' in low per capita national income. Frequently, then, 'developed' urban communes in the midst of backward areas (e.g. Titovo Užice, Čačak, Kraljevo, Kruševac and Niš in Serbia) were excluded for purposes of receiving federal or republic grants although it is precisely these areas which must provide the solution of the problems of backward areas: employment outside agriculture. Such an approach resulted in a decade of frequently irrational transfers of capital from urban areas 'to small upland settlements which did not possess elementary pre-conditions for the agglomeration of non-agricultural activities and population'.[50]

Radical changes in regional thinking among economists and planners since 1960 have become more influential in policy-making circles recently, although as yet it is too early to see positive results. The evolution of the 'new economic system' towards parity prices and ever freer operation of 'market forces' has given the ascendancy in investment allocation to the criterion of greatest 'rentability'—the greatest capital effectiveness of investment in raising productivity, employment and social provision at the lowest production cost—over social, political and strategic criteria. Integrated spatial planning for the whole federation is now regarded as essential though not yet actual. The recent economic reforms demand the establishment of strict sector and locational priorities to exploit regional potentials in order to achieve a larger measure of regional specialisation according to comparative advantages in production for both the home and overseas markets. This will, it is hoped, stimulate the adjustment of population density to regional economic potentials and equalise interregional standards through interregional labour migration. Nevertheless, there is clearly a need to co-ordinate the greater capital mobility, achieved since the 1964 reform, with carefully guided labour mobility because 'developed regions (especially Slovenia) with the greatest ability to accumulate capital, generally possess more limited growth potentials than many less developed or underdeveloped areas (Pannonia, central mountains, Dalmatia), and because labour reserves are sometimes separated from natural resources (as in parts of the Karst, north Bosnia or Sandjak), while regions with abundant labour and natural resources (in central and south-eastern mountain and basin areas) lack the means to accumulate capital.'[51]

The regional development strategy now conceived in Yugoslavia consists in investment priority for broad 'growth zones' along the major river valleys and transport arteries, where development potentials are greatest, and to which labour should be encouraged to migrate on a federal scale from overpopulated areas; these zones should be supported, in areas with limited potentials, by selected 'growth centres' for population regroupment on a regional scale. Unfortunately, as always, a national economic choice of priority regions falls victim to ethnic sentiments and ethnic barriers. Serbs stress the advantages of locations along those transport arteries that focus on Belgrade and the Danube international waterway, the Croats underline the nodal advantages of the Zagreb–Sisak area and the Adriatic seacoast. Very limited labour migration into developed Slovenia and out of underdeveloped Macedonia, reflecting strong linguistic and other cultural barriers, complicates economic issues, yet must clearly affect the order and nature of priorities.

However, it is agreed that the major 'priority growth zone' (*Prioritetna Zona Razvoja*) is the Pannonian region. Strategic vulnerability and agricultural structure made this region unattractive until 1957, when more decentralised agricultural and industrial investment began to redress the situation. Today it is realised that the region lying northward of a theoretical line joining Jesenice, Ogulin and Niš offers unique advantages for economic development. Capital is most readily available here. Existing transport facilities, road, rail and river, are the best in Yugoslavia, provide easy interlinkage within the region and with the remainder of the federation, and, with other infrastructure facilities, can be expanded the most cheaply. Postwar economic development largely in other regions has left much spare railway capacity in Podravina and Vojvodina as well as a virtually unutilised Sava waterway; proper exploitation of these 'social capital advantages' may be expected to stimulate greater growth in areas of only average economic standards. The major rivers—the Sava, Drava, Danube, Tisa, Morava and their tributaries—provide abundant water supplies for agriculture, industry and large potential urban populations. With flood protection, drainage and irrigation, highly fertile— but at present extensively used—land could support a very intensive mixed agriculture which, in turn, could supply food cheaply to a much larger population. Relatively large farms and substantial modernisation of agriculture through socialisation and co-operation facilitate progress in this direction. The expansion of manufacturing is encouraged by cheaply-expanded existing capacity (in textiles, shoe, food, engineering and chemicals), skilled labour and good training facilities (important in electrical, engineering and chemical industries), presence of or proximity to varied resources (oil and gas in the plain and lignite, non-metallic minerals and timber in the southern hill country), supplies of agricultural produce, a complex market for industrial and agricultural capital goods and for consumer goods, and by accessibility to home and overseas markets. Traditional immigration of younger people from less developed areas, enriching the demographic resources of the region, is an additional growth factor which economists stress must be not only tolerated, but encouraged. One model of Serbian economic growth, for example, predicts the immigration of 705,000 people into Vojvodina, Belgrade, Šumadija, Mačva and the Morava valley by 1980; most will migrate from Kosmet, Sandjak and Timok, although some will move from Bosnia, Montenegro and Macedonia.[52] It is important, too, that population densities are low in much of Slavonia and Banat;

substantial capital investments here could attract large numbers of immigrants as a means of avoiding excessive immigration to and agglomeration around Belgrade or Zagreb.

Development potentials are very different in the mountain region which lies between Pannonia and the coast or Greece. Without the protective umbrella of guaranteed investments and subsidies this region has been suffering, since the economic reform, from a poor competitive position which results from unskilled, often illiterate, labour, overpopulation, lack of capital and limited industry, and which works under the handicap of poor infrastructure and transport. This, then, is the chief source region of migrants to the north. Yet the persistence of high over-population will demand investment to provide employment locally for many decades to come. Capital is most urgently required for the improvement of transport facilities that is the pre-condition of growth. Firms in northern and coastal Yugo-slavia, however, are likely to invest in the region, in agriculture to increase marketable supplies of livestock products from in-land *polja*, in branch industries to serve local markets or to employ cheaper labour and especially in plants to process a variety of bulky raw materials which are in short supply in northern or coastal areas: lignite, lead and zinc (Kosovo), ferrous metals (Bosnia), bauxite (the Karst), non-ferrous metals and food and tobacco (Macedonia) and timber and water power in many areas. Within the region two regions are to be differentiated for policy-making: first the priority growth zones which comprise the gravitational areas along and to the Bosna–Neretva and the Ibar-Southern Morava–Vardar axes which, in addition to transport, infrastructure and water, also provide access to and from ports and the 'economic spine'; and second, 'complementary growth zones', the Karst uplands and eroded hill country, which are scheduled for depopulation, re-afforestation and water-power development, and the *polja*, which will become areas of population re-groupment and irrigated agriculture. A scheme for Bosnia–Herzegovina[53] proposes a 'T'-shaped priority growth zone along the Sava river and the Banja Luka–Doboj–Tuzla railway on the north and the Bosna–Neretva transverse axis to the south. The remainder of the republic is to become tributary to these axes.

The third region, the coast, is to receive priority for expanded industries processing imported materials and local materials in or near the ports and railheads, with the careful separation of planned growth in the tourist industry in other centres along the coast, served by road, and on the islands.

Clearly these policy concepts represent the active encouragement of broad trends in the location of economic activities which have been emerging since 1948 (Figure 12) and which have been tolerated hitherto only because an apparent effort was being made to develop backward areas. Now, however, stress is laid upon the location of more activities in the less developed areas which have development potentials within the framework of priority growth zones. Such a policy is justified by an analysis which shows that the social costs of providing infrastructure and the costs of operation of urban services are optimal in Yugoslavia in towns with 40,000–60,000 people.[54] These are, potentially, most of the third-order regional or secondary regional centres (Figure 28) that are located in less developed parts of the priority zones, in Slavonia, northern Bosnia, Vojvodina, north-west Serbia, Šumadija and central Serbia and the Morava/Ibar-Vardar areas. Active development of 76 such centres as 'poles of growth', 48 of them in the Pannonian growth zone, is seen as a means, first, of counteracting the agglomerative forces of the larger cities, and hence, of reducing the total social costs of economic progress by rational dispersion, and, second, of achieving a more 'efficient' hierarchy of central places with a rank-size distribution.[55]

Between the population censuses of 1953 and 1961, however, cities with more than 100,000 inhabitants grew almost as quickly (28 per cent.) as those with fewer than 50,000 inhabitants (32 per cent.).[56] Growth in smaller towns does bear witness to some dispersion of postwar economic development. The growth trends of the larger cities, however, represent a degree of 'deviation' from socialist urbanisation theory.[57] Three reasons are apparent. First, the greater attraction of the 'big city' over the smaller settlement has been marked especially as many smaller towns still lack, in large measure, basic urban facilities such as piped water. General 'disinvestment' in housing before 1961, however, shifted the social costs of urbanisation to commuter transport or to less productive labour in industry for large and small settlements alike. Second,

Yugoslavia has no urbanisation policy with which to 'steer' the location of economic activities. Third, this has left unfettered the apparent desire of each republic government to make its own capital a 'Yugoslav metropolis'. Zagreb is to be the 'million city' on the Sava to rival Belgrade, while Skopje is being rebuilt (after the disastrous 1963 earthquake) on its old site to rival Sarajevo and Ljubljana. 'National pride' has thus tended to inflate the fine nodality of the cities in question (except Ljubljana), and hence, to unleash, particularly as the new economic system took effect, centripetal economic forces which have hastened agglomeration in and around the republic capitals to the relative neglect of excellent small or medium town nodes nearby (e.g. Sisak near Zagreb) and of towns which approach 'optimum' size in regions which appear to be 'peripheral' from the capital (e.g. Slavonia, north Bosnia, the southern crescent rimlands of Macedonia). In consequence, fine opportunities have been frequently overlooked for inter-republic co-operation in exploiting common assets along their frontiers. The most striking example is the Sava valley which, with its excellent agricultural and industrial potentials based on water supplies and access to major material and energy sources and to major markets, could become a leading growth zone which, with activities located on both the Slavonian and the Bosnian banks, could support both large numbers of immigrants from interior Bosnia and much higher living standards for people in currently overpopulated north Bosnia. Only time will tell how far Balkan politics will continue to shape the patterns of economic growth and change in Yugoslavia.

REFERENCES

1 Branko Kubović, *Regionalni Aspekt Privrednog Razvoja i Samoupravljanje*, Savez Ekonomista Jugoslavije, Belgrade, 1962, p. 4.

2 Svetozar Ilesić, 'L'état et les méthodes des recherches sur la regionalisation économique en Yougoslavie', *Geographia Polonica*, 4, 1964, Warsaw, p. 125.

3 V. Nenadović, 'Socijalistički Razmeštaj Proizvodnih Snaga', *Ekonomist*, 3/4, 1951, p. 81.

4 S. Dodjan, 'Regionalni Razvoj u Nacrtu Sedmogodišnjeg Plana', *Ekonomist*, 3/4, 1963 (published 1964), p. 704; Mihailo D. Mladenović,

2A

Regionalni Razvoj i Ekonomska Rejonizacija, Savez Ekonomista Jugoslavije, Belgrade, 1962, 20 pp: R. Stojanović, 'O Potrebi Potpunijeg Uključivanja Regionalnog Aspekta pri Planiranju Dugoročnog Privrednog Razvoja', in: Radivoj Uvalić, editor, *Problemi Regionalnog Privrednog Razvoja*, (Ekonomska Biblioteka 18), Belgrade, 1962, pp. 48–67.

5 Branko Kubović, *Regionalni Aspekt Privrednog Razvitka Jugoslavije*, Zagreb, 1961, pp. 112–13.

6 Marijan Hubeny, *Ekonomska Geografija Jugoslavije*, Belgrade, 1958, p. 190.

7 Savezni Zavod za Privredno Planiranje, *Neka Pitanja iz Metodologije Perspektivnog Planiranja Regionalnog Razvoja*, Belgrade, 1956; B. Srebrić, 'Nužnost Potpunijeg Obuhvatanja Teritorialnog Aspekta Razvoja', *Ekonomist*, 3/4, 1963 (published 1964), pp. 686–7.

8 M. Tepina, N. Dobrović, F. Gašparović, B. Petrović, and S. Žuljić, *Regionalno Prostorno Planiranje*, Belgrade, 1957, pp. 96–97;; also see: M. Tepina, V. Nenadović, N. Stefanović and P. Ivandekić, 'Urbanizacija i samofinansiranje u Komunalnu Zivotu', *Godišnja Skupština Stalne Konferencije Gradova*, Zagreb, 1957.

9 B. Kubović, *op. cit.*, p. 29.

10 C. Malovrh, 'Problemi Razgraničenja Geografskih Regiona u Jugoslaviji', *Zbornik Radova V Kongresa Georgrafa F.N.R.J.*, Cetinje, 1959, pp. 323–32.

11 An exception was the simple identification of similarities in existing economic conditions with physiographic regions (which was clearly made before planning was initiated) given in: B. Ž. Milojević, *Glavne Doline u Jugoslaviji*, Srpska Akademija Nauka, Belgrade, 5, 1951, pp. 130–50. This was later translated into French as *Les Vallées Principales en Yougoslavie.*

12 Examples of this kind of approach may be found in: A. Melik, 'Prirodno-Gospodarska Sestava Slovenije', *Geografski Vestnik*, 18, 1946, pp. 3–20 and 'Gospodarski Rajoni v Jugoslaviji', *Ekonomska Revija*, 1, 1950, pp. 47–63; R. Petrović, 'O problemi geografske rajonizacije Jugoslavije', *Geografski Pregled*, 1, 1957, pp. 104–35 and 'Geografske Regije Jugoslavije' in *Ekonomska Geografija Jugoslavije*, Zagreb, 1958, pp. 71–104.

13 C. Malovrh, 'Važnost Strukturne Diferencijacije Antropogenih Faktora Privrednog Prostora za Rajonizacija', *V. Sastanak Jugoslovenskog Statističkog Društva*, 1958. Also see: M. Popović, 'Études de Géographie Économique sur les Régions Économiques de la Yougoslavie', *Problems of Economic Region* (Geographical Studies 27), Warsaw, 1961, p. 160.

14 R. Petrović, *Ekonomska Geografija Jugoslavije*, Sarajevo, 1961 and *Geografski Atlas Jugoslavije*, Zagreb, 1961.

15 S. Žuljić, 'Položaj kao Faktor Regionalno-Gospodarske Strukture Jugoslavije' *Geografski Glasnik*, 25, 1963, pp. 61–80.

16 Readers are reminded also that the concept of national income in Yugoslavia, as in all other socialist countries, excludes income from 'non-productive activites', i.e. state administration, cultural, educational and social welfare activities, and personal services. See, for example, 'Metodološka Objašnjenja-Narodni Dohodak i Privredni Bilansi', *Statistički Godišnjak SFRJ.*, 1964, pp. 28–9.

17 *Ibid.*, p. 28.

18 'Stanovništvo i Domaćinstva-Osnovne Strukture prema Popisu 1961', *Statistički Bilten*, 250, 1962, pp. 22–168. Justification for using this data is given in a number of works in Yugoslavia which stress the limitations on using national income to define 'levels of economic development' in classifying areas. See, for example, R. Lang and D. Gorupić, 'Neka Pitanja Analize Stepena i Mogućnosti Regionalnog Privrednog Razvoja', *Ekonomski Pregled*, 8–9, 1956, pp. 553–72; B. Ivanović, 'Nov Način Odredjenja Otstojanja izmedju Višedimenzionalnih Statističkih skupova sa Primenom u problemu Klasifikacije Srezova F.N.R. Jugoslavije prema Stepenu Ekonomske Razvijenosti', *Statistička Revija*, 7 (2), 1957, pp. 125–54; and D. Vogelnik, 'Ka Pitanju Klasifikacije Srezova F.N.R.J. prema Stepenu Ekonomske Razvijenosti', *Statistička Revija*, 7 (2), 1957, pp. 167–74. A counter-argument is that 'national income in fact gives some indication of potentials since it represents the effects of maximum and rational use of fixed assets'. (B. Kubović, 'O Privrednoj Snazi Naših Kotareva i Gradova', *Ekonomski Pregled*, 7, 1954, pp. 353).

19 Originally this section was included in Chapter 8, but it was transferred to this chapter on account of its 'concluding' nature. Since the section was written the Yugoslav communes have been ranked according to indices of development by factor analysis. See Jack C. Fisher, *Yugoslavia —A Multinational State*, San Francisco, 1966, pp. 154–65 and Appendix Three.

20 It should be borne in mind that communes vary greatly both in area and in population. In 1964 the largest commune, Nikšić (Montenegro) covered 2065 km², mainly Karst, while the smallest, Ljubljana-Centar, covered 5 km² of built-up city. Novi Sad had the largest population (162,100), the island of Lastovo the smallest (1449). However, the average populations of communes in five areas—Croatia, Vojvodina, Serbia Proper, Bosnia-Herzegovina and Kosovo-Metohija—showed remarkable uniformity, varying between 33,000 and 37,000. Averages for Slovenia, Montenegro and Macedonia ranged between 23,000 and 26,000.

21 In some works figures are combined for Vojvodina, Serbia Proper and Kosmet as figures for the Serb Republic. Such practice hides the sharpest intra-republic economic and cultural contrasts in Yugoslavia. That contrast may be summed up in national income per capita terms. In Novi Sad (Vojvodina) income is 346,000 dinars per head whereas in Zjum (Kosmet) it is only 16,000 dinars per head!

22 Boris Kidrič, *Narodna Država*, Belgrade, 1947, p. 6.

23 Trgovinska Komora Split, *Željeznička Veza Srednje Bosne s Morem*, Split, 1957, p. 232.

24 Kosta Mihailović, 'Regionalni Aspekt Privrednog Razvoja', *Ekonomist*, 1, 1962, pp. 3–20.

25 Handicrafts are often key indicators of service functions in predominantly agricultural areas, especially in Pannonia and Serbia. In former Turkish areas handicrafts are very much a part of 'commerce', as sales are made direct by handicraftsmen and their workshops are also retailing establishments.

26 The date used may be found in: *Statistički Godišnjak SFRJ.*, 1964, pp. 358–654. Readers should note that there are 40 districts and their

average size is 6,400 sq. km. and their average population is 465,000 inhabitants—large enough then, to be equitable with urban 'spheres of influence'. The data had to be used with care because higher levels of cultural and economic development tended to raise the rank of northern towns in relation to southern towns. The 'size of open markets' often corrected this, however, since towns in more developed areas tend to have many more shops and fewer and smaller open markets than towns in less developed areas. Equally, towns in the upland and central areas tend to have larger markets for livestock than towns in the northern lowlands where food markets are dominant.

27   D. Vogelnik, *Urbanizacija kao Odraz Privrednog Razvoja*, Ekonomska Biblioteka, 13, Belgrade, 1961, Chapter 5, pp. 122–57.

28   This was supplemented by information, gained on field work during 1960 and 1962, on suburban bus services around Zagreb, Banja Luka, Zenica, Sarajevo, Belgrade, Novi Sad, Niš, Skopje, Bitola, Split and Rijeka.

29   Data for this purpose, albeit now outdated, are available in 'Dnevna Migracija Zapeslenog Osoblja 1957', *Statistički Bilten*, 101, 1957, pp. 11–18. The information contained there was supplemented in 1960 from field work which involved the investigation of the labour supply area for some fifty large factories located in 31 towns from Jesenice (Slovenia) to Zrenjanin (Banat) and Bitola (Macedonia). It was also supplemented by information from the following sources: S. Žuljić, 'O Dnevnim Kretanjima Radne Snage u Zagreb', *Geografski Glasnik*, 1957, pp. 135–47; V. Klemencić, 'Geografski Problemi i Metode Proučavanja Svakodnevnog Putovanja Radne Snage od Mesta Stanovanja na Rad i Obratno', *Zbornik VI Kongresa Geografov F.L.R.J. v L. R. Sloveniji*, 1961, pp. 291–301; and Muhibija Kreso, *Problematika Dnevne Migracije u N.R.B. i H.*, Sarajevo, 1961, 198 p.

30   W. Christaller, 'Das Grunderüst der räumlichen Ordnung in Europa: Die Systeme der Europäischen zentralen Orte', *Frankfurter Geographische Hefte*, 1, 1950, pp. 51–59.

31   B. Kubović, *op. cit.*, p. 20.

32   Veljko Rogić, 'Fizionomska i Funkcionalna Regionalizacija Hrvatske', *Zbornik VI Kongresa Geografov F.L.R.J. v. L. R. Sloveniji*, 1961, pp. 279–90.

33   R. E. Dickinson, *City and Region: A Geographical Interpretation*, London, 1964, p. 64, quoting W. Christaller, 'Die Hierarchie der Städte', *IGU Symposium in Urban Geography*, Lund, 1960.

34   Compare for example S. Dodjan, *op. cit.*, p. 705, and M. D. Mladenović, *op. cit.*, p. 170.

35   Sekretarijat Saveznog Izvrsnog Veća za Socijalnu Politiku, *Sistem Komunalne Privrede u Petrogodišnjem Planu 1961–1965*, Belgrade, 1960.

36   R. Petrović, 'Determiniranje Nekih Prostornih Relacija u Komunalnom Sistemu F.N.R.J.', *Zbornik VI Kongresa Geografov F.L.R.J. v L.R. Sloveniji*, 1961, pp. 303–14.

37   In fact Kosovo-Metohija began to receive federal assistance only in 1957; before that some funds had been supplied from the Serbian Republic budget.

38   Restrictions on the area which nomadic pastoralists could use came as a result of the growth of Adriatic city states, the expansion of the

Venetian Empire, the limitation on pastoral areas written into the Karlovac Treaty (1699), the organisation of the Military Frontier in Lika by Austria and with it settlements and the occupation of Bosnia-Herzegovina by Austria in 1878. See Aleksander Ugrenović, 'Krš Kao Naučni Problem', *Krš Jugoslavije*, 1, Zagreb, 1957, p. 8.

39 These calculations were based on figures of income for Karstland communes; see *Statistički Godišnjak SFRJ.*, 1964, pp. 563–74.

40 An aluminium combine was planned for location at Mostar already in the first Five-Year Plan, 1947. *Petogodišnji Plan Razvitka Privrede F.N.R.J. 1947–51*, Article 10.

41 Detailed studies on problems on the Karst, though predominantly physiographic, may be consulted in *Krš Jugoslavije*, 3 vols, Zagreb, 1957–62. Particularly useful papers in vol. 2 are: Jura Medarić, 'Područje Krša Kao Ekonomski Problem u Svijetlu Savjetovanja o Kršu Jugoslavije 1958 i Naših Ekonomsko-Političkih Ciljeva', pp. 21–58, and Zlatko Gračanin, 'K Pitanju Odnosa Poljoprivrednih i Šumskih Tala na Degradiranom Kršu' pp. 99–104.

42 After 1929 the regional name 'Macedonia' was replaced by 'Southern Serbia', and the use of the Macedonian language in schools and books was made illegal. All Macedonians had to learn Serbian.

43 Readers may find further information on the problems of Vojvodina in: *Aktuelni Problemi Privrede Vojvodine i Perspectivne Mogućnosti Njenog Razvoja*, Ekonomski Institut N. R. Srbije, Belgrade, 1957; *Društveni Plan Privrednog Razvoja N. R. Srbije 1961–65*, Belgrade, 1962; and M. Nikolić, Regionalni Aspekt Akumulacije i Prosirene Reprodukcije', *Ekonomist*, 3–4, 1963, pub. 1964, pp. 694–9.

44 Toussaint Hočevar, *The Structure of the Slovenian Economy 1848–1963*, Studia Slovenica V, New York, 1965, p. 196.

45 Branko Petrović and Stanko Žuljić, editors, *Kotar Krapina: Regionalni Prostorni Plan*, Urbanistički Institut N. R. Hrvatske, Zagreb, 1958, 176 p. and Urbanistički Zavod Kotara Split, *Regionalni Prostorni Plan Kotara Split*, 2 vols., 1961 and 1965. A number of other plans are in preparation in various republics.

46 In this respect it should be noted that planners in Slovenia, for example, lack even the regional planning experience that has been gained in Croatia. Work began in this field in 1960 under the guidance of V. Kokole of the Slovenian Town Planning Institute, Ljubljana.

47 Zagreb district absorbed Krapina district, while Split district now comprises the former districts of Split, Dubrovnik, Makarska, Šibenik and Zadar.

48 B. Čolanović, 'Methods of Industrialising Underveloped Regions in Yugoslavia', in: A. Winsemius and J. A. Pincus, editors, *Methods of Industrial Development*, O.E.C.D., Paris, 1961, p. 153.

49 Boris Kidrič achieved a stature, as chief planner at the Federal Planning Institute, in a way which none of his successors have been able to do, largely because of the outstanding importance of his position in the centralist planning system before 1950, but also because of his original and prolific writings. He died in 1951 from overwork.

50 B. Srebrić, *op. cit.*, p. 686. This transfer was marginally increased when, after 1960, communes taxed workers salaries according to their place of residence. Previously, salaries had been taxed according to

the place of work. Financial 'transfers' in this way were important only where marked commuting by workers occurred from outlying communes to a central urban commune.

51 Kosta Mihailović, 'Regionalni Aspekt Privrednog Razvoja', in *Problemi Regionalnog Privrednog Razvoja*, Savez Ekonomista Jugoslavije, Ekonomska Biblioteka 18, Belgrade, 1962, pp. 40–41.

52 Pajo Ivković-Ivandekić, 'Politika Urbanizacije Kao Izraz Koncepcije Regionalne Organizacije Privredjivanja', *Ekonomist*, 18 (4), 1965, pp. 688–9.

53 Hasan Hadžiomerović, 'Jedan Model Regionalizacije Primjen na Projekciju Privrednog Razvoja Bosne i Hercegovine', *Ekonomist*, 18 (1–2), 1965, pp. 112–31.

54 P. Ivković-Ivandekić, *op. cit.*, p. 682. According to the analysis, costs became uneconomically high in towns with fewer than 10,000 people and, it is assumed, also in cities with more than 1,000,000 people.

55 P. Ivković-Ivandekić, *ibid.*, pp. 682–3.

56 V. Klemenčić, *Problemi Urbanizacije u Jugoslaviji*, XV Skupština Stalne Konferencije Gradova Jugoslavije, Ljubljana, 1964, p. 7.

57 According to several authors socialist urbanization theory emphasises the need to avoid urban agglomeration by spreading economic growth 'among medium- or small-sized settlements in such a way as to minimise the social costs of urbanisation and to attract that level of immigrants or commuters which still permits easy contact with nature for excursions for purposes of health and recreation'. Kosta Mihailović, *op. cit.*, p. 577.

The Pronunciation of Yugoslav Names

Inevitably, the foregoing text contains words and place names which many readers will find bewildering to pronounce and also difficult to remember. A brief note, then, is included here which, it is hoped, will give every reader the necessary equipment with which to become acquainted with the correct pronunciation of the Yugoslav words and names included in this book. At the outset, it should be stressed that the Yugoslav languages are entirely phonetic; this simplifies, to a considerable extent, the task of learning, but it does not diminish the need to practise pronunciation.

Vowels and diphthongs are always pronounced in the following manner:

a	as in 'bar'
e	as in 'pet'
i	as in 'machine'
o	as in 'pot'
u	as in 'rule'
aj	as 'i' in 'hide'
oj	as 'oy' in 'boy'

Consonants are pronounced exactly as they are in English with the following important exceptions:

c	as 'ts' in 'bits'
č	as 'ch' in 'church'
ć	as 't' (ty) in 'picture', but transliterated here as 'ch'
dj	as 'dg' in 'midget'
dž	as 'j' in 'jack'
g	is always hard as in 'give'
h	as 'ch' in the Scottish 'loch'
j	as 'y' in 'yet'

lj   as 'lli' in 'million'
nj   as 'ni' in 'union'
š   as 'sh' in 'shell'
ž   as 's' (zh) in 'pleasure'
r   is always rolled (as in Scots pronunciation)

The stress in Serbo-Croation words never falls on the last syllable, but usually on the antepenultimate syllable. Examples of the pronunciation of selected names are given below, indicating, in italics, the stressed syllables:

Aleksinac	Al-*ek*-si-nats
Brčko	*Burch*-ko
Cetina	*Tset*-ina
Čevljanovići	Chev-*lya*-no-vi-chi
Djakovica	*Dgak*-o-vi-tsa
Ilidža	*Il*-i-j-a
Jajce	*Yay*-tse
Ljubinje	*Lyu*-bi-nye
Nikšić	*Nik*-shich
Mežica	*Mezh*-i-tsa
Rijeka	Ri-*ye*-ka

Occasionally in Slovene the 'v' is pronounced as a 'u', as, for example, in: Pivka — *Piu*-ka.

Throughout the text the Serbo-Croatian spelling of place names is adopted with the exception of (1) *Belgrade*, which is the accepted English form of Beograd, (2) *Koper* which is Slovene (Kopar in Serbo-Croat), (3) *Skopje* and (4) *Bitola* which are Macedonian (respectively Skoplje and Bitolj in Serbo-Croat).

Readers who wish to have a more detailed guide to the pronunciation of Yugoslav place names are referred to: R. H. Osborne, *East Central Europe: A Geographical Introduction to Seven Socialist States*, London and New York, 1967, Appendix 2, pp. 335–7.

Select Bibliography

In addition to the many references cited in the text, it has been thought desirable to note here some of the more important books, statistical sources and journals that may be consulted by readers who wish to gain a broader background knowledge or to pursue specific topics in greater depth.

BOOKS

Auty, P., *Yugoslavia*, London, 1964; New York, 1965.

Avsenek, Ivan, *The Yugoslav Metallurgical Industry*, New York, 1955.

Bakarić, Vladimir, *Aktuelni Problemi Izgradnje Našeg Privrednog Sistema*, Zagreb, 1963.

Basch, A., *The Danubian Basin and the German Economic Sphere*, London, 1944.

Betts, R. R., *Central and South-East Europe 1945–1948*, London, 1950.

Bićanic, Rudolf, *Ekonomska Politika*, Zagreb, 1962.

Bjeličić, Sreten, *Communal System in Yugoslavia*, Belgrade, 1961.

Blanc, A., *Géographie des Balkans*, Paris, 1965.

Bobrowski, C., *La Yugoslavie Socialiste*, Paris, 1956.

Carter, F., 'A Bibliography on the Geography of Yugoslavia', *King's College Department of Geography Occasional Papers Series A*, 1, 1968.

Chataigneau, Y., and Sion, J., *Géographie Universelle*, 7: *Méditerranée, péninsules méditerranées*, 2: *Italie, Pays Balkaniques*, Paris, 1918.

Čalić, D., *Izgradnja Industrije u F.N.R.J.*, Zagreb, 1957.

Čobeljić, N., *Politika i Metodi Privrednog Razvoja Jugoslavije*, Belgrade, 1959.

Čolanović, B., 'Methods of Industrialising Underdeveloped Regions in Yugoslavia', *Methods of Industrial Development*, editors, A. Winsemius and John A. Pincus, O.E.C.D., Paris, 1962, pp. 153–68.

Cvijić, J., *La péninsule Balkanique: géographie humaine*, Paris, 1918.

Dimitrijević, S., *Strani Kapital u Privredi Bivše Jugoslavije*, Belgrade, 1952.

Energetski Izvori Jugoslavije: Vodne Snage Jugoslavije (Yugoslav Energy Sources: Yugoslav Water Power), Yugoslav National Committee of the World Energy Conference, Belgrade, 1956.

Fisher, Jack C., *Yugoslavia—A Multinational State*, San Francisco, 1966.

Hoffman, G. W., and Neal, E. W., *Yugoslavia and the New Communism*, New York, 1962.

Hubeni, Marijan, *Ekonomska Geografija Jugoslavije*, Belgrade, 1958.

Jelavich, C., *The Balkans in Transition*, Berkeley, 1963.

Kardelj, E., *Problemi Socijalističke Politike na Selu*, Belgrade, 1959.

Kerner, Robert J., (editor). *Yugoslavia*, Berkeley, 1949.

Kidrič, Boris, *Privredni Problemi F.N.R.J.*, Belgrade, 1948.

Kostić, C., *Seljaci—Industrijski Radnici*, Belgrade, 1955.

Kreso, Muhibija, *Problematika Dnevne Migracije u N.R.B. i H.*, Sarajevo, 1961.

Krndija, D., *Industrializacije Jugoslavije*, Sarajevo, 1961.

Kubović, Branko, *Regionalni Aspekt Privrednog Razvitku Jugoslavije*, Zagreb, 1961.

Lah, Augustin, *Gospodarstvo Jugoslavije: Prispevek k Ekonomski Geografije F.N.R. Jugoslavije*, Ljubljana, 1950.

L'économie Collective en Yugoslavie, Geneva, 1959.

Lovrenović, Stjepan, *Ekonomska Politika Jugoslavije*, Sarajevo, 1963.

Macura, Miloš, *Stanovništvo kao Činilac Privrednog Razvoja Jugoslavije*, Belgrade, 1958.

Marković, Petar, *Strukturne Promene na Selu kao Rezultat Ekonomskog Razvitku 1900–1960*, Belgrade, 1963.

Melik, A., *Jugoslavija: Zemljepisni Pregled*, Ljubljana, 1958.

Melik, A., *Slovenija.*, 4 vols, Ljubljana, 1956–60.

Mellen, M., and Winston, V. H., *The Coal Resources of Yugoslavia*, New York, 1956.

Milojević, B., *Les Vallées Principales en Yugoslavie*, Paris, 1956.

Mirković, Mijo, *Ekonomska Historija Jugoslavije*, Zagreb, 1954.

Mišić, Dimitrije, *Ekonomika Industrije Jugoslavije*, Belgrade, 1956.

Mitrović, M. M. *Gradovi i Naselja u Srbiji*, Belgrade, 1963.

Moore, W. E., *Economic Demography of Eastern and Southern Europe*, Geneva, 1945.

Newbigin, Marion I., *The Geographical Background to Balkan Problems*, London, 1916.

Pavić, Radovan, *Regionalna Ekonomska Geografija Jugoslavije*, Zagreb, 1966.

Petrović, R., *Ekonomska Geografija Jugoslavije*, Zagreb, 1958.

P.E.P. (Political & Economic Planning), *Economic Development in Southeastern Europe*. London, 1945.

Pounds, N. J. G. and Spulber, N., (editors), *Resources and Planning in Eastern Europe*, Bloomington, 1957.

Proizvodne Snage Srbije, Ekonomski Institut N. R. Srbije, Belgrade, 1953.

Razvoj Privrede F.N.R. Jugoslavije, 2 vols., Belgrade, 1958.

Seton-Watson, H., *The East European Revolution*, London and New York, 1956.

Sirotković, J., *Problemi Privrednog Planiranja u Jugoslaviji*, Zagreb, 1961.

Sirotković, J., *Odnosi u Nivou Razvijenosti Komuna i Politika Pomaganja Nerazvijenih Područja*, Zagreb, 1962.

Sirotković, J., (editor), *Suvremeni Problemi Jugoslavenske Privrede i Ekonomska Politika*, Zagreb, 1965.

Stevanović, Milan, *Ekonomska Saobraćajna Geografija*, Zemun, 1957.

Stojanović, Radmila, *Teorija Privrednog Razvoja u Socijalizmu*, Belgrade, 1961.

Spulber, N., *The Economics of Communist Eastern Europe*, New York, 1957.

Todorović, Mijalko, *Problemi Privrednog Planiranja u Jugoslaviji*, Belgrade, 1959.

Tomasevich, J., *Peasants, Politics, and Economic Change in Yugoslavia*, Stanford, 1955.

United Kingdom, Naval Intelligence Division, *Yugoslavia*, 3 vols., London, 1945.

United Nations Economic Commmission for Europe, *Economic Survey for Europe*, annually.

Uvalić, R., editor, *Problemi Regionalnog Privrednog Razvoja*, Belgrade, 1962.

Vinski, I., *Procjena Nacionalnog Bogatstva po Podrucjima Jugoslavije*, Zagreb, 1959.

Vinski, I., *Kretanje Fiksnih Fondorva Jugoslavije 1947–1962*, Zagreb, 1963.

Vogelnik, D., *Urbanizacija kao Odraz Privredng Razvoja F.N.R.J.*, Belgrade, 1961.

Vujević, P., *Podneblje F.N.R. Jugoslavije*, Belgrade, 1953.

Waterston, A., *Planning in Yugoslavia*, Baltimore, 1962.

Warriner, Doreen, editor, *Contrasts in Emerging Societies*, London and Bloomington (Indiana), 1965.

Warriner, Doreen, *The Economics of Peasant Farming*, London, 1939, (rev. 1966); and New York, 1964 (2nd. ed.).

STATISTICAL SOURCES

Statistički Godišnjak, annually, 1954 to the present.

Statistički Bilten; some 500 numbers have been published since 1948 on income, wages, social security, health, culture, education, population, agriculture, industry, trade, transport, tourism and peasant households.

Jugoslavija 1945–1964 : Statistički Pregled, Belgrade, 1966.

SELECTED PERIODICALS

Agronomski Glasnik
Ekonomika Poljoprivrede
Ekonomika Preduzeća
Ekonomska Revija
Ekonomski Pregled
Ekonomist
Geografski Glasnik
Geografski Pregled
Geografski Vestnik
Glasnik Srpskog Geografskog Društva
Gospodarski Vestnik
Jugoslovenski Pregled (English version: Yugoslav Survey)
Sociologija Sela
Tehnika
Vestnik Investicione Banke

Index

2B

M